BLOCKING KAMPFGRUPPE PEIPER

BLOCKING KAMPFGRUPPE PEIPER

The 504th Parachute
Infantry Regiment in
the Battle of the Bulge

FRANK VAN LUNTEREN

CASEMATE
Philadelphia & Oxford

First published in Great Britain and the United States of America in 2015.
Reprinted as a paperback in 2022 by
CASEMATE PUBLISHERS
1950 Lawrence Road, Havertown, PA 19083, US
and
The Old Music Hall, 106–108 Cowley Road, Oxford OX4 1JE, UK

Copyright 2015 © Frank van Lunteren

Paperback Edition: ISBN 978-1-63624-128-9
Digital Edition: ISBN 978-1-61200-314-6

A CIP record for this book is available from the British Library

Printed and bound in the United Kingdom by Short Run Press

For a complete list of Casemate titles, please contact:

CASEMATE PUBLISHERS (US)
Telephone (610) 853-9131
Fax (610) 853-9146
Email: casemate@casematepublishers.com
www.casematepublishers.com

CASEMATE PUBLISHERS (UK)
Telephone (01865) 241249
Email: casemate-uk@casematepublishers.co.uk
www.casematepublishers.co.uk

CONTENTS

MAPS

Dedicated to all the officers and men who served in the 504th Regimental Combat Team in World War II. Their sacrifices will *not* be forgotten.

As the stars that shall be bright when we are dust,
Moving in marches upon the heavenly plain;
As the stars that are starry in the time of our darkness,
To the end, to the end, they remain.

—Laurence Binyon, *For the Fallen* (1914)

"There is very heavy fighting going on there now between American paratroops and German SS-men."

—BBC reporter Robert Barr at Cheneux,
   December 21, 1944

"Our casualty rates, including those of my platoon, were high, not only because of combat injuries but also because of the brutal weather conditions."

—2nd Lt. Robert E. Bramson, F Company

"Began wondering if this Siegfried Line wasn't just a big hoax. We changed our minds fast—all hell broke loose."

—2nd Lt. Charles E. Zastrow, E Company,
   Letter to his parents, February 10, 1945

FOREWORD

I served in F Company of the 2nd Battalion of the 504th Parachute Infantry Regiment of the 82nd Airborne Division, briefly in Holland and subsequently in Belgium, until I was wounded on February 2, 1945. The 82nd to this day is considered a very famous division. I was proud to have served in such a fine unit, and especially one led by General Gavin, an aggressive leader who was often seen up with the forward units.

I believe the successful and necessary use of airborne troops in infantry ground operations in Belgium for an extensive period, though lightly armed and equipped and under very adverse conditions, further fostered the unmatched reputation of the 82nd Airborne. At that time few, if any, units had as much front-line duty as the 82nd, having fought in Sicily, Salerno, Anzio, Normandy and in Holland.

In this second volume Frank van Lunteren's very exhaustive research describes the 504th operations during the Battle of the Bulge, leading up to the breaching of the Siegfried Line. As I was a young paratroop officer rather low in the chain of command, van Lunteren's research in essence has given me information about the regiment's operations through a different set of eyes than my own. My knowledge, on the other hand, was at most times limited only to what I was able to hear or observe. Conditions during this period were often physically difficult due to the nature of the terrain, the extreme cold, and at times the deep snow. Our casualty rates, including those of my platoon, were high not only because of combat injuries but also because of the brutal weather conditions. For example, the morning I was wounded I had to be carried off the Mertesrott Heights by just-captured German

9

soldiers, under guard, as no rescue vehicles were able to penetrate the hilly forest trails due to the difficult weather.

After the victorious breaching of the Siegfried Line on the German–Belgian border, the regiment and the division's other units continued successfully into Germany, where they subsequently served as the occupation troops in Berlin. Upon returning to the United States, the 82nd was given the honor of leading the gala Victory Parade in New York City—a very proud moment.

Second Lieutenant Robert E. Bramson
F Company, 504 PIR, 1944–1945

INTRODUCTION

The Ardennes Campaign, popularly known as "the Battle of the Bulge," is probably the sole military campaign fought by the U.S. Army in World War II that is characterized by defeat followed by ultimate victory after weeks of fighting in extremely adverse weather. Both Malmédy and Bastogne are iconic geographical names that trigger memories of the Malmédy Massacre by Kampfgruppe Peiper, and the "Battered Bastards of Bastogne," whose defense of the town earned the 101st Airborne Division collectively a Presidential Unit Citation in March 1945. But these places, along with the Elsenborn Ridge, Skyline Drive, Lanzerath, and the so-called "twin towns" of Krinkelt and Rocherath are only a few of the many important battle sites in the Belgian Ardennes. Nor was Kampfgruppe Peiper first and foremost defeated at Trois Ponts by the 505th Parachute Infantry Regiment and the 291st Combat Engineer Battalion. As the late Clay Blair wrote in the outstanding *Ridgway's Paratroopers*, the most important defeat occurred "at Stoumont and La Gleize, [where] Peiper's kampfgruppe was blocked and under heavy attack from the north by Hobb's 30th Infantry Division, supported by Rose's CCB [Combat Command B] and, from the southwest, by Tucker's 504th Parachute Infantry Regiment."[1]

Historians have well covered the actions of the 30th Infantry Division and the 3rd Armored Division led by Rose, but the heroic stand of the 504th Parachute Infantry Regiment against the 9th SS-Panzer Division between Bra-sur-Liennes and Les Villettes is little known, as is the brave, successful counterattack by the 1st and 3rd battalions staged from Rahier on elements from Kampfgruppe Peiper at Cheneux and Monceau. Historians who have viewed these battles as an unimportant sideshow have limited their research to other books about the 82nd Airborne Division, the division's official After Action Reports, and Capt. Thomas Helgeson's dramatic "Narrative of Action of the First Battalion, 504th Parachute Infantry at Cheneux, Belgium." *Blocking Kampfgruppe Peiper* is the first examination to draw extensively on Morning Reports and S-2 and S-3 Journals, and incorporates much new material from written and oral interviews I personally conducted with numerous 504th veterans who participated in the Ardennes Campaign. I believe the story that emerges from this new research significantly clarifies and expands our knowledge of the course of the war in the Bulge, and demonstrates that the actions of the 504th Parachute Infantry Regiment—which include breaching one of the most difficult sections of the Siegfried Line—have unjustly been long overlooked.

It is my over-all aim as an historian to provide, as much as possible, an equal amount of information on each campaign fought by the 504th Parachute Infantry Regiment. *Blocking Kampfgruppe Peiper* introduces replacements to the regiment as they join it, and presents new background material on the disbanded units and other pools from which replacements came, the dates they were sent overseas, and the experience of arriving in a new front-line unit in the midst of a battle—sometimes to be immediately placed on an outpost position. What is it like to participate in night patrols? How did replacements respond to their first battle? Also included are lesser-discussed aspects of garrison life such as Prop Blast parties and division reviews. For these and many other aspects of daily life in and out of battle, I was fortunate to have access to numerous letters by and to Tucker's troopers, battle reports, Company Morning Reports, rosters, and telegrams, all of which helped me to reconstruct the epic story of the 504th Parachute Infantry Regiment in the Battle of the Bulge.

ACKNOWLEDGMENTS

Foremost among those who contributed to the making of this book are the veterans of the 504th Parachute Infantry Regiment, the 307th Airborne Engineer Battalion, the 325th Glider Infantry Regiment, the 376th Parachute Field Artillery Battalion, and all the veterans' wives and families. They kindly answered numerous questions, and in several cases the veterans spoke about their experience in World War II for the very first time. The generosity with which they shared their stories made this a better, and far different, book than it would have been had they not participated.

My goal has been to let the veterans tell their own stories while readers "listen in" as they relate their memories. Sadly, several of those who contributed eyewitness accounts for *Blocking Kampfgruppe Peiper* are no longer with us. I especially think of my long-time friends David K. Finney and Fred J. Baldino, who passed away before my first book—*The Battle of the Bridges*, about the 504th Parachute Infantry Regiment in the Holland Campaign—was published. Fred was the first to get me interested in the regiment, and several of David's unique wartime photographs are included in this book.

Relatives of paratroopers who were killed in action or who have died since the war have equally provided much-needed information. Sometimes the letters and telegrams they shared were very personal, but gave me as an author a clearer view of the impact of each paratrooper's death, both on the front lines and at home. Families who decided to bring their fallen loved ones home after the war often went through a second period of grief when the reburial took place in their home town or at a national cemetery; in some cases, the grief was even so powerful that they could not bear to repatriate the remains. This was the case for the family of John G. Allen, Jr., G Company, who was killed in the battle of Cheneux. As Mark King, the veteran's nephew, recalls, "To the best of my knowledge, it was my family's choice to have him buried with his fellow troopers in Belgium. Knowing my mother and John's mother (my grandmother), it would be easier for the family to get past this loss, if his grave were not here in the States. It also felt like it was the right thing to do to honor him and his sacrifice. To the day my mother died, it was very hard for her to speak of John. As a young kid, I was taught that the subject of John was off-limits with Grandma. I learned not to ever talk about John to Grandma because it made her relive all her memories of her only son."[2]

Mark kindly shared a photo of his uncle and a letter his family received from Lt. Harry J. Frear, his uncle's platoon leader. It was a pleasure to connect Mark with the lieutenant's daughter, Joy Frear, who sent me scans of her father's medal citation and photographs. Among the moving contributions of many others was correspondence I received from the Jajowka family: wartime letters about the death at Cheneux of Pvt. Frank A. Jajowka, C Company, showed me the crucial, but difficult role of Chaplains Kozak and Kuehl as they answered letters from family members asking how their loved ones had been killed. Many thanks to Chelsea Williams for sharing Private Jajowka's letters with me.

Frederick Lindley also opened his family archives to supply several photographs and another moving letter from Chaplain Kozak to his grandparents, describing how Frederick's uncle, Lt. Howard Kemble, was mortally wounded at Cheneux. Steve Howerter sent photographs on behalf of the family of Cpl. Harold Stevenson, and David Faile supplied photographs of his uncle, Sgt. Voyd Faile of C Company, also killed at Cheneux. Greg Korbelic provided various letters, photographs, and documents regarding his uncle, Pfc. Angus M. Giles, Jr., A Company, who was killed near Manderfeld.

Susan Repke and her husband Neil sent me numerous photographs and letters written by Susan's late father, 1st Lt. Charles E. Zastrow of E Company. His letters are a treasure trove of information on the Battle of the Bulge and provide rich insight into a platoon leader's experience at that time. Once again, Steve Mandle stepped up to the plate, just as he had done for my first book on the 504th PIR, *The Battle of the Bridges*, and provided dozens of photographs and letters from his father, 1st Lt. William D. Mandle, who passed away in 1962. Steve's wife Barbara and his siblings Kim and Shannon have been equally supportive for the past five years. It was Shannon who dug up a copy of the 3rd Battalion Unit Journal for the Battle of the Bulge, which helped me to reconstruct numerous events.

In the late 1980's James M. McNamara, Jr., from Clinton, Massachusetts, conducted a dual interview with his father and B Company veteran Robert Waldon about their World War II experiences. I thank him for kindly sharing both this unique interview and several other documents with me. Although I have not thus far had the honor to meet him in person, Mike Bigalke is another long-time friend. He contributed several documents concerning the late Cpl. George D. Graves, Jr., as well as invaluable A Company Morning Reports for December 1944.

Dominic Biello—named after his uncle who was killed at Floret in December 1944—is the dedicated webmaster of <www.ww2-airborne.us>, a goldmine of information about U.S. airborne forces in World War II. He freely shared information and photographs from his collection. Dominic and his family had been trying to find out for years what had happened to his uncle. It was very special when I was able to find D Company veteran Virgil Widger and email him numerous questions via his good friend Jim Patten. Virgil had been wounded by the same sniper who had killed Dominic's uncle.

Unfortunately Jim died in May 2011 of injuries sustained in a traffic accident and Virgil passed away in January 2014. Not long after Virgil's death I learned of his passing and got in touch with his daughter and son-in-law Rhonda and Robert Schum. They visited the Netherlands in June 2014 and I was able to show them the places where Virgil fought during Operation Market Garden. Rhonda and Robert gave me reproductions of unique photographs from Virgil's collection, some of which are included in this book.

Richard Gariepy sent photocopies of the diary the late S/Sgt. William V. Rice of H Company kept during the Ardennes Campaign. Char Baldridge, historian of the 359th Fighter Group, kindly provided a digital version of the memoirs of the late Capt. Paul D. Bruns, a battalion surgeon. Airborne historian Phil Nordyke contributed witness statements testifying to the actions of Pfc. Daniel Del Grippo and S/Sgt. William Walsh, both of whom were awarded the Distinguished Service Cross for outstanding heroism at Cheneux. At my request, Eileen Mahon interviewed her father George Mahon about his experiences with E Company in the Battle of the Bulge. Beth Tweed, daughter of Lt. Wayne Fetters of C Company, and Pamela Chase, daughter of Lt. Col. Richard Chase, shared various wartime pictures from the collections of their late fathers.

My long-time friend Chris Lucas shared several documents regarding his late grandfather Leslie Lucas of A Company. James R. Allmand III and Jeff Anderson sent photographs and scanned documents regarding their late fathers, who served as platoon leaders in G Company. Vera and Victor Abramson supplied information and pictures of their late husband and father, Lt. Myles Abramson of F Company. Cody Mann scanned his late grandfather S/Sgt. Paul Mann's diary, photographs, and a rare translated German account of the Cheneux battle. Mary Gagliano sent photographs and information about her late father, Oscar Smith, and Craig Caba provided the same for his uncle, Sylvester Barbu. Robert Wolfe again generously opened his father's archives on B Company. Karen Wald provided photographs of her late father, boxing champion George Silvasy of G Company. Terry Swartz sent a wartime photo and information on his late father, Elmer Swartz of C Company. I also thank Joe Bass, who kindly shared information about his late uncle, Lt. G.P. Crockett; Roland Dew and his sister Janeen Ralston for letters and photographs of their late uncle, Sgt. Robert Dew of I Company; and Patsy Murphy Wells for the photo of her late father, Lt. Ernest Murphy of H Company.

In Europe probably no one is more knowledgeable on Ross Carter than Jörgen Rosenquist from Denmark. He spent decades studying Carter's life and met several of his family members. Rosenquist sent me numerous postwar photographs and information on the Belgian battlefields, Ross Carter, and James Megellas. I am indebted to Mike St. George, secretary of the Colonel Reuben Tucker Chapter, for identifying many of the real names of the characters mentioned in Carter's classic account of the 504th PIR, *Those Devils in Baggy Pants*.

My father Wim again helped me to digitally enhance various old photographs and scan large 1:20,000-scale topographical maps of the Belgian Ardennes, which I used with some 1:25,000-scale wartime maps to indicate various actions and movements. The text is enriched by clear maps by Carl Mauro II, an expert graphic designer with whom I previously had the pleasure of working on *The Battle of the Bridges*.

Gayle Wurst of Princeton International Agency for the Arts once more believed in the importance of telling the unique story of the 504th Parachute Infantry Regiment, and I owe warm thanks and appreciation for her work as both literary agent and editor. It was from the outset once again a pleasure to work together!

Robert Bramson, a former assistant platoon leader in F Company, kindly wrote the foreword to this book. He joined the regiment in the last month of the Holland Campaign and got through the Battle of the Bulge unscathed until he was severely wounded while attacking a pillbox on the Siegfried Line.

Corresponding with the families of paratroopers was one of the most enjoyable aspects of my research. I especially enjoyed these exchanges, as I often could provide families with company photos or other information they wanted to know, while I learned much from them about family members who had been in the 504th. If you, too, have a relative or friend who was in the 504 PIR in World War II, I would love to hear from you. Please don't hesitate to contact me at macfrank82@hotmail.com.

So many people contributed to helping this book come to pass that it is impossible for me to mention them all, but I deeply thank all who contributed whose names may not here appear. My final word of thanks must go to the 504th Parachute Infantry Regiment Association for making me an Honorary Member in appreciation of my on-going research on the 504th PIR during World War II. Col. Trevor Bredenkamp, the current commander of the 1st Brigade Combat Team (504th Parachute Infantry), 82nd Airborne Division, presented me with this honor on September 18, 2014—exactly 70 years to the day after a cousin and four nieces of my late paternal grandfather were liberated by A Company of the 504th Parachute Infantry Regiment at the beginning of the Holland Campaign. I could receive no greater honor. Thank you!

Frank van Lunteren
Arnhem, the Netherlands
November 22, 2014

Private First Class Hugh Wallis of H Company after recuperating
from wounds received in the Waal River Crossing.
Courtesy: Hugh Wallis

CHAPTER 1

CAMP SISSONNE
SISSONNE, FRANCE,
NOVEMBER 15–DECEMBER 15, 1944

While the 504th Regimental Combat Team [RCT] and the remainder of the 82nd Airborne Division [ABD] were still fighting in Holland and Germany, preparations had been made by Maj. Gen. Matthew B. Ridgway's XVIII Airborne Corps Headquarters to install new base camps in the French towns of Sissonne and Soissons, some thirteen miles east of the city of Laon and twenty-six miles north of Reims. A number of recent jump school graduates of the Parachute School at Ashwell, along with some veteran paratroopers—both officers and enlisted men—of the 82nd Airborne Division who had not participated in Operation Market Garden were sent to France to prepare the camps.

Private First Class Hugh D. Wallis of H Company, who had recuperated from wounds received during the Waal Crossing, eagerly waited at Camp Sissonne for the remainder of the regiment to arrive from Holland, wondering who would return alive and well and who would not. Waiting with him were S/Sgt. Leroy M. Richmond, Pfc. Charles L. Zlamal, and his best friend, Pfc. Cletus J. Shelton, of H Company: "We had all come out of hospitals. We were waiting for our battalion to return from Holland."[3] Among the other returning veterans were S/Sgt. Ernest W. Parks of D Company and Sgt. Charles L. Peers of C Company, who had both missed the Holland Campaign due to wounds received on the Anzio Beachhead.

One of the recent jump graduates sent to Sissonne was 23-year-old Pfc. Edwin R. Bayley, born on November 25, 1921, in the small town of Canton, Maine: "My father was the principal of the small high school. I was raised in the town of Whitman, Massachusetts, about 20 miles southeast of Boston.

It was from that town that I entered the army."[4] Bayley was inducted at Fort Devens, Massachusetts, and further trained at a chemical warfare training camp in Gadsen, Alabama. Here he was placed with a couple of other northerners in a company that was made up almost entirely of southerners, including the officers and cadre. Although it took a while to prevent a small-scale recurrence of the Civil War, the rifle range competition with .30 Springfield rifles helped establish both an esprit de corps and unit cohesion. Having played trumpet as a civilian, Private Bayley became one of the battalion buglers, spending each tour of guard duty in a guard house, leaving it only to blow the requisite calls several times a day.

After several weeks of infantry and specialized chemical training, including the use of smoke generators and handling hazardous chemicals, Bayley and some of his comrades were assigned to the Army Specialized Training Program [ASTP] and returned to college life. He opted to study Mechanical Engineering at the University of Florida, but his studies were interrupted when the government broke up the ASTP program in early 1944. The need for replacements for the European Theater of Operations exceeded the number of men in the infantry pool. Assigned to the 347th Infantry Regiment of the 87th Infantry Division in South Carolina, Bayley was one of thousands of young ASTP students assigned to an active outfit due to the shortage in manpower.

"It was a tremendous and abrupt change from a sheltered academic life in nice, warm, comfortable college dorms in a nice, comfortable climate," Bayley recalled. "The reality of military life had returned. The time at Fort Jackson was spent in intensive infantry training. A great amount of firing-range time was spent on qualifying and familiarization with the M1 rifle, the .45 automatic and the carbine. I also qualified for the Browning Automatic Rifle [BAR]. We were trained in the use of bayonets, hand grenades, rifles and incendiary bombs, hand-to-hand combat, the laying of several types of mines and of barbed wire, and learned how to crawl for several hundred feet below barbed wire entanglements while under continuous machine-gun fire directed just over the top of the wire. If anyone stood up, he would have been cut to pieces by the bullets.

"In August, when the company returned from several days of field manoeuvres, we found that our company had grown to nearly double its normal size. We thought that we were being reinforced prior to going overseas as a unit for combat. We were shocked to learn that the new personnel had completed a very short training schedule and in reality were practically raw recruits. Then we found out what was happening. Congress had promised the mothers of the boys in the States that their 18-year-old sons would not be shipped overseas to combat, unless they were a member of a combat division or regiment, so they moved all these young kids in, the 18-year-olds, and at the same time they moved us old guys to a general replacement depot at Fort Meade, near Washington D.C. The big day finally came when names were called out for shipping rosters to Camp Kilmer, New Jersey, the port of embarkation. At that point we knew we were probably headed for Europe."[5]

After being shipped across the Atlantic Ocean as a general replacement, Private First Class Bayley ended up in a replacement depot outside of Liverpool, England: "One day a parachute colonel came by and addressed our large group. The airborne troops had suffered great losses and quickly needed replacements. If we volunteered, were accepted after a physical and completed an intensified physical- and jump-training program, we could become full-fledged paratroopers and double our base pay.

"A few of us close friends thought about this, and concluded that we had no real choice as to when our time would be up. So why not join the troopers, get twice as much money, and have twice as good a time while we were alive? About this time I was given another tempting choice. The camp bugle calls were being played on a record player and amplifier. I was given the chance to become the official bugler, have a jeep to drive, etc. In my abysmal ignorance of what combat would be like, I said that I had come to fight and not be a replacement depot bugler.

"A few days later a bunch of busses with the smallest seats I have ever seen came to the camp and took the soon-to-be paratroopers off to the nearest rail station. After about a two-hour ride on the London, Midland, and Scottish Railroad, we were dumped off at a small town station outside the city of Leicester. We were met by several non-coms [non-commissioned officers] with red, white and blue shoulder patches with the letters 'AA' on them. Immediately we all said we didn't come to be in the antiaircraft artillery. We were going to be paratroopers. We were informed that we were now at Camp Ashwell Jump School of the 82nd Airborne Division—the 'All American' Division—the reason for the 'AA'. We were assigned sleeping quarters, some in steel huts and most in tents. I got the steel hut, which was most welcome when the wind and the rains came.

"Training started early the next day with long stretches of double-time running, push-ups and other strenuous physical training, rope climbing and tests for mental alertness. In the afternoons we were given instruction and practice on handling parachutes, using harnesses suspended from the training building roof. We were awed by the ability of the trainers to do several hundred push-ups on one hand. They also made rope climbing with one hand look easy as well. We found that many of them were said to have been circus personnel in civilian life. We heard all sorts of war stories and trooper adventures.

"We practiced exiting planes through use of a mock door. After a week of this we were taken to a nearby airport for our first jump. We had no 250-foot jump towers like they had in the States. Our first jump was to be the real thing. We were issued main and reserve parachutes, instructed on how to put them on, and told to count for three seconds after leaving the plane. If the main chute didn't open then, we were to pull the reserve and hope for the best.

"Eighteen of us were put into the plane along with a jumpmaster and instructor. For most of us this was the first time we had been in a plane. We took off and after gaining about 1000 feet altitude headed for the drop field. We were given the command 'Stand up and hook up.' This we did and then we inspected the chute and hook-up of the man in front of us. A jump trainer inspected the last man in the string.

"Next came the command, 'Stand in the door.' This was the big moment. What was going to happen? Would anyone refuse to jump? If we did, would there be a second chance? We remembered we had been told not to look down but to look up at the distant horizon as we positioned ourselves in the door.

"Everybody in the string left the plane in seconds. The opening shock was just as violent as predicted. I found myself drifting down and feeling great that I had actually jumped. Then came the ground shock, equal to jumping off the back of a truck going about 15 miles per hour. We walked back to our nearby camp and went to our tents and huts. We found that one person had apparently been killed in practice that afternoon, and another had clean, complete breaks of both legs just above the ankle.

"The next day there was another jump—this one was a little easier for me. There were some refusals. The penalty for returning with the plane was the removal of your shoes and having to walk back barefoot several miles to the camp. The final punishment was assignment to the 325th Glider Infantry Regiment [GIR] as an infantryman. No one wanted to be in the gliders since they were thought to be very life-hazardous during crash landings.

"Our first jump was from a plane at 1000 feet. Each day we dropped about 100 feet lower, and on the fifth day we came down to 500 feet and jumped. Our final jumps had to be taken under less than ideal conditions because our training camp time was running out. The wind speed was much higher than would usually be considered safe. My final jump landed me in the middle of a turnip patch where the tops of the turnips were about one to two inches above the ground level. I wasn't able to collapse the chute right away, so was dragged a hundred feet or so. It was like being dragged over a cobblestone road.

"The training was hard and rough, but we were all the better for it as later events proved. At the beginning I weighed about 186 pounds and had a 36-inch waist. At the end of the two weeks I weighed about 205 pounds and the same clothes fit perfectly. The successful trainees got their jump boots and were awarded the coveted winged parachute, identifying us as qualified jumpers.

"A few days later we boarded trucks and went to the former Leicester City golf course to the 504th Parachute Infantry Regiment tent city. We were assigned tents, shown the mess hall, the recreation room, and the Red Cross doughnut line. Every evening a Red Cross girl served us doughnuts and coffee. The camp sanitary facilities were very primitive, an outdoor latrine with a canvas wall and big buckets below wooden seats for toilets. The camp prisoners had the detail of cleaning and emptying these every morning. In the middle of a small field in the camp was a small, closed structure about three feet high and maybe six by ten feet wide. This was said to be solitary confinement for incorrigible prisoners. I believe it had at least one tenant.

"The regiment was over in Holland near Nijmegen, having jumped into a very successful phase of the ill-fated Market Garden operation in which the British parachute brigades were decimated. We went through minor training exercises, including night marches and night compass drills. There were other minor training exercises during the day, but generally the camp was a relaxing type of life without much to do. Passes were issued for evenings and Saturdays and Sundays in town, where we could go to the movies, to pubs for a beer, and out with the girls.

"After a few weeks, we were told to get our gear ready for transfer. We went to an airport, boarded C-47 transports and found ourselves on the way to north central France. We landed at a small, isolated airfield. After a long wait, trucks picked us up and took us several miles to a nearby empty French army barracks just outside of the town of Sissonne. The barracks consisted of many large, concrete-constructed, two- and three-story buildings, several large, one-story mess halls, and a lot of small, one-story warehouses, garages, and other such buildings.

"Our mission was to prepare the barracks and related buildings for the arrival of the 504th, 505th and 508th PIRs and the 325th Glider Infantry Regiment [GIR] returning from Holland. The camp had been recently cleaned of mines after the Germans left. Many of the dangerous antipersonnel mines were still piled around the place, but they supposedly had been defused.

"It was now late October and very cold at night, but we did have stoves, for which we had to go to the woods and cut fuel. The green wood did not always burn very well and troopers would help it with a little gasoline now and then. Some of the stove pipes were hooked up to chimneys and some to the building ventilating system. It was a wonder we didn't kill ourselves with carbon monoxide. One day, in our barracks section, one of the troopers threw on a little more than the usual amount of gasoline while trying to light the fire. Ignition was delayed, and finally, when it did occur, the evaporating gasoline fumes had spread into the ventilation ductwork. There was a loud explosion followed by falling ceilings. Fortunately, nobody got hurt.

"One day a bunch of us were selected to ride trucks to a large city about two or three hours' drive from our Sissonne campsite to get a lot of wood-constructed double-decker beds so that the returning troops would have a place to sleep. We had very large, long tractor trailer units. During the way to the city we stopped near an apple orchard. Foolishly, I ate one or two apples, never realizing that the Germans might have poisoned them. I paid dearly. The next day I was taken to see a camp doctor and found myself in an ambulance on the way to a general hospital in Reims. After about a week I recovered. In an ordinary ward for a few days awaiting discharge, I began to get an idea of what might occur in the future. The ward was full of soldiers who had been in a very serious battle near Metz. Many had trench foot and some had serious battle-inflicted wounds.

"On the day of discharge I was sent outdoors to an ambulance waiting to transport me and others back to Sissonne. During the several-hour wait some of the ambulance crew filled time by drinking champagne, of which there appeared to be a non-ending supply.

"Back at Sissonne I now had a problem. The regiment had returned to camp while I was in the hospital. I had no idea where I belonged or where my stuff was. I went to the barracks from which I had gone to the hospital and found exactly where I had been assigned and where to find my clothes and equipment. I was assigned to A Company, 1st Platoon. I was the only one from my jump class that I know of who was assigned to the 1st Platoon. I went to the orderly room and was surprised to find that my arrival was no big deal. They said to go find an empty bunk in the platoon squad room and settle in. That's all there was to it—immediate acceptance by the more experienced troopers without question of where I came from. Later I realized that replacements and new arrivals were non-events because they were always occurring. Sometimes during combat a replacement would appear and be gone without ever getting to know anyone or be known other than a temporary name on a roster."[6]

Bayley became close friends with Pfc. Harold ("Harry") Freeman of Willimantic, Connecticut, one of the veterans in the 1st Platoon: "Freeman was one of the guys that had been around for a long time. The first day I joined the platoon in November, I didn't know anybody. We went to the Red Cross place, the coffee and the donut line, and he made me welcome to the platoon and we became real close friends. He was a good guy. Harry was one of the old guys because he had one of the desert uniforms, the light-colored uniforms.

"Within a company or platoon the only people you might know well were the few in your squad, and maybe not all of them. One usually had a few close friends that stuck together and went to town, USO shows, etc. You might know by sight that a fellow soldier belonged to the company or platoon, but never really know that person. The squad operated as sort of a family group, all for one and one for all."[7]

On November 16, a long file of British trucks arrived in the old French army cantonment at Sissonne, about twenty-five miles northwest of Reims, France. A cold drizzle fell while the trucks stopped near the three-story barracks. Aboard a number of trucks were the tired paratroopers of Col. Reuben H. Tucker's 504th Regimental Combat Team. The 504th would be stationed in Sissonne, while the 505th PIR, 325th GIR and the division artillery units would camp at Suippes, east of Reims. Thus the 376th Parachute Field Artillery Battalion [PFAB] was separated from the 504th for the time being. The airborne engineers of C Company, 307th Airborne Engineer Battalion [AEB], however, stayed at Sissonne as well, but in a different area.

Camp Sissonne, as the army barracks were called, was just a few miles east of the city of Laon, although many men preferred to see the famous cathedral in Reims or to receive a pass to visit Paris. First Lieutenant William D. Mandle of the Regimental Demolition Platoon wrote to his parents that evening: "I am now attempting to recover from a sad case of soritus feetius—meaning my feet hurt. That's the bad thing about this outfit—we get to fly into combat, but they make us walk back!

"We have a fair setup here—social life is nil, but the quarters and food so far have been OK. It really was swell to get a shower and some clean clothes again—my jumpsuit was so dirty that I had to practically peel it off. No mail has come in yet but the rumor is that truck loads will arrive tomorrow—I'm hoping so, 'cause it's been over two weeks since my last letter; our packages should be in this bunch too.

"My travels now include 13 countries—I'm beginning to feel like Gulliver. Of all that I've seen, I believe Tunisia was the worst and Holland and Germany the best, for cleanliness, food and scenery. The prettiest gals are to be found in Belgium. As far as England—well, they have Big Ben and Montgomery. Sicily and Italy have good wine and numerous prospects from which to pick future New York mayors. They also have plenty of mud and mountains, but I became allergic to them this time last year. The people I liked best were the Scots. Morocco, Algeria, Sardinia and Egypt, I will remember namely because I've been there—your leather goods came from Morocco. France hasn't made much of an impression as yet. So much for the travelogue—I wonder what the United States is like?"[8]

As 1st Lt. Reneau G. Breard, who led Private First Class Bayley's platoon, remembered: "We arrived at a French cantonment at Sissonne near Reims, France, on 16 November 1944. I think the weather was awful the whole time we were there. I did get to Reims once and saw the cathedral. It was mostly sandbagged on the outside, but untouched. I did not get to Paris, but we did go into Sissonne to the railroad station café where we ordered French champagne and large ham or beef sandwiches on French bread. They were good.

"We spent most of our time getting new and reconditioned equipment and a few replacements. We were also issued K-rations for three days. I sent my khaki jumpsuit (We wore them the first 10 days in Holland and then changed into olive green after a shower at the power plant at Nijmegen, making our unit look like a new unit to the Germans) and also my olive green to the GI cleaners, but I never got them back."[9]

A new assistant platoon leader, 1st Lt. James A. Kiernan, was assigned to Lieutenant Breard's platoon on November 17. Born in June 1920, Lieutenant Kiernan had joined the U.S. Army in 1942 and arrived in England in the late summer of 1944: "I was born and raised in Eau Claire, Wisconsin, and I was drafted into the army in April 1942. I went to Officer Candidate School [OCS] in Fort Benning and got out of there in March 1943. When I got out of OCS I tried to get into the paratroopers, but they assigned me elsewhere so I just kind of went with the flow. Then I was assigned to the 71st Infantry Division.

"From the 71st I went to England as a replacement officer. While I was in England they had some recruiters around from the 82nd, recruiting people that wanted to go to jump school. I was in a replacement center in England and I still wanted to go jump school, so I applied and joined the 82nd. The 82nd ran its own jump school in Oldham, outside of Leicester, England. Major Zakby was in charge of the base camp in England."[10]

Kiernan graduated from Jump School on October 22, 1944, and was flown to Holland in a C-47 together with a number of other officers and enlisted men. They landed on the provisional air strip at Keent, near the city of Grave, and were sent by truck to the 504th PIR assembly area: "I just barely had joined the 504th in Holland when they left. I think they were still waiting to assign me to a company when they pulled out. It was at Sissonne that I was assigned to A Company. It was nothing unusual to have a replacement officer coming in. I was a 1st lieutenant then, and therefore I became the assistant of Reneau Breard, who was also a first lieutenant."[11]

On November 18, a notice appeared on the 3rd Battalion bulletin board informing officers and enlisted men they were now permitted to write to their parents about the Holland Campaign, as long as they did not include any data. The senior medic in H Company, T/5 Seymour Flox was one of the first to do so that day. Captain Henry B. Keep, the 3rd Battalion S-3 officer, wrote a long letter to his mother two days later: "To begin with, we are no longer at the front. We have been withdrawn and are now somewhere in France, getting a rest and reorganized. I am fine and hope to put on some of the weight I lost during the last couple of months. We are living in old barracks and sleeping on hard wooden cots and washing in cold water, but everyone is so thankful to be here, to have a roof over one's head, to be able to sleep in peace and to have the leisure to wash, that this spot has taken on many of the aspects of Heaven in the eyes of the men and officers. The weather is foul—cold, raw and constant rain—but perhaps it is just a squall and not customary."[12]

Meanwhile, two 504th officers had been sent to England to train the men from various American infantry divisions or quartermaster companies who had applied for the paratroops. These men had to be well trained before being assigned to the 82nd Airborne Division to bring the regiments back to authorized strength. Maj. Abdallah K. Zakby, former executive officer of the 3rd Battalion, had been sent to England in early October 1944 to supervise the training of the replacements. He performed the job of regimental commander in England, using Colonel Tucker's car with his permission. Eighty percent of the training was done at night to prepare the new soldiers for night patrols and realistic combat situations.[13]

First Lieutenant James Megellas, a platoon leader from H Company, was sent with three sergeants to England in the middle of November 1944 to help Major Zakby: "I was ordered along with three sergeants to return to the regimental rear headquarters in Leicester, where about 250 paratrooper replacements were waiting to join us. My mission: organize and train them based on combat experience and generally prepare them for assignment to combat squads and platoons. When they were ready, we would move to France.

"The replacements consisted almost entirely of enlisted men with a sprinkling of non-commissioned officers but no officers. Their average age was about twenty. I was an old man to them. All had volunteered for parachute training school, had made the requisite five jumps, and were proudly wearing jump boots and paratrooper wings. [...] Most of the men in this group qualified as paratroopers in newly established schools in England. The course was an abbreviated two weeks, including the required five jumps." [14]

Also in England was the former battalion commander of the 504th Parachute Battalion and subsequently the first regimental executive officer of the 504th Parachute Infantry Regiment, Lt. Col. Richard Chase. He had closely followed the operations of his old regiment in the newspapers while in charge of the war room at General Omar Bradley's 12th Army Group Headquarters. In late November 1944, he was transferred to the same function in the staff of Lt. Gen. Lewis Brereton's First Allied Airborne Army.

A few days after the 504th PIR arrived in their new base in France, they celebrated Thanksgiving Day in the old army buildings at Camp Sissonne, which did not offer much in the way of comfort, but were still preferable to the cold, muddy foxholes the companies had occupied in Holland. "The 504th, having returned from Holland, enjoyed passes to Paris and other points, [and] had a very satisfying Thanksgiving," remembered Bayley. "The food service personnel went all out for that day. They managed to get white table cloths on every table and prepared a magnificent Thanksgiving dinner with all the conventional fixings.

"After that we were looking forward to Christmas. According to the reports, all was going well with the war at the front and it looked as though the troopers might not be needed again. Rumors were rife though with plans of jumping into Berlin ahead of the Russians or the outfit being returned to the United States for refitting and assignment to the invasion of Japan."[15]

The Holland Campaign had caused an obvious and lasting change within the 504th. Many of the original junior officers who remained after the Anzio Campaign had become casualties in Holland. The casualty rate had also been high among the non-commissioned officers and company commanders. This lack of officers was mainly due to battle losses, but it was increased by Major General Gavin's decision to transfer a number of experienced officers like Captain Beverly T. Richardson and 1st Lieutenant G.P. Crockett, and recently commissioned 2nd Lieutenant Reginald J. Gowan to the 325th Glider Infantry Regiment. After observing glider troops in action in Normandy and Holland, Gavin felt that their ranks needed to be bolstered by tough paratroopers. Richardson would miss the next combat mission due to battle-inflicted wounds received in Holland and return to the 325th on February 1, 1945.[16] Although they operated primarily out of sight, Maj. John S. Lekson and 1st Lt. Elbert F. Smith performed numerous assignments as members of the Division G-3 Section.

Because of the losses sustained in the Holland Campaign, it was necessary to appoint, assign, promote and transfer officers and non-commissioned officers so that each company would be prepared for another eventual combat mission. The 1st Battalion staff changed little, apart from Maj. Willard E. Harrison's promotion to lieutenant colonel on November 24. Captain Charles W. Duncan transferred to 1st Battalion Headquarters as Battalion S-3 officer, and was replaced by 1st Lt. John N. Pease, who rejoined A Company after serving eight months as Battalion S-3, and was placed in command of the company. First Lieutenant Ernest L. Walker still served in the 3rd Platoon with 2nd Lt. James G. Douglass as his assistant and 1st Lt. Earl V. Morin continued to command the 2nd Platoon. Both had been promoted on the same day as Lieutenant Breard. Second Lieutenant George A. Johnson was transferred to the 2nd Platoon as an assistant platoon leader and 1st Lt. Joseph G. Wheeler left A Company and was made a platoon leader in Headquarters Company.

Captain Thomas C. Helgeson and 1st Lieutenant Henry C. Dunavant, from Waynesville, North Carolina, still presided over B Company; 1st Lt. William A. Meerman was with his 3rd Platoon; and 2nd Lt. Ralph S. Bird,

Jr. and 2nd Lt. Richard A. Smith remained in charge of their 1st Platoon. Three new officers also arrived: 1st Lt. David L. Thomas joined the company to take command of the 2nd Platoon, and 2nd Lt. Robert J. Brantley and 2nd Lt. Thomas H. Keating were new assistant platoon leaders.

In C Company, Capt. Albert E. Milloy said goodbye, transferred to change leadership with Capt. Roy E. Anderson of Headquarters Company. At the same time, 2nd Lt. Charles W. Battisti was transferred to command the Mortar Platoon. Second Lieutenants Robert Magruda and Wayne M. Fetters remained assistant platoon leaders and 1st Lt. Bruno J. Rolak stayed with his 2nd Platoon, while 1st Lt. John M. Randles joined the company as 1st Platoon leader. Last to arrive on December 17 from Service Company was 1st Lt. Vern G. Frisinger, assigned to the 3rd Platoon.

Lieutenant Fetters wrote a long letter to a friend in his native Wisconsin on November 23: "Our mail was held up for quite some time. Two days ago it came in. Consequentially I received it all at one time. It surely made me homesick to say the least. There are some deer around here. Some of the guys were out rabbit hunting (with M1 rifles) and they came across pheasants, rabbits, deer and they even saw a wild boar. [...] How are things back there? I imagine everyone is getting all set for Christmas. I may not be home for it this year, but from the way things look, I won't be sitting in some hole like I did last year, I hope. I am not going to say much about France, as I haven't been around too much. Personally, I don't think much of these French people. They are just a shade better than the Italians and that isn't saying too much.

"The weather here is much like the fall weather back home. It has rained almost every day for the past week. We are living in barracks so I'm not complaining too much. From some of the holes I've been in, it doesn't take much to satisfy me.

"Today was payday. Some of the enlisted men drew as much as $800.00. When we get in combat the fellows don't spend a cent. I'm really saving the dough over here. However, it is a problem to get home to spend it. I'm salting away at least $200.00 each month."[17]

The 2nd Battalion staff of Lt. Col. Edward N. Wellems remained unchanged since leaving Holland, as did Capt. Adam A. Komosa's D Company and Capt. Robert J. Cellar's Headquarters Company. Captain Herbert H. Norman's E Company, however, had lost several officers on October 3 and was strengthened soon after with the transfer of 1st Lt. Roy L. James of Headquarters Company. At Camp Sissonne two replacement officers—2nd Lt. Glen R. Simpson and 2nd Lt. Charles E. Zastrow—were officially assigned, although they had already joined the regiment in the latter days of the Holland Campaign. With 1st Lt. John S. Thompson serving as company executive officer, 1st Lt. William E. Sharp, Jr. of the 2nd Platoon was now the most experienced platoon leader.

Lieutenant Zastrow wrote to his parents on the afternoon of Monday, 11 December: "Have about half an hour to write before we fall out for a Division review—presentation of medals to those who won them in Holland. Our company is pretty well represented, as is our Regiment within the Division. Things have been very dull the past several days—rained almost daily the past week. Sun does shine more frequently than it does in England— that's not saying a great deal for the sun though. We have training in the morning—afternoons we play football for about two hours, then return to beautify the barracks. Starting next week our schedule becomes more rugged.

"Looks as if I'm going to get to see Paris within the next month or so— 48 hours of it. Not long, but better than nothing. Haven't seen much of the French countryside, except by air. We're pretty well confined to camp. Seems the paratroopers get a bit playful when they get to town, and the Frenchmen have no sense of humor. So the military authorities put the taverns off limits for a while. If we stay here long enough, all France will probably be off limits to us.

"Enclosing a couple of pictures a friend took and gave to me. Had them developed in a small town nearby, went in yesterday to get them—had some more taken. It's a real workout, talking to these people—very friendly—get along OK by pantomime. All the talk about French girls being beautiful is just a myth, or else they have all vacated this area, because there are certainly none around. [...]

"Went to church yesterday morning—nice service—enclosing the program. Have a swell Chaplain [Delbert A. Kuehl]—been with the Regiment since it was formed. Made all combat jumps with it—sticks around the front line with the men—everyone has the utmost respect for him. [...] Had a good meal on Thanksgiving Day: turkey and all the trimmings—including real potatoes in place of all the usual dehydrated variety."[18]

In 1st Lt. William J. Sweet's F Company three new (assistant) platoon leaders—1st Lt. Robert E. Manning, Jr., 2nd Lt. Robert E. Bramson and 2nd Lt. James H. Peerson—were assigned on November 6 in Holland. Twenty-two-year-old Lieutenant Bramson had joined the paratroopers in Fort Benning after graduating from OCS at Fort Hood: "It was exciting, especially because I had not been up in a plane before joining the airborne. The physical training was very exhausting even though I was in pretty good condition, having played basketball on a university team plus all the intramural sports in college—actually my major was physical education—and obviously the airborne selection process dwelt heavily on physical condition. My only problems were a little air sickness and a slight fear of heights. The training sergeants made no distinction between officers and enlisted men. Student officers were yelled at and treated the same as everyone else and I recall seeing majors and lieutenant colonels chastised by the training cadre.

"The paratroop boots were a distinguishing feature of the paratroop uniform with the pant legs inserted in the boots and bloused. I remember seeing a trooper who had refused a jump order on a practice jump and in the evening formation he was singled out and instructed to remove or de-blouse his pants from his boots, as he was in effect dismissed from the jump school training. After we made the required five training jumps and were awarded our paratroop wings, I and several others were sent to Pathfinder school for a short time before we were sent overseas."[19]

The 3rd Battalion had been more badly mauled in Holland than the 1st or 2nd. At the time the regiment arrived in Camp Sissonne, some 13 men had been captured from each of the 3rd Battalion rifle companies, in addition to those who had been killed or wounded. Captain Thomas' G Company was the worst off of all—all platoon leaders and assistant platoon leaders, except one, had been captured, killed, or severely wounded. Six replacement officers were assigned to the company to take their places. First Lieutenant Harry J. Frear assumed the leadership of the 1st Platoon, while James R. Pursell, the acting 1st Platoon leader, was promoted to first lieutenant and became permanent 2nd Platoon leader. This enabled 1st Lt. Roy M. Hanna to concentrate once again on his duties as executive officer. Also assigned to G Company were 2nd Lt. Robert T. Tennyson and former 1st Sgt. James C. Hesson of B Company, who had received a battlefield commission to second lieutenant. Tennyson was assigned to the 2nd Platoon as assistant platoon leader and Hesson joined the 3rd Platoon. Second Lieutenant James R. Allmand, Jr., remained leader of the 3rd Platoon.

I Company was strengthened by the arrival of 2nd Lt. George A. Amos and 2nd Lt. Chester R. Anderson, who came from Sioux Falls, South Dakota, and 1st Lt. Harold G. Weber, while 2nd Lt. Joseph Shirk rejoined the 2nd Platoon. The assistant platoon leaders were 2nd Lieutenants Robert M. Rogers (1st Platoon), Bernard E. Karnap (2nd Platoon) and Anderson. First Lieutenant Harry H. Price remained in charge of the 3rd Platoon. Lieutenant

Anderson would be transferred to G Company in early December. H Company saw fewer changes, since only in the 1st Platoon had leaders been captured or promoted elsewhere. Headquarters Company, 3rd Battalion, retained its commander, Captain George M. Warfield, who had taken command right after the Waal River Crossing.

All the new officers, including those who had joined the 504th in the weeks preceding the Holland Campaign, had to participate in the traditional Prop Blast ceremony. Lieutenant Bramson was sent out with another officer to buy spirits: "I understood that the Prop Blast party was a sort of tradition to be celebrated by the survivors upon the return from a mission or campaign. After the return from Holland to the camp in Sissonne, as one of the new young officers, I was sent along with another second lieutenant, outfitted with a jeep and some money, to Reims to purchase whatever liquid refreshments we could obtain. We found champagne at what we thought to be very inexpensive prices. In addition we were only able to find and buy cognac—that was the sum total of our purchases.

"Our party was held in our company area room on the post. The area was not too large, but it was near where my bed was located. Because of the size of the area, I assume the party was only for F Company. The one thing I remember, other than it was a loud affair, was that my platoon leader, [Lt. Stuart] McCash, fell and had an accident. As a result I temporarily became the new platoon leader and handled the platoon on the road march later from Sissonne to Belgium, until he subsequently returned to the platoon."[20]

As Capt. Paul D. Bruns, the 2nd Battalion Surgeon, recalled: "I was formally inducted into the 504th Regiment by standing in front of the commanding Colonel Tucker, being handed a pitcher of straight alcohol, and told not to stop drinking while my fellow officers counted—'1001, 1002, 1003'—which was the rate you were supposed to count when you jumped in combat before opening your auxiliary chute. This was staged as the traditional sobriety party and called the 'Prop Blast,' that blast of air you get when you jump out the door."[21]

While the 82nd Airborne Division was resting up at Camp Sissonne, Major General Gavin was making preparations so the division could move promptly in case it was called upon. It seemed unrealistic that the 82nd would be called from Theater Reserve, but the division gathered a basic load of ammunition and enough rations for two days. There were several opportunities to obtain a pass. One was to win the marksmanship competition held among the enlisted men, where the prize was a pass to the city for a few days. The winner, Pfc. Julius Lasslo of A Company, was a determined guy. A little nearsighted, he needed glasses to see at a distance, but he dropped them the day before the competition, shattering the lenses. Not to be deterred, he found the largest piece of glass for his right eye and used cellophane tape to hold the bit of glass in the frame. This he used to sight his rifle and ended up winning the competition.

Apart from participating in marksmanship competitions, the newly assigned paratroopers also needed additional training to prepare them for their first battle. Colonel Tucker and his officers knew that previous replacements had been ill-prepared and needed to learn a great deal before they could be depended on in battle. They were not untrained, but basic infantry training and parachute school were still an insufficient basis for combat. Bayley recalled of one of the courses at Camp Sissonne, which involved the remains of the many World War I trenches in the area: "We had some of the troopers dress in German uniforms and rise out of the remnants of the World War I trenches to show us new guys what German soldiers would look like when we met them. I can still picture that training in my mind."[22]

Maj. Ivan J. Roggen made Captain Bruns responsible for checking the whorehouses in and around Sissonne and Laon to keep the rate of venereal diseases [VD] as low as possible: "My first rest and recuperation duty after coming out of the line was to make certain none of our spirited troops picked up any nasty venereal diseases in the local whorehouses. The first one I visited in a village outside of Sissonne (pronounced 'Swassown') had been servicing the Yanks during World War I, and was delighted to do so during World War II. The Madam had not lost much of her verve from a quarter of a century ago. She assured me that her girls were clean, were inspected regularly, and would comply with all my new regulations. Hell, I saw GI's going in the side door while I was talking to the Madam at the front door. I am not a man with scruples, so her house was OK'd for anything and anybody. I emphasized that if I happened to treat any of her customers for one of those bad diseases, her place would be off limits. Her fear of losing money, chocolates and cigarettes reassured me that none of my troops would get clap or syphilis. She should thank God she didn't have to worry about AIDS and herpes. [...] It beat treating soldiers, who on night patrol duty were damn near killed in Holland. I'll take treating VD any day."[23]

Captain Bruns visited the cathedral and the nearby monastery of Laon several times. He drove almost daily from Camp Sissonne to Laon and back in his ambulance: "Driving to and from Laon along the plains, flatter than

North Dakota, afforded me an opportunity to go from farm to farm asking for *oeufs*. I called them *erfs*. Anyway the farmers knew I was looking for fresh eggs. (Hadn't the Krauts been looking for the same thing before the Yanks came?) When bored with driving my meat wagon, I would take my commandeered motorcycle and speed up and down the Laon-to-Paris highway, looking for anything, eggs included.

"The artillery range in our rest area offered a great opportunity for hunters—as all 504th men are—to bag rabbits, if they could hit them. I tried with a .45, my friend with an automatic rifle, but we got nothing but experience. Another relief in the rest area of Sissonne was to go to Reims. I could not go there often enough. The Reims Cathedral, a magnificent structure, is the most beautiful church in Europe. However, there happened to be one slight problem. When the enlisted men came off the line they were ready for a holiday. Reims took the brunt of every drunken paratrooper in the 82nd, and I laid low and explored the underground caverns where champagne was stored. The Huns had so depleted the supply of champagne bottles that Pieper Heidseck [the champaign house] promised to give me a full bottle of champagne for every empty bottle I brought in. Need I say more? My room at the rest area was the 'champagne room.' A word of caution: never get sick on champagne. I can't drink more than a glass of it to this day. Another diversion was driving my Catholic Chaplain to Paris to buy perfume. Little did I know that he was a personal friend of the Guerlain family. I acquired every perfume known to womankind and eventually brought most of it back to my wife."[24]

Pvt. Morris ("Mike") Holmstock of B Company felt glad to be in a rest area after surviving half of the Anzio and the entire Holland Campaign: "When we got to Camp Sissonne, Colonel Tucker said to us, 'We are finished for a while. I can guarantee that we will be two months off the line.' I turned 22 years old on December 13, 1944."[25] Little could Holmstock and others in the 504th RCT know that their next call to arms was fast approaching.

Lieutenant Colonel Richard Chase in the War Room of the First Allied Airborne Army, December 1944. *Courtesy: Pamela Chase Hain*

CHAPTER 2

A SERIOUS BREAKTHROUGH
WERBOMONT AND RAHIER, BELGIUM,
DECEMBER 16–19, 1944

On the early morning of Saturday, December 16, just before dawn, a massive German artillery barrage opened up along a 65-mile front on the Belgian–German border. The sector was mainly held by one battered and two green divisions of VIII Corps, Lt. Gen. Courtney Hodges' U.S. First Army. The Germans broke through the front line and moved deeper into the densely forested region of the Ardennes Mountains in the Belgian province of Wallonia and through the Grand Duchy of Luxembourg. Hodges was faced with a difficult situation, since the bulk of his 14 divisions were deployed north of the Belgian Ardennes. Behind VIII Corps, roughly in a triangle formed by the cities of Liège, Verviers, and Spa, lay large gasoline and map supply installations built in preparation for an offensive toward the Rhine. The city of Liège, twenty miles northwest of Hodges' headquarters in Spa, was the second largest American supply depot on the Continent.

The American fuel dumps in the Belgian Ardennes were extremely valuable to the Germans, who had insufficient fuel to go all the way to Antwerp and Liège. If the move were successfully accomplished, Hitler hoped to literally divide the Allied forces, encircle and destroy four Allied armies and negotiate a favorable peace treaty. The biggest obstacle to success was not the dense forest of the Belgian Ardennes, but rather the Meuse River at Liège and the Amblève River and its series of tributaries flowing south from the springs and swamps of the rugged Hohes Venn region. The Amblève, situated south of Spa and flowing westward, is joined at the town of Trois Ponts by the Salm River, a north-flowing tributary out of the Hohes Venn. By blowing

37

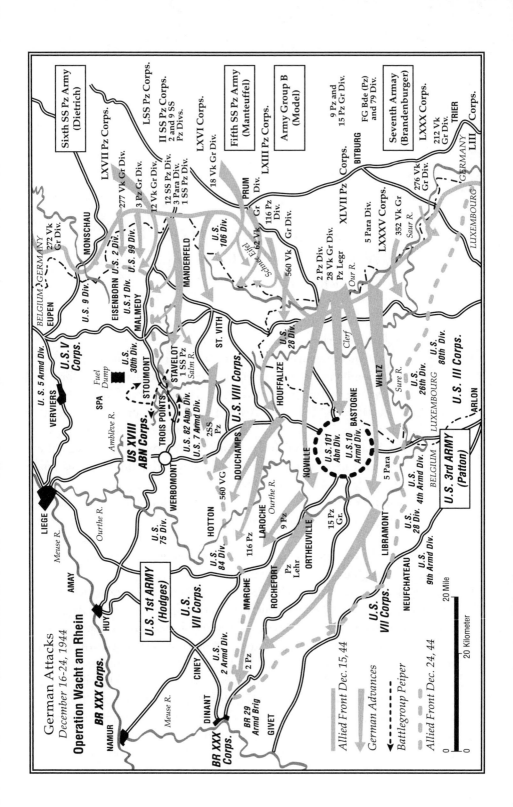

German Attacks
December 16-24, 1944
Operation Wacht am Rhein

Sixth SS Pz Army (Dietrich)
LXVII Pz Corps.
LSS Pz Corps.
II SS Pz Corps. 2 and 9 SS Pz Divs.
LXVI Corps.
Fifth SS Pz Army (Manteuffel)
LXIII Pz Corps.
Army Group B (Model)
9 Pz and 15 Pz Div.
FG Bde (Pz) and 79 Div.
XLVII Pz Corps.
BITBURG
Seventh Army (Brandenburger)
LXXX Corps.
TRIER
LIII Corps.

272 Vk Gr Div.
LXVII Pz Corps.
277 Vk Gr Div.
3 Pz Div.
12 Vk Gr Div.
12 SS Pz Div.
3 Para Div.
1 SS Pz Div.
18 Vk Gr Div.
PRUM
116 Pz Div.
560 Vk Gr Div.
2 Pz Div.
28 Vk Gr Pz Legr
Our R.
5 Para Div.
LXXXV Corps.
352 Vk Gr Div.
Saur R.
276 Vk Gr Div.

MONSCHAU
BELGIUM GERMANY
EUPEN
U.S. 9 Div.
EISENBORN U.S. 2 Div.
U.S. 1 Div.
U.S. 99 Div.
MANDERFELD
U.S. 106 Div.
62 Vk Gr Div.
ST. VITH
U.S. 28 Div.
Clerf
WILTZ
GERMANY
LUXEMBOURG

U.S. 5 Armd Div.
VERVIERS
U.S. V Corps.
SPA Fuel Dump
U.S. 30th Div.
STAVELOT 1 SS Pz
STOUMONT Salm R.
TROIS POINTS
US XVIII ABN Corps.
2SS Pz
U.S. 82 Abn Div.
U.S. 7 Armd Div.
WERBOMONT
U.S. VIII Corps.
HOUFFALIZE
NOVILLE
BASTOGNE
U.S. 101 Abn Div.
U.S. 10 Armd Div.
5 Para
Sure R.
U.S. 26th Div.
ARLON
U.S. 80th Div.
U.S. III Corps.

LIEGE
Ambleve R.
Meuse R.
AMAY
HUY
U.S. 1st ARMY (Hodges)
U.S. VII Corps.
Ourthe R.
U.S. 75 Div.
HOTTON
U.S. 84 Div.
DOUCHAMPS
560 VG
LAROCHE
9 Pz
116 Pz
Ourthe R.
ORTHEUVILLE
15 Pz Gr.
Pz Lehr
ROCHEFORT
MARCHE
LIBRAMONT
U.S. 28 Div. 4th Armd Div.
NEUFCHATEAU
U.S. 9th Armd Div.
U.S. VII Corps.
BELGIUM LUXEMBOURG
U.S. 3rd ARMY (Patton)

BR XXX Corps.
NAMUR
Meuse R.
CINEY
DINANT
U.S. 2 Armd Div.
2 Pz
BR 29 Armd Brig
GIVET
BR XXX Corps.

Allied Front Dec. 15, 44
German Advances
Battlegroup Peiper
Allied Front Dec. 24, 44

20 Mile
20 Kilometer
0   0

up or defending the bridges across these rivers and the Ourthe River to the south, Lieutenant General Hodges could probably at least temporarily halt the German advance. But where could he find at least two of the required divisions? He immediately sent out all independent tank battalions [TB], combat engineer groups, and other small units at his disposal, but it was clear their forces were insufficient to stop the German advance alone.

The strongest division in the German Sixth SS-Panzer Army, *SS-Brigadeführer* [Brigadier General] Wilhelm Mohnke's 1st SS-Panzer Division "Leibstandarte Adolf Hitler," was tasked to move forward as soon as the American front lines had been crushed. This division was the strongest fighting unit of the Sixth SS-Panzer Army, with about a hundred Mark IV and Panther tanks, and the attached 501st Schwere SS-Panzer-Abteilung consisting of 42 Tiger tanks. Mohnke had to capture the fuel dumps, a number of important bridges across the Salm River and the Amblève River, and one or more bridges across the Meuse River, thus enabling the remainder of the Sixth SS-Panzer Army to continue its advance without delay.

Mohnke divided his division into four battlegroups whose mission was to break through the U.S. 99th Infantry Regiment near Lanzerath on the Belgian–German border and advance on prefixed lines. Kampfgruppe Peiper, commanded by the 29-year-old *SS-Obersturmbannführer* [Lieutenant Colonel] Jochen Peiper, captured a large gasoline dump at Büllingen, and Peiper became notorious after shooting Belgian civilians and American prisoners of war in the towns of Büllingen, Honsfeld, and Stoumont. The most infamous of Peiper's war crimes was committed on December 17 at the Baugnez crossroads southeast of the city of Malmédy, when some of Peiper's men opened fire point-blank on 113 American prisoners. Sixty-seven of them were either killed instantly or shot when Germans later walked through the field to pick off wounded survivors. Forty-six Americans, some of whom were from the 285th Field Artillery Observation Battalion, managed to slip away into the woods and link up with other American units.[26] War correspondents quickly spread their gruesome story.

In the early evening of December 17, Colonel Tucker's paratroopers were still unaware of events in the Belgian Ardennes. The first notice was a telephone call from Division Headquarters of the 82nd Airborne Division at Camp Sissonne. First Lieutenant Rufus K. Broadaway, junior aide to Major General Gavin, picked up the phone and heard an almost incoherent story from Col. Ralph P. Eaton, Chief of Staff of the XVIII Airborne Corps. When Eaton stressed he urgently need to speak with Gavin, Broadaway called his commander, who learned that Supreme Headquarters of the Allied Expeditionary Force [SHAEF] had ordered the XVIII Airborne Corps to prepare to move to the front within the next 24 hours.

Eaton made clear that there had been a serious German breakthrough at the front in Belgium. But there were some problems with issuing orders: Maj. Gen. Maxwell D. Taylor, the commanding officer of the 101st Airborne Division, was in Washington discussing a change in the structure of the airborne divisions; the corps commander, Maj. Gen. Matthew B. Ridgway, was on leave in England. Given their absence, Gavin was effectively in charge. He instructed Eaton to warn Brig. Gen. Anthony C. McAuliffe and have him prepare the 101st Airborne Division for immediate movement in accordance with the SHAEF estimate, then assembled his staff to prepare a tentative plan for the move to Bastogne—an important town at the meeting of seven roads in the Ardennes—and called for all the regimental commanders to issue his plans.

Several junior officers of the 504th PIR were unaware of the German breakthrough that weekend. In A Company, First Lieutenant Kiernan spent the whole Sunday at the rifle pits: "As I returned I heard that the S-4 had issued a basic load of ammunition, so I knew that something was going on. I had been promised a pass for a short leave for the next week because I had been at the rifle pits all that Sunday, but as it turned out I never got that leave."[27] Kiernan's platoon leader, 1st Lt. Reneau G. Breard, was watching a movie with fellow officers when he noticed Colonel Tucker and Lieutenants Colonel Harrison and Warren R. Williams were called away: "Immediately, I went to my quarters and rolled up my bedroll and packed. Later, I went down to the company and finally got a used, but clean combat jumpsuit and a pair of galoshes to fit over my boots. I think we worked all night getting ready to leave. A three-day-supply of K-rations was issued to each man."[28]

In the barracks, non-commissioned officers and enlisted men remained uninformed of the German breakthrough "until late in the evening of December 17," according to Bayley, when "our company commander came into the barracks and announced that the Germans had broken through. We were told that we would be moving out to combat early in the morning of the 18th. The non-coms were conferring with their squads and platoons, the lieutenants with their platoon leaders and the company commander.

"My platoon sergeant said that I would be the machine gunner, mostly because I was big and strong enough to carry this weapon. I told him to get someone else since I had no training on the machine gun and did not know how to set it up and operate it. He got the normally assigned platoon machine gunner out of the stockade where he was serving time for something he had done or not done. This was a rather suave, smooth character who had a custom-made shoulder holster for a small automatic that he carried inside of his shirt or coat. He looked like a professional gunman."[29]

Private First Class Ervin E. Shaffer, from the 3rd Platoon of 1st Lt. John N. Pease's A Company, was "in the company room when they told us that the Germans had broken through. We would have to be ready to leave in a few hours: 'Go to the supply room, draw any equipment you need and be ready to leave in about four hours.' We were all ready to go and the trucks were late. They came in about 0900 hours in the morning. We stayed there until the orders came for us to load up."[30]

Sergeant Meldon F. Hurlbert of C Company, 307th AEB, was watching a movie at Camp Sissonne with some of his buddies when someone stopped it and turned on the lights. They were told to go back to their respective company barracks. Startled by his order, Hurlbert and his friends went back to the barracks and were told to go through the ammunition dump and help themselves to 'all you want.'[31] Some men like Pvt. George H. Mahon, 3rd Platoon of E Company, had turned in their jumpsuits at the laundry shops: "When this news came, all we had was our dress clothes. So we had to wear them. They redistributed our arms, like my BAR, and rifles for the riflemen. All that stuff had to be redistributed."[32] Second Lieutenant Robert E. Bramson of F Company recalled they had been "bunking in a large room, probably previous office space," when they received the alert "to prepare to leave early next morning—giving us time to resupply equipment and ammo. I don't believe we were given much information other than news of a serious German attack and breakthrough. I for one had no information as to specifically where we were heading."[33]

Capt. Victor W. Campana, who had been made the 2nd Battalion S-3 officer only a few weeks earlier, shared a room with Capt. Charles Duncan and Capt. Henry B. Keep, the S-3 officers of the 1st and 3rd Battalions, respectively. Training at Camp Sissonne, Campana remembered, "consisted mainly of small unit training to include night compass problems, range-firing and road marches. Regimental and division reviews, intermingled with three-day passes to Paris filled out our program. Christmas was just eight days away and everyone had visions of a peaceful Christmas holiday accompanied by that very appetizing turkey dinner which does not come too often in the army.

"On Sunday evening about 2130 hours, December 17, word was passed through the officers' quarters that Colonel Tucker had been summoned to Division Headquarters for an important meeting. Some of the officers who had been listening to the radio stated that the announcer mentioned a series of German attacks in the Ardennes, and this was likely the reason for the meeting. Many officers discredited their assumption and prepared for bed. However, word traveled around again that Colonel Tucker had called a battalion commanders' meeting."[34]

Campana, Duncan and Keep decided that action might be in the offing and returned to their respective battalion headquarters to await further information. At approximately 2230 hours, the battalion commanders arrived at their battalion headquarters with operational orders. Lieutenant Colonel Wellems, Campana recalled, "instructed the adjutant, 1st Lt. Chester Garrison, to phone the company commanders for an immediate meeting. He then gave me an overlay and some French road maps. The overlay was very scanty, merely showing the proposed route of march to a general area in the vicinity of Bastogne. The company commanders soon arrived. They were Capt. Robert Cellar of Headquarters Company, Capt. Adam Komosa of D Company, 1st Lt. William Sweet of F Company, and 1st Lt. John Thompson, executive officer of E Company. Capt. Felix Simon and 1st Lt. Ross I. Donnelly, the battalion surgeon and supply officer respectively, were also present. Capt. Herbert Norman, commanding officer of E Company, was on pass in Paris as were 1st Lt. [Lauren W.] Ramsey, the 81mm Mortar Platoon leader, and other key officers and non-commissioned officers.

"The battalion commander immediately acquainted us with the situation. Extracts of this meeting were as follows: 'The Germans have made a breakthrough in the Ardennes sector, near Bastogne. Some American units have already been overrun, particularly the 106th U.S. Infantry Division. We move out tomorrow at 0900 hours in 10-ton semi-trailers. Lieutenant Donnelly will issue K-rations and ammunition tonight to the companies. One machine gun, half loaded, will be manned on the cab of each truck in case of enemy air attacks. [First] Lieutenant [Earnest H.] Brown, from D Company, will be in charge of the battalion rear echelon. Each company will leave at least two men behind for the rear echelon. Kitchen personnel will also be left behind initially. All weapons that are in ordnance will be returned to us before we leave.'

"Upon the completion of this meeting, the company commanders returned to their respective orderly rooms and started immediate preparations for the move the next morning. Equipment being left behind was packed and stored. K-rations and ammunition were distributed to the men. All sections of the battalion staff packed and stored material not vital for the move.

"About 0100 hours 18 December, replacements came to the battalion direct from England. These replacements included men without combat experience plus former members of the unit who had been wounded during the Holland operations. It was not until 0230 hours, 18 December, that everyone finally went to bed for a few hours' sleep, tired and somewhat concerned as to how serious the German counterattack was."[35]

As Colonel Tucker's troopers were preparing for the upcoming combat mission, a large number of trucks came in with Major Zakby, 1st Lieutenant Megellas and 250 replacements. The timing was coincidental, as their arrival had been scheduled in December to bring the 504th Parachute Infantry Regiment up to full combat strength. Flown in transport planes from the base camp in Leicester to the Continent, the replacements had boarded 40 & 8 boxcars in France and travelled by train to Sissonne. There was no welcoming committee at the train station, only trucks and drivers commanded by 1st Lt. Dick Owen, the motor pool officer. Owen had bad news for Megellas and Zakby: the replacements would move out with the regiment the next morning.[36]

About 200 replacements were assigned to various companies, while the remaining men were temporarily assigned to Service Company. The hectic situation at Camp Sissonne allowed them no time to get to know their fellow platoon members as the regiment prepared to move out in the next few hours. Private First Class Bayley remembered their arrival late that night: "They were very tired after having been trucked across France in rainy, chilly weather. They had been cheered to some extent, as they had been told the 82nd would probably be in barracks for the next month or so, where they would be able to meld with the division, get to know the other men and get some more training. They were shocked and frightened when they were told that they were going directly into combat the next day or so. We were instructed to go to the supply room and get needed blankets, emergency food rations and whatever ammunition we could carry. We were told to take plenty, as we would be needing it."[37]

It was still dark when the paratroopers of the 504th went to the mess to eat a hastily prepared breakfast, which was probably the only food they would get that day. Some men had managed to sleep, others had not. The most recent replacements especially lost out on sleep, since they had arrived around midnight and were awakened at 0500 hours. Large ten-ton open trucks and trailers and the standard two-and-a-half ton trucks from the Oise Section of the Communications Zone around Paris arrived at 0800 hours, over two hours late. Because the 82nd ABD had been given a little more rest than the 101st, and would therefore be prepared earlier, it was selected to lead the motorized march into the Ardennes. The only absent men were the Pathfinders, who were training in England.

"At 0830 hours 18 December," recalled Captain Campana, "the battalion was assembled and loaded into huge semi-trailers. Approximately sixty men with all their personal equipment plus crew-served weapons were loaded into each truck. The 2nd Battalion followed the 1st Battalion serial with a five-minute interval. The battalion commander and the S-3 led the battalion serial in a jeep. The route to be followed was from Sissonne to Charlesville, Sedan, Recogne, Sprimont and Bastogne—a distance of 150 miles.

"About 1900 hours, the 2nd Battalion motor serial halted in the vicinity of Sprimont. The road ahead was crowded with vehicles, almost bumper to bumper. We discovered that we were behind Division Artillery; somehow or other the artillery serial had managed to insert itself between the 1st and the 2nd Battalion. After waiting in the cold night for almost two hours in open vehicles, we finally moved on again. However, we discovered that instead of turning south towards Bastogne, we were now headed towards Werbomont."[38]

Bayley recalls going to early chow, and discovering "some of the largest open stake-bodied tractor trailer trucks we had ever seen" in the company streets to transport the troops to the front-line assembly area. "Only the officers seemed to have any information as to our destination. We and the 101st Airborne were the only active reserve troops in the theater. We found out later that our original destination was Bastogne. […] My platoon was among those climbing into the lead trucks. There was a small area covered with canvas at the front of the truck trailer. I and about four others jumped into the truck real fast and got these choice semi- weather-protected positions. We only got up when really necessary to pee, and did it over the side while standing in our spots so we wouldn't lose them."[39]

Bayley's platoon leader, Lieutenant Breard, sat in the leading truck of the group transporting the 1st Platoon. Breard had received a map of the area to which the trucks were going: "We pulled out in open supply trucks (similar to cattle trailer trucks) on the morning of the 18th. On leaving, I was given a strip map listing the towns and villages that we were to pass through, Bastogne being the last."[40]

The weather was cold and very misty as the 504th drove north on the muddy, wet roads. "It was chilly and misting all day long as we trekked along about a 150 mile drive," Bayley recalled. "We were directed to Werbomont, north of Bastogne, as there was a very dangerous thrust through that area toward Liège and the port of Antwerp with a complete severance of connections between the First U.S. Army and the Ninth U.S. Army and the British to our north. First U.S. Army headquarters was in grave danger of being overrun."[41]

Pvt. Mahon of E Company recalled the dazed looks on the faces of the weary infantrymen as they passed through Bastogne: "On our way to the front we passed these young infantry troops. They gazed at us like we were replacement troops from the United States. I was standing at the back of the trailer and one of them yelled, 'You're going to be sorry!' I answered, 'The Germans will be sorry for messing up our return to the States!' It was raining, mixed with snow."[42]

Lieutenant Breard fell asleep in the early evening, as he had slept very little the previous night. He had been told that Bastogne was no longer their destination, but he had not been informed of their new destination: "Sometime during the night we were diverted north. I dozed off and when I woke, there was not a truck ahead to follow. We were leading our convoy serial, so we kept north and were stopped at Werbomont, Belgium, by none other than General Gavin. After reporting to him that I had 50 men, nearly half of A Company 504th, he told me to de-truck and go into a defensive position on the right side of the road to the east approximately two miles. I think this was about 0100 hours on December 19. Later, 1st Lieutenant John Pease came along with the rest of the company. We could hear artillery fire to the east."[43]

Private First Class Bayley remembered that the trucks in Breard's serial stopped near a farmhouse where Gavin had set up his command post [CP]: "Long after dark, about 2000 hours, we arrived in the woods just outside of the small village of Werbomont on the road from Bastogne to Liège and Antwerp. There were major supply dumps and warehouses in these cities where the German armies could replenish themselves with much-needed materiel and gasoline. During this time it was impossible for the Air Force to assist in the operations because of heavy, low, overcast weather.

"We debarked from the trucks near a farmhouse which we were told was the division or regimental headquarters. It was guarded by a single Sherman tank with an idling engine, ready for action. We asked our sergeant, who was dispersing us into the woods, if he knew where the Germans were. Those of us facing combat for the first time were worried about what might be happening. He said that the Germans were several miles away. About that time we heard a .50-caliber machine gun firing, so we knew they were not very far away. Two troopers were assigned as buddies by the platoon sergeant. My first partner was [Pvt. Clarence E.] Sonntag—a newly arrived replacement I had never met before this night. Most of us tried to get some sleep on the cold, wet ground. No snow had fallen in this area yet."[44]

Second Lt. Hubbard D. Burnum, Jr., in charge of the 1st Battalion Demolition Squad, had been with the regiment since August 1944. Burnum recalled that Headquarters Company was assigned to take up positions around a church situated at a crossroads at Werbomont. His group would spend their first night in Belgium in the local cemetery. It was hard to dig a foxhole in the hard, frozen ground and the eeriness of the place did not make it any easier to get some sleep.[45]

T/5 Herbert C. Lucas of the 3rd Battalion thought "the trucks were jam-packed, but it was better than hiking."[46] To Pfc. Walter E. Hughes of I Company, "it seemed like we rode for days in those huge, open trailer trucks. Actually it was more like 14 hours, I think. Twice MP's who seemed anxious to be rid of us diverted us away from their positions. Our convoy made too much noise and was too much of a tempting target. We arrived at a place called Werbomont, which was in a state of mass confusion. We formed up on the high ground above the town and were told to dig in. It was a relief from the trucks. We could hear the rumblings of large caliber guns toward the opposite side of town and some small arms closer in. Most of us fell asleep and I figured better get some rest, who knows what tomorrow will bring."[47]

While paratroopers and glidermen from the 82nd were on their way to Bastogne, Maj. Gen. Troy H. Middleton, VIII Corps, was alerted by radio that a rear command post of engineers had been overrun just east of Houffalize. Changing plans, he sent the 82nd north toward Werbomont, and placed the 101st ABD and the 10th U.S. Armored Division at Bastogne, creating a strong front line in the hope of blocking the German assault.

First Lieutenant Garrison, the 2nd Battalion S-1, recalled that "within 15 hours of the time we first heard of the German attack, we were in a different country seeking to know specifically what we were in for. With our vehicles stopped along the road, I joined the other members of the staff on the rounded top of a hill that dominated the snowy countryside. We could hear from afar the dull sound of artillery fire. Even with binoculars, we searched aimlessly in all directions for the enemy, who could have been anywhere. Colonel Tucker joined us with a plan: our companies were assigned to nearby towns that commanded roads."[48]

Captain Campana was left in charge of the 2nd Battalion serial "at a road intersection where other units had been dismounting. It was now 2300 hours. [First] Lieutenant [George H.] Fust, the Battalion S-2 who had preceded the battalion to Werbomont earlier that day, met us at the dismount point along with company guides. The battalion was given a sector to defend on the high ground about one-half mile northeast of the town. The battalion command post was located in a small wooden shack next to an odious pig pen and outhouse. By the time the companies were in position it was long after midnight."[49]

One truck, carrying Captain Thomas of G Company and some of his headquarters personnel, failed to arrive. Private First Class David K. Finney, a radio operator in Headquarters and Headquarters, remembered that his company "took up positions on the high ground surrounding Werbomont. Most of us didn't have the slightest conception of what the big picture contained or what was at stake, or what the next few days had in store for us."[50]

A sad affair took place when Capt. Jack M. Bartley, the Service Company commander for more than a year, was relieved from command and received no new duty. First Lieutenant Irving Silver, the company executive officer, replaced him. The reason for this command change is not mentioned in any report.

The following morning Colonel Tucker and his S-3 officer, Capt. Mack C. Shelley, made a personal reconnaissance of the surrounding area. Before he left, Tucker instructed every battalion to send out a patrol. Lieutenant Colonel Julian A. Cook, 3rd Battalion, decided to do this personally at 0930 hours, accompanied by his S-3 officer, Captain Keep and his company commanders. While they were away, Captain Thomas' truck arrived, and appeared to have skidded off the road.

Lieutenant Colonel Wellems also sent out a patrol, led by a replacement officer. "On the following morning, 19 December," remembered Captain Campana, "the battalion commander had a patrol from E Company dispatched with instructions to contact American troops located somewhere to our front. Five hours later, the patrol returned and 2nd Lieutenant Simpson, the patrol leader, reported that he had contacted a battalion of the 119th Infantry Regiment, 30th U.S. Infantry Division, some three miles to the east of Werbomont. The battalion commander of that unit [Major Hal D. Mc-Cown] had been overjoyed to learn that the 82nd Airborne Division had now come up into the lines. He stated that the 106th Infantry Division and the 7th Armored Division were having a difficult time warding off frequent German counterattacks. The report from this patrol was immediately forwarded to regiment. That afternoon Captain Norman, Lieutenant Ramsey and the other members of the battalion who had been on pass in Paris reported to the battalion."[51]

The German attacks in Stoumont were carried out by Kampfgruppe Peiper. Peiper's battlegroup was composed of the 84th Luftwaffe Flak Battalion under Maj. Wolfgang von Sacken, the 3rd Battalion of SS-Panzergrenadier Regiment 2, 1st SS-Panzer Battalion, 502nd SS-Heavy Panzer Battalion, 1st SS-Panzer Artillerie Battalion, and two panzer engineer companies. The sudden appearance of Peiper's vanguard on the morning of December 18 at the bridge across the Amblève River at Stavelot had completely surprised the engineers from the 202nd Combat Engineer Battalion stationed nearby.[52]

The 1st SS-Panzer Battalion tanks advanced south at full speed to bridges across the Salm River at Trois Ponts, which Peiper was obliged to cross in order to continue his advance to the Meuse River. Foreseeing the danger, the American 291st Combat Engineer Battalion blew up the Amblève River Bridge at 1100 hours, and shortly afterwards blew the lower Salmbridge south of town. As Lt. Col. David Pergrin, battalion commander of the 291st, recalled in his memoir: "The destruction of the Trois Ponts bridges forced Kampfgruppe Peiper far to the north of its route [... and] the objectives of the 1st SS-Panzer Division it was spearheading. [...] When knowledgeable engineers looked at their maps of the region and factored in Peiper's actions and probable aims, it was clear that he had two options upon clearing La Gleize. Since there was no way of knowing that Peiper was out of his divisional zone and needed to run back in a southerly direction, it was easy to assume that he would leave La Gleize in the direction of Spa, at which the First Army headquarters was still located. Considerable efforts were thus made to defend Spa. On the other hand, it was possible that Peiper was on his way to Werbomont, in which case he needed to cross the Amblève at the first available bridge, the span at Cheneux. [...] And there was nothing we could do to blow the Cheneux Bridge—no time and no engineers left."[53]

Peiper had indeed decided to advance to Werbomont via the Cheneux Bridge, which was right on the advance axis of the 504th PIR the following day: "Blocked at Trois Ponts, we continued on to La Gleize, where we encountered little resistance," Peiper later recalled. "There was another important bridge near Cheneux, which we prevented from being blown. However, in the afternoon of 18 December 1944, we had a bad break when the weather cleared and American fighter bombers came over. We lost two to three tanks and five armored half-tracks. The tanks blew up in the road, and the road was too narrow to by-pass them, thus causing additional delay. About 1800 on 18 December 1944, we moved up towards our old route of advance near Habiemont and started to cross the Lienne River. Just when we started to cross, this bridge also was blown up. [...] Not being able to find another bridge, it was decided to turn north to Stoumont and La Gleize."[54]

In the morning of December 19, Peiper's men fought for over two hours before they managed to take the town of Stoumont, west of La Gleize, and halted by the railway station some three kilometers to the west. At 1400 hours Peiper ordered the balance of his force to consolidate his positions at Stoumont and to defend the town of La Gleize against American counterattacks from the north and northeast. To the 84th Luftwaffe Flak Battalion he assigned the mission of blocking the area around Cheneux in order to secure the Amblève crossing. They would were reinforced by *SS-Obersturmführer* [1st Lieutenant] Heinz Tomhardt's 11th Kompanie of the 3rd Battalion, SS-Panzergrenadier Regiment 2.[55]

Meanwhile on the American side, Major General Gavin decided to send the 504th PIR to the east of Werbomont. The 3rd Battalion was relocated that day to another position, but in the early evening conflicting orders were received from regimental headquarters. "Big picture is SNAFU" [Situation Normal, All Fucked Up], wrote a member of the battalion staff. Major Zakby was assigned as battalion executive officer, replacing Capt. Arthur W. Ferguson, who became a liaison officer for the regiment. Cook finally called his company commanders to the Battalion CP and told them that the whole regiment would march that night to Rahier, where Colonel Tucker would set up his regimental headquarters. Here they were to be prepared to repel any attacks or spearheads coming from the east. The 2nd Battalion would lead, followed by the 1st and 3rd, in that order.

"Immediately after dark on 19 December," Captain Campana recalled, "the regiment received orders to attack east of Werbomont and seize the town of Rahier. The regiment moved off in a column of battalions; each battalion in a column of companies and each company in a column of two's. The 2nd Battalion was the advance guard. The order of march for the battalion was F Company, E Company, D Company and Headquarters Company. F and E Companies each had a light machine-gun section attached from Headquarters Company. The 2nd Battalion was ordered to attack, seize and hold the town. The battalion moved out on foot at 1900 hours 19 December. Except for a long, six-hour trek over some very hilly terrain, the march was uneventful. There was no enemy in Rahier. The battalion immediately prepared defensive positions to hold the town.

"A perimeter defense was established with the companies disposed on the outskirts of town from right to left as follows: F Company, E Company and D Company. The Battalion CP was set up in town and 81mm mortars were placed on the west edge of the town. A platoon of Company C, 307th Airborne Engineer Battalion, was attached to us during this movement. Later on, this platoon under [1st] Lieutenant [Travis] Womack was given a sector to defend on the left of D Company. I obtained extra hand grenades when requested by Lieutenant Womack, but was unable to get him any automatic weapons."[56]

As Lieutenant Breard remembered the eight-mile advance to Rahier: "After daylight, the battalion moved out, crossing Lienne Creek at Habiemont. The engineers had already demolished the bridge the day before when a German recon unit had come that way from La Gleize via the road through Cheneux. I think, but am not sure, we moved out B Company, C Company, Headquarters Company, followed by A Company."[57]

Private First Class Bayley and other replacements in A Company wondered about their first fight, as they did not know where the company was going: "Late in the evening of the 19th we began to realize that something serious was about to occur. We were instructed to assemble our squads and platoons and prepare to move out. I was in the lead group directly with the officers. We went through the bushland, cutting barbed wire fences and pushing brush aside as we probed our way through the dark.

"Eventually we came to a paved road. We passed through some groups of army engineers and kept moving. When we did take rest stops, some of us were so tired and hot, even though it was a chilly night, that we flopped down into puddles of rain water along the roadway to cool down. We turned down a side road toward the village of Rahier.

"After several minutes (seemed like hours) we stopped for a rest and to listen. We heard machine guns firing close by, just ahead on the road. The officers concluded that we were stymied and better get off the road. We climbed steep hills and attempted unsuccessfully to dig-in on the high, open ground, in event an attack came."[58]

Lieutenant James Roberts leading his two tank destroyers from B Company, 703rd Tank Destroyer Battalion, at Werbomont on December 19, to come under command of the 504th Parachute Infantry Regiment.
Courtesy: U.S. Army

CHAPTER 3

THE ROAD TO CHENEUX
CHENEUX, BELGIUM, DECEMBER 20, 1944

As a heavy ground fog developed in the early hours of December 20, the military situation was also far from clear to Colonel Tucker. After over 24 hours in the Belgian Ardennes, there were still no Germans to be seen. He had placed his 3rd Battalion about a mile to the southwest in the town of Froidville, with G Company designated as regimental reserve, since it was uncertain how long Captain Thomas would be away and 1st Lt. James Pursell had just taken over. The 1st Battalion was set up 1500 yards to the north on the Roftier hill and the 2nd Battalion was centrally positioned in Rahier itself.

During the night 1st Lt. Marshall W. Stark's platoon of four 57mm antitank guns from the 80th Airborne Anti-Aircraft Battalion [AAAB] was attached to the 1st Battalion. In Stark's description, "a visit to the regimental command post disclosed that the 1st Platoon, Battery C, was now attached to the 1st Battalion. This unit was generally located on the northern part of the high ground northwest of Rahier. At this time, about 0700 hours, 20 December, I went on reconnaissance with the battalion commander for possible gun positions. The road leading south from the Amblève River through Xhierfomont appeared to be the only approach for enemy armor into the area, so the two sections, of two antitank [AT] guns each, were placed in depth along this road in general locations recommended by the battalion commander. One section was located between the crest of the hill and Rahier, and the other, near a church at Xhierfomont. While the platoon sergeant supervised the emplacement of the guns near Rahier, I was with the other section.

"As the gun positions of the forward section were being improved, I looked around the area to determine in which company's sector my guns were located, but I could find no one. I started back toward the battalion command post, when, most to my surprise, after going back on the road about 500 yards, I came to a hasty antitank minefield, which had been laid on the road after I had taken my guns forward. This minefield was being covered by a few riflemen who stated they were 200 yards in front of the main line of resistance.

"This deployment of antitank guns and troops was unsound, and consequently I suggested to the battalion commander that the two forward guns be withdrawn to the rear of the minefield and preferably back to where they would have proper infantry protection. The request was granted and the guns were hastily moved back to approximately the line of resistance, where they were emplaced covering the road.

"During the remainder of the morning, considerable firing could be heard and seen in the vicinity of Stoumont, which was in the 30th Infantry Division sector. This town was approximately two miles from the platoon location. At that time several reports had been received, from civilians in and around Rahier, to the effect that about 125 German vehicles, including 30 tanks, had moved east through that town during the preceding day. The indications were growing stronger that we were coming closer to the enemy than we had been at any time since arriving in the area."[59]

Colonel Tucker made a full daylight reconnaissance of the immediate area, and spoke with civilians in Rahier, who told him that a large column of German armored troops had moved through the preceding day in the direction of Cheneux, two miles to the northeast. Tucker requested and received permission from Gavin to take the town of Cheneux, where he had noticed that the terrain was higher than the area around Rahier; if the Germans were in Cheneux, they could dominate the Rahier area with artillery and tanks. Calling his battalion commanders to Rahier, Tucker gave the mission to lead the attack on Cheneux to Wellems' 2nd Battalion, while Harrison's 1st Battalion would follow, with the 3rd Battalion in regimental reserve.

At 1115 hours, Capt. T. Moffatt Burriss' I Company and two 57mm antitank guns took over road blocks from the 2nd Battalion at Rahier. Five men from the 3rd Battalion intelligence section were sent out at 1600 hours to recon a blown bridge to the north across the Amblève River. Captain Campana, 2nd Battalion S-3, recalled questioning civilians in Rahier about the location of enemy troops. "The civilians reported that many enemy vehicles, about 125 in number, including 30 tanks, had moved through the town the afternoon of 19 December on the way to Cheneux, located on the very high ground about two miles to the northeast of Rahier.

"This information was passed on to General Gavin by Colonel Tucker when the former visited the unit later that morning. Gavin then ordered Tucker to seize Cheneux and the nearby bridge which crossed the l'Amblève River. The reason for this order was that the heavy German armor was unable to cross the creek obstacle at Habiemont after engineers had blown up the bridge. The enemy, therefore, intended to use the main road through Stoumont and La Gleize. An advance of the 504th Parachute Infantry Regiment would threaten the flank of Kampfgruppe Peiper and force him to pull out of Stoumont and withdraw to La Gleize.

"Therefore, a patrol from D Company led by Sergeant [Elton R.] Venable [of the 1st Platoon] made its way towards Cheneux. On the ridge about one-half mile west of the town, they fired on a German motorcyclist accompanied by a small patrol. Sergeant Venable was wounded in the hip during the brief exchange of shots that followed."[60]

The point of the 2nd Battalion, Captain Adam Komosa's D Company, got only 200 yards farther when they were pinned down. Wellems deployed his E and F Companies on either side of D Company. Tucker, who was up with the 2nd Battalion, decided to go to the rear to find Roberts' 2nd Platoon of B Company, 703rd Tank Destroyer Battalion [TDB], which had been assigned to the 2nd Battalion on division order but had not yet come up.

The 2nd Battalion had captured a German half-track with a mounted 77mm gun intact during Tucker's absence. On his return at approximately 1500 hours, he at once radioed Lieutenant Colonel Harrison, ordering him to tell Lieutenant Stark to send two of his men up to the 2nd Battalion to man the half-track. Tucker informed Harrison that he intended to advance and take Cheneux before nightfall. The 2nd Battalion had spotted tank and infantry movement to their front, but could not determine their strength. He therefore would leave the 2nd Battalion in position and Harrison's 1st Battalion would pass through them to attack Cheneux. He sent A Company to the town of Brume several miles to the east to guard the northern flank of the 505th PIR and prevent a German flanking attack from that direction.

"I was requested to furnish two men to operate a German 77mm howitzer mounter on a half-track which had been abandoned somewhere in the area," recalled Lieutenant Stark of the 80th Airborne Anti-Aircraft Battalion. "Prior to this request, one or two test rounds had been fired, and apparently the entire half-track and its gun were in perfect operating condition. Two of the best men from the platoon [Pfc. Harold Kelly and Pfc. Harry Koprowski] were selected to perform this mission. At this time, the point of the column was all set to move out and was awaiting the scheduled time to advance. The battalion commander desired that this reinforcing armor, as he called it, accompany the point during the advance. Therefore, he decided to delay the advance until these two men were briefed on the operation of the weapon.

"For two men who had never seen a weapon of this type other than in pictures, the five-minute interval allotted to me for orientating them was rather brief, and only the minimum knowledge necessary for operation could be imparted. Actually, this was the first time that I myself had ever seen one of these weapons."[61]

Private First Class Russell P. Snow from the Regimental S-1 section volunteered to drive the vehicle and Captain Helgeson, the CO of B Company, designated Pvt. Thomas R. Holliday and Pvt. Buland Hoover of his own 1st Platoon to cover the driver and gunners with their BAR's. At the outskirts, Harrison quickly briefed the battalion executive officer and company commanders on Tucker's regimental order. First Lieutenant Pease received the task of leading his company to the small village of Brume, situated on a high hill northwest of Trois Ponts. A Company was to defend this town and regularly send out patrols. Captains Helgeson and Anderson were given a tougher assignment: to attack and capture the defended village of Cheneux. Harrison told his officers that a D Company patrol had been fired upon from the town. Cheneux's strategic position near two bridges across the Amblève River made it imminently important for the Americans to gain control of the town, against all odds.

Helgeson's B Company was directed to lead the attack, followed by Anderson's C Company and Milloy's Headquarters Company. First Lieutenant William Meerman and his 3rd Platoon would lead the B Company column, followed by 1st Lieutenant Thomas' 2nd Platoon, Company Headquarters, and the 1st Platoon led by 2nd Lt. Ralph S. Bird, Jr.

B Company was still set up in perimeter defense when Captain Helgeson sent out runners to inform his squad leaders on the outposts [OP's] to report to the Company CP. Corporal Robert E. Waldon was surprised when "a runner came down and said, 'The captain wants you in the CP.' I went up there and he said, 'Get your men ready to move out. We are moving out in a half hour.'"[62] Hastening back, Waldon ran "around from this hole to that hole," telling his men to gather up. One, Pvt. J.B. Hill, carried a bazooka. "We were short of men," Waldon remembered, "so I had to carry his ammunition. It gets real heavy after a while. Plus there were two machine guns, so everyone was carrying weapons or ammunition, plus the mortar."[63]

Corporal Waldon took his gathered squad back to the 3rd Platoon assembly point, where his platoon leader, Lieutenant Meerman, informed him that their platoon would be leading: "We left there before dark and marched all night that night, and it was a couple of days before Christmas. Marched all night, no rest. You're supposed to rest every couple of hours or so, but we went the whole night without a rest. We were supposed to reinforce the battalion, because B Company was off by itself for some reason. There was a tank attack coming. We got up to where we were going to stay and we got all dug-in."[64]

While Waldon's men were digging foxholes in an open field, he walked up to Private Hill and told him to "get his bazooka ready. And he says, 'I don't have it. It got too heavy for me to carry, so I left it alongside the road.' I said, 'Aw, Geez! Well, saddle up! (I said this very nicely, of course!) We're going back to get it.' So we hiked back about three or four miles. I couldn't believe it. We're doing all this hiking because of an upcoming tank attack and he leaves behind the bazooka. What did he figure he was going to do? Go *bang, bang* with a rifle at a tank? I made him carry it the whole way back."[65]

In the midst of these preparations, Lieutenant Colonel Cook received instructions at 1645 hours to send out a platoon of G Company to recon Bois le Chere, a large wooded hill north of the Rahier–Cheneux road. Colonel Tucker wanted to make sure that no Germans would flank the 1st Battalion from the north as it approached Cheneux. They returned at 1950 hours to report that the woods were empty.

Unknown to Colonel Tucker, D Company's patrol and the capture of the half-track had been brought to the attention of *SS-Obersturmbannführer* Jochen Peiper, who was visiting one of his engineer companies in Stoumont. He had earlier established his command post in a farm building near the Château de Froidcour, perfectly centered among Stoumont, La Gleize, and Cheneux. The castle served as first aid station and makeshift detention quarters for prisoners of war [PW or POW]. Peiper alerted his artillery guns at the Vaulx Renard farm, beyond the Cheneux bridge on the east side of the Amblève River, and directed the 6th Kompanie of SS-Panzergrenadierregiment 2 to Cheneux as reinforcements for Major von Sacken.[66]

Meanwhile the 1st Battalion had set off from Rahier with B Company in the lead, deployed on either side of the road. Lieutenant Stark saw the column as they moved away: "The battalion commander expected that he would be in Cheneux before dark and that as soon as he arrived there, he would want the platoon of antitank guns to come forward to aid in the accomplishment of his mission, which was to seize and hold the bridge crossing the Amblève River to the east of Cheneux. About the time that the head of the main body of the 1st Battalion went out of sight, considerable small arms fire, augmented by a great deal of 20mm fire and some larger caliber direct-fire weapons, could be heard coming from the direction of the advance of our troops. Information received at Regimental Headquarters at about dusk indicated that the advancing 1st Battalion had met a strong German force, consisting of infantry supported by armor, advancing toward Rahier on the high ground west of Cheneux. The battalion commander did not want the antitank guns brought forward at that time."[67]

Captain Helgeson recalled that the leading elements of his company "met enemy resistance 500 yards east of Rahier. The leading platoon deployed and attacked the enemy resistance, strength of about one squad armed with a MG42, and drove them east along the axis of the Rahier–Cheneux road; one enemy was killed and one enemy captured. The enemy fought a very vigorous rear-guard action, inflicting casualties on our troops. Our leading elements pressed a vigorous and aggressive action against the enemy along the axis of the road. This attack was pressed for about 1000 yards toward Cheneux until the forward elements of the leading company contacted the enemy's main line of resistance."[68]

According to the 1st Battalion After Action Report, "with 3rd Platoon on the left of the road and 2nd Platoon on the right, the company continued the advance, handicapped by ground haze which limited visibility to 200/300 yards, and heavy machine-gun fire from the outskirts of the town. First Platoon was ordered by Captain Helgeson to turn the enemy's right flank. The captured enemy half-track was put between the attacking platoons, thus enabling the return of fire against the machine guns and 20mms. After receiving heavy fire, however, the half-track moved back. First Platoon advanced 200 yards past the other platoon's base of fire, where it was pinned down by a 20mm and two MG42s with a squad of riflemen 100 yards from the enemy forward lines.

"Contact was lost with battalion, and C Company's mortars were falling on the rear of the company. The position then held by B Company was a table top crisscrossed by barbed wire fences. Ground haze made the adjustment of artillery difficult. At 1700 hours Captain Helgeson ordered the company to withdraw 200 yards to the edge of the woods. An orderly withdrawal was made, one platoon at a time, and the company reorganized and set up a perimeter defense at the wood's edge. At 1845 hours Captain Helgeson gave the CO the situation."[69]

Captain Helgeson's official account of the action reports that "the left platoon [the base of fire] was engaged by a vicious counterfire. The right platoon was pinned to the ground by devastating crossfire from two 20mm cannons, supported by two MG42's. Enemy SP mortar fire swept the two elements of attack, killing six men and knocking out the company's radio."[70] It is to be noted that Captain Helgeson does not mention the C Company mortar fire in his report. Even more interesting, neither the Roll of Honor nor the Morning Reports list the names of six B Company men killed in action on December 20. For this phase of the attack, only one man is listed as KIA: 20-year-old Pfc. Emil E. Bauer, who had received his jump wings in England just eight weeks earlier. [71]

Private First Class Snow drove the captured half-track down the road to the edge of the forest during the attack, while Private First Class Kelly fired on seven well-hidden 20mm flak wagons and heavy machine-gun nests. Behind the sights of the 77mm gun, he could not clearly see his targets because of ground haze, and therefore aimed at flashes of enemy fire. At one point Kelly raked a column of German infantry coming down the road from Cheneux, forcing them to scatter. Private Hoover meanwhile spotted a machine-gun nest and put it out of action with his BAR.

When Kelly was wounded in his lower lip and chin by fragments of a 20mm shell that hit the brace of his gun, Snow maneuvered the half-track in the direction of enemy tracer fire and took Kelly's place at the gun. At the crossroads just outside of Cheneux, a German half-track moved perfectly into the sight of his gun and went up in flames by a direct hit. Two probable scores were made on machine-gun nests before the 77mm ran out of ammunition. Snow resumed his place at the wheel and drove back to the regimental aid station to get Kelly's wounds dressed. Privates Holliday and Hoover jumped off the half-track at the rear of B Company and rejoined their 1st Platoon. For their actions, the makeshift crew would all be awarded the Bronze Star.

"Platoons were withdrawn one platoon at a time, covering one another," recalled Captain Helgeson. "The slight ground haze facilitated the withdrawal. At this time a company runner reported that contact had been gained with Company C to our rear. Company B was reorganized and set up a perimeter defense in the edge of the woods. The company commander was called for a meeting by the battalion commander. The time was now 1845."[72]

Lieutenant Colonel Harrison conferred with his company commanders and Captain Duncan, the Battalion S-3. Helgeson first gave a resumé of the attack and an estimation of enemy strength. Harrison then radioed Colonel Tucker to give him an update. Tucker had just learned that the 3rd Battalion intelligence section had encountered a patrol of the 119th Infantry Regiment of the 30th Infantry Division at the blown bridge across the Amblève River. There were no Germans in or west of Bois le Chere, so the only Germans encountered so far were in Cheneux. Tucker also knew that the 505th PIR had set up defenses at Trois Ponts, a few miles south of the town, and another friendly regiment was to their south. Cheneux thus formed the only German bridgehead west of the Amblève River, a position which enabled the Germans to influence the battle in Stoumont and range their guns from the high ground on the 1st Battalion between Rahier and Cheneux.

Helgeson recounts that Tucker "ordered a night attack against the enemy positions and the town of Cheneux. The battalion commander ordered Companies B and C to attack abreast astride the road, Company B on the right and Company C on the left, with two M36 tank destroyers [TDs] in support on the road. The time for attack was 1930 with a ten-minute artillery barrage preparation preceding the jump-off time. The companies were oriented and formed into four assault waves 50 yards in depth from each other. The order was given, 'We will take that town!' During the organization of the battalion for the attack, the enemy mortared the battalion assembly area incessantly and fired 75mm AT [antitank] tracer shells into the area."[73]

At H-Hour there had been no artillery barrage, nor was there any sight of Lieutenant Roberts' two tank destroyers. In hindsight, it might have been better to delay the attack, but the 1st Battalion jumped off exactly on time at 1930 hours, crossing 400 yards of flat, open terrain with numerous barbed wire fences. Second Lieutenant Bird's 1st Platoon formed the first wave of B Company on the right side of the road and was soon pinned down by 20mm and machine-gun fire from multiple guns. The advance seemed to stall, while the remainder of the company attempted to cross the open fields as quickly as possible to catch up to Bird's platoon, working their way through and over the barbed wire fences. "We were pinned down," recalled Pfc. Morris ("Mike") Holmstock, 1st Platoon, "and you could see the tracers going over your head. Fortunately, the road to my left was elevated, and we were on the slant on this open field. We must have been five or ten feet below the level of the road."[74]

The open field was dimly illuminated from the intense tracer-laced fire being laid down in both directions, producing a spooky atmosphere. S/Sgt. William P. ("Knobby") Walsh, platoon sergeant, 1st Platoon, realized many of the green replacements who had joined his platoon after the Holland campaign were not moving now. Some of the "old timers" also naturally hesitated given the suicidal condition of the frontal assault. Some, like Lieutenant Bird and Pfc. Melvin D. Isbel, were wounded and unable to proceed. Reasoning they were sitting ducks in open terrain, Walsh decided to lead the platoon forward again and take the risks. Still "pinned to the ground by heavy grazing fire, Staff Sergeant Walsh, though seriously wounded, rose to his feet and voluntarily led a charge upon an enemy-held village."[75]

Sgt. William L. Clay couldn't believe his eyes when Walsh stood up and waved for his men to follow him. "Come on, let's get 'em, men!" he shouted, and started to run towards the town. Clay and the rest of the platoon jumped up and ran behind Walsh, shooting all the way. Sgt. Edwin M. Clements and Pvt. Mack Barkley each jumped on a flak wagon and killed the crews with their trench knives. Barkley cut the throat of a 20mm flak gunner and Sgt. Dock L. O'Neal saw Clements kill at least three Germans with his knife.[76]

Barkley was decorated with a military medal for "pick[ing] up the rocket launcher of a wounded man and assault[ing] a German flak wagon which was delivering direct fire upon his comrades. Suffering severe wounds, Private Barkley continued to a point within 75 yards of the enemy vehicle where he fired an additional two rounds, scoring direct hits and setting the wagon on fire. Although his wounds prevented him from advancing forward with his company, Private Barkley took up a position from which he supported the assault. These gallant and courageous actions were an inspiration to his comrades and greatly facilitated the advance of his company."[77]

Other troopers, many out of ammunition, also used their rifle butts to kill Germans occupying "spiderholes" in the ground nearby. O'Neal was out of ammunition by the time he was just half way across the field. He picked up an M1 rifle from a wounded paratrooper and kept charging forward with his platoon. Nearing a German soldier in a spiderhole, O'Neal, again out of ammunition, clubbed the German with his rifle butt, breaking the stock off completely.

The assistant platoon leader, 2nd Lt. Richard Smith, also played a vital role in reorganizing and leading his men on toward Cheneux. As "his platoon came under murderous crossfire from enemy machine guns and cannon, he bravely and calmly organized his firing line and led his platoon forward. The platoon knocked out two German machine guns and overran the enemy positions."[78]

Especially hindering the 1st Platoon were two enemy machine guns. One was destroyed by 21-year-old Pfc. Daniel T. Del Grippo of the 2nd Platoon, who received the Distinguished Service Cross "for extraordinary heroism in action against the enemy on 20 December 1944, in Belgium. During an attack on the village of Cheneux, Belgium, Private First Class Del Grippo, in the face of murderous machine-gun and 20mm fire, personally reduced an enemy machine-gun position, killing one German and capturing the other.

"That night in another attack, Private First Class Del Grippo observed an enemy self-propelled gun firing on his comrades. Although painfully wounded, he dashed toward the vehicle firing his submachine gun, and killed the four-man enemy crew. The singular gallantry and heroism displayed by Private First Class Del Grippo exemplify the highest traditions of the Armed Forces."[79]

Private First Class Holmstock "was scared," but did follow his platoon leader. "I crawled forward a bit and came across a buddy of mine by the name of [Pfc.] Raymond [R.] Ault, who had a belly wound and was begging for water. We were always told that if somebody has a belly wound, don't give them water. I called for the medics and I said, 'I've got to go, Ault, I can't stay here. The medics will be up here soon.' About that time I heard Knobby Walsh up on the road, yelling for hand grenades."[80]

Advancing some 300 yards, Walsh "encountered devastating flanking fire from a 20mm flak wagon. Unable to pull the pin from a hand grenade because of a severe hand wound, he moved quickly to a comrade who armed the grenade. Returning to within ten feet of the weapon, he tossed the grenade into the vehicle, destroying the gun and annihilating the crew. Staff Sergeant Walsh's courage and personal bravery exemplified the highest traditions of the military service."[81]

According to his Silver Star Citation, assistant squad leader Cpl. Henry B. Klee was "advancing with his squad to attack a strongly held enemy roadblock. When he was 400 yards away the enemy opened fire, pinning down the entire squad. At this crucial moment, Corporal Klee jumped to his feet and dashed forward into the intense direct fire, calling on his squad to follow.

At close range he opened fire on a flak wagon, forcing the crew to abandon their vehicle. Corporal Klee was hit in the leg and head. Badly wounded and unable to move, he shouted instruction to the men following, enabling them to advance and destroy another enemy flak wagon without further casualties."[82]

On the way to Cheneux, Sergeant O'Neal spotted at least two flak wagons and one tank along the road to their left. He was with the leading squad when Staff Sergeant Walsh dropped a hand grenade down the hatch of one of the vehicles, taking it out. S/Sgt. James M. Boyd, the 2nd Platoon platoon sergeant, followed closely behind the 1st Platoon. It seemed to him that B Company troopers were going down like flies. He saw Walsh closely approach an enemy flak wagon and toss a grenade into it. The explosion knocked out the entire crew. Seeing that Walsh was hit in the left arm and left leg, Boyd moved over to him and suggested he get his wounds treated. "Later," Walsh said, and ran on with his group.

As the 1st Platoon reached the first buildings of Cheneux, the fighting became even more confused. A quick head count revealed only about a dozen men were left standing. The remainder had been too severely wounded in the open fields. The enemy fire, however, was still as strong as ever. Those still capable of fighting included Lieutenant Smith, Staff Sergeant Walsh, Sergeants Clay, Mann and O'Neal, Cpl. John L. Barton, Privates First Class Donald C. Graham and Holmstock and Privates Edward Focht, Thomas R. Holliday, Jr., and perhaps two or three others.

At about this time S/Sgt. Curtis L. Aydelott, a former C Company noncommissioned officer from Nashville, showed up. Aydelott, who worked in the 1st Battalion S-2 section, had been sent forward by Harrison to ascertain what was going on and bring back the first German prisoners. Having become separated from his small patrol on the way to Cheneux, he decided to join Lieutenant Smith's group. Smith "was leading his company's advance elements toward the heavily defended town of Cheneux when his unit came under withering mortar and machine-gun fire, pining it down. He boldly and calmly organized his firing line, exposing himself with utter disregard of his personal safety, until two machine guns were silenced and the enemy had suffered many casualties. Later that night, Second Lieutenant Smith was with the leading platoon when the attack was resumed. Although the platoon suffered extremely heavy casualties, he organized the remaining men and personally led a charge which overran another enemy strongpoint, destroying two armored vehicles and another two machine guns. Hastily reorganizing his platoon, which was now cut to eleven men, he led his men on still another charge against two houses and a flak wagon. While exhorting his men onward through a hail of enemy fire, he was killed. The few remaining men were so inspired by his unsurpassed heroism and exemplary leadership that they overran this objective in the face of overwhelming odds. His conduct during this entire action will be a source of lasting inspiration to all who were associated with him."[83] Smith would be posthumously awarded the Silver Star for his heroic actions. Aydelott thought the lieutenant had been hit by sniper fire as they made a wide swing around a German strongpoint, and this was also the opinion of Sergeant O'Neal.

Almost simultaneously the group ran into another 20mm flak wagon parked near a fork in the road into Cheneux, just east of a house. The flak wagon was on an incline, firing 20mm rounds into the trees, attempting to frag the paratroopers below. O'Neal, Aydelott and Pfc. Arley O. Farley, one of the attached bazooka men from Headquarters Company, worked their way around the house to approach the flak wagon from its left flank. O'Neal directed Farley to fire into its side. The explosion set the German vehicle alight as Aydelott sprayed it with his tommy gun.

The shrapnel from the last round fired from the flak wagon wounded O'Neal in his right leg, and the impact sent him rolling down the incline, but he climbed back up, got around the west side of the house and onto the road. Discovering a German attempting to escape the flames of the burning flak wagon, without hesitating, O'Neal shot him with his .45 pistol.[84]

Private First Class Farley's action, which saved the lives of the light machine-gun crews who had moved up to support B Company, earned him the Silver Star. His citation reads: "During an attack on this stubbornly defended enemy town, the advance of the right flank company of the attacking battalion was stopped and pinned down by fire from a 20mm cannon and supporting fire from automatic weapons. This fire had destroyed or neutralized five of the unit's eight machine guns.

"Realizing that further loss of firepower by his unit would be disastrous, Private First Class Farley, a bazooka man, crawled in the face of this fire to a position from where he could deliver effective bazooka fire on the enemy cannon. With utter disregard of his personal safety, Private First Class Farley succeeded in reaching a position from where he was able to engage and destroy this cannon. This gallant and unselfish act enabled his unit to successfully continue its assault on the enemy MLR [Main Line of Resistance].

The devotion to duty and initiative displayed by Private First Class Farley typifies the spirit and caliber of the parachute infantryman."[85]

The same 20mm round that wounded O'Neal also wounded Pfc. Mike Holmstock. After emptying his M1 into a flak wagon on the road leading into Cheneux, Holmstock had made his way to the first house, using a water-filled drainage ditch on the right side of the road, certainly a safer (albeit wetter) way to reach the house than by the road. "Up toward the first house, the third flak wagon that I can remember started backing up [from behind a house]. I opened fire and I guess some other guys did, and he pulled forward behind the house again. So I had to hit that water. I didn't want to be hit.

"I decided to go down by my side to the rear of the house. I worked my way down there, and behind the house about 10 or 15 yards the land went off into a steep drop. I was crawling behind that when I saw this flak wagon from behind the edge of the house, firing. I remember two guys with a machine gun [one was Pvt. Paul E. Hayden, Headquarters Company, 1st Battalion] up on the road level above me open fire on the flak wagon. The flak wagon returned fire.

"When I got up there the machine-gun team was gone. I took my shot at the flak wagon, and he took a shot at me. I had ducked just in time behind this tree, when one of those 20mm shells exploded, and I got a piece of it right above my left eye. I thought first I was hit by some dirt or something from the tree.

"When I started to fire again, I couldn't see. I checked myself and I tasted blood. [...] I was bleeding so I worked my way back to the first part of the house up near the road. There was a little room that had had sheep in there, and [someone] had converted that into an aid station. I got to the medic, and he said, 'I'm going to evacuate you.' I said, 'No, no, I'm not hurt. I'm just cut someplace.' He cleaned me up and put a patch on my eyebrow."[86]

After Sergeant O'Neal was wounded, command of the platoon fell to Sgt. Paul V. Mann, who was aided by Corporal Aydelott. Aydelott's helmet was shot off his head during the advance but miraculously, he was not hit. A sergeant who had been shot in the chest gave him his own helmet with the words: "I don't think I'll be needing it again very soon."

A few hundred yards back, the remainder of B Company had lost its platoon leaders: Lieutenants Ralph Bird, Robert Brantley, Thomas Keating, William Meerman and David Thomas were all wounded. "Captain Helgeson went berserk when he saw what was happening to his company," recalled

Holmstock later. "He went out of his mind and Sgt. [Amadeo] Castagno, who became the first sergeant after the battle of Cheneux, told me that he had to sit on Helgeson all the time during the battle."[87]

A few days after the fateful attack, Captain Helgeson was decorated with the Silver Star: "During the initial stage of a battalion attack on that town, Company B, 504th Parachute Infantry, commanded by Captain Helgeson, suffered heavy casualties. Unmindful of concentrated close-range fire from flak guns, automatic weapons and artillery, he courageously reorganized his command and moved among his men to exhort, advise and encourage them, and led them across 400 yards of open terrain protected with barbed wire.

"While breaking through entanglements, they sustained further casualties, including all officers. Captain Helgeson quickly regrouped his men and led them again in an assault which was stopped by the enemy. Disregarding hostile fire, he reorganized once more and keeping the determination of his men at high pitch by his own exemplary fearlessness, drove the enemy from the objective and held it against all enemy counterattacks.

"Throughout the three hours of this action Captain Helgeson exhibited complete disregard for enemy fire, magnificent bravery and outstanding leadership. The successful accomplishment of the company mission against a numerically superior foe backed by greater fire-power was due to his heroism, determination, and inspiring conduct in the high traditions of the Airborne Forces of the United States Army."[88]

First Lieutenant Harold C. Allen, the last remaining officer in B Company, came forward with the fourth and final wave of B Company. He attempted to reorganize the troopers and rallied them in another attack, but was also wounded. His Silver Star Citation reads as follows: "First Lieutenant Allen's platoon was in the fourth wave of his company's assault upon this heavily defended town. In the initial advance the Company Commander and platoon leader had become casualties along with many enlisted men due to the fierce hail of enemy cannon, machine-gun and mortar fire which the first assaulting units had encountered. First Lieutenant Allen came forward and reorganized the remaining elements of the company. While directing the operations of the assault, he was exposed to the full concentration of enemy fire, and painfully wounded. Despite his wound, he led two men forward and knocked out a machine-gun nest which was holding up the advance.

"When the advance was again halted by machine-gun fire, First Lieutenant Allen crept forward and knocked out an enemy machine-gun nest of two men. In this action he was again wounded but still refused evacuation until he had established a line of fire for the continuance of the advance. The intrepid and inspiring leadership and unselfish courage which First Lieutenant Allen demonstrated during this entire action contributed largely to the success of his company's accomplishment of this vital mission against superior odds of men and armor."[89]

Staff Sergeant William P. Walsh (standing) of B Company, photographed on May 1, 1942. Walsh was a cadre member of the regiment and took part in all campaigns, knocking out a German flak wagon at Cheneux. *Courtesy: John Walsh*

CHAPTER 4

THE BATTLE OF CHENEUX
CHENEUX, BELGIUM, DECEMBER 20, 1944

On the left side of the road from Rahier to Cheneux, Captain Anderson's C Company also charged forward. He had only five lieutenants in his company; 1st Lt. John M. Randles was on detached service with Service Company and 1st Lt. Bruno J. Rolak was still on leave in Paris. Sgt. Ross S. Carter from 1st Lt. Vern G. Frisinger's 3rd Platoon vividly describes the action: "The thirty-three men in our platoon, spearheading for the two platoons following us, ground into motion and began to advance in a dressed skirmish line, noisily and clumsily breaking sticks as they went. At any second we expected *it* to come like a wind-driven gust of burning hail. The silence continued, save for the steady sound of a string of men picking their way through a dry forest. A few cords of stacked wood lying between us and the field made it necessary to form in a single file. We formed again in a skirmish line on the edge of the field, crisscrossed at forty- or fifty-yard intervals by barbed wire fences. An enemy dressed in skirmish formation advancing across such a terrain was a machine gunner's dream. [...]

"Our men, strung out unevenly now because of difficulty in getting across, under and through the wires, had nearly reached mid-field and were beginning to climb another fence when it happened. Suddenly thousands of tracer bullets, uncannily beautiful despite their lethal purpose, arched and crisscrossed above us. Their flickering flames turned the night into day and men into targets. The air was filled with the yellow glow of hissing 20mm cannon shells, the sputter of machine guns and the roar of exploding mortar shells dumped on our comrades just below us."[90]

Assistant machine gunner Pfc. Raymond D. Levy spotted a 20mm flak wagon on the right side of the field, just on the left of the road that separated

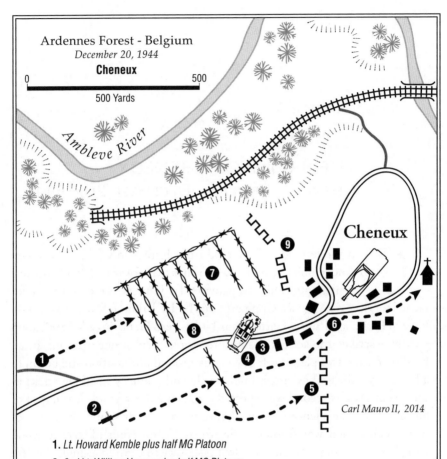

1. *Lt. Howard Kemble plus half MG Platoon.*

2. *2nd Lt. William Yepsen plus half MG Platoon.*

3. *2 Lt. Richard Smith (B Co.) killed about here, after reading outskirts of Cheneux. Sgt. Dock O'Neal wounded here by 20mm shrapnel.*

4. *Pfc. Paul E. Hayden (HQ1) killed while firing .30 caliber at half-track. 2nd Lt. Yepsen takes over gun but mortally wounded by cannon fire.*

5. *Enemy MG42's knocked out by Pvt. L.N. Emmons (HQ/1 MG Platoon).*

6. *Advance route of Sgt. Paul Mann and other survivors of 1st Platoon, B Company.*

7. *1st Lt. James Dunn assumes command of C Co. after Capt. Roy Anderson wounded.*

8. *Pfc. Raymond Levy (C Co.) killed here. Sgt. Elmer Swartz finds his body.*

9. *2nd Lt. Wayne Fetters leads 2nd Platoon forward and wounded about here.*

the company from B Company. He charged towards it, firing his weapon as he ran, aiming for the gunners. Suddenly he was struck and his hand grenades went off, setting him on fire. He ran a few feet back and collapsed mortally wounded in a barbed wired fence. "Kill the bastards who killed Levy!" shouted T/Sgt. Frank L. Dietrich, the 3rd Platoon's platoon sergeant, encouraging his men to move forward. He recounts how, near Cheneux, he "ran into three men at a machine gun. They were dug-in and I was moving. I spotted them about the same time they saw me. I knocked out the guys on the right and left. Rounds struck my hand on the submachine gun grip, and the Thompson stopped firing. I ran to the side and toward [the shooter] while he was firing at me. I threw the Thompson and hit him in the chest. [Pvt. Orin B.] Guidry came up with his BAR and shoved the muzzle into the foxhole and shot him."[91]

More casualties were sustained during the advance across the open ground: Sgt. Voyd L. Faile and Privates Dale E. Bean, Robert H. De Doncker, John L. Hays, Frank A. Jajowka and Paul F. Nelson were all killed. It often took many months before their family members learned what had happened—and in some instances even years. Valerie Seborg, Frank Jajowka's sister, wrote to Catholic Chaplain Kozak of the 504th PIR to ask how her brother had died. He replied on March 12, 1945: "Dear Mrs. Seborg. Received your sorrowful letter inquiring about your brother's death. It is true that Frank met his death in action as reported by the War Department. It happened during an attack and he was killed by an enemy shell. Frank's death, however, and that of his comrades was not in vain, for it was this battle that not only stopped the new German drive but which ended in their retreat from the Belgian Bulge."[92]

Another man killed during the charge across the barbed wired field was 23-year-old Cpl. Harold D. Stevenson of Ellisville, Illinois, who saw a German SdKfz 234/3 Puma heavy reconnaissance vehicle positioned in the middle of the road. The eight-wheeled vehicle, which looked almost like a tank, was creating havoc with its 75mm gun. Corporal Stevenson unhesitatingly took up his bazooka and moved closer to the armored vehicle, but he was killed outright by enemy fire while trying to knock it out. It was a brave, but tragic ending for the life of a man who was studying to become a minister before the war, and had delivered his first sermon when he was just 14 years old.[93]

As casualties mounted, the radios of both B and C Company went off the air, giving way to chaos as platoon leaders and squad leaders went down one after the other. Bleeding, the 1st Platoon leader in C Company, 2nd Lt. Robert Magruda, came up to Captain Milloy of Headquarters Company: "I remember him giving up his platoon to me and I saw him going back to the aid station," Milloy later recalled.[94] Magruda made his way to Tucker's forward CP, several miles back. As he burst into the farmhouse he gasped, "We've been catching hell! Get some ambulances up there in a hurry!"[95] Moments later Captain Duncan, the Battalion S-3, came in. "We've been cut to pieces!" he grimly declared.[96]

Captain Roy Anderson's company encountered approximately two platoons of well-dug-in German infantry, four 20mm flak wagons, and four MG42s on the outskirts of Cheneux. They killed 20-some Germans in hand-to-hand combat and the remainder fled further into the town. Anderson was also hit and moved back to the rear, handing his company over to 1st Lt. James E. Dunn, the company executive officer. At about the time Dunn took over, a devastating enemy mortar barrage hit the third assault wave of the company, further increasing casualties. Soon about 70 men figured among the killed, wounded and missing. But Americans were not the only ones to amass heavy casualties. Although exact figures for German losses are not known, in Kampfgruppe Peiper, the 6th and 11th Kompanies of SS-Panzergrenadier Regiment 2, commanded by *SS-Obersturmbannführer* Rudolf Sandig, were estimated to have lost at least 50 percent of their men.[97] They were supported by Major Wolfgang von Sacken's Leichte Flak Abteilung 84, a Luftwaffe unit equipped with 20mm flak wagons; and a mortar detachment and artillery unit situated at the Vaulx Renard farm east of Cheneux. One of the Germans killed that evening was 24-year-old *Obergefreiter* (Corporal) Karl-Heinz Nehring from *Leutnant* (Lieutenant) Schmidt's 2nd Battery, Leichte Flak Abteilung 84. According to his *soldbuch* (pay book) from February 1940, he had served in the Luftwaffe with various antiaircraft units in France (1940 and 1944) and the Soviet Union (1943).[98]

Led by 2nd Lt. Wayne M. Fetters, the assistant platoon leader of the 2nd Platoon, the third wave of C Company assaulted, passing by the dead and wounded who had fallen in earlier waves, to clash with the 11th Kompanie of SS-Panzergrenadier Regiment 2. Fetters was wounded in the fighting, but he and his group managed to rout the Germans from their entrenched positions, an action for which he was awarded the Silver Star and promoted to 1st lieutenant. His citation reads: "Lieutenant Fetters, a Platoon Leader in Company C, commanded the support platoon which made up the third assault wave on the town. In the initial stages of the attack, the Company Commander was wounded, and most of the officers and non-commissioned officers were either killed or wounded. The attack was moving across flat, open ground, and through numerous barbed wire fences running perpendicular to the direction of advance. Intense grazing fire from machine guns and 20mm cannons inflicted heavy casualties on the assault waves and threatened complete disorganization of the unit. Seeing the seriousness of the situation, 2nd Lieutenant Fetters, quickly and unhesitatingly, led his platoon through the assault waves and reached the objective. He continually exposed himself to the heavy fire while moving around among his men to better direct and urge them onward. His own fearless example was an inspiration to his company's mission."[99]

Some of the advancing troops managed to remain unseen as they advanced the first few hundred yards. Some of these lucky men were in the Mortar Squad of the 3rd Platoon of C Company, commanded by T/5 Elmer W. Swartz. He recalled that before the attack jumped off, a soldier in the mortar squad shot himself in the foot. This unfortunate event not only reduced their numbers (the trooper was evacuated); it gave their presence away to the German defenders in Cheneux. The C Company platoon leader who was given command of all the mortar squads instructed them to fire as many HE shells as possible into the center of the town, where he expected enemy armor to be amassed. Swartz believed the lieutenant's next decision saved a lot of lives: "The 1st, 2nd and 3rd Platoons crossed the open fields in full view of the enemy, but we went down the road. That is why we didn't suffer so many casualties in my squad."[100]

Sergeant Carter, a rifle squad leader in the 3rd platoon, was also wounded by shrapnel from the 20mm flak wagon as he advanced down the road. Just before he was hit, Carter saw S/Sergeant Walsh from B Company, who knocked the gun out with a hand grenade minutes later. Carter staggered on in the direction of Cheneux until he collapsed from the loss of blood: "When I regained consciousness," he recalled, "[Pvt. Dominic J.] Ciconte was kneeling beside me. He took off my jacket and coat, slipped loose my belt and put it on my arm as a tourniquet. Suddenly he picked up his gun and threw a fast shot. 'That Krauthead won't try to slip up on anybody else!' Then he knelt gently by me again, gave me a shot of morphine and rechecked my tourniquet. I think I must have fainted about every 50 yards on the way to the station."[101]

At one point Carter collapsed against a barbed wire fence. Cpl. George W. McAllister pulled him up and detailed Pfc. John F. Esman to escort him back to the aid station. On the way they were passed by more wounded 3rd Platoon members: Pfc. Bethel D. Nix and Sgt. William D. Serilla, who had received a serious head wound. Of the original 3rd Platoon members in C Company, only Corporal McAllister and Technical Sergeant Dietrich were still standing at the end of the battle.

A diary written by *Stabsfeldwebel* [Staff Sergeant] Karl Laun, Leichte Flak Abteilung 84, that was found after the fighting sheds a good light on the German view of the battle: "The din in the village is maddening, a fact to which I personally can testify as I have been selected to remain at the bridge. In vain have I tried to point out to Major [von] Sacken that employing our pieces near the bridge is plain and simple suicide, because incessant artillery and mortar fire seems zeroed in on this point. On inspecting the first piece, I found one crew member was already wounded. He was evacuated and I returned to hear that another man had disappeared without a trace, probably expedited into the murky river by a hit. And then I found *Leutnant* Porep severely wounded. When I placed the unfortunate fellow at the major's feet, [von] Sacken became concerned about his own safety. In the meantime, I had already taken it upon myself to order the survivors of my platoon to retreat.

"In the meantime, the threats, kicks, and curses of their officers cajoled the SS into new positions behind Cheneux. American infantry counterattacked twice at night. We suffered heavy casualties, while the SS officers sat in bunkers and basements. Prior to taking cover, they displayed their courage by ordering all the civilians in Stoumont to be herded up. Somewhere in the night we heard the anguished screaming of women."[102]

According to the battalion history, the 376th Parachute Field Artillery Battalion opened fire with their 75mm howitzers at 1950 hours—20 twenty minutes late. No explanation is given for the delay. The history also states that the battalion "fired numerous missions in support of the 504th and inflicted many casualties among the Germans," but does not provide details on how many shells were fired.[103]

Lieutenant Colonel Harrison meanwhile tried to put some order in the chaotic situation that emerged around 2130 hours. First of all, there was still no sign of Lieutenant Roberts' tank destroyers. Secondly, attempts to make radio contact with B and C Companies had failed, but judging from the number of wounded streaming to the rear, the situation was not going well. When Harrison decided he and his headquarters group would move forward, they encountered a few C Company men. He tried to radio the tank destroyers by radio, but the radio was out. He selected five men as runners, including Pfc. Donald L. Leonard, and sent them off with a message in the attempt to contact the various components of his dispersed battalion. The body of Private First Class Leonard was found later that evening, but how he was killed remains unknown. Over the next few days, three more C Company men, Sgt. Leon R. Duquette, Sgt. Edward E. Fox and Pvt. Wesley J. Groffen, succumbed to wounds sustained during the assault on Cheneux.

First Lieutenant Howard A. Kemble's Light Machine Gun Platoon became heavily involved in the attack on Cheneux. "The Germans held part of the town and we had to cross a wide open field with barbed wire," recalled Pvt. Stanley S. Kaslikowski, one of the machine gunners. "We had to crawl like snails. It was cold and there was snow on the ground. Some of the guys would straighten up to climb over the barbed wire and were shot immediately. I was able to crawl over to a small group of trees. It was night and we could hear the enemy but couldn't see them. They had these big flak wagons that were opening fire on us. We fired back, but with one machine gun we really couldn't do that much damage. Then a round came in, hit a tree, and part of the shell got me right in the chest. It felt like I got hit with a sledgehammer. I fell down to my hands and knees and that was it for me."[104]

Private Paul E. Hayden, another machine gunner, was posthumously decorated with a Silver Star for giving his life in a diversionary action that enabled C Company's advance. The citation reads: "Private Hayden was a member of an advance machine-gun crew during an attack on this strongly defended town when the left flank assault company was held up by the fire from an enemy cannon and supporting machine-gun elements. Casualties were becoming heavy when Private Hayden, realizing the seriousness of the situation, picked up his machine gun and rushed to a forward position in an effort to draw fire [away] from his comrades engaged in a flanking movement. While engaged in this gallant and unselfish act, Private Hayden was killed. Due to his supreme sacrifice, his company was able to take advantage of the diversion he created in its flanking assault on the enemy."[105]

A third machine gunner, Pvt. Robert M. Kinney, who knocked out a German flak wagon with hand grenades, also received the Silver Star: "Private Kinney, a member of a machine-gun crew, was attached to the left element of the attacking force, which had advanced about 200 yards when it was stopped by a vicious crossfire from an enemy cannon and machine guns. The fire from this strongpoint destroyed five out of eight machine guns. Private Kinney, realizing further casualties would result in disaster, advanced with three other men under this crossfire of enemy automatic weapons for about 200 yards. His path was constantly crossed by barbed wire fences, causing him to silhouette himself while advancing.

"With complete disregard for his personal safety, he cut these wires and continued his advance. Although small arms fire was hitting within a short distance, Private Kinney crawled within 25 yards and threw two hand grenades, destroying the gunner and neutralizing the enemy cannon. The actions of Private Kinney were an inspiration to his comrades in the subsequent assault, which was successfully concluded."[106]

Suddenly a German tank appeared and opened gunfire on the machine-gun crews. Without hesitation, 2nd Lt. William G. Yepsen, the assistant Light Machine Gun Platoon leader, took a machine gun from one of his crew who had been hit and started crawling forward to an exposed position: "Although enemy automatic weapons fire came within six inches of him, Lieutenant Yepsen returned the fire and eliminated a machine-gun position before turning his attention to the tank. Firing prolonged bursts of AP and tracer ammunition at the driver's slit, he caused the enemy tank to remain buttoned up, hampering its efficiency. He held this exposed position and continued to harass the tank until mortally wounded by direct cannon fire."[107]

Lieutenant Kemble, platoon leader of the Light Machine Gun Platoon, led his platoon's assault across the open fields and had them set up on either side of the road that served as an axis for attack by B and C Companies. Kemble took up position north of the road in the C Company sector, where his machine guns got hit one after the other by fire from the Puma armored car that had remained impervious to C Company's attack. According to his posthumously awarded Silver Star Citation: "First Lieutenant Kemble's platoon was pressed into action after the first two assault waves on the town were badly depleted and disorganized by heavy casualties. While moving forward over the flat, open terrain crossed with barbed wire fences, the platoon came under the observed fire of two cannons and a freshly committed enemy platoon. Only through the cool courage and superior leadership displayed by First Lieutenant Kemble as he moved fearlessly around among his men in order to better direct and exhort them onward was the platoon able to advance 200 yards. Five out of the platoon's eight machine-gun crews had now been killed or wounded; further advance would have been suicidal.

"First Lieutenant Kemble, after ordering his men to dig in on a defensive line, took a machine gun to a position 50 yards in front of his men and gave them covering fire until they were safely dug-in, expending five boxes of ammunition in the process. The full concentration of the enemy fire was placed on this lone target; bullets ripped through his clothing and ricocheted off his gun, but First Lieutenant Kemble remained steadfast. After his men had been entrenched safely without further casualties, he returned to the rear and collected all the company overhead with which he strengthened his defensive line so expertly that this regrouped unit was able to break up two determined enemy counterattacks with heavy casualties. Throughout this entire vital action, the unsurpassed courage and inspiring leadership displayed by First Lieutenant Kemble made such a profound impression on his men that their performance was above that expected in the call of duty. The eventual successful completion of his company's mission can be attributed largely to the impetus provided by First Lieutenant Kemble at a critical juncture in the attack. First Lieutenant Kemble was killed in action the next day while leading a subsequent assault. The memory of his actions at Cheneux, Belgium, will serve as a lasting inspiration to all who witnessed them."[108]

Chaplin Kozak wrote in reply to Lieutenant Kemble's parents to describe how he was killed while checking one of his outposts at Cheneux: "It is true that Howard died in action as reported by the War Department. It happened on December 20 [sic], when your son led an attack upon a Belgian village in the hands of an SS-Panzer unit. The fighting was fierce, enemy mortars, cannon, and machine guns made the mission a hazardous one. Your son injected his men with good natural coolness as he moved amongst them. Finally, the assault—and, as one sergeant reported, Lieutenant Kemble leaped from his foxhole, yelling 'Let's go, you guys!' Firing from the hip, he led his men through the village. One building was left intact in the village—the church. Howard warned the men not to harm it unless they received fire out of it. Looking inside, they beheld a touching sight—an elderly priest leading old people and tiny children in prayer. Howard and his men knelt and joined them.

"A little later, Howard went on a tour, inspecting his outpost. Darkness was settling. In a doorway, he beheld what seemed to be an American soldier. Howard stepped up to see who it might be. It was a German, who fired and struck your son in the chest. The sergeant who accompanied Howard [Sgt. Al N. Vrabac] immediately dropped the enemy. Howard was surprised and joked about his wound. An aid man and a captured medical officer attended to his wound. He never realized his condition for he felt no pain and talked to the very end. Then smiling, he closed his eyes and met his God. The sergeant, standing by, sadly said: 'He died like a Christian and a hero.' The

German doctor, adhering to the medical code of ethics, tried in vain to save his life and was very much upset over your son's death.

"The day before that day, Lieutenant Kemble attended Mass and received the Sacrament. He was buried with full military honors in an American cemetery—a Catholic Priest officiating at the funeral service. For his exemplary leadership and courage, Howard received the award of the Silver Star.

"Mr. Kemble, you have lost a brave son—we, a good leader and a pal, yet it was heaven's gain. He died fully prepared spiritually. His death and that of his comrades was not in vain. For it was this battle that stopped the German counteroffensive and marked the beginning of our offensive in the Belgian Bulge.

"While there is no earthly compensation for the loss of your son, I hope that you shall find consolation in Howard's complete devotion to duty. I further trust that our mutual faith in God shall sustain you in this hour of bereavement. May his soul, through the mercy of God, rest in peace."[109]

Sergeant Vrabac, who had shot the German who had killed Kemble, was awarded the Bronze Star: "With the assistant platoon leader [Lt. Yepsen] and platoon sergeant casualties, Sergeant Vrabac took command of the machine-gun platoon, organized defensive positions and held a line against repeated tank and infantry counterattacks. Late that afternoon [December 21], Sergeant Vrabac again took command of the platoon when the platoon leader [Lieutenant Kemble] was killed during a bayonet charge into the village. Sergeant Vrabac and his men routed superior numbers of the enemy and successfully occupied the village."[110]

Around 2100 hours the remnants of B Company, led by Sgt. Clyde A. Farrier, dug in on the outskirts of the company position, east of the road. Farrier's Military Medal Citation reads: "When his commanding officer and all non-commissioned officers of his platoon became casualties, Sergeant Farrier, in the midst of heavy enemy artillery and small-arms fire, reorganized the platoon. He then led it in two successive assaults, killing 13 Germans, knocking out two hostile machine guns, and capturing the objective. While his platoon consolidated its newly-won position, Sergeant Farrier assisted three wounded comrades through fierce German small-arms fire to the medical aid station. These voluntary and courageous acts were an inspiration to all the officers and men of his organization."[111]

Private First Class Hubert A. Wolfe from the 2nd Platoon was in a slit trench not too far from a radio when a 20mm shell hit the radio and steel fragments struck him in the back of the head. All the B Company medics were busy evacuating men and tending the dozens of wounded fallen during the attack, so Wolfe knew there were no medics in his immediate area. It nevertheless was urgent that he obtain medical attention, because was bleeding from his head wound and the blow had rendered him partially paralyzed on the left side. Wolfe somehow managed to drag himself out of the slit trench and was crawling to the rear when an unknown soldier suddenly grabbed him under his arms and carried him to the aid station. Wolfe's long road to recovery started with a five-month hospitalization, including the insertion of a steel plate in the back of his head. He gradually regained full use of the left side of his body, but the war was over for Wolfe. Only at the regimental reunion in Philadelphia in 1983, did Wolfe and his wife learn that the man who had dragged him to safety was Sgt. Ian G. ("Red") McKee from the 3rd Platoon. "It was an emotional time," he recalled. "I think we all had tears. I couldn't say much of anything to him—I was too choked up."[112]

In the C Company sector of Cheneux, Pfc. Albert S. Ianacone drove off a strong enemy combat patrol that threatened to overrun the recently gained position. As his Silver Star Citation sums up: "After capturing the village of Cheneux, Belgium, the badly depleted and disorganized units were in the process of reorganizing to prepare for the defense of the town. Private First Class Ianacone and another man were placed in an outpost position which was soon attacked by the enemy. Private First Class Ianacone, realizing that his platoon was not completely dug-in at the time, remained in position until the enemy forces of approximately 15 men reached a point within ten yards, then opened fire. The enemy patrol deployed and attacked Private First Class Ianacone with a machine gun, automatic pistols, rifles, and grenades, causing Private First Class Ianacone to be painfully wounded. Despite his almost hopeless situation, Private First Class Ianacone continued to fight until he knocked out the enemy machine gun with a hand grenade. After losing their machine gun and four of their men, the enemy patrol withdrew. Private First Class Ianacone's gallant action in the face of overwhelming odds delayed an enemy counterattack in force. His exemplary conduct reflects great credit upon himself and the unit in which he serves."[113]

Another paratrooper who distinguished himself that night was S/Sgt. Norman B. Angel, the 1st Battalion supply sergeant. Angel received a Silver Star "for gallantry in action while serving with Headquarters Company, 1st Battalion, 504th Parachute Infantry Regiment, 82nd Airborne Division, in action on 20 December 1944, near Cheneux, Belgium.

"During the height of an attack on Cheneux, Belgium, the First Battalion had expended nearly all of the basic load of ammunition and was in danger of being without ammunition for the defense of its hard-won position. Staff Sergeant Angel, Headquarters Company Supply Sergeant, realizing this, and with complete disregard of his personal safety, made repeated trips in a jeep over an exposed section of road about 1,000 yards long, which was continually swept by fire from enemy cannons, machine guns, and small arms, to deliver ammunition to a point 50 yards behind the foremost riflemen. From this point he personally carried the ammunition to the individual riflemen and machine gunners of the entire battalion, crawling as much as 200 yards under intense small arms fire to reach the battalion's flanks.

"Despite the fact that his vehicle was frequently hit by hostile fire, Staff Sergeant Angel never hesitated or faltered in his assigned task. By his unselfish devotion to duty, he played an important part in the successful accomplishment of his battalion's mission. The heroism and gallantry displayed by Staff Sergeant Angel upheld the highest traditions of the United States Army."[114]

By 2200 hours the tank destroyers had not moved one inch forward and were still out of sight. Lieutenant Colonel Harrison left his Battalion CP and ran back along the road. Passing Sergeant Swartz's C Company 60mm mortar squad, Harrison spotted the tank destroyers in a large patch of woods behind them. A heated discussion broke out between Harrison and Lt. James Roberts, commanding officer of the tank destroyer platoon. Roberts claimed his tank destroyers were no match for German armor and could not be deployed into combat. Harrison then returned to the mortar squad and issued an extraordinary order to Pvt. Ross Pippin and another man: "If these men don't get into the battle, shoot them!"[115]

Led by Pippin and the other trooper, two tank destroyers started to move forward, Lieutenant Roberts being in the leading vehicle. The After Action Report of the 703rd TDB omits the exact times the platoon moved forward and gives the misleading impression that the two tank destroyers moved out simultaneously with B and C Companies: "One section of this platoon constituted the entire available armor for this attack, there being no tanks attached to the regiment, and two TD's being deadlined for repairs. The mission of the TD's in supporting this attack was to move along with the leading infantry elements, to make as much noise as possible, giving the impression of great strength, and to shoot at anything that moved in front of them. At the time of the attack it was so dark that visibility was limited to about 25 yards, and the destroyers could see very little as they moved toward the town.

"As the infantry moved just ahead of them, a 20mm flak wagon opened up, pinning the infantry down, and stopping their advance. The destroyers were not in a position to take the 20mm under fire, and it was necessary to move further ahead before this could be accomplished. One destroyer moved up the road while the other remained in position, covering its advance.

"As the leading destroyer moved forward, it all but ran into a German half-track on the right side of the road, and as the gunner swung the gun around, the tube struck the other vehicle. The driver immediately reversed the destroyer, and at the same time the crew of the half-track began to abandon it. They were helped along considerably by a round of HE, which completely destroyed the vehicle and crew. Then in rapid succession the destroyer knocked out the 20mm flak wagon and a tracked prime mover.

"With this resistance eliminated, the infantry pushed forward toward the center of the town until it was held up again by another flak wagon. This was hidden from the destroyer by a stone house, and the gunner had no way of maneuvering into a good shooting position. Therefore, the next best choice was made—to knock away one protection and then go after the vehicle. Using APCBDF ammunition [armor-piercing shells] the gunner fired directly at the building, blasting away the wall, and then destroyed the exposed flak wagon. A few moments later, two half-tracks left their hiding positions behind buildings in front of the TD, and were destroyed as they attempted to retreat down the road. This concluded the action of the destroyers for the balance of the night, and the infantry consolidated the gains they had made up to that point."[116]

Also advancing with the tank destroyers were 1st Lt. Melvin C. Ullrich and two squads of his 1st Platoon, C Company, 307th AEB, whom Lieutenant Colonel Harrison had sent to protect the tank destroyers from panzerfaust attacks and reinforce his battered companies. It was obvious from the many wounded walking to the rear that the battle was not going in favor of Colonel Tucker's troopers. With the arrival of the engineers, the mortar men returned to their position. Hardly had the tank destroyers advanced a few hundred yards before they received heavy fire. Lieutenant Roberts wanted to stop and reverse, but Lieutenant Ullrich urged him to go forward and support the pinned-down infantry. Reaching the town, the tank knocked out several vehicles, as described in the previously cited report. Ullrich then joined B Company and took command until Captain Duncan, the Battalion S-3 officer, arrived. Harrison had designated him as the acting company commander while Captain Helgeson remained out of his mind. At approximately 2300 hours 1st Lt. Michael G. Sabia arrived with the remainder of the engineer platoon and they dug in on the high ground near Cheneux.

While the attack on Cheneux continued with support by the tank destroyers, Harrison moved his 1st Battalion CP forward, first to a knocked-out German half-track, and subsequently in the first house on the right side of the road. His executive officer, Maj. John T. Berry, recalled that he was going up the stairs with a runner when a shell came through the window, killing the runner instantly. A tiny fragment pierced a hole in the sleeve of Berry's uniform, a very close call. The unfortunate runner may have been Pfc. Donald L. Leonard from C Company, who was killed while delivering messages.

At 2300 hours Colonel Tucker walked into the CP and enquired about the situation. Harrison gave him the appalling total losses: B Company was down to less than 20 men and all the officers had been wounded; C Company had three officers left and about 40 men, and all the company commanders had been wounded. Harrison placed his Headquarters Company on the far left flank, the engineer platoon to their right on high ground, and a mixed company of remnants from both B and C Company in the center and on outposts, and positioned the three machine guns on the right flank. Cheneux was now about half under control, but without another company, the rest of the town could not be taken. Tucker, fortunately suspecting the need for reinforcements, had radioed Lieutenant Colonel Cook at 2115 hours to send G Company down to Cheneux.

CHAPTER 5

THE CAPTURE OF CHENEUX
CHENEUX AND MONCEAU, BELGIUM,
DECEMBER 20–21, 1944

C aptain Thomas' G Company moved out at 2130 hours, nearing the village around midnight. In the lead, 1st Lt. Harry Frear's 1st Platoon was suddenly pinned down by enemy machine-gun fire. It was at this point that Pfc. John Allen, Jr. was most likely killed. Frear described the battle in a letter to Allen's sister: "My platoon and of course myself were ordered to lead an assault upon an enemy-occupied town. We suffered heavy casualties in the first phase of this battle and the true spirit and character of your brother once again comes to light. At a time when under heavy enemy fire, my platoon became disorganized. John was of invaluable assistance to me. A combat-wise soldier, he moved everywhere, cheering up men who were new to the war, doing all within his power to keep the platoon working as a unit. When my Thompson submachine gun was shot from my hands, John secured for me an enemy weapon, which he put into operation for me. He was a definite guiding influence on the men in my platoon, and performed duties and services there that I would ask from no man.

"To say that he died for his country is a small way of putting it. John gave his life so that I and the other men of my platoon might live; he gave his life so that you and his friends and his countrymen might live and that we, as a people, might never allow this to happen again.

"I have commanded many men in my five years of service, but never before has it been my privilege to command as fine and heroic soldier as your

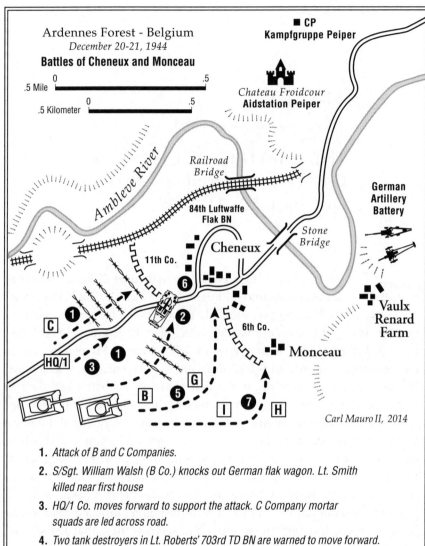

Ardennes Forest - Belgium
December 20-21, 1944
Battles of Cheneux and Monceau

■ CP
Kampfgruppe Peiper

Chateau Froidcour
Aidstation Peiper

Ambleve River

Railroad Bridge

German Artillery Battery

84th Luftwaffe Flak BN

11th Co.

Cheneux

Stone Bridge

Vaulx Renard Farm

6th Co.

Monceau

Carl Mauro II, 2014

1. *Attack of B and C Companies.*
2. *S/Sgt. William Walsh (B Co.) knocks out German flak wagon. Lt. Smith killed near first house*
3. *HQ/1 Co. moves forward to support the attack. C Company mortar squads are led across road.*
4. *Two tank destroyers in Lt. Roberts' 703rd TD BN are warned to move forward.*
5. *Flanking attack by G Company 2330 hrs.*
6. *Lt. Kemble (HQ Co.) mortally wounded on the afternoon of Dec. 21.*
7. *Flanking attack 1400 hrs. Dec. 21. Captain Bartley (composed platoon) killed.*

❶ *Notes* Ⓐ *Parachute Co.* ◄---- *U.S. Troop Movement*

⋈⋈⋈ *Barbed Wire* ⊓⊔⊓⊔ *German MLR*

brother. I may not live to return to my home, but whether I do or not, I will say that I will never meet a finer man, better soldier, or a more heroic figure than John E. Allen, Jr."[117]

One of the lead scouts had been Pvt. Francis J. Bardon, who was awarded the Silver Star: "Private Bardon, a lead scout, ran into heavy fire from three enemy machine guns, one flak wagon, and numerous small-arms weapons. Even though seriously wounded, Private Bardon refused to withdraw and returned the enemy's fire, holding them off until his platoon had maneuvered to an attacking position. Private Bardon personally accounted for five of the enemy killed and many more wounded, including one entire machine-gun crew. Only when he had received a direct order from his platoon leader, did he consent to be evacuated."[118]

Another G Company soldier, Pfc. Clarence E. Ables, was most likely wounded around the same time. He also later received a Silver Star: "Private First Class Ables, a machine gunner, was a member of the squad designated to attack an enemy strongpoint. There was no cover available and Private First Class Ables was forced to set up his gun out in the open under heavy machine-gun, mortar, rifle and 20mm fire. He was immediately knocked from his gun and seriously wounded, but in spite of this, he crawled back to his gun and moved it to a position where it could be manned by his assistant gunner. When the gun was back in action, Private First Class Ables allowed himself to be evacuated."[119]

S/Sgt. Marion Shagdai, a recently assigned squad leader in Lieutenant Frear's platoon, moved forward and knocked out one machine-gun team while he scared away a second. For his bravery he would later be awarded the Silver Star: "During a night assault the platoon of which Staff Sergeant Shagdai was a member became pinned down by intense crossfire from two enemy machine guns. Staff Sergeant Shagdai made a lone assault on the enemy gun positions. With utter disrespect for the enemy fire focused upon him, he crawled close to the first gun, threw two grenades and fired upon the crew with his submachine gun, killing them all. The second gun immediately turned its fire upon him, but Staff Sergeant Shagdai coolly and courageously stood his ground and forced the crew of the second gun to flee. Staff Sergeant Shagdai's courage and unflinching devotion to duty enabled his platoon to proceed without further delay."[120]

Pvt. Henry E. Schmid, a rifleman in the 2nd Platoon, recalled "taking fire from a half-track that was on a side of a hill that sprayed the whole area we were in. The shells hit all around us and I got hit twice by shrapnel in the leg. My platoon leader, Lieutenant Hesson, was severely wounded at that time and I believe 1st Sergeant [Wayne C.] Long was killed then. I spent five weeks in a hospital in Liège, Belgium, before I rejoined G Company again."[121]

Schmid's platoon leader, 2nd Lt. James C. Hesson, received a Silver Star for his leadership in the battle: "While leading his platoon against a well-dug-in and numerically superior force of enemy, Second Lieutenant Hesson was fired upon by a machine gun. He immediately returned their fire and knocked out the gun as well as killing two members of the crew. A 20mm flak wagon and two machine guns then opened up with point-blank range into the platoon, causing many casualties. Second Lieutenant Hesson, seriously wounded, insisted on remaining with his men until all the wounded had been given first aid and evacuated. Second Lieutenant Hesson's complete disregard for his own personal safety was greatly responsible for keeping up the morale of the men for the assignment still ahead of them."[122]

Another assistant platoon leader, 2nd Lt. Paul M. Nance, was wounded while attacking a German-held house in Cheneux with hand grenades. For his gallantry in action he also received the Silver Star: "As the platoon designated to attack the town from the right, their progress was blocked by intense rifle and machine-gun fire from a large house to their front. Taking one man with him, Second Lieutenant Nance, assistant platoon leader, moved forward to attack the house with grenades. Second Lieutenant Nance then rushed the house and was wounded in the leg by 20mm flak-gun fire. Continuing, he succeeded in killing three of the enemy, wounding two more and forcing the remaining three members of the enemy group to flee. During this action, Second Lieutenant Nance was wounded twice more, in the right leg and shoulder. He returned to his companion and found him seriously wounded. Despite his own wounds, Second Lieutenant Nance carried the soldier to safety and returned to his platoon, refusing evacuation until so ordered. His heroic and courageous actions reflect great credit on the Airborne Forces."[123]

Dug-in on the right flank of C Company, 2nd Lt. James R. Allmand, Jr. and his 3rd Platoon and bore the brunt of the German counterattack that morning. One of Allmand's men, Pfc. Raymond S. Holsti, would receive a Distinguished Service Cross "for extraordinary heroism" in repelling the sudden counterattack: "As a machine gunner, Private First Class Holsti was dug in position on the far left flank of his company's defense line, protecting the link with C Company to its left. At approximately 0800 hours, the enemy mounted a determined attack with at least of company of infantry supported by two flak wagons and artillery. Private First Class Holsti, seeing the casualties being caused by the fire from the 20mm cannons on the vehicles, immediately placed all the fire possible from his light machine gun upon the advancing vehicles.

"In consequence, the flak wagons focused their firepower on the harassing gun position. Private First Class Holsti was seriously wounded several times. Despite these wounds, he continued to fire effectively at the vehicles, until bazooka men were able to get into a firing position from which they were able to knock out one vehicle and force the other to withdraw. Seeing their supporting armor eliminated, the enemy infantry broke off the attack. Private First Class Holsti continued to fire unassisted at the retreating infantry until he collapsed in his hole from great loss of blood. As a result of Private First Class Holsti's unsurpassed courage and unswerving devotion to duty, a serious threat to his company's whole defensive perimeter was eliminated."[124]

Despite Holsti's heroic actions, there were casualties among the American defenders. First Sergeant Long and Pvt. Melesio Perez, Jr. of G Company were killed and Pvt. Lawrence H. Bishop, also in G Company, was mortally wounded by 20mm gunfire and died later that day.[125] Other wounded included the company medic, T/5 William M. Peeples, Jr., 2nd Lieutenants Anderson, Hesson, Nance and Tennyson, and 30 enlisted men. Private First Class Melvin S. Kessler recalls that Lieutenant Anderson was wounded in the leg on top of a ridge and that he dragged him with help from Pfc. Leo J. Estenson to a safer spot. According to G Company Morning Reports, Captain Thomas was hospitalized due to reasons not related to battle on December 20. He was succeeded by 1st Lt. James H. Goethe, the former 1st Battalion S-2 officer, and did not return to the 504th Parachute Infantry Regiment.

Lieutenant Ullrich's engineer platoon suffered casualties due to shelling. Sgt. Russell H. Fritz was wounded in seven places in his head, chest and arms by 20mm shrapnel; Pfc. Roy A. Bachellor and Pfc. Joseph A. Dickson were also hit, and all three were evacuated. Cpl. Carmen J. Western and Pfc. Albert J. Middlemiss, more lightly wounded, were patched up and remained on duty.

The 3rd Platoon of C Company, 307th AEB was sent up around dawn to strengthen right flank defensive positions. Pvt. Leo R. Cardin was killed by a direct hit on his chest. Later that morning two more men from the 1st

Platoon were hit by shrapnel: Pfc. Francis W. Byrnes was wounded in the hand and Pfc. Garo Krikorian in the knee.

At 0745 hours, just as the German counterattack was beginning, Lieutenant Stark was contacted by radio. He was ordered to bring his four 57mm antitank guns up front as the two tank destroyers had pulled back during the night and were once again "lost": "During the night of 20-21 December, bitter fighting continued on the outskirts of Cheneux. Much of the 20mm flak that was missing the troops in the forward areas was exploding in and about the town of Rahier. A platoon of tank destroyers was also attached to the 1st Battalion during the night, and before dawn, at approximately 0400 hours, this unit moved toward Cheneux to contact the battalion commander. At 0730 hours, the battalion commander had not yet seen them, and called for the antitank platoon to move forward, in the belief that the Germans were massing their armor for an all-out attack against his positions. Since all gun squads had been on the alert, movement toward Cheneux was started in a matter of minutes. The battalion commander wanted me to come to his command post, which he said was located in the first house on the right-hand side of the road, as one moved toward Cheneux.

"When the platoon reached a point 400 yards west of the command post, the tank destroyers were seen halted along the road. Their commander stated that he did not know where the battalion commander was located, and also that he was unable to move forward any further. I decided that if the tank destroyers were not able to advance beyond this point, the further advance of the quarter-ton trucks towing antitank guns would not be a wise move. Therefore, after dismounting and directing the troops to disperse, I moved forward on foot to contact the battalion commander.

"Upon going about 100 yards, I saw some 81mm mortars firing from the eastern edge of these same woods. I inquired of the personnel manning them as to the exact location of the front lines and the command post. Through some bushes, they pointed out a house about 300 yards forward, stating that that was the command post. They further stated that they were firing in that direction at a range of 350 yards. With this knowledge, I moved forward along the ditches of the road.

"About half way to the house, I met the battalion commander running toward the rear. He had just learned that the tank destroyers were sitting back in the woods, and he was going after them. I led him back to the commander of the tank destroyers. After a brief heated discussion between the battalion commander and the tank destroyer platoon leader, in which the latter said little, the tanks were finally moved forward to the edge of the woods, about 100 yards. The platoon leader refused to move them any further forward. The situation appeared critical, as many armored vehicles could be heard moving about in the town. Since the tank destroyers were of no value, the order was given to move the antitank guns forward so that the road and the broad open fields north of the road would be covered. On the south side of the road, the terrain dropped off sharply and was considered to be sufficient antitank protection.

"I made a reconnaissance and found some excellent locations for positions, if the weapons and crews could reach these points without being knocked out. To arrive at these sites, open spaces within sight of the enemy had to be traversed. Two of the guns were attached to the front of the vehicles, permitting them to be pushed into their positions. Then they would be quickly disconnected, so that the vehicles could go in reverse for a short distance and be relatively safe from direct fire. The other two vehicles and guns, using standard towing procedure, were to rush across the open ground into a defiladed area, disconnect the guns and then push them forward slowly into barrel defilade. Two men from each squad were to go individually to these positions by crawling or rushing. Only the driver would go with the vehicles to the positions. The other members of the squads were to remain back in the woods and were to dig foxholes.

"After the battalion commander had approved the proposed positions and plan, each man in the antitank platoon was told how and what he was to do. From the time I had first contacted the battalion commander, about one hour had elapsed, and it was then 0845 hours. The first of the men had barely started to move toward their positions, when a fog or mist, which reduced the visibility to less than 100 yards, covered the entire area. With this situation prevailing, rather than have the vehicles rush across the open spaces as previously planned, they moved across very slowly, making a minimum of noise. This move was accomplished quickly, the guns were dug in to give them added protection, and all personnel went to the vicinity of their weapons, rather than remaining back in the woods. The heavy part of the fog remained a sufficient length of time to permit the entire position preparation to be accomplished unobserved or about 30 minutes. By 1000 hours, the visibility was back to normal.

"Though the battalion commander had feared that the Germans were massing their armor and forces for an all-out attack against his positions, this apparently was not the German plan, for the vehicular movement that had been heard continuously was becoming more distant. Not one vehicle of any type was seen during the day from any of the gun positions."[126]

Lieutenant Stark was apparently unaware of the counterattack that had taken place that morning before he was called forward. Capt. Charles Duncan, acting B Company commander, became livid with anger as he spotted the tank destroyers once again to the rear of his severely depleted company. To Pfc. James M. McNamara of the Regimental Demolition Platoon, "the tank destroyers seemed to be conspicuous by their timidity. The next morning I saw Captain Duncan from Headquarters, 1st Battalion, threaten a tank destroyer commander with his .45 in order to get him to move forward."[127]

At 0845 hours the field telephone in the 3rd Battalion CP in Froidville, west of Rahier, rang. Battalion XO Major Zakby picked up the phone and heard the voice of his regimental counterpart, Lieutenant Colonel Williams. "Alert battalion and prepare to move," Williams said. "Lieutenant Colonel Cook and Captain Keep are to report to Cider." Zakby immediately passed the word to Cook, who left with Keep in a jeep to regimental headquarters in Rahier. An hour later Major Zakby noted in the 3rd Battalion log: "Colonel and Captain Keep returned from Cider [call sign for the 504th PIR]. Called meeting of commanding officers. Battalion less G will move as soon as possible to sweep area to our east."[128]

Cook instructed Captain Kappel to lead off with H Company, followed by Captain Burriss' I Company, with Captain Warfield's Headquarters Company bringing up the rear. Trucks would transport the men forward under the guidance of Capt. Jack M. Bartley of Service Company, who would lead a composite platoon of replacements and two reconnaissance cars as part of the 3rd Battalion. The battalion column pushed off by 1030 hours, and by early afternoon had reached the assembly area south of Monceau, from whence the attack on the town would commence. The terrain seemed to favorize the paratroopers: they were on high ground, whereas the Germans defending Monceau were on lower ground.

First Lieutenant Harold Roy, 376th PFAB, was assigned as a forward observer [FO] to Headquarters Company, which would support the H Company assault. He and his five assistants were handed cups of coffee, and after they finished, Roy was told "'From here to here is your position.' I didn't know what the objective was. If I had known the objective I could have arranged better adjustment points for artillery. It was very misty and there was poor visibility. I used the church of Cheneux as a reference point to adjust the artillery fire. We could see the church well through the haze."[129]

Captain Kappel meanwhile assembled his platoon leaders and gave them the order of attack. They would attack from the southeast, with 1st Lt. Richard G. La Riviere's 2nd Platoon on the left, near the road leading into Monceau, and 1st Lt. James Megellas' 3rd Platoon on the right. Kappel would follow with 2nd Lt. Henry S. Furst's 1st Platoon and Company Headquarters. The objective was to overrun the German defenders in Monceau, and move on to Cheneux to attack the German force in their rear. Meanwhile, time had been passing; it was now 1500 hours.

Megellas recalled that the leading platoons "were fired upon by enemy 20mm flak wagons and machine guns. [...] I was about halfway down the hill heading for the Amblève River. The shrapnel from the exploding 20mm shells initially took a heavy toll in wounded men, forcing those who had just started down the forward crest to seek cover behind the hill. I was at least halfway down the forward slope, so instinctively I charged down the hill in the direction of enemy fire. [...] In my combat experience, I learned that in a situation such as this, the best course of action was to charge in the direction of the enemy fire. The enemy certainly had to be confronted if we were to achieve our objective.

"I reached the bottom of the hill along with five other men, including [2nd] Lieutenant [Ernest] Murphy and Pvt. Donald Herndon. We took cover along the banks of the Amblève River in a growth of brush and saplings hidden from the view of the flak wagons."[130]

Sergeant Tarbell, Captain Kappel's radio operator, recalled that "as we charged down the hill, the flak wagons turned their weapons on us. We had many casualties from that encounter. There was a Captain [Bartley] with us from Service Company who was severely wounded and eventually died. Another of our men was wounded in the leg and was yelling like a stuck pig. The officer told him to quiet down, that he was not hit that bad. I helped with the wounded by getting them out of the line of fire and onto the trucks which were parked nearby to get them to a medical station. We were pinned down a while from the 20mm shrapnel. The trucks with wounded were unable to move for quite a while."[131]

Meanwhile, the remnants of H Company were reorganized behind the hill and Captain Kappel soon learned that the 3rd Platoon of H Company was without both its officers; Lieutenants Megellas and Murphy and four enlisted men were missing. Lieutenant Colonel Cook was informed and came up to see the result of the assault. He decided to attack once more, this time with I Company on the left.

At 1600 hours Captain Burriss received a distress call from Lieutenant Colonel Cook to bring his I Company forward because H Company was being pinned down by flak wagon and small-arms fire. Captain Kappel and Lieutenant Furst had both been wounded by 20mm gunfire. Artillery support had also been requested. Burriss quickly assembled his platoon leaders and instructed 1st Lt. Harold Weber to move out with his 1st Platoon on the left—across the open barren hill crest southwest of Monceau—while 1st Lieutenant Harry Price, the 3rd Platoon leader, was to advance between the 1st Platoon and the road. H Company was to attack from the southeast as soon as they had regrouped.

By 1750 hours the 3rd Battalion jumped off once more on Monceau. "We now split our three platoons," recalled Sgt. George Leoleis of I Company. "The 1st moved a little to the left but could still see the main road in the middle of the town, and the 3rd (mine) worked its way to the right, which sloped into the town, and we went in. From house to house we worked our way and from half-track to flak wagons."[132]

Second Lieutenant Joseph D. Shirk, leader of the 2nd Platoon, was wounded by one of the two 20mm flak wagons in Monceau, which had early spread havoc among the assaulting H Company troopers. Also wounded were Pfc. Vern O. Hanners and Privates Martinez, Parenti and Wynn. Shirk would rejoin I Company a couple of weeks later. Their I Company comrades captured one 20mm flak wagon intact and Captain Burriss immediately ordered his men to use its fire power against the enemy. The crew of a second flak wagon was knocked out by Lieutenant Megellas' group, who shot all eight gunners down and then turned to run back in the direction of the remainder of H Company. Private Herndon was wounded and carried back on Megellas' shoulder to safety. Megellas was awarded the Silver Star: "While attacking across the barren crest of a hill toward their ultimate objective, Lieutenant Megellas, with utter disregard for his personal safety, fearlessly charged down the hill toward the enemy, calling his men to follow him. Reaching a small patch of woods, Lieutenant Megellas sighted a large force of enemy armor and infantry and a gun firing on friendly tank destroyers. Unhesitantly, Lieutenant Megellas opened fire upon its crew, killing all eight. The enemy raked the trees with a curtain of intense fire, wounding one of the men. Lieutenant Megellas fearlessly picked up the wounded man and led his small force to cover, re-formed it, and led them to seize the objective."[133]

Corporal Eldon F. Young of Megellas' platoon, wounded while trying to render first aid to a wounded soldier, was also be awarded the Silver Star:

"While proceeding north through the town of Monceau, the platoon in which Corporal Young was an assistant squad leader was pinned down in open terrain by a crossfire from enemy cannons and machine guns. While attempting to crawl back to the safety of the reverse slope of the hill, one of the men of Corporal Young's squad was seriously wounded. Corporal Young unhesitatingly left a position of cover and crawled to his aid through a curtain of fire. While in the process of dragging his wounded comrade to a position where he could receive medical aid, Corporal Young was himself seriously wounded in both legs by machine-gun fire."[134]

Lieutenant Roy, the forward artillery observer of the 376th Parachute Field Artillery Battalion, took command of the remnants of H Company and later received a Silver Star for his leadership: "Suddenly a withering crossfire from three enemy guns split the company and pinned down about a platoon in an open area. The company and platoon commanders were both wounded and evacuated. In the absence of any infantry officers, First Lieutenant Roy took command of the composed troops and directed them to cover behind the ridge. Despite the crossfire and lack of cover, First Lieutenant Roy remained in this hazardous position, set up his radio and fired his artillery battalion almost constantly for more than an hour; knocking out three tanks, two scout cars, and inflicting heavy personnel casualties against the enemy. First Lieutenant Roy's gallant action saved our troops many casualties and assured the accomplishment of the mission. Entered military service from San Antonio, Texas."[135]

As the battle report of the 740th Tank Battalion sums up its contributions to the day: "The Germans were offering stiff resistance and it was evident that they had no intention giving up the remainder of the town without a struggle. The battalion commander therefore decided to send a force around the town and attack from the rear, supported by a frontal attack. The TD's were given the mission of driving through the town, clearing out whatever they could find, until they met up with the flanking force. When the attack started, one TD almost immediately knocked a 105mm gun and prime mover out of action, which blocked the road, making it necessary for them to find an alternate route. Moving cautiously through farmyards and alleys, the destroyers made their way through the town and finally joined the flanking force. The infantry following behind mopped up pockets of resistance and by 2100 hours the town was cleared. The section set up a road block on the east side of the town, overlooking the approaches from that direction, and later that night destroyed another flak wagon which had remained in concealment and was trying to escape across the river toward La Gleize.[136]

Colonel Tucker was awarded a Silver Star "for gallantry in action on 21 December 1944 near Monceau, Belgium. In the the development of the attack of his regiment across the Amblève River during a critical phase of the Ardennes Campaign, Colonel Tucker, Commanding the 504th Parachute Infantry Regiment, 82nd Airborne Division, personally directed the pincer operations designated to capture two strategic towns. While one reinforced battalion was struggling for Cheneux, he advanced with the lead elements of the Third Battalion against Monceau through densely wooded and mountainous terrain under intense 20mm and artillery fire. Colonel Tucker coolly coordinated the attack on the town, exposed to and with calm disregard of enemy action. His encouraging and inspirational presence served to stimulate his troops to greater endeavor. Monceau was quickly captured. Supporting fire delivered from its heights insured the successful completion of the assault on the other wing. Colonel Tucker's courage and front-line leadership was thus instrumental in the elimination of a most dangerous group of enemy strong points, troops and material."[137]

After fighting for over two hours, the 1st Battalion was finally reached at 2015 hours and by 2230 hours that evening the 3rd Battalion companies were all in position. Cook and Keep made a round along the battalion perimeter to check on the various outposts.

"Just before dark," remembered Sergeant Tarbell, "I walked over to see some of the wounded, as they had not moved out yet. All of our casualties were wounded, except for the one captain from Service Company. There again, a lot of casualties were unknown to us, having just joined us as replacements for losses in Holland. The same thing always enters your mind after things cool down a little. 'When is my time coming?' Men are being hit all around you and you are not hit, but you worry about the law of averages."[138]

Captain Bartley came up at the head of his platoon of replacements in the trail of H Company. He was killed by a 20mm shell, along with three other men: Privates Alvin Bains of I Company; James A. Diemert, a medic with Headquarters Company; and Joseph J. Quinn of Service Company. The 2nd Battalion had one fatal loss in the evening, Pvt. Charles Luca, who was killed in a friendly fire incident when a machine gun fired on E Company's extreme left flank at 2125 hours. This was reported to the Regimental S-2 section; at 0025 hours the S-2 Journal reads: "Called White [2nd Battalion] regarding MG firing in E Company's extreme left flank. E Company challenged a figure, figure did not answer, he was fired upon and killed. It turned out to be a member of E Company who did not answer the password."[139]

During the attack on Monceau and Cheneux, H Company counted two officers—Captain Kappel and Lieutenant Furst—and 14 enlisted men wounded. Kappel would return on December 23 to resume his command. In all, the 3rd Battalion had lost three officers (of which one returned soon), one unattached officer, three men killed, one man captured and 18 enlisted men wounded.

Losses in the 1st Battalion had been excessively high compared to 3rd Battalion losses. Of B Company, only 18 men plus Captain Duncan remained; Lieutenant Smith and Private Bauer had been killed, and 1st Sgt. James R. Lowe and Lieutenants Allen, Bird, Brantley, Keating, Meerman and Thomas had been wounded along with 66 enlisted men. C Company fared little better, with Captain Anderson and Lieutenants Branca, Fetters, Magruda and 67 men either killed or wounded. Some of the wounded would die, bringing total fatalities to 14 men. Lieutenant Branca, although wounded, decided to stay with the company, as there were only two other officers left: 1st Lieutenants James E. Dunn (executive officer) and Vern G. Frisinger (3rd Platoon), along with 1st Sgt. Michael F. Curran and 37 other ranks. In Headquarters Company, Lieutenants Kemble and Yepsen had been killed along with one enlisted man and Lieutenants Alvin T. Hudgins and Joseph G. Wheeler, and 29 non-commissioned officers and enlisted men were wounded. Requests for replacement resulted in the transfer of numerous men from Service Company: seven men to Headquarters Company, 20 enlisted men to C Company, and 20 to B Company. It was less easy to find replacement officers: 1st Lt. Reneau Breard and 2nd Lt. James Douglass of A Company were transferred to B Company on December 23 as platoon leaders. The 18 survivors and 20 replacements were divided over two makeshift platoons, designated as the 1st Platoon under Breard and the 3rd Platoon under Douglass.

Large credit must be given to the medics and surgeons of the 504th RCT, who treated approximately over 170 wounded and whose actions and bravery saved many lives. Captain Helgeson's official report of the battle for Cheneux, written while he was S-3, just days following the fighting, paints a gloomier picture of his own B Company than the Morning Reports. True, his company suffered many wounded, but "only" two men were killed, versus six in his report. C Company's losses were almost equal in number, although more of these casualties were fatal. Why does Helgeson's report contain these inconsistencies? Is it because of rumors about the number of casualties that inevitably circulated after the fight? Or because of his own, perhaps overdrawn, perception of the battle?

Although Helgeson wrote about his wartime experiences after the war, he never mentioned the traumatic experience he had endured at Cheneux, when his whole company was decimated in a firestorm of German machine-gun bullets and 20mm shells. His temporary mental collapse in the battle most probably contributed to the decision to send him on a 30-day leave in the United States. This gave him the opportunity to see his family and recover so he could resume the excellent service that his record reflects prior to the Pyrrhic victory at Cheneux.

The entry for December 21 in the dairy of *Stabsfeldwebel* Karl Laun from the Leichte Flak Abteilung 84 reads: "A German counterattack at dawn is stifled by enemy fire. Nobody shows any inclination to fight—not even the SS. As a matter of fact, they are the first ones to withdraw. Suddenly, one of our tanks makes an appearance near the bridge. Again a frantic request for gasoline. Draining all vehicles, including the Volkswagen and the wrecker prime movers, we scrape 30 gallons together. The Tiger continues forward to Cheneux.

"I am damned glad I don't have to be in the inferno prevailing in that village. Down here the enemy artillery curse has somewhat subsided. In the morning hours two of my best comrades and I are selected to form a *Panzer-vernichtingsstörungstrupp* [antitank squad]. Six panzerfausts, one machine pistol—and now we constitute a formidable force which will be able to stop all enemy tanks. Our battle plan concentrates around the selection of the most favorable route of withdrawal.

"Everything in our old AA position is quiet now. The piece lies at the roadside neatly segmented. I am just to inspect one of my platoon's quadruple guns, when all of a sudden 12 Americans, shouting continuously, their rifles and machine pistols raised above their heads, break out of a thicket. They shout, *Nicht schiessen!* [Don't shoot!] At first I think this is a ruse and tell my men to go into firing positions, but then I remember the *Greif* boys. Yes, indeed, these are the fellows who've returned, accompanied by some sizzling hot farewell messages from the Americans. They'd posed as the 68th Headquarters but the Yankees refused to swallow it. The 'gangs,' as they call themselves, quickly change uniform and continue fighting as harmless antiaircraft boys.

"I don't know how it's come about, certainly nobody gave orders to this effect, but suddenly everything on the Cheneux road is making a dash for our bridge. There is no more stopping; the situation has become hopeless.

SS-Obersturmbannführer Jochen Peiper led the infamous Kampfgruppe Peiper that was driven back at Cheneux and Monceaux by Colonel Tucker's paratroopers.

Captain Moffatt Burriss and Lieutenant Robert Rogers of I Company at Camp Sissonne, November 1944. *Courtesy: Moffatt Burriss*

Second Lieutenant Robert Bramson of F Company in Camp Sissonne, November 1944. Bramson was severely wounded on February 2, 1945, while attacking a bunker in the Siegfried Line. *Courtesy: Robert Bramson*

Captain Paul Bruns, one of the battalion surgeons, at Camp Sissonne, November 1944. *Courtesy: Char Baldridge*

Corporal David Stanford of I Company, killed at the Den Heuvel farm in the Netherlands. His remains have never been recovered. *Courtesy: Rob Stanford*

Sergeant Robert Dew of I Company is still missing after he was killed at the Den Heuvel farm in the Netherlands. *Courtesy: Janeen Dew Ralston*

Unknown, PFC Joe Edgerly and PFC Lorenzo Jim Davis of the 551st PIB with mascot Furlough in Fort Kobbe, Panama, summer 1943. Davis was transferred to E Company in Remouchamps after his battalion was dissolved. He was severely wounded in the head by a sniper in Herresbach and died of wounds on January 29. *Courtesy: Mike Davis*

Technical Sergeant Hubert Kendall of I Company at Camp Sissonne, November 1944. Kendall was a veteran of all previous campaigns. *Courtesy: Tom Kendall*

Second Lieutenant Ernest Murphy of H Company would earn a battlefield promotion and Silver Star in Belgium. *Courtesy: Patsy Murphy Wells*

Opposite page, top: The 3rd Platoon of C Company in November 1944, immediately following the Holland Campaign. *Front row:* Corporals George McAllister and Fred Gruneberg, Sergeant Ross Carter, Privates Orin Guidry, Lloyd Shipp and Dominic Ciconte. *Backrow:* unknown, Privates Bethel Nix and Ernest Kong, unknown, Privates Frank Lucas and Raymond Levy (Finklestein). *Courtesy: John Walsh*

Left: Staff Sergeant Ernest Parks, operations sergeant in D Company, rejoined his unit after missing the Holland Campaign for wounds sustained in Italy. He was wounded once more in January 1945. *Courtesy: Ernest Parks*

Lieutenants Leonard Harmon and William Mandle at Camp Sissonne. Mandle was one of the authors of the regimental history published in 1946. *Courtesy: Mandle family*

Some of "Those Devils in Baggy Pants"

Winters — Gruening — Nix — Kong — Ross — Breidey — Lucas — Shipp — Finkelstein — Ciconte

Sergeant Elmer Swartz (Destiny's Tot in Ross Carter's book) of C Company survived the severe fighting in Cheneux and led his mortar squad throughout the remainder of the Ardennes Campaign. *Courtesy: Terry Swartz*

Sergeant Ross Carter of C Company in December 1944. Carter was wounded at Cheneux and wrote the famous *Those Devils in Baggy Pants*, posthumously published in 1947. *Courtesy: Mike St. George*

Three "founding fathers" of the 504th Parachute Infantry
Regiment on May 1, 1942. Left to right: Major Reuben
Tucker, Lieutenant Colonel Richard Chase and Colonel
Theodore Dunn. *Courtesy: John Walsh*

Lieutenant Colonel
Chase being awarded
the Bronze Star by
Lieutenant General
Lewis Brereton in
early 1945. *Courtesy:
Pamela Chase Hain*

Pre-war postcard of the La Gleize area showing the bridge at
Cheneux and the Vaulx Renard farm to the right. *Author's collection*

Pathfinders of the 504th Parachute Infantry Regiment on Comiso, Sicily,
in October 1943. William Clay would fight as a squad leader in Cheneux,
while Lieutenant Rolak just missed the battle. *Courtesy: Walt Lowery*

Private First Class
Thomas J. McCarthy
504

Private First Class
John W. DeCourcy
B/504

Private First Class
Valentine L. Dobrychlop
B/504

Private Eugene
R. Elliott
HQ/1

Private First Class
William L. Clay
B/504

Private First Class
James J. Adams
A/504

1st Lieutenant Bruno J. Rolak
C/504

Technician 4th Grade
Robert W. Lowery
C/504

Corporal Carlos B. Guttry, Jr.
C/504

PFC John Gallagher standing on the far right and his 60mm Mortar Squad of I Company. *Courtesy: Dain Blair*

Corporal Harold Stevenson of C Company was killed at Cheneux while engaging a tank. *Courtesy: Stevenson family via Steve Howerter*

Sergeant Voyd Faile joined C Company in November 1944 and was killed in his first battle at Cheneux. *Courtesy: David Faile*

Second Lieutenant Wayne Fetters was awarded the Silver Star for his leadership during the fighting in Cheneux. *Courtesy: Beth Tweed*

First Lieutenant Howard Kemble of Headquarters Company, 1st Battalion, was mortally wounded at Cheneux. *Courtesy: Frederick Lindley*

Howard Kemble's grave at Henri Chapelle Cemetery, 1945. *Courtesy: Frederick Lindley*

Howard Kemble's remains lay in state in a closed coffin before his reburial in 1948. *Courtesy: Frederick Lindley*

Captain Moffatt Burriss standing in front of a captured flak wagon. Private
John Gallagher sits in the driver's seat. *Courtesy: Moffatt Burriss*

Two I Company troopers on a captured flak wagon at Monceau. *Courtesy: Moffatt Burriss*

Private Raymond Holsti of the 3rd Platoon, G Company, was wounded at Cheneux. He received the Distinguished Service Cross for his heroic actions. *Courtesy: Ginger Steciuk*

PFC John Allen, Jr. of G Company was killed at Cheneux. Lieutenant Frear wrote a moving letter to his family. *Courtesy: Mark King*

Catholic Chaplain Edwin Kozak in 1945. He served with the regiment from activation until July 1945. The sad expression in his eyes seems to reflect the moving letters he wrote to the next-of-kin of paratroopers who fell on the battlefields. *Courtesy: Mandle family*

PFC James Perham (with rifle) and Staff Sergeant Myrl Olrogge of the Regimental Recon Platoon perch on a captured German half-track. *Courtesy: David Finney*

Catholic Chaplain Edwin Kozak and D Company troopers after prayer at Rahier, ready to march to Cheneux, December 22, 1944. *Courtesy: US Army photo*

Lieutenant Colonel Willard Harrison of the 1st Battalion was severely injured in a traffic accident just after the capture of Cheneux. *Courtesy: Jerry Harrison*

Major John Berry joined the 1st Battalion just before Operation Market Garden and assumed command of the 1st Battalion after the battle of Cheneux. *Courtesy: Caroline Berry*

Crossroads near Trois Ponts, December 1944. *Courtesy: David Finney*

Bridge across the Amblève River near Cheneux with the railroad bridge in the distance, photographed in 1980. *Courtesy: Edwin Bayley*

Houses in Trois Ponts occupied by A Company before Christmas
1944, photographed in 1980. *Courtesy: Edwin Bayley*

Second Lieutenant George Amos (standing far right) and his I Company patrol,
photographed on December 31, 1944, before carrying out a daylight reconnaissance.
One of the enlisted men was wounded during their mission. *Courtesy: Moffatt Burriss*

Second Lieutenant Harry Rollins of D Company was captured in Floret with part of his platoon on December 26, 1944. During the Hammelburg Raid he was a free man for a few hours before being recaptured. *Courtesy: Harry Rollins*

Private Dominic Biello of D Company was an original member of the regiment. He was killed by sniper fire at Floret, December 26, 1944. *Courtesy: Dominic Biello*

Private Robert Frank Cunningham of D Company was one of the men who moved the badly wounded Private Widger to the rear. *Courtesy: Rhonda Schum*

Private Virgil Widger in 1945 after being severely wounded in Floret by the same sniper who killed Private Biello. *Courtesy: Virgil Widger*

I swing aboard the first vehicle that comes along and we make a mad dash for La Gleize. In front of a bridge, the self-propelled gun, overloaded with its human cargo, starts sliding, and I pick myself out of a ditch. In the meantime the Americans have been able to occupy the heights to the right (east) of the road and their guns pay careful attention to all moving vehicles. I barely succeed in clamping myself onto a passing truck to escape towards La Gleize."[140]

The "*Greif* boys" referred to above were from Operation *Greif* [Seize], a false flag operation by *SS-Obersturmbannführer* Otto Skorzeny's Panzer Brigade 150, employing British jeeps captured in the Battle of Arnhem repainted as American vehicles. Clad in American uniforms, a few hundred English-speaking officers and men were deployed early in the Ardennes offensive to cause confusion behind enemy lines and capture bridges across the Meuse River. Some of Skorzeny's commandoes also operated at Cheneux. Of all people in the regiment, the regimental intelligence officer Capt. Fordyce Gorham was the first to be deceived by a jeep load of English-speaking Germans at the Regimental CP in Rahier. Gorham was approached by a captain, who leapt out of the jeep and walked right up to him. "I'm from VIII Corps," he said. "I'm looking for my tanks. Have you seen any going along the road to the next village?"

"I hear some have, but you can't go across the river because the bridge is out," Gorham replied. "How are things going?" asked the other captain. "All fouled up." The captains started a conversation and after half an hour the captain borrowed a cigarette and took off. Gorham, a native of Coudersport, Pennsylvania, on learning later that the "captain" he had spoken with was a German, stated: "I'm a boy from the hills, and this time I was taken in by a city slicker. Me—who's supposed to know about things like that!"[141]

Readying to move his 57mm antitank guns into Cheneux that morning, Lieutenant Stark was the next to encounter a jeep-load of disguised Germans. "Intelligence information received in higher headquarters had indicated that as a part of the overall German plan, small groups of Germans, who could speak English with an American accent, would be dressed in American uniforms, drive captured American vehicles, and operate behind our front. Some would work close to the front line, while others would operate far in the rear areas to locate supplies, unguarded bridges, and other items of information that would be of value to them. This information was not disseminated to the front-line troops.

"At about 0845 hours, 21 December, when plans had been completed for moving the antitank guns into position, two quarter-ton trucks from the 99th Infantry Division came along the road from Rahier. In each were four people who looked like American officers and enlisted men. They were forced to stop because the tank destroyers and antitank guns, which were about to move out, were effectively blocking the road. A major in the leading vehicle dismounted and stated that he was anxious to see Colonel Harrison. I had never seen this officer, but since he desired to see Colonel Harrison, the 1st Battalion commander, the guns were moved so that he could advance. I told him that driving his vehicles more than 200 yards further would be excessively dangerous, for the road was effectively covered by small-arms fire.

"After telling me in an offensive tone that he was capable of making his own decisions, he mounted his jeep and drove on toward the Battalion Command Post. I watched him go and then stood dumbfounded as all the German small-arms fire in that area ceased while the vehicles sped by the command post, through the front lines, and on down into Cheneux. Obviously these men were Germans, though this fact was unsuspected until too late."[142]

The third time the jeeps stopped, it was in front of the 1st Battalion CP, where their trick failed to work. The timing was peculiar: as the Germans jumped out, a Mark VI King Tiger tank was shelling the Battalion CP. "Where is it?" one of them asked with a German accent. This aroused the attention of Pvt. Theodore S. Watson, a medic from Brooklyn in Headquarters Company who took nothing at face value. "What's your outfit?" he called. "Ninety-ninth Infantry," the "captain" replied. S/Sgt. Edgar P. Lauritsen, the Headquarters Company operations sergeant, who had just emerged from the CP, joined the conversation: "What outfit in the 99th?" "Headquarters," the "captain" answered with a slightly guttural growl, and the eight Germans walked on in the direction of the town center. "Halt!" shouted Lauritsen, raising his M1 as they started to run. He opened fire and hit the "captain" in the back. The other Germans grabbed him and hurried away, while occupants of the CP rushed outside and jumped on Lauritsen. They were about to shoot him when they suddenly realized what had happened.[143]

Corporal George D. Graves, Jr., a clerk in the regimental S-1 section, arrived in Cheneux with 1st Lt. Vincent E. Voss on the evening of December 21 to take stock of the casualties at the 1st Battalion CP: "Lieutenant Colonel Harrison, 1st Battalion commander, said the assault across the top of the hill crossed with many barbed wire fences was far worse than any nightmare he had ever imagined. The surrounding terrain was the worst example I had ever seen of what results when a large number of men are out to kill each other. Broken rifles, loose ammunition, countless helmets, bloody GI clothes and bandages, belts of machine-gun ammo, mortar shells—all sorts of miscellaneous items were strewn about the bald hill and ditches along the sides of the road. Dead bodies were everywhere. Living troopers, glassy-eyed and expressionless, were hugging holes scraped out of the banks bordering the road."[144]

Lieutenant Stark found parachuted German supply containers: "After Cheneux had fallen, there were indications that perhaps the Germans had been unable to launch a mass attack, supported by armor, against the American forces because of the lack of gasoline. A few scattered parachutes and empty gasoline containers were found in the vicinity of the town and a few were discovered that the Germans had overlooked. During the night of 21–22 December, the Luftwaffe either had not received word that Cheneux had fallen to the Americans, or else they missed their drop zone, for the entire surrounding area was showered with supplies, principally gasoline."[145]

German pilots had indeed dropped supplies for Kampfgruppe Peiper at the wrong place—the badly needed gasoline for his armored vehicles and tanks at La Gleize was firmly in the hands of the 504th PIR. *Obersturmbannführer* Peiper recalled of this day that "around noon on 21 December, the situation in the pocket was discussed with all unit commanders of the Kampfgruppe in a conference at the Kampfgruppe's command post. This conference was the result of the following radio message from the Division: 'Division intends to advance through Trois Ponts, Petit Coo, Grand Coo, and to relieve Kampfgruppe Peiper.'

"However, neither Stoumont nor Cheneux could be held any longer under prevailing conditions. In order to keep in line with Division's intention, it was decided to concentrate all available elements of the Kampfgruppe around La Gleize, a village of about 30 houses, and to keep open the bridge at Cheneux.

"The necessity of concentrating forces became particularly manifest once more when a U.S. engineer assault detachment succeeded without incident in pushing forward from the north toward the Stoumont–La Gleize road, blocking the road effectively by blasting trees and subsequently mining it. In a counterthrust against that assault detachment, which had dug in at the road, a number of U.S. soldiers were captured, including a Major [Hal McCown] with his radio operators.

"In the evening of 21 December, the German lines were withdrawn to La Gleize. The withdrawal from the Stoumont area as well as the withdrawal of the defense line at Cheneux to the area immediately behind the bridge was carried out without any incident or enemy interference."[146]

Peiper wrote this account himself: it expresses his own point of view on the situation, and is meant to depict him as a skilled commander. First of all, he used more than one bridge at Cheneux. There was also a nearby railroad bridge, constructed of brick with large roman arches, situated just north of the Amblève River Bridge at Cheneux. Secondly, Karl Laun's account of the 84th Luftwaffe Flak Battalion shows that the SS-troops pulled out in a hurry, leaving before their colleagues at the flak guns. Thirdly, the 3rd Battalion was not ordered beyond the Amblève River in the evening of December 21, since the 1st Battalion had been badly mauled and Tucker and Gavin still did not know Kampfgruppe Peiper's total strength in men and armor. His artillery battery at the Vaulx Renard farm was also still in place, screened by several 20mm guns and machine guns. It was withdrawn during the night. Peiper also withdrew from the Château de Froidcour, leaving one of his surgeons and two American medics behind to take care of over a hundred American and German wounded who could not be taken to La Gleize due to lack of transportation.

The total casualties inflicted on the Germans consisted of: one Mark VI King Tiger, four 20mm flak wagons, two 75mm Puma self-propelled guns, two personnel carriers, six half-tracked vehicles, one 105mm howitzer, and approximately 150 Germans killed. Tactically viewed, it had been a failure, because the 1st Battalion was down to a sole (A Company) rifle company capable of operating as such. Strategically seen, however, the attack was a complete victory: Kampfgruppe Peiper was forced to withdraw to La Gleize, and the Americans took a vital bridge across the Amblève River.

Tucker's 504th RCT counterattack on the strong German battlegroup at Cheneux denied Peiper the possibility of staging a flanking attack from the south on Stoumont, or shelling the 119th Infantry Regiment across the Amblève River. Peiper's withdrawal from Cheneux had nothing to do with the situation at La Gleize. David Cooke and Wayne Evans erroneously state in *Kampfgruppe Peiper at the Battle of the Bulge*: "all the [German] vehicles had empty fuel tanks, and the guns had run out of ammunition. While the 1/504th consolidated their position in Cheneux, the 3/504th continued to push up to the Amblève, where after receiving fire from the Germans across the river, they dug in."[147] This unfounded criticism clearly shows the failure to consult the lower-level unit reports of the 504th PIR, which reveal what actually took place at Cheneux, Monceau, La Gleize, and Stoumont. Focusing on the 30th Infantry Division, it neglects to take into consideration the bigger picture on the American side.

German prisoners from Kampfgruppe Peiper being marched off through Trois Ponts, December 1944. *Courtesy: David Finney*

CHAPTER 6

THE END OF KAMPFGRUPPE PEIPER: CHENEUX AND TROIS PONTS, BELGIUM, DECEMBER 22–24, 1944

D uring the night of December 21–22, a higher-level G-2 report was telephoned in from 82nd Airborne Division Headquarters stating that the U.S. 7th Armored Division had been heavily attacked late that afternoon and pushed out of the Belgian city of St. Vith to the east. A serious accident occurred later that morning when Lieutenant Colonel Harrison broke his jaw when an American truck crashed into his jeep in Cheneux. The injured battalion commander was sent to an aid post and then evacuated to the rear. His loss was another blow to the remaining 1st Battalion members who had recently lost so many others. It seemed almost unbelievable that the officer who had encouraged his men in the attack on Cheneux from his forward command post, who had crossed the Waal River with them under enemy fire in broad daylight, and who had parachuted into Normandy on D-Day had been put out of commission by a traffic accident.

Major Berry, executive battalion commander, succeeded Lieutenant Colonel Harrison as commanding officer. Captain Milloy of Headquarters Company became acting battalion executive officer, being the most senior officer present. He was not only the youngest company commander, but also the most experienced, having led C Company in all previous campaigns. Major Berry learned at the same time that more replacements were on the way, and would arrive the next day. Milloy was temporarily replaced as company commander by 1st Lieutenant Peyton C. Hartley.

It was difficult for the officers and men of A Company who had moved to Trois Ponts to take in the fact that they had seen no action, whereas many other units in the division had been committed in heavy fighting. Their first casualty was sustained when a sergeant was wounded in a German shelling that morning. "When our house was hit by German cannon fire we ran to a house with a back having open land for about 25 to 30 feet to the river front and settled in there," recalled Private First Class Bayley. "Our houses were just to the north of the town center on the west bank. This was a very quiet area, nothing happening. A few hundred yards to the north of us and a few hundred yards to the south, some of the most vicious fighting of the war was taking place and would extend over the next several days. We could hear some of it, especially the tank and artillery shells, but nothing was coming into our area and there were no engaged firefights. Germans on the other side of the river were keeping out of sight, as we were on our side.

"It was strangely quiet. It is hard to realize that such quiet could occur on an extremely active battle front. We posted lookouts in the upstairs rooms, being careful to keep away from the windows. During the night the platoon members would take observation turns in a foxhole at the back left-corner of the house. We had our rifles and some very powerful plastic Gammon grenades on the front lip of our foxhole to warn the soldiers if an attack was started. We never had to use them.

"We had our first snow the night of the 22nd. I made my bed in a concrete-constructed coal bin. I don't know why it seemed safer, but it did. This quiet state of affairs went on through the 24th and was apparently going to last into Christmas Day."[148]

In the early afternoon, heavy German artillery fire rained down on the 3rd Battalion positions at 1330 hours, appearing to come from the direction of the Château de Froidcour on the other bank of the Amblève River. Fifteen minutes later, 3rd Platoon, I Company, paratroopers sighted a white bed sheet hanging out one of the windows of the château. Captain Burriss sent out a contact patrol to investigate, led by 1st Lt. Harold E. Reeves. According to his Silver Star Citation, Reeves "volunteered to lead a combat patrol with the mission of trying to make contact with friendly troops that had been cut off by the German offensive. First Lieutenant Reeves led his patrol through two miles of enemy-held territory under heavy shelling by the enemy and our own artillery. First Lieutenant Reeves pressed his patrol on through all this until contact was established with friendly troops. As a result of this action, First Lieutenant Reeves' patrol captured 50 Germans and liberated eight

American soldiers that had been captured by the Germans a few days before. Information gained by First Lieutenant Reeves as to the location of Allied Prisoners of War and the enemy troops was invaluable in the attack that was launched shortly on his return."[149]

As 30th Infantry and 82nd Airborne artillery hammered Kampfgruppe Peiper all day long in La Gleize, some of the shells landed in I Company's position, but fortunately did not hit anyone. At 1650 hours Lieutenant Reeves' group reported at back to the 3rd Battalion CP. Reeves informed Lieutenant Colonel Cook that there were both American and German wounded at the Château de Froidcour, and delivered a slightly wounded soldier from the 2nd Armored Division who had returned with them.

"On the afternoon of 22 December," recalled Captain Campana, "the 2nd Battalion was ordered to relieve the 1st Battalion at Cheneux. On arriving in the town, we saw evidence of the bitter fight which had taken place. German dead and equipment lay strewn on the main road and adjacent fields. A disabled self-propelled gun and tank were on the road. Some of the enemy dead were clad in American olive-drab shirts and wool-knit sweaters beneath their uniforms. The battalion took over the defense of the town and bridge and waited for events to happen. Sounds of brisk fighting on our left flank could be heard, intermingled with tank-gun fire. It was the 119th Infantry attacking the Germans in La Gleize with assistance from the 740th Tank Battalion."[150]

While Captain Komosa's D Company occupied positions in Cheneux itself, cameramen filmed their reception by Chaplain Kozak on the western outskirts of the town. As the Catholic chaplain prayed with several troopers clustered around him, a platoon radio operator stood behind him, looking sideways into the camera, smiling feebly. Captain Norman's E Company took up positions just north of Cheneux; to the south, the battered remnants of C Company were emplaced along the Salm River with B Company to their south, followed by A Company in the northern outskirts of Trois Ponts.

Early in the evening, 1st Lt. Thompson, the 3rd Platoon leader in E Company, was ordered to send out a security patrol to the east to screen the vicinity of La Gleize and find the position of the new German lines. Pvt. George H. Mahon describes the five-man patrol: "I walked down in the middle of a street, two men on either side of me. Our mission was not to get into a skirmish but just to locate [the Germans] and get back. First thing I know, I was looking at a wooded area and I saw a flicker like a cigarette. About the same time I saw a concussion grenade go off in front of me. It blew me down and my helmet was blown off. [No one was hit.] We got up and got back to our lines."[151]

Around 2045 hours the patrol reported to Lieutenant Thompson that they had heard vehicular movement in the town of La Gleize. During this debriefing, Thompson noticed that Mahon was hobbling: "By the time I got near our lines I couldn't bend one knee. I told Lieutenant Thompson and he said I should go see the doctors. I said, 'It's just swollen from the concussion. It wasn't a fragmentation grenade. I'll be all right.' It was about 2300 hours at night. He told me, 'Go over and see the doctor anyhow. We aren't going to hit them until about 0230, so go over there and see what he has to say.'

"I went to the aid station and there weren't any other wounded in there. They had already been evacuated. The doctor said, 'Take your pants off.' I took my boots off, my pants off, and then when I pulled my socks off, he said, 'Wow!' He stopped me and said, 'Put them back on. You are going nowhere. Lay down on that stretcher.' I said, 'I came walking in here from my company.' He said, 'Damnit, I am not requesting you to do it. I am telling you, it's an order!' I went over there, lay down, and fell asleep. Next thing I woke up in France in a warehouse-kind of building and then moved to a hospital in England because of frozen feet. It took another two months before I could return to the unit. I was still in my dress uniform from when we left Camp Sissonne."[152]

Lieutenant Stark of the 80th AAAB requested permission to test-fire a 57mm shell on an abandoned German Mark VI King Tiger tank: "With the taking of Cheneux and the bridge across the Amblève River, offensive action was temporarily halted. All antitank guns were placed in positions so that they covered all angles and approaches to the bridge across the river. I, desiring to replenish the supplies, principally rations and gasoline, tried to locate these supplies. The 1st Battalion had failed to draw supplies for its attachments, and in turn, the regiment had not made any provisions for the resupply of the attached antitank platoons, as it believed the battalions had included them in their requests. The battery commander and I finally received supplies from our own battalion headquarters. All echelons of the unit to which the platoon was attached were contacted, so that the situation would not recur.

"Near one of the gun positions overlooking the bridge was a knocked-out German Tiger tank. I was curious to know exactly what effect a shell fired from a 57mm gun would have on the front of the tank. Such an opportunity had not previously been afforded. Permission to fire the gun was received from the battalion commander. A special round of super high-velocity armor-piercing shell was fired from a distance of about 200 yards, and the front of the tank was penetrated slightly above the axle."[153]

Lt. Col. William B. Lovelady of the 33rd Armored Regiment supported the 119th Infantry Regiment between Stoumont and La Gleize, with a CP situated at Roanne, east of La Gleize. He recalled that "on December 22, 1944, about 9:30 PM, a young lieutenant from the 82nd Airborne was brought to my command post. He was wet, cold, and his face was all blackened. He had swum, waded, or whatever across the Amblève River to contact one of our outposts. He told them he had information for the Commanding Officer and asked to be taken there. You can imagine my surprise and gratitude to see him, since we had not been in contact with friendly forces for three days, and to learn that the paratroopers were just across the river cheered us. His message was that we were now attached to the XVIII Airborne Corps. He gave me a sketch of the disposition of forces just across the river, and asked me for a similar sketch or diagram of our forces. (Generally, just strung out across the road with the Amblève River on the right, and a steep wooded hill on our left.)

"Just before he left, he asked if we needed anything. We told him that the Germans were dug-in on the hill to our left and we needed artillery or mortars. He offered help. He said he would shoot a line across the river at dawn and we could call for and direct the fire from their Howitzers. This was done and we soon neutralized the enemy on the hill. This experience was one of the greatest in our five campaigns. We have no record of this incident in our book, Regimental or Combat Command B logs, and most, if not all, of the individuals that knew of this have either passed on, or are out of contact. Perhaps there is a mention of this incident in the Airborne or Regimental Journals."[154]

That same evening in La Gleize, bad news came through for *Obersturmbannführer* Peiper: "The last hope for relief through units of the Division had to be given up. In the last radioed order which was received, Division ordered the encircled forces to fight their way out of the pocket. For unknown reasons the U.S. infantry and tank units [of the 30th Infantry Division] failed to resume their attack against La Gleize on 23 December, but the situation in the pocket nevertheless remained grave. Ammunition and fuel supplies were practically exhausted and no food supplies had arrived since the first day of the attack. Ammunition and fuel supplies by air on 22 December admittedly had arrived, but only about 10 percent of the supplies dropped by the three planes reached the target area, an amount which could have no effect whatever."[155]

On 23 December 1st Lt. Bruno J. Rolak returned to the 1st Battalion CP from leave in Paris and learned to his horror what had happened to his company and battalion at Cheneux. Although the need for an acting executive officer in C Company was urgent, Rolak did not return to his C Company platoon but transferred to B Company. That morning orders came through for the 2nd Battalion to move out. Captain Campana recalled that "the destination turned out to be the town of Lierneux, where we were attached to the 325th Glider Infantry Regiment commanded by Colonel Billingslea. The battalion was placed in division reserve on the high ground some 5000 yards southwest of Lierneux. The 325th Glider Infantry CP was located in the town of Verleumont on the high ground southeast of Lierneux. This move was part of the division plan to hold the Lierneux ridge since it dominated the road nests at Regne, Fraiture and Hebronval.

"The [2nd] Battalion of the 325th Glider Regiment, which was originally in reserve, had been returned to its mother unit when division orders had required the regiment to further extend its right flank to include Regne and Fraiture. This extension was necessitated by the failure of the 3rd Armored Division on the right flank to maintain physical contact with the 82nd Airborne Division. It was imperative for all the airborne units, in keeping with orders from XVIII Airborne Corps, that contact be made and maintained with American units in the Vielsalm–St. Vith area and provide an exit for their extrication. [...]

"The 2nd Battalion, 504th Parachute Infantry immediately prepared and occupied defensive positions astride the Regne–Lierneux road. The battalion CP and aid stations were located in two adjacent houses about 800 yards to the rear. Shortly afterwards, the battalion commander and I went to the CP of the 325th Glider Regiment for instructions. While there, we heard reports over the radio stating that 7th Armored Division tanks were still coming through the road blocks.

"That afternoon, 23 December, the enemy attacked and captured the town of Regne. The division commander immediately ordered the recapture of the town, which was accomplished by the 325th Glider Regiment with the aid of supporting armor. During the recapture of Regne, the regimental adjutant of the 2nd SS-Panzer Division was captured with orders for the advance of the following day. These orders were quickly relayed to higher headquarters. That same afternoon, the important crossroads at Fraiture were taken by the enemy.

"Just before dusk that afternoon, the 2nd Battalion, 504th Parachute Infantry was ordered to retake the [Baraque de Fraiture] crossroads at Fraiture [where elements of the 2nd SS-Panzer Division had overwhelmed F Company, 325th, in the afternoon]. An artillery liaison officer from the 320th Glider Field Artillery Battalion came down to the CP but could not promise us any artillery support, except possibly from corps artillery. At this time all division artillery was busily engaged along the 25,000-yard sector which was then being held by the division. Thus, without artillery support and without armor, the battalion moved out at 1930 hours to recapture a terrain being held by an enemy superior in numbers and fire power. The only prior reconnaissance made was from a map. The outlook was very black indeed, and the battalion commander had accordingly designated his succession of command before we moved out."[156]

First Lieutenant Garrison, 2nd Battalion S-1, recalled Colonel Tucker attended the company commanders' briefing "that Wellems had called to explain the particulars of the attack. We gathered around a table with a spread-out map that Colonel Tucker poked at vaguely. Logic quickly made us realize that the project was deadly. The battalion was to go down a slope near Trois Ponts to a draw that led to a stream in the woods, where Germans were certain to be entrenched. Discussion failed to make the proposal any more palatable than an inevitable trap.

"After Colonel Tucker left, the gathering tried without success to arrive at a less pessimistic interpretation. Eventually, Wellems made assignments. I was to be in charge of the battalion headquarters in the house, of communications, and of response to emergencies. I would have a phone line to regimental headquarters and radio contact with Wellems. Before closing the meeting, he asked, 'Any questions?' I did not have essential information that he had several times delayed in giving me—in emergency, who succeeded whom; so I had to ask, 'What is the chain of command?' Wellems gave me a hard stare. Concentrating on the matter, he named two officers.

"At the designated time, the battalion led by Wellems started down the snowy hill. He must almost have reached the danger area when I had a call from regiment to cancel the attack because Montgomery had changed his mind. I yelped to the radio operator to get Wellems. Through disruptive static, the far operator finally responded and quickly put Wellems on. The connection was barely clear enough for him to hear, 'Turn back!'"[157]

When the call came, Lieutenant Colonel Wellems was already in Fraiture, having preceded his battalion to contact the 325th GIR. Moving out with the battalion column, Captain Campana recalled that "suddenly Major [William] Colville, the executive officer, received a radio message stating that the attack had been called off. I suggested that this message be authenticated before adopting any action whatsoever. This was done. The message was from the battalion commander announcing that the attack had definitely been cancelled. The entire battalion did an about-face and returned to Lierneux much happier."[158]

The recall of the attack order for the 2nd Battalion was decided by British Field Marshal Bernard Montgomery, whose 21st Army Group had temporarily received command responsibility over the U.S. First Army a few days earlier. Montgomery had ordered Major-General Ridgway to withdraw from St. Vith on December 22, and to shorten the defensive lines on the northern side of the German pocket—or bulge—in the Ardennes. As Ridgway's biographer Clay Blair explains: "Early that evening—December 23— Ridgway took a drastic step of ordering all the forces withdrawing from St. Vith to immediately regroup on his southern front near Manhay. Hasbrouck's full 7th Armored Division, plus the 424th Infantry Regiment, would block the highway at Manhay. Bill Hoge's CCB, plus the 112th Infantry Regiment, would be attached directly to Gavin's 82nd Division at Malempré."[159]

In the evening another group of replacements was assigned to B Company on the Salm River. One of them, 21-year-old S/Sgt. William L. ("Bill") Bonning of Hazel Park, Michigan, was among those taken to 2nd Lt. Douglass' 3rd Platoon. Born in Hazel Park near Detroit, in December 1922, Bonning entered the service in Royal Oak, Michigan, as a 20-year-old draftee in January 1943. Wanting to choose his own branch of the U.S. Army after basic training, he opted for the paratroopers but was turned down twice because he was two inches shorter than the 5 foot 6 inch minimum.

The third time he attempted to get in, luck was with him. Recognizing Bonning, a medic tossed him a handful of matchbooks to put in his socks to lift his feet up. The trick worked: he began jump training at Fort Benning, Georgia, in August 1944, and was shipped to Europe in the fall with the rank of staff sergeant.

Along with a few others, Bonning was brought to the 3rd Platoon CP where "they introduced me to Lieutenant Douglass. He looked a lot younger than me. I said, 'You have to be kidding.' I thought they were making a joke.

It was night time when we were assigned. Lieutenant Douglass didn't appreciate my remark and I got admonished."[160] Surprisingly, no one told Bonning the name of the company commander: "You learned the name of your company commander after a few weeks. Basically you were with your platoon most of the time."[161] Veterans of the 504th did not like it when high-ranking non-commissioned officers came in with the replacements from parachute school, because they had no combat experience but were required to lead at least a rifle squad. It also meant that promotions that had been in the offing were frozen until new vacancies in the cadre were created. In Bonning's case, it was only a few weeks before they found some reason to demote him to private, but he eventually earned his stripes back.

The 3rd Battalion found several red-colored parachute equipment bundles on December 23 that later transpired to be from a German resupply drop for Kampfgruppe Peiper. The supplies unfortunately added nothing to the battalion's meager K-rations, since they consisted of gasoline and 88mm ammunition.

At 1130 hours a patrol of I Company was dispatched to contact the 119th Infantry Regiment south of the Château de Froidcour. They returned at 1400 hours to report the exact location of that regiment. At the same time a call came into the 3rd Battalion CP from 1st Lieutenant Megellas of H Company, who had spotted a German crew setting up an 88mm gun. Artillery was called in, but XVIII Airborne Corps vetoed artillery fire on the gun later that afternoon. Nothing remained than to try it with 1st Lt. Allen F. McClain's 81mm Mortar Platoon. When the gun unfortunately appeared to be out of range, the 376th Parachute Field Artillery Battalion was called in and fired a few shells, but the forward observer was not sure if they scored a direct hit or not.[162] Another three-man contact patrol sent out to check on the 119th Infantry at dusk returned at 1900 hours with the news that the 119th had been stopped by tanks and infantry and was still in the same position.

Meanwhile *Obersturmbannführer* Jochen Peiper decided to pull his forces out that night. Leaving approximately 50 of his remaining 850 officers and men as a rear guard to disable his remaining vehicles, he withdrew with the rest of his men and a few unwounded American prisoners. Conditions could not have been better as he withdrew across the La Venn bridges on the Amblève River in a southern direction, searching for a bridge across the Salm River to move east. First, it had begun to snow and frost, creating a perfect natural cover in the dark. Second, by moving the 2nd Battalion to Fraiture in the afternoon, Major General Gavin had seriously thinned 504th defensive lines. These now stretched all the way from Rahier to Cheneux, Monceau, Brume and on to Trois Ponts through heavily wooded terrain, the screening of which called for two battalions at full strength.

Peiper recalled that his "forces started breaking out of the pocket during the night of 24 December at about 0200 hours, after all armored vehicles had been blown up. Without encountering resistance, the Kampfgruppe moved southward from La Gleize via La Gleize railway station, crossed the Amblève valley over a small bridge, and in a long, drawn-out column reached the wooded area west of Trois Ponts under most difficult conditions."[163]

In the early morning of December 24, the 3rd Battalion was alerted to break up as soon as possible for a truck ride to Jevigné, almost two dozen miles southwest of Cheneux. The 30th was expanding its sector, and the 82nd was pulling back to a shorter defensive line. At 0940 hours the 3rd Battalion cleared Cheneux, arriving in Jevigné at 1030 hours. Second Lieutenant George A. Amos of Weston, Illinois, a recently assigned platoon leader in I Company, earned a Silver Star "while leading his platoon on a reconnaissance for a road block position, [where] two enemy machine guns and several riflemen unexpectedly opened fire on the platoon. With utter disregard for his own safety, Second Lieutenant Amos single-handedly charged the nearest machine-gun nest, killing the four occupants with his submachine gun. From this position he delivered a withering fire, knocking out the other machine gun and forcing the remaining enemy to withdraw from a vital spot, thus enabling the platoon to accomplish its mission."[164] Despite Amos' bravery, Pvt. Donald W. Johnson was killed and several others were wounded. Cut off from the remainder of the company, Amos' platoon set up a road block and was on its own for several hours. Only when G Company was sent in with a sweeping move to clear the area, did I Company manage to link up with the platoon and drove the Germans back.

Captain Campana recalled that "late in the afternoon of 24 December, the 2nd [Battalion] was informed that the 82nd Airborne Division had been ordered to withdraw to a new and shorter defensive position eight miles to the rear. Each unit was ordered to leave a covering force equivalent to one third the size of the unit. This covering force would remain in position until 0400 hours on 25 December and would then return by truck to the new defensive positions. Accordingly, one platoon from each rifle company was left behind with Lieutenant Fust, Battalion S-2, designated as covering force commander for our battalion.

"Just after dusk, 24 December, the battalion minus the covering force started its withdrawal. I and the executive officer were not informed of the location of the new defense positions, nor were they informed of the route to be followed to the rear. Christmas Eve was a very cold, bright, moonlit night. Along the route, we saw evidence of prepared demolitions and road obstacles executed by our engineers. For the most part, the withdrawal was accomplished without any difficulty, except in the sector to the north where the 505th and 508th Parachute Regiments were constantly being harassed by a very persistent foe."[165]

Sergeant Mitchell E. Rech of A Company spent Christmas Eve singing Christmas Carols in Trois Ponts: "My buddies [Pfc.] Roger ("Frenchy") Lambert and [T/5] Les Lucas and I were singing Christmas carols aided by a bottle of wine. New snow on the ground, moonlit night. The Germans did not appreciate good singing and gave us a few rounds of mortars. They missed, but we got the hint."[166]

A Company was still holding its position at Trois Ponts along the Amblève River, unaware of the plan to withdraw the entire division. The 1st Battalion was defending a front from Trois Ponts in the south to D Company in Cheneux with the order to hold their ground against any new German attack. But there would be no other attack—the 1st SS-Panzer Division was unable to reach the encircled remnants of Kampfgruppe Peiper at La Gleize.

Peiper led his 800 men behind B Company that night and moved on to Bergeval, where in the confusion of a firefight, his foremost prisoner, Maj. Hal McCown, 119th Infantry Regiment, managed to escape. At Rochelinval Peiper's depleted force swam "across the icy and turbulent Salm River, [and] broke through the American front. Contact with German advance elements was established only in Wanne, six kilometers east of the American positions in the Salm Valley."[167] The remaining covering detachment at La Gleize had meanwhile been overwhelmed: Kampfgruppe Peiper was disbanded, its mission a failure. Only 770 officers and men came through the American lines.[168]

First Lieutenant Breard, the 1st Platoon, B Company commander, describes the action on the "freezing cold" night when Peiper's men passed his sector near Trois Ponts. "At Christmas Eve our mortars behind the CP were infiltrated and a firefight started. They had 800 men and went down in several positions and came through us. We didn't know who it was. [...] No casualties occurred. [...] B Company left that position after midnight and marched through Trois Ponts passing Basse-Bodeaux, where we were finally shuttled to Bra by truck. We went into position just south on the road to

Manhay. First Battalion was in reserve near Hill 463. It had started snowing when we left our position on the Salm."[169]

At 2000 hours 3rd Battalion company commanders gathered in the CP, where Lieutenant Colonel Cook informed them of the decision to withdraw to a new defensive position in the small village of Bra-sur-Lienne, several miles to the northwest. The 2nd Battalion would be on their left flank as far as the next hamlet of Bergifaz with an outpost at Floret, and the battered 1st Battalion would be in regimental reserve. Colonel Billingslea's 325th GIR would tie in on their right flank. One rifle platoon was to act as a shell while G Company rejoined the battalion. By 0045 hours on December 25 the move had been successfully carried out and the new CP was set up in Bra.

Relieved during the night from its positions along the Amblève River, Major Berry's unit also made its way to Bra. "Finally, just after dawn on Christmas Day we came to a little village with a church and a few farm-houses," Private First Class Bayley recalled. "The villagers had awakened to find paratroopers swarming through their village. They feared for the worst and were gathering belongings together and fleeing the area with wagons, carts and bicycles, but no powered vehicles. We saw no sign of their owning any cars or trucks. We never knew where they went, but in a few minutes the village was completely evacuated of civilians. It was sad to see this, but they did this for their own safety, as they did not know what was going to happen."[170]

The villagers, however, did not depart of their own free will, but on orders to evacuate because their town was now on the front line. Division head-quarters had been established in the Chateau Naveau de Bra-sur-Lienne in the center of the village, but had moved out to the northwest during the night. Colonel Tucker in turn made the chateau his regimental headquarters. "I well remember the spooky Christmas Eve at the 504th headquarters when the regiment was withdrawing on Montgomery's orders from the salient we occupied," recalled Capt. Frank D. Boyd, an attached officer of the 376th Parachute Field Artillery Battalion. "The 307th Engineers were blowing bridges behind us and left us only one over which to withdraw. We had orders to retire to Bra and Colonel Tucker asked a Belgian civilian if there was a landmark building in Bra that was easy to identify and find. The man told him there was a big, well-known chateau on the east edge of town and Colonel Tucker said, 'That is my CP.'"[171]

It was clear to the paratroopers of the 504th Parachute Infantry Regiment, 376th Parachute Field Artillery Battalion, and C Company of the

307th Airborne Engineer Battalion that they were to hold their defensive positions at all costs. They had given ground on orders—but not in battle.

INA284 30 GOVT=WUX WASHINGTON DC 21 733P

C H LUCAS=

15 BENTON ST ROCHESTER NY=

:REGRET TO INFORM YOU YOUR SON TECHNICIAN FIFTH GRADE LESLIE H LUCAS WAS SLIGHTLY WOUNDED IN ACTION TWENTY TWO DECEMBER IN BELGIUM MAIL ADDRESS FOLLOWS DIRECT FROM HOSPITAL WITH DETAILS=

ULIO THE ADJUTANT GENERAL.

Telegram sent to the parents of Technician 5th Grade
Leslie Lucas of A Company. *Courtesy: Chris Lucas*

CHAPTER 7

ENTRAPMENT AND ENDURANCE
BRA-SUR-LIENNE, EN FLORET, BELGIUM,
DECEMBER 25–26, 1944

Proceeding through Bra, Private First Class Bayley and his unit "came to a big open field. We were told to dig in for protection. We watched as the American fighter planes engaged the German planes in dog fights and bombed villages, tanks, troops, etc. It seemed so sad to see planes being shot out of the sky on Christmas Day.

"A short while later we were told to move into a nearby wooded area and hold. Artillery shells began landing in our area, which resulted in tree bursts. This was not a pleasant experience. We moved again within the woods, but there was no digging yet. A very serious battle suddenly began a few hundred yards from us. Artillery from our side began firing over our heads. This battle lasted about two hours or so. It was frightening because we did not know what was happening or what would happen if the Germans broke through. We moved further into the woods.

"The army decided that all servicemen should have a Christmas turkey feast. Each squad had a frozen turkey, which was no problem to keep as the temperature was well below freezing! Our medic carried no gun, only a shovel for necessary digging and burial. I can remember seeing him carrying the turkey over his shoulder as we marched through the woods. Sometimes another soldier would help out by carrying the turkey for a while.

"Finally, we arrived at a wooded location with plenty of previously dug foxholes, some with partial log cover. I had been paired off with a soldier named [Pfc. Harold J.] Freeman, from Connecticut. We promised each other [that] if we survived the war, we would buy each other a steak dinner.

"As luck would have it, we both survived and I met him while having breakfast at a short-order restaurant in Connecticut several years later. At that time he had a bunch of kids and I was busy travelling as a fire inspector. We weren't able to work out a dinner date and lost contact later, so we never did get to treat each other.

"We had a real good foxhole, big enough to get into our sleeping bags and comfortably stretch out. Unless we had guard or patrol duty, we would go to bed about dark and get up in the early morning. We were a half mile or so from the active front. During the night we could hear artillery but no rifle fire. To get to sleep I would smoke a cigarette while closing the top of the sleeping bag. I would stay awake long enough to snub the cigarette just before going to sleep. I had some of the best sleep of my life in that fox-hole.

"About one or two days after Christmas, a few soldiers took a chance and went down into the village, lit a fire, and cooked the turkey, sort of frying it piece by piece. When the cooked turkey was brought back, we sat around in a sort of circle near our foxholes on that sunny, cold day and enjoyed our Christmas repast, ever thankful to those of our group that had the courage to prepare the turkey in a possibly dangerous situation."[172]

Staff Sergeant Bonning of B Company had a close call that day when the regiment came in range of German artillery: "It was decided to bring those on line a hot meal on Christmas Day. Four or five of us at a time would go back about a hundred yards behind the lines in the woods. There was six to eight inches of snow on the ground. […] Capt. Delbert Kuehl from Minnesota, standing against a large tree, gave a short sermon or prayer to the five of us who were scattered in the woods, but within hearing distance. We assumed there was a cease fire that Christmas Day as it seemed very quiet on line.

"When Chaplain Kuehl was about half way through his prayer, two German 88s came whizzing in. Everybody dove for cover, of which there was none! The 88s exploded nearby! We automatically started yelling, 'Is anybody hit? Is anybody hit?' I looked up at Chaplain Kuehl, and he was standing there against that tree, Bible open—no movement! I thought he was dead! All of a sudden his eyes opened slowly, him saying, 'Is anybody hit?' The four cooks, the five of us, the guide, the chaplain—unbelievably, no one got hit, but the two cooking stoves were destroyed! Many in B Company did not get a hot meal that Christmas 1944; however, many lived to tell this true Christmas story."[173]

Even within a few miles, conditions on the front line could vary quite widely. First Lieutenant Marshall W. Stark of the 80th AAAB, who was stationed in Bra, recalled that "after satisfactory positions were prepared by both the infantry and the attached weapons, everyone breathed a sigh of relief, for no enemy attack had been launched before the unit was adequately prepared. It was Christmas Day and the weather was clear and sunny, with the skies filled with all types and numbers of friendly aircraft.

"Once again it was time to consider the supply situation. No ammunition had been expended, therefore only rations and gasoline were required. The antitank platoon may have been forgotten once, as far as food was concerned, but on Christmas Day both the battalion and the regiment of the 504th and battery and battalion of the 80th delivered to the platoon command post a hot meal consisting of turkey and all that goes with such a dinner. Each man had the opportunity to eat four turkey dinners that day."[174]

T/5 Herbert Lucas from the 3rd Battalion Communications Platoon was proud of his battalion commander: "I admired Colonel Cook for visiting each trooper in a foxhole and wishing them a Merry Christmas."[175] That same day, First Lieutenant La Riviere took out a patrol and captured a young soldier from the 2nd Battalion of SS-Panzergrenadier Regiment 19. A combat photographer took a photo as he returned. The presence of a regiment of the 9th SS-Panzer Division "Hohenstaufen" was definitely not good news. The division, presently commanded by *SS-Brigadeführer* (Brigadier General) Sylvester Stadler, had previously defeated the British 1st Airborne Division at Arnhem during Operation Market Garden, despite being down to a strength of 3,000 men. They had been refitted and reorganized in the Siegen–Dillenburg area, where about 30 percent of their replacements were transferred in from the Luftwaffe.[176]

To the east of the 3rd Battalion the H Company lines bordered the 2nd Battalion. As Captain Campana recalled the layout of the 2nd Battalion defenses: "At 0030 hours 25 December, the battalion arrived in the vicinity of Bra. The company commanders were then given definite instructions for the defense of the battalion sector and immediately made their ground reconnaissance and placed their troops in position. The positions occupied by the battalion were as follows: F Company on the right, contacting the 3rd Battalion of our regiment; E Company in the center along the high wooded ground; and D Company minus the 1st Platoon on the left in the vicinity of Bergifaz, contacting the 3rd Battalion, 508th Parachute Infantry. The 81mm mortars were set up on the reverse slope of the hill behind E Company. The battalion CP was set up in a house about 400 yards to the rear of F Company and the battalion aid station was located about one mile to the rear of the MLR in the vicinity of Trous de Bra.

"About 1000 hours 25 December, the regimental commander visited the battalion CP on his tour of inspection. The battalion commander was out checking the battalion defensives. He [the regimental CO] asked for, and was shown, the disposition of the battalion defensive system. However, he noticed the village of Floret about 1000 yards to our front and astride the Bergifaz-Lierneux road, and inquired what the battalion had done to outpost that town. When I replied that nothing had been done yet, Colonel Tucker instructed me to tell Lieutenant Colonel Wellems to outpost that town immediately.

"Not long after Colonel Tucker had departed, Lieutenant Colonel Wellems returned to the CP and the regimental commander's order was transmitted to him. He then phoned D Company and told Captain Komosa to send the reserve platoon to outpost Floret. An additional SCR-300 [portable radio transceiver] was given to this outpost from Headquarters Company."[177]

Captain Komosa gave the assignment to his acting 1st Platoon leader, 27-year-old 2nd Lt. Harry W. Rollins from Chicago, Illinois, whose platoon acted as battalion reserve after several patrols and the wounding of Sergeant Elton R. Venable on the 20th. "After being told that my platoon had been carrying more than our share of the load and that we would be in company or battalion reserve, my platoon was selected to establish a combat outpost approximately one and a half miles in front of the regiment," Rollins recalled. "The platoon strength was only 23 men. We were organized as two squads, one to cover each of the two roads into the area and the platoon HQ. This was all near the tiny village of En Floret."[178]

The two 1st Platoon rifle squads were commanded by Sgt. Harold M. Dunnagan and Cpl. Jack C. Larison, while Pfc. Bert Davis led the 60mm Mortar Squad. T/Sgt. Charles L. Anderson, the platoon sergeant, set up the Platoon CP in the village of En Floret, better known as "Floret." Second Lieutenant Rollins meanwhile placed Sergeant Dunnagan's reinforced rifle squad at the main roadblock across the Lierneux–Bergifaz road. This would be roadblock #1, and a squad of C Company engineers from the 307th Airborne Engineer Battalion under Sergeant Alfred P. Nitz assisted in laying antitank mines. Corporal Larison's squad was positioned at another roadblock, designated as #2. Wire communication was established between these roadblocks and the Platoon CP, where a third line ran to the mortar squad some 200 yards away. Rollins returned to the Platoon CP at dusk: "Christmas Day was fairly uneventful. We established locations forward as well as several fallback positions. We received mail and one ration for every three men and were happy to get it."[179]

Everything remained quiet until 0125 hours on December 26 when Sergeant Dunnagan reported a small German patrol on the Lierneux–Bergifaz road. Rollins submitted this report to the 2nd Battalion CP using the SCR-300 radio and was instructed to ambush and wipe out the patrol. "The 26th would prove to be a momentous day," Rollins recalled later. "Dunnagan's squad reported the approach of an enemy patrol that appeared to be repositioning mines. I told him to hold their fire until they were close enough to engage with hand grenades. They hit a vehicle carrying a machine gun, igniting the gasoline and killing all of them" in the vehicle.[180]

At 0350 hours a larger German patrol opened fire on roadblock #1 at the Lierneux–Bergifaz road, using grenades and small arms fire. Also driven off by Sergeant Dunnagan's reinforced squad, they left one man wounded in the road, who most likely had been shot in the abdomen. Pvt. Virgil W. Widger recalled that they didn't know for sure if the Germans were baiting someone to come to the aid of this man and then be ambushed or whether the German had really been wounded. He screamed and groaned for a few hours, but as dawn broke there was not a single German to be seen.

Around 0730 hours some 40 German 105mm artillery shells started to rain down between roadblock #1 and the Platoon CP. The bombardment knocked out the field telephone wire, thereby cutting off all communication with Sergeant Dunnagan. Some smaller German patrols had an hour earlier been reported to be roaming the area near the blown bridge northeast of Floret, so Rollins decided to take no chances. The German shelling had abruptly stopped and that worried him. Despite the chance of another barrage it was vital that communication with his squads be maintained. He decided to accompany his platoon radio operator, T/5 Emmett E. Coffin, and his assistant, Pvt. Luther E. Krantz, on their journey to repair the broken telephone wire. Private First Class Vernon P. West, the platoon runner, fortunately went along as well. They found the break in the line and Coffin and Krantz quickly repaired it. They were proceeding across the open field toward roadblock #1 when mortar shells from their own unit came raining down on them. "The friendly fire killed Private Krantz," Rollins recalled. "Shrapnel ripped his leg open and he bled to death in seconds. Coffin, my radio operator, lost the end of his penis in the same attack."[181]

Private Widger, who had been a medic, tried in vain to save Krantz by placing a tourniquet around the stump of his right leg. Krantz just groaned and died. Widger then applied first aid to Coffin while Rollins sent West back to the Company CP for litters and litter bearers. After a while, four medics appeared and carried the casualties back to the 2nd Battalion aid station. Rollins and his runner returned to the Platoon CP and Widger rejoined his rifle squad.

At 1130 hours Sergeant Dunnagan called the CP and reported that one German group had moved around through the woods on the east side of the road and was attacking from the north with MG42's and Schmeisser automatic weapons. Dunnagan's men returned fire, but suddenly found themselves pinned down as another German group came up the road from Lierneux. Dunnagan reported that his position was becoming untenable.

It was at this point that Pvt. Dominic T. Biello was sighted by a sniper and instantly killed with a bullet to the head.[182] Private Widger was near Biello when the sniper started shooting at them. The sniper was after Biello first and Widger called out to Biello to get down low as the sniper was aiming for him. Biello cried that he had to get out of there and exposed himself in an attempt to escape. The German then turned his attention on Widger, hitting him twice. The first bullet grazed his butt, but the next hit was much more serious, in the back. He lay there for some time until troops moving through the area discovered him and administered first aid. They told him they would pick him up on the way back, as Rollins had given Dunnagan permission to withdraw some 1200 yards to set up another road block (#3) with a view to protecting a possible route of withdrawal for the entire platoon.

About 30 minutes after Sergeant Dunnagan's call, Corporal Larison reported enemy activity in the woods near outpost #2 where he was posted. Using the radio of a forward observer, Larison requested and received artillery fire on the woods and roadblock #1. Rollins had heard reports of a 20mm flak wagon and German infantry firing on Dunnagan's men. He called up Captain Komosa at the D Company CP around 1300 hours and requested permission to withdraw: "We heard the Germans drinking and a good bit of pep talk, suggesting that they were getting their courage up for an attack. Despite all the indications and reports, the combat outpost was not pulled back. It is my understanding that the Regiment considered the platoon to be a company asset to recall, but Komosa did nothing because it was a regimental combat outpost."[183]

At 1500 hours two 20mm flak wagons were reported coming down the

Lierneux–Bergifaz road, as reported in the Regimental S-2 journal: "White OP reports two flak wagons coming up the main road—not seen yet."[184] About two hours later Corporal Larison's squad spotted a lone German on a horse-drawn cart coming down to their outpost. They opened up at the wagon with small-arms fire, but did not shoot at the horse or the man—they wanted the German alive. The German raised his hands and was signaled to come down to the roadblock. Larison moved over to the cart and found two MG42 machine guns and eight K98 rifles. While his men destroyed the weapons, Larison escorted the prisoner to the Platoon CP. The young SS-trooper from 4th Company, 1st Battalion, SS-Panzer Grenadier Regiment 19, 9th SS-Panzer Division, stated that his battalion was planning a night attack on the town. A soldier was sent back with the prisoner to Les Villettes to have him further questioned by Lieutenant Fust, the 2nd Battalion S-2 officer.

Around 1730 hours a barrage of Nebelwerfers, 88mm gunfire, and mortar fire rained down on Floret and its surrounding area as German troops closed in on three sides. Rollins estimated them to be a battalion strong—most likely the entire 1st Battalion of SS-Panzer Grenadier Regiment 19. "Around suppertime," he remembered, "all hell broke loose. I ordered the platoon to one of the fallback positions."[185] But no telephone contact or radio contact with roadblock #2 could be obtained. Rollins sent the men in the Platoon CP back four or five at a time, and instructed Technical Sergeant Anderson also to be prepared to withdraw himself to roadblock #3 if he (Rollins) did not return from his visit to roadblock #2.

Along to way to roadblock #2, accompanied by Private First Class West, Lieutenant Rollins was approached by an excited trooper from Larison's squad who stated that they had been hit hard by an enemy force. Rollins nevertheless decided to press on and found roadblock #2 unoccupied. There was no sight of Corporal Larison or any of his men, apart from the soldier he had encountered. He returned to the Platoon CP and got on the SCR-300 to inform Lieutenant Colonel Wellems of the situation. Wellems finally gave him permission to withdraw and ordered him to dismantle the radio. Enemy small arms tracer fire was already traversing up and down the main road of Floret, so Rollins pulled out his .45 and put the set out of action with two rounds.

There was no sight of Technical Sergeant Anderson, who had left the Platoon CP just before they returned and had covered the withdrawal of the mortar squad with his tommy gun. Private First Class Bert Davis and Private

Connor Dilbeck had argued that they wanted to remain in position to fire their 60mm mortar, but the appearance of a platoon of Germans and a 20mm flak wagon forced them to retreat with Anderson.[186] Private First Class Davis was awarded the Silver Star: "When his platoon was fiercely attacked by approximately two companies of enemy infantry shortly before dusk, Private First Class Davis, acting mortar squad leader, instructed his men to leave, stayed at his position and continued to drop effective mortar fire into the ranks of the onrushing enemy. Despite heavy fire on his unprotected position, Private First Class Davis fought single-handedly until all his ammunition had been expended. The enemy rushed his position, but he stopped them with two hand grenades and got away in the resulting confusion. His heroic stand at his mortar contributed directly to the safe withdrawal of his comrades."[187]

At roadblock #3 Sergeant Dunnagan gave the order to withdraw, as the opposing force would soon overwhelm their position. Meanwhile, 2nd Lieutenant Rollins and Private First Class West left the CP and made their way to the northern outskirts of Floret, passing by the abandoned 60mm mortar, which been knocked over as though someone had tried to disable it in a hurry. "Running down the hill," Rollins recalled, "I vaulted over a stone wall, and found myself in the midst of ten Germans huddled against the wall waiting for their artillery to lift. I emptied my .45 into the crowd. One of the Germans threw a concussion grenade. I recall being thrown four feet into the air and then waking up in a food cellar. A German soldier wrapped in bandages was also in the room. He had a bottle of schnapps and passed it to me. A little later, I was taken upstairs. I was able to clean up a little and was given a small piece of cheese.

"Then the interrogation began. They kept asking over and over again: 'Where is the 509th?' They would slug me, ask the question, and give me a little piece of food. This went on for some time. I knew that the 509th was not part of the 82nd, but had no idea where they were or if they even existed."[188]

Another seven members of the 1st Platoon were captured: Corporal Larison, Privates First Class Edward C. Rosella and Kenneth M. Smithey, Privates Kenneth G. Shelton (platoon medic), David J. Sturgeon, Lester F. Vogel, and Rollins' runner, Pfc. Vernon P. West. Second Lieutenant Rollins was sent to Oflag XIIIB at Hammelburg, while West was sent to Stalag IXC in Bad Sulza. Larison, Rosella, and Sturgeon were likely taken to the same place. Smithey was shot while attempting to escape on January 2.

The troopers who managed to move out of Floret made their way to Captain Norman's E Company lines. From there they were sent to the D Company CP where Technical Sergeant Anderson was placed in charge of the platoon, until 1st Lt. Earnest Brown returned from his supply detail to reassume command. Sergeant Dunnagan received the British Military Medal in April 1945 for his leadership in the battle of Floret.

It seems likely that the stubborn defense of Floret by Rollins' platoon caused the Germans to underestimate the situation. *SS-Obersturmbannführer* Emil Zollhöfer, commanding officer of SS-Panzergrenadier Regiment 19, had heard of a battle between the 509th Parachute Infantry Battalion and elements of the 2nd SS-Panzer Division on Christmas Day south of Manhay, and believed Rollins belonged to this battalion. Although Rollins told his interrogators that he didn't know where the 509th was, they probably did not believe him. Thinking, without sending out patrols to check, that the villages of Bra and Les Villettes were defended by one, maybe two platoons at most, Zollhöfer ordered *SS-Hauptsturmführer* (Captain) Josef Altrogge to send only two companies of his 2nd Battalion down to take them. This was a serious tactical error, which turned out well for Tucker and his men, for it gave them the chance to deal with the Germans piecemeal. Some paratroopers regarded it as an opportunity for payback for the losses sustained at Cheneux and Floret.

Captain Campana recalled that "a clouded message from Lieutenant Rollins' platoon stated that the Germans were making an all-out attack against their positions. Instructions were issued to withdraw and destroy the SCR-300 if necessary to prevent its capture by the enemy. The battalion was soon engaged in a bitter fight all along its sector. All companies reported that they were engaging the enemy, who was attempting to cross the creek obstacle in front of our positions.

"At about dusk, the enemy attack waned and stopped. Casualties were received mainly in the sector defen---ded by E and F Companies. Late that night, stragglers from the outpost in Floret drifted through E and F Companies."[189]

After Private Widger lay alone for hours near the abandoned outpost #2, Pvt. Robert F. Cunningham and Sgt. Dunnagan showed up to carry him out. He was taken to the 2nd Battalion aid station and then transported by ambulance to a field hospital. Widger spent almost two and a half years in various hospitals before he could be discharged. In a hospital in France, he met Technician 5th Grade Coffin, who thanked him for saving his life. Private First Class Biello's body was left behind in the withdrawal process, and was recovered several weeks later.

The British Military Medal Citation for Sergeant Dunnagan at Floret reads as follows: "Sergeant Dunnagan, a rifle squad leader, was commanding a ten-man outpost covering a minefield near Floret, Belgium, on 26 December 1944, when he observed approximately thirty-five German riflemen approaching his position from three directions. During the bitter firefight which ensued, Sergeant Dunnagan, displaying marked bravery, manned the only remaining machine gun and heroically covered his comrades' withdrawal.

As he made his way across a fire-swept field, Sergeant Dunnagan encountered a severely wounded soldier [Widger]. With selfless devotion to duty, he picked up his comrade and carried him through intense enemy fire to safety. His gallant actions and cool-headedness permitted the escape of his men and saved the life of a wounded soldier."[190]

CHAPTER 8

BREAKING UP THE GERMAN
ASSAULT: Bra-sur-Lienne,
Bergifaz, Belgium,
December 26–31, 1944

n the late afternoon of December 26, Colonel Tucker's troopers experienced a trying time as *SS-Hauptsturmführer* Josef Altrogge's battalion closed in on their objective at Bra. Earlier that day, Altrogge had sent out a small patrol ahead of his 6th Company, which made fire contact but managed to pull back without casualties. The patrol reported that a frontal assault would be suicidal, but the hills to the left and right of the village seemed to be less defended and thus a better route. Altrogge called up his regimental commander, *SS-Obersturmbannführer* Emil Zollhöfer, and asked permission to change his orders from a frontal assault to a pincher moving attack. But Zollhöfer disagreed, as the orders were to take Bra before nightfall and to change the outlay of the attack required valuable time.

After a short barrage of 105mm guns by the SS-Panzer Artillerie Regiment 9, two of *Hauptsturmführer* Altrogge's companies charged out the woods facing the 3rd Battalion, wave after wave crossing open ground. Running up the hill they made perfect targets for the American defenders. "Just as we came out of the edge of the forest," recalled *Oberjunker* Johannsen of 6th Company, "a dive bomber strafed us with his board guns. The first casualties were sustained. Facing Bra, the attacking companies were forced down the bare ridge by raging defensive fire. Judging by the rate of fire, the Americans were firing at us with German MG42s that they had probably

Carl Mauro II, 2014

1 Notes 🏰 504 CP ◄----- U.S. Troop Movement

◄═ German Assault ▨▨▨ U.S. Roadblock

1. German patrol and half-track fires on Roadblock 1. Driven off by Sgt.
   Dunnagan's squad, one German wounded, 03:50 hrs.
2. 07:30 hrs. German 105mm shells knock out telephone wire. Lt. Rollins,
   T/5 Coffin, Pvt. Krantz and Pfc. West set out to repair wire.
3. Approximately 08:15 hrs. friendly mortar fire falls short. Pvt. Krantz KIA
   and T/5 Coffin wounded.
4. Litter bearers from 2nd BN Aid station evacuate Coffin and Krantz.
5. 11:30 hrs. Germans flank through woods with MG42 and small-arms fire,
   pin down Sgt. Dunnagan's squad. Pvt. Biello KIA and Pvt. Widger severely
   WIA by same German sniper.
6. 11:45 hrs. Lt. Rollins allows Sgt. Dunnagan to fall back to Roadblock 3.

captured in Normandy—every fifth round seemed to be tracer ammunition. A flanking attack broke through the enemy line and made it to the first houses in Bra. The Americans immediately launched counterattacks that forced us to give up the captured part of town. There was heavy fighting until night fall, when the 2nd Battalion of the SS-Panzergrenadier Regiment 19 returned to its starting position at the edge of the forest east of Bra."[191]

First Lieutenant James Megellas, commanding H Company, 3rd Platoon, recalled that "the Germans opened up with mortar fire on our entrenched positions, then followed with heavy artillery. Behind the artillery barrage, the infantry charged out of their concealed positions. They came at us waving their arms and weapons and letting out bloodcurdling yells. Behind them, German machine guns opened up, providing overhead fire for the advancing troops, while their artillery kept pounding our positions. We kept low in our deep foxholes until they got into range; then we opened up with everything we had.

"Our first volley dropped a number of the enemy, but a second wave soon followed, screaming and yelling and charging past their fallen comrades. Repeatedly they kept streaming out of the woods, still employing the same tactics. But in the face of our withering small-arms fire, they were unable to penetrate our positions.

"In this action, I laid aside my trusted submachine gun. The tommy gun was an excellent weapon for close-in fighting and patrols, but it was not accurate at long range. On this occasion, with a barren and open field of fire, I relied on a sniper rifle, which was more accurate and had much greater range. [...] Suddenly the Germans withdrew to the cover of their concealed positions in the woods, leaving the battlefield littered with their dead."[192]

Captain Frank Boyd of the 376th PFAB saw the Germans enter the east side of the village, near the Regimental CP in the chateau: "The Germans attacked in force. I remember standing in a window of the heavy stone building directing artillery fire with a telephone in one hand and a radio microphone in the other as [Sergeant] Barr and [Pvt. Abel] Fernandes killed German soldiers with their rifles, firing from the same window. They got that close. The 376th dropped a concentration only 100 yards in front of the 504th line of foxholes and broke the assault. We got a lot of praise from the doughboys.

"I lost a jeep at Bra by artillery fire in the courtyard of the chateau that we had taken over for the 504th CP. Fortunately we were all inside the building and there were no casualties. A horse that was wandering about the place was badly injured and Major Gorham put him out of his misery with a .45 pistol. The jeep had a large hole through the engine block and several smaller holes in the seats, but my bedroll, which was strapped to the front bumper, was undamaged."[193]

German artillery fire meanwhile took its toll. Pvt. Rodney V. Buchman of Service Company was killed while loading supplies on a truck. Pvt. Donald Dukovich, a medic in E Company, was wounded and later decorated with a Silver Star for "action on 26 December 1944, about one and one half miles from Bra, Belgium. During a tremendous barrage of artillery and mortar fire from the advancing enemy, Private Dukovich, Company Medic, set out to give aid to a squad of men, of which many had been wounded by the heavy combat action. On his way forward, he was wounded but he kept going and efficiently administered necessary first aid to the men. He then made many trips to evacuate the men safely to the rear slope of a nearby hill.

"When all the men had been cared for, Private Dukovich had his own wounds dressed. His swift actions and steadfast devotion to duty were directly responsible for saving the lives of the more seriously wounded and bringing immediate relief to all of the wounded. Private First Class Dukovich's gallant actions and selfless devotion to duty, without regard for his own safety, were in keeping with the highest traditions of military service and reflect great credit upon himself, his unit, and the United States Army."[194]

First Lieutenant Marshall W. Stark of C Battery, 80th AAAB, had set up his four 57mm guns in support of the 3rd Battalion defensive line: "Considerable activity and movement could be observed in the woods to the front of the positions at several points along the division defensive line. Not only could movement be observed, but as the afternoon progressed, shouting and yelling such as one might hear at a football game could also be heard. Finally, at about 1600 hours, an attack was launched. It was unsupported by anything other than numerous machine guns and mortars, and consisted of great numbers of the enemy running forth from the woods, shouting, yelling and cursing in the American language. In crossing the wide open spaces between the woods and our front lines, they made little or no attempt to use any natural protection like ditches, but just kept running. Devastating fire from our weapons rained down on them, but still they continued to pour forth from the woods.

"All members of the antitank squads had been trained to be cautious about disclosing gun positions against targets other than tanks, but at that time if they had good targets, squad leaders could use their own judgement about opening fire. Many mortar and machine-gun positions could be easily seen from the antitank gun positions, so two of the squad leaders elected to open fire and in a short time all four guns had joined in the fight. Those men from squads not engaged in hauling ammunition or loading were firing their individual weapons. Numerous of these mortar and gun positions were knocked out by direct high explosive fire from antitank weapons. Two of the guns were located on the front lines, so that during the attack a few Germans came to within 100 yards of the guns before they fell, killed or wounded.

"After all the high explosive ammunition carried by these forward squads had been expended, a few rounds of armor-piercing shells were fired at personnel who were within close range. Finally, the attack was driven off along the entire front without giving up any ground. Enemy casualties had been extremely heavy, while our own, from prepared positions, were few. The antitank platoon did not suffer a single casualty."[195]

On December 27 American dive bombers spotted and successfully bombed the positions of SS-Panzer Artillerie Regiment 9. Their regimental commander, *SS-Obersturmbannführer* Ludwig Spindler, was killed while he drove from his command post at Gernechamps near Lierneux to visit one of his three batteries when a dive bomber spotted his vehicle and dropped a bomb that exploded nearby. Bomb splinters fatally hit him in the chest and wounded his driver. Command passed on to *SS-Sturmbannführer* (Major) Franz Jakob.[196] Unfortunately, Spindler's death did not bring about any decrease in German artillery.

Meanwhile the SS-Panzergrenadier Regiment 20, 9th SS-Panzer Division, made another attempt to take the villages of Vaux and Chavanne, held by the 325th GIR on the regiment's right flank, and SS-Panzergrenadier Regiment 19 once again attempted to take Bra and Les Villettes. Despite its concentrated efforts, the 9th SS-Panzer Division was unable to break through the lines of the 82nd ABD, which was backed up by the 703rd Tank Destroyer Battalion and A Company of the 740th Tank Battalion, among other units.

"An enemy flak wagon was destroyed on the road between Floret and Bergifaz by members of E Company," recalled Captain Campana, describing the events of December 27. "Occasional artillery and mortar fire fell on our positions, particularly in the E Company sector. Several casualties were caused by tree bursts."[197] Most likely killed by tree bursts, Pfc. Ferris E. Dunton from E Company and Cpl. Urban M. Shirley from D Company were the two fatalities that day in the 2nd Battalion sector. Pvt. Albert C. Lodovici of E Company earned a Silver Star for destroying the flak wagon: "Private Lodovici, when an enemy armored vehicle penetrated to within a few hundred yards of his company's lines, moved out voluntarily without orders and alone to meet it. Despite heavy small arms and artillery fire sweeping the open ground, Private Lodovici ran and crawled to close range and stopped the vehicle with a single rifle grenade. As he moved closer, one enemy soldier leaped from the vehicle and attempted to run but Private Lodovici killed him. Another enemy soldier attempted to fire from the vehicle but Private Lodovici wounded him. Securing five other enemy soldiers from the vehicle, Private Lodovici returned them to his own lines over the fire-swept open ground. Information obtained from the prisoners played an important part in successful attacks of a few hours later."[198]

Captain Kappel's H Company was not so fortunate: their outpost #4, manned by a rifle squad of First Lieutenant La Riviere's 2nd Platoon, was attacked around 1500 hours. Ten minutes later the news came through that the position was pinned down and one man had been killed. La Riviere immediately gathered some men and headed for his outpost, whose occupants had been forced to fall back before he arrived. First Lieutenant Harold A. Stueland, the forward artillery observer, was at the outpost with his assistants and directed 60mm mortar fire and later also artillery fire on the assaulting Germans. He estimated at 1700 hours that about 100 Germans had been hit and one tank had been knocked out.

At 2300 hours La Riviere again took a few men out and located the bodies of the squad leader, Sgt. Robert A. Tague, and Pfc. Clarence T. Smith. Tague had distinguished himself during the Waal River Crossing and was well known in the 3rd Battalion, so his death was especially a great shock.

"On the morning of 28 December," wrote Campana, "the regimental commander made another inspection tour and paid us a visit. After he left, I ate my Christmas dinner, which consisted of a small piece of cold turkey, supplemented with crackers and jelly obtained from the artillery liaison party, who always seemed to be well fed. About half an hour later, we noticed shells being dropped about 200 yards from the CP. Seconds later, the rounds came much closer, showering dirt against the window panes.

"The battalion commander immediately ordered everyone down to the cellar. There we huddled, listening to the shells shattering the window panes and shades. Suddenly, a terrific noise was heard and a gaping hole in the

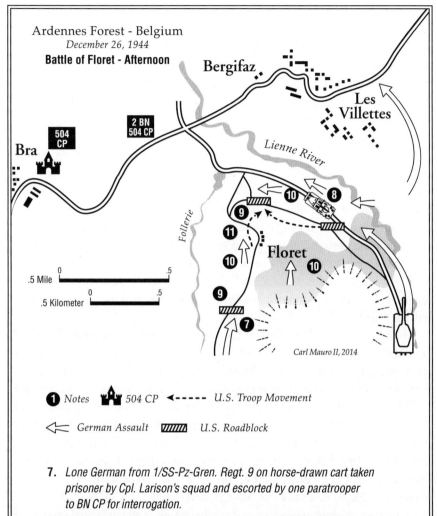

Ardennes Forest - Belgium
December 26, 1944
Battle of Floret - Afternoon

Bergifaz

Les Villettes

504 CP

2 BN 504 CP

Bra

Lienne River

Follerie

Floret

.5 Mile   0   .5
.5 Kilometer 0   .5

Carl Mauro II, 2014

❶ *Notes*   🏰 *504 CP*   ◄----- *U.S. Troop Movement*

◄═ *German Assault*   ▨ *U.S. Roadblock*

7. *Lone German from 1/SS-Pz-Gren. Regt. 9 on horse-drawn cart taken prisoner by Cpl. Larison's squad and escorted by one paratrooper to BN CP for interrogation.*

8. *15:00 hrs. Two flak wagons appear on Lierneux–Bergifaz road.*

9. *Lt. Rollins and Pfc. West visit Roadblock 2 and find it unoccupied. Platoon CP and mortar squad fall back.*

10. *Approximately 17:30 hrs. 1/SS-Pz-Gren Regt. overruns Roadblock 2 and attacks Floret from three sides.*

11. *Lt. Rollins taken POW.*

cellar wall became visible. Some of the men were showered with debris. The battalion commander immediately ordered the artillery liaison officer to get some artillery fire on the enemy weapon, which appeared to be a self-propelled gun. Orders were then issued to evacuate to the new CP located in the wooded draw. The battalion commander later told me that the gaping hole in the cellar wall had been caused by a dud from at least a 105mm gun. The dud had rolled underneath the cellar stairway a few feet from where we had gathered.

"The next few days were spent in relative peace, except for the occasional enemy artillery and mortar fire on the company positions and in the draw occupied by the battalion CP group. The only bright feature of my stay in Bra was an invitation to dine with Captain Komosa, D Company commander, whose CP was the only one in the battalion that was located in a house. The CP contained desirable livestock to supplement the daily K-ration, which we had been eating since the operation started. It was during this period also that Lieutenant Fust, our Battalion S-2, was assigned to regiment as assistant regimental S-3. Consequently, in addition to my other duties, I also became Battalion S-2."[199]

The German artillery fire on December 28 came once more from the 2nd Abteilung of SS-Panzer Artillerie Regiment 9, set up in the vicinity of Ramont, east of Floret. At 1428 hours three 105mm rounds landed near the Regimental CP. German mortar fire pounded the company positions. Around 1545 hours five mortar rounds landed in the right flank of E Company and slightly wounded Privates First Class Homer G. Eckerman, Robert L. Farrington and Samuel R. Shepler and Privates Peter E. Gallagher and Albert C. Lodovici. In a different barrage that day, two other E Company troopers, Privates Max W. Fleming and Leonard M. Lilley, were more seriously wounded. Lilley died of his wounds the next day.

SS-Brigadeführer Sylvester Stadler's division was the principal opponent of the 504th RCT until December 30, when it was extracted piecemeal from the front lines and replaced by the 560th Volksgrenadier Division. The capture of Bastogne required more German armor; they had failed to get through the 82nd ABD, but the German field commander in the west, *Generalfeldmarschall* Gerd von Rundstedt, thought the 9th SS-Panzer Division might be able to crush the 101st ABD like it had previously crushed the British Airborne at Arnhem. Little did he know that he would get a bloody nose in Bastogne too, where the 101st was backed up by elements of two U.S. armored divisions.

December 29 was the last day that the German panzer division made its presence felt in the 504th positions. Heavy artillery shells rained down on the I Company area at 0055 hours, and three hours later it was discovered that the company telephone line had been cut in three different places. By 0930 hours one of the forward artillery observers from the 376th PFAB spotted an enemy gun that had poured some 15 shells into Bra and fired a counterbattery on it.

Captain Kappel called the 3rd Battalion CP to report he had successfully placed another 20 concertina wires and 30 antipersonnel mines in his sector, and requested that a shot-down B-17 bomber that he was using as outpost #2 out in no-man's land be prepared for demolition. German shelling of the town continued throughout the day, including phosphorus grenades that set two houses on fire. At 1840 hours, OP #5, manned by I Company troopers, was fired on and one man was wounded in the leg.

December 31 saw various patrols, including an I Company patrol led by 2nd Lt. George Amos, which Capt. Moffatt Burriss photographed as they were setting out to recon the German lines to the south near the village of Xhout-si-Plout. When Amos returned at 1400 hours, he reported that they had located three positions where Germans had dug in along their defensive line and discovered one of the enemy's outposts. They had inflicted heavy casualties: three Germans killed and probably eight wounded. One of the ten troopers in Amos' patrol had also been wounded. Second Lieutenant Burnum, 1st Battalion Demolition Squad, had a bad cold and felt so miserable after marching through the snow on patrol that he finally checked in at the 1st Battalion Aid Station. It was determined he also had a serious case of trench foot and he was evacuated to a hospital in England.[200]

Also killed that day were Privates Wayne E. Mack and Anthony S. Kavaleski, two E Company troopers. It is probable that they, too, were lost on patrol duty, but this cannot be confirmed due to lack of information. Private First Class William K. Myrick of F Company and 1st Lt. Patrick C. Collins of E Company lost their lives on December 31 as well.

At approximately 2230 hours on New Year's Eve, First Lieutenant Garrison, the 2nd Battalion S-1, was severely wounded near the CP: "I was called out of my foxhole to organize an emergency patrol to locate an earlier patrol that had not returned or communicated. In addition, medics had to be stationed at the take-off point of the new patrol in case it brought back bodies. I had just conferred with Colonel Wellems, who was in a double-sized foxhole with a tarpaulin over it so that he and the executive officer could sit up side-by-side with their legs stretched before them and use flash-lights to study maps. As I started on my way, a single German artillery shell landed about 20 feet behind me. The expression that one does not hear the incoming shell that hits him is true. I don't even recall the sound of the explosion, because I focused on the force of the blast that buckled my knees and tilted me forward. As I fell, I threw myself in the direction of the flap entrance to Wellems' set-up. I went in head-first, landed crosswise on the outstretched legs of the two officers, and pinned them down."[201]

Captain Campana, also in the makeshift Battalion CP, recalled that "an enemy rocket barrage struck the CP area. A combination white and red flash was visible as the blackout curtain was blown aside. Suddenly Lieutenant Garrison, the adjutant, staggered into the dugout bleeding from the mouth. Lieutenant Colonel Wellems immediately gave him a morphine injection. In the meantime, the radio operator, who was also in the dugout, complained that his hand had been cut and also his back had been hit by some terrific force. Upon investigation it was discovered that the radio operator's back had been hit by a rock fragment and was merely bruised. I assisted in the evacuation of Lieutenant Garrison shortly afterwards."[202]

Garrison remembered that "I managed to gasp, 'Shrapnel!' When they maneuvered out from under my weight so as to have some freedom of movement, Wellems asked, 'How bad is it?' I answered, 'I've an internal injury. […] I'm spitting blood—I taste it.' He untied the morphine kit attached to the side of my jump boot and gave me the shot that we were trained to administer. Either I fainted from my shock or reacted quickly to the morphine; but some time passed, because Wellems' voice came through a mental fog to me when he said, 'Chester, we have problem. The stretcher-bearers are here. We are trying to figure the best way to get you out.' I remember saying, 'Tell them to grab my ankles and pull.' They did, and we started down the nearby field to the road where a jeep waited. Whether or not my drugged condition stimulated my imagination, I had the impression that the four stretcher carriers, including Victor Campana, twice slipped on the icy slope and fell with the stretcher in slow turns. Thirty years later, Victor complained that I had been unwieldy.

"I do not recall the next hour. The stretcher was secured to the medics' jeep for the trip to the regimental aid station at Werbomont. With the doctors, two close friends—[Captains] Lou Hauptfleisch and Bob Halloran—waited for my arrival. Wellems had phoned Lou at regimental headquarters, and Bob, a dentist, in combat became the medics' administration officer. [...] An ambulance took me to a field hospital in Verviers with a medical tag attached to me with the time 0001, January 1, 1945—one minute after midnight."[203]

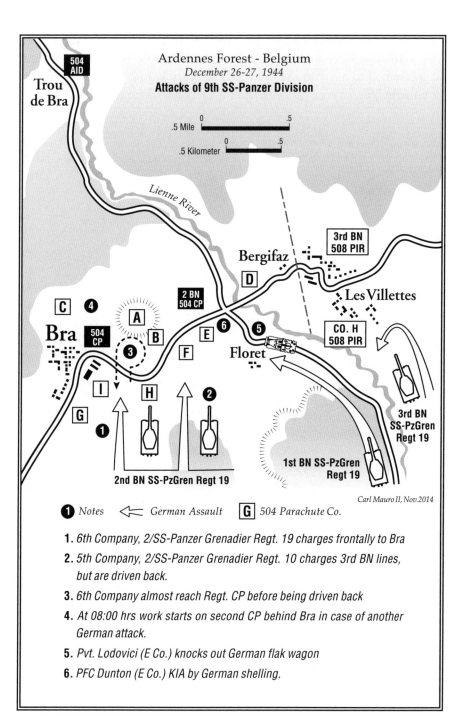

Ardennes Forest - Belgium
December 26-27, 1944
Attacks of 9th SS-Panzer Division

504 AID

Trou de Bra

.5 Mile — 0 / .5
.5 Kilometer — 0 / .5

Lienne River

3rd BN 508 PIR

Bergifaz

D

Les Villettes

2 BN 504 CP

C 4

A

Bra 504 CP

B

3

E

6 5

CO. H 508 PIR

F

Floret

I

H 2

G 1

2nd BN SS-PzGren Regt 19

1st BN SS-PzGren Regt 19

3rd BN SS-PzGren Regt 19

Carl Mauro II, Nov.2014

1 *Notes*   ⬅ *German Assault*   **G** *504 Parachute Co.*

1. *6th Company, 2/SS-Panzer Grenadier Regt. 19 charges frontally to Bra*

2. *5th Company, 2/SS-Panzer Grenadier Regt. 10 charges 3rd BN lines, but are driven back.*

3. *6th Company almost reach Regt. CP before being driven back*

4. *At 08:00 hrs work starts on second CP behind Bra in case of another German attack.*

5. *Pvt. Lodovici (E Co.) knocks out German flak wagon*

6. *PFC Dunton (E Co.) KIA by German shelling.*

CHAPTER 9

STRIKING BACK
BELGIUM, JANUARY 1–6, 1945

By the end of December 1944, plans had already been laid out for a counterattack, which General Dwight D. Eisenhower wanted to carry out on a broad front. This meant that the Allied forces had to retake every village, town, and city—a costly undertaking that would take a heavy toll on riflemen, tank crews and other ground troops. Although Field Marshal Montgomery had proposed a flanking attack north and south along the Belgian–German border to cut off the German "bulge," Eisenhower swept his idea aside. A second "Battle of the Bulge" was set to begin: this time not to prevent the enemy from enlarging his territory, but to strike back with all possible strength and determination.

This meant that the 504th front line was widened on January 1 and 2, so the 505th, part of the 517th PIR and the 325th GIR could be withdrawn and assembled for a counterattack. Part of the 517th, and the 504th and 508th PIRs were to defend the front lines. Enemy artillery fire was still inflicting casualties: Pvt. Ozzie A. Johnson of C Company and Pfc. Kenneth P. McDowell of E Company were both killed on January 1.

Three replacement officers were assigned from the 11th Replacement Depot that day: 1st Lt. John D. Nolan became a platoon leader in C Company, 2nd Lt. David M. Sniderman was assigned to G Company and 2nd Lt. Robert L. Spitz joined B Company. That evening Pfc. Ervin E. Shaffer, 3rd Platoon, went along on an A Company combat patrol ordered by 1st Lt. John N. Pease: "I don't remember how far we went, maybe five miles. We were to attack the German town on a diversionary maneuver to make them think that a full-scale attack was coming. We were to shoot at anything we wanted to. When we first came into the German lines, Sgt. [Clifford E.] De

First Lieutenant Peyton Hartley led Headquarters
Company for two weeks after the Battle of Cheneux,
where he was one of the few surviving officers of
his company. *Courtesy: Daniel Hartley*

Camp was killed by two Germans on a machine gun. I knocked it out with the bazooka—fired one round into it and killed both of them. I think that there was one other German killed at that time. The patrol was successful and we made it back into our lines without any incidents."[204]

A Company Pfc. Edwin Bayley experienced his first outpost duty that night. "The worst part of this duty on the front was being sent out with another trooper into no-man's land on outpost duty, as on New Year's night. Our squad leader guided us out through the minefield and left us in the open on the small road several hundred feet beyond our front line. We were told to take our sleeping bags with us to help keep us warm while we stood upright on watch.

"I believe that night was the coldest two hours I ever experienced in my entire life. Even with the sleeping bags around us we were terribly cold. To make it worse, it was bright moonlight and we must have been really visible. I thought about this later and realized that we were truly expendable. We could have fired our rifles to warn others of an impending attack, but there was no way to protect ourselves or to get back behind the lines. We had no foxholes by the road and no way of finding our way back through the minefield.

"Our machine gunners were on constant duty within the minefield. I was sure glad that I had refused the machine-gunner job when we started for the front. The job was so dangerous that one of the machine gunners who had served for a long time could not take it anymore and disappeared. We had one or two other long-time troopers who went absent without leave at times because they couldn't take it anymore. They were burned out. They had our sympathy.

"The foxhole was unbelievably comfortable after that session. If our feet got wet during the day, we never took our shoes off, but slept with them inside of our sleeping bags and let body heat dry the shoes. Otherwise we would have been in serious trouble with swollen feet, frozen, rock-hard shoes, etc. Foot care was essential for survival. I had learned that when I was in the Reims general hospital in October when I had a serious internal illness, possibly poisoning, from eating apples in an area previously occupied by German soldiers. In the hospital I had seen many men with severely swollen and infected feet (trench foot infection). I believe some of them had one or both feet amputated."[205]

On January 2, the patrolling continued. Cpl. Fred R. Gruneberg of C Company, who had been severely wounded at Cheneux, died of sustained wounds that day in an evacuation hospital. At 1400 hours Privates Warren H. Anderson, Horace M. Biddle, and George P. Haydu of C Company telephoned from their OP and reported, "We think we're being surrounded. Looks like enemy in American uniforms." Rifle shots at the outpost could be heard through the woods as far as the 1st Battalion CP, and then it was all quiet again. Major Berry decided not to send out any rescue patrols until well after dark. At 1940 hours an investigating patrol reported that the telephone line had been cut, the phone was gone, and broken weapons were lying around the OP. There was no sign of Anderson, Biddle and Haydu, who now were prisoners of war.

That same afternoon, at 1700 hours, Lieutenant Colonel Cook called his company commanders to the 3rd Battalion CP and told them that the counterattack would take place the following day. The 504th RCT would remain in position until called up into division reserve. G and H Company patrols dispatched that evening encountered Germans but no losses were suffered and no prisoners were taken.

That night Private First Class Bayley was on an A Company patrol which also was dispatched to take prisoners. "There is nothing that can create more tension and foreboding fear than to go into a deserted village near the battle front day or night, especially at night. Even walking across fields and through brush and woods is scary. As we went through a field, a lonesome dog decided to come along. Somehow we managed to get rid of him. Then a lonesome cow decided to keep us company. Somehow we discouraged her. We finally got beyond our front line without setting off any trip wires or mines and saw our future prisoner, a short, chunky German soldier standing guard, or so we thought. We rushed him and found we had captured a fir tree. After this we decided we better get out of there. We made it back through our line safely."[206]

The Germans launched their counterattack on the morning of January 3, 1945. Enemy light mortar fire rained down around the G Company CP in the afternoon, but there were no casualties. Two E Company troopers were killed by artillery fire that day: Privates First Class Willis H. Lamberson and Gerald R. Poehlman. Late in the afternoon the news came through that the battalions would be relieved that evening and night. Guides were provided for the relieving units, and by the early hours of January 4 the 3rd Battalion had left Bra and started on foot to the assembly area near Fosse.

Lieutenant Colonel Wellems' 2nd Battalion left its positions a few hours later and were repositioned northeast of Bra, around Les Villettes, closer to

Fosse. At 0900 hours the companies moved out in columns of two's. "The S-4 and his assistants passed out ammunition, K-rations, and heat tablets as we passed by," recalled Captain Campana. "The battalion marched for hours over ice-covered roads, uphill and downhill, stumbling and cursing as the individual pack became heavier. By late afternoon we arrived in the town of Fosse, which the 505th Parachute Infantry had captured the day before. The battalion commander reported to the Regimental CP, which was set up in that town. The battalion commander received the regimental attack order to seize the high ground southeast of Fosse, overlooking the crossings of the Salm River in the vicinity of Grand-Halleux.

"Lieutenant Colonel Wellems then issued orders to his company commanders, whom I had assembled. The battalion was to advance approximately four miles through dense woods, void of any good roads except a few trails and firebreaks covered by waist-high snow. The formation for this advance was D, F, E and Headquarters Companies, with a platoon of tank destroyers attached to D Company. One LMG [light machine-gun] section was attached to both D and F Companies. One platoon of 57mm towing AT [antitank] guns was attached to the battalion."[207]

Just before the 2nd Battalion moved off, the Catholic chaplain visited the troopers of D Company. "Just before engaging the Germans near Fosse, a small group of soldiers, including myself, were gathered together," recalled the D Company supply sergeant, S/Sgt. Ernest W. Parks, "Father Kozak approached us. It was not my idea originally, but I was dared to ask the chaplain for the bottle of wine he carried to administer last rites to dying soldiers. As near as I can remember, I addressed him, 'Father Kozak, knowing perhaps most of us will not survive the coming battle, I was asked to request of you the wine you use concerning the Catholic dead.' I prepared myself for a blistering rebuke from the chaplain, but to our amazement and shock, he handed me the bottle, it being, I believe, about half full. To my shame now, we drank every drop of it, passing it around from mouth to mouth. Our predicament did not afford us the luxury for the concerns of hygienic matters.

"It turned out to be the last of wine for some in our group. I hope I am wrong, but I personally do not remember a single soldier, regardless of his religion, profess faith in Christ Jesus as his Lord and Savior."[208]

The battalion commander set out leading the way, searching and finally discovering the trail, Campana recounts. "The unit progressed for at least 300 yards and then stopped. While the battalion commander was checking his map along with his compass, a mortar round landed next to the lead tank destroyer, killing one man [Pvt. Willard E. Pike, D Company] and wounding the platoon leader of the advance party [1st Lt. John W. Gardner, D Company] and the field artillery liaison officer. The battalion commander then dispatched Lieutenant [Stuart] McCash of F Company to take a patrol and reconnoiter another trail which he had just discovered. By this time it had become dusk and the cold air began to penetrate our clothing. Lieutenant McCash finally returned with the good news that it was the right trail. The battalion, after slight confusion, was turned around and proceeded along the trail, which was narrow and traversed with frequent streams. The attached tank destroyers and 57mm AT guns could not advance and consequently were left behind.

During the next seven hours the battalion trudged along in deep, knee-high snow. The weather had suddenly turned very cold and the wet, stiff web equipment stuck to our outer garments. The battalion commander made frequent but short halts to check his route of march by compass. The battalion had now been marching for 15 hours from the time it left the assembly area that morning, but not once did we have an opportunity to stop for any length of time to even eat a K-ration.

"At 0100 hours, 5 January, the battalion arrived at what we thought was the objective. It was a black, dreary, wooded area void of everything but snow and one or two firebreaks. D Company was placed into position on the left flank and set up a roadblock across the trail, which formed the boundary between the 2nd and 3rd Battalions. F Company was on the right flank, and it too set up a roadblock. E Company was put in reserve approximately 200 yards from where the Battalion CP was established. Since it was still dark, positions for the 81mm mortars were not set up. The battalion aid station was located in Fosse, the only place where there were any houses.

"Our bed rolls did not come up that night and the men did not sleep. Everyone was completely exhausted by hunger and the 16-hour march in intense cold over deep snow and iced-glazed trails. The situation was so bad that the men could not lie down on the cold snow for fear of freezing to death, nor could they move about too long to provide body circulation because of their exhausted condition. Fires were not possible because of the close proximity of the enemy.

"About 0300 hours, six mortar rounds dropped into the area occupied by D Company. Soon a phone call from Captain Komosa was received requesting several litters immediately. The mortar rounds had landed among his CP group. Unfortunately, no litters were on hand, nor were any members of the battalion aid station present. It certainly was a sad state of affairs. Half an hour later, the wounded men from D Company stopped at the Battalion CP on the way to the rear. Captain Komosa's runner had been seriously wounded in the head and was being carried on a makeshift litter formed by tree limbs and an overcoat. S/Sgt. Parks, the supply sergeant; Sgt. [Raymond A.] Kimball, the communication sergeant; T/4 [Lacy R.] Starbuck, the SCR-300 radio operator; and a first aid man had all been wounded. I immediately obtained some men from the 81mm Mortar Platoon to assist the wounded men back to the rear."[209]

Staff Sergeant Parks recalled that "it was still dark when a group of about eight of us formed together to watch a German tank maneuvering about a thousand feet ahead. Many small trees separated us from the enemy tank but, even in the darkness, our position was sharply revealed against the whiteness of the snow. We were careless in our formation, for we should have stayed several feet apart and in a straight line while facing our enemy. I remember the flash of fire and exploding rounds. It was many years later when I learned the full truth of the carnage of that encounter. Three soldiers were killed and five wounded.

"In the list of wounded appeared the name of Lacy Starbuck. Lacy was from Pinnacle, North Carolina, and we were dear friends. I had a reunion with Lacy some years after the incident and he enlightened me on some of the details as we discussed our battle experiences. But our encounter with the German tank ended my military career. I was struck with shrapnel in my left leg. Heavily medicated with morphine, I vaguely remember being brought back to the rear with two other wounded soldiers. Even wounded, we were required to walk as we were still in no-man's land. The bridges had been blown away and there were no medical facilities to care for the wounded and dying except for the barest means. The dead would be picked up later. My wound would eventually heal.

"While I was being treated by medical personnel for the shrapnel wound to my thigh, I remember few of the details, but some of the transactions I remember very distinctly. The wounded, including myself, were treated in a makeshift emergency structure erected as close to the front as feasibly possible. I requested the medic to 'Please keep the shrapnel for me when you remove it from my leg.' He replied, 'Soldier, it may look more terrible than it really is. The shrapnel did not enter. It's only a flesh wound.'

"I told him I still had a little sense left, and informed him the shrapnel was still in my leg. Stressed by his multiple responsibilities and the sheer number of his patients, the medic informed me in return that he had been on duty for at least the past 19 hours and suggested that maybe I should be the one doing the operating. Naturally, I felt ashamed and said no more. But he was mistaken! Even though the x-ray did not disclose it, the shrapnel had entered deep in my thigh beyond the penetration of the diagnostic x-rays.

"I will not attempt to describe the condition of most of the soldiers that were brought to that medical facility. It was a very gruesome sight indeed. I have always had the deepest respect for the medical personnel and thank the Lord profusely for them and their sacrifices."[210]

Parks would never return to the battlefield, but the war continued for his battalion. "As day broke on 5 January," wrote Captain Campana, "all company positions were moved forward at least 600 yards when it was discovered that the 3rd Battalion, on our left, was unable to make contact with us because we were too far behind. That same morning approximately 65 men from the battalion had to be sent to the rear because of trench foot.

"Later still, Lieutenant Colonel Williams, the regimental XO, visited the Battalion CP and wanted to know why the 81mm mortars had not been set up in position. He stated that German troops, consisting mainly of horse-drawn artillery, were reported to be leaving the town of Mont, some 2,000 yards away, and he wanted something done about the situation immediately. Accordingly, the 81mm mortars were set up approximately 30 yards from the Battalion CP and began firing as soon as their observers were in position near D Company's observation post. After several minutes of firing and when no further lucrative targets had appeared, the mortars were displaced forward. Nothing exciting happened for the remainder of that day."[211]

The 3rd Battalion also had a trying day on January 5. Second Lieutenant Amos of I Company was dispatched with a patrol at 0200 hours to contact the neighboring 551st PIB near Dairomont, which they were preparing to attack at 0530 hours. The patrol returned nearly three hours later and reported back to the Battalion CP. Outposts observed German horse-drawn artillery, tanks and infantry at 0900 hours withdrawing in the direction of Mont. Immediately artillery support was requested and small arms fire opened on the Germans, killing about 15 of them.

At 0915 hours a serious situation developed: the 81mm Mortar Platoon was surrounded and five infiltrating Germans were captured. Within ten minutes Lieutenant Colonel Cook alerted an I Company platoon and some machine gunners under Lieutenant Reese to help them out. Reese returned

STRIKING BACK • 147

at 1000 hours with 34 German prisoners, reporting all was quiet. But in the early afternoon, 1st Lt. Virgil F. Carmichael, the Battalion S-2, reported more Germans near a wood to the battalion's rear. Seven troopers sent from the CP to round them up returned at 1345 hours with another 28 prisoners. Fifteen minutes later, 1st Lt. Richard La Riviere arrived with seven Germans from H Company's position. Radio contact was established between Lieutenants Colonel Cook and Wood G. Joerg of the 551st Parachute Infantry Battalion, who said they were moving to the high ground near Dairomont. The battalion shifted its positions in the afternoon to be closer to the 551st. An I Company patrol dispatched to a bridge across a creek southeast of the town reported that the 551st was in a fire fight between I Company's position and the bridge.

On January 6 the 504th RCT consolidated terrain gained the previous day, and their neighboring 551st Parachute Infantry Battalion was placed under Colonel Tucker's command at 1320 hours. It transpired that they had suffered numerous casualties the previous day, but had taken their objective and driven off the enemy patrol that had harassed them the night before. H Company was placed in reserve and traded places with I Company. Four 57mm antitank guns and four tank destroyers were also attached to the 3rd Battalion during the day. Second Lieutenant Lawrence Pickard of I Company was wounded during the advance and returned weeks later.

At 2130 hours Colonel Tucker issued orders to his four battalion commanders: Lieutenant Colonel Joerg's attached 551st PIB in the north was to take the town of Rochelinval. They would receive tank support from a 740th Tank Battalion company. South of the 551st, Cook's 3rd Battalion had to take three towns: Petit-Halleux and Mont on the west bank of the Salm River, and Grand-Halleux on the east. They would come in from the northwest.

Lieutenant Colonel Wellems' 2nd Battalion, directly south of the 3rd, was tasked to attack Mont from the west with a D Company platoon and launch an F Company attack on the town of Farnières to the south. E Company would be in regimental reserve, following in the wake of D and F Companies. Finally, Major Berry's 1st Battalion was ordered to attack east to the Salm River, sending C Company to Farnières to provide support as needed, and then advance northwards to Mont. A and B Companies were to dig in on the west bank of the Salm and generally prevent any flanking counterattack from the south or from across the river.

Information received from various patrol reports and prisoner interrogations had disclosed that the reinforced 504th RCT was facing the 62nd

Volksgrenadier Division led by *Generalmajor* (Brigadier General) Friedrich Kittel. According to Lieutenant Colonel Cook, the German garrison at Petit-Halleux had been "estimated at a regiment of infantry, supported by artillery. Visibility was poor."[212] Cook ordered H and I Companies to attack the village, while G Company was assigned to capture Mont. Two tank destroyers from the 1st Platoon, C Company, 628th Tank Destroyer Battalion, were attached to each rifle company.

Captain Campana recounts his battalion commander, suddenly summoned to the regimental CP for a meeting at 2200 hours, "returned about midnight and had the company commanders assembled for a meeting. Crowded into the CP, which consisted mainly of the battalion commander's dugout with a field phone inside, we heard the attack order: The regiment was to attack at dawn 7 January and seize the town of Mont and the west bank of the Salm River in its sector. The 3rd and 1st Battalions were to attack in their zone of action, in a pincers movement, while the 2nd Battalion would make a secondary attack from the front, using only two platoons. Lieutenant Druener's platoon from D Company and [1st] Lt. [Richard R.] Harris' platoon from F Company would make the assault. The meeting then broke up at 0130 hours."[213]

That same day the independent 551st Parachute Infantry Battalion was detached from the 517th PIR and attached to the 504th RCT. The battalion moved out to consolidate positions west of the Salm River, receiving casualties in the evening due to artillery fire. According to 1st Lt. Richard ("Dick") Durkee, A Company was still holding a reserve position two days after he had led a bayonet assault at Dairomont: "We dug in and stayed there a day and a half getting resupplied with ammunition and clothing, set up our guards and outposts for B Company, and sent out reconnaissance patrols. Many of our men had to be evacuated then because of frozen feet. [...] On the 6th we got in two new officers: [First] Lieutenant [Charles E.] Dahl and Lieutenant [Joseph] Kienly. Neither of them had any experience in combat. Dahl told me that all he wanted was to get the Combat Infantry Badge. Our Company had then been divided into two platoons, one commanded by Lieutenant [Charles] Buckenmeyer [Platoon A] and the other [Platoon B] by me. Kienly went to Buckenmeyer and I got Dahl."[214]

In the afternoon of January 6, 1st Sgt. Roy McGraw lined A Company up on a road and sorted out the sick and wounded. Several men with black, frozen feet were loaded on trucks and sent back to an aid station. Only four officers and 42 enlisted men, including the company cooks, remained. The cooks were pressed into service as radio operators, most of whom had been killed or wounded.[215]

Colonel Tucker had instructed Lieutenant Andy Titko to lay down a line between both command posts, as it was a custom for a subordinate unit in the U.S. Army to furnish communications to the larger unit to which it had been attached. Titko replied he had only six men left in his battalion communications platoon and tried to explain why he needed help from the 504th, but Tucker brushed his protests aside with strong words. According to Lieutenant Titko, Tucker "is still waiting for that line, because I never laid it. He was a good man though."[216] The lack of a field telephone line made it far more difficult to follow the progress of the 551st in the upcoming attack, especially if the radios faltered in the densely wooded area.

It was therefore a radio call that alerted Lieutenant Colonel Joerg that day to prepare his depleted battalion for an assault on Rochelinval. Sgt. Bill Hatcher, a SCR-300 radio operator who had been moved from B Company to Headquarters Company the previous day, was at the Battalion CP on January 6, where he overheard a conversation between Lieutenant Colonel Joerg and another senior officer. Joerg was "pleading with someone on the phone. [...] He wanted to get us relieved because of the incidence of frostbite. The way he was talking, I would assume it was not General Gavin but probably a colonel. The language he was using was forceful—not four letter words, but words you might use in speaking to an officer of about your own rank."[217]

That evening Joerg called a meeting of his company commanders and principal staff officers. Maj. William N. Holm, his battalion XO, recalled: "Company B was to swing around the right side of the town, Company A was on the left and was to make a near-frontal attack, and Company C was to lay down fire from the center."[218]

The 551st Parachute Infantry Battalion was in a bad shape after severe fighting during the previous week. Their Battalion S-3 officer, the commanders of A and C Companies, and their executive officers had all become casualties or had been evacuated due to trench foot. A Company was now led by 1st Lt. Donald A. Booth, who had originally been the Battalion Demolition Officer. C Company was commanded by 1st Lt. Leroy C. Sano with three other officers remaining, one of whom would be evacuated with frozen feet. C Company numbered some 50 officers and men and A Company would attack with 46 paratroopers. B Company, led by Capt. James Evans, numbered two platoon leaders and some 65 enlisted men on the morning of January 7.[219] Headquarters Company, comprising an 81mm Mortar Platoon and a Light Machine Gun Platoon, as well as demolitionists and a seriously depleted communications section, consisted of some 60 officers and men. The overall strength of the 551st PIB just before the attack on Rochelinval was thus about 230 officers and men. Their opponents in Rochelinval were estimated to be at least double the strength.

The Headquarters Company executive officer, 1st Lt. John M. Hill, recalled that Lieutenant Booth had a premonition: "Don Booth visited me that night, and he was worried that there would be a lot of bloodletting. [Capt.] Bill Smith [of Headquarters Company] was pretty upset too, to the degree that the Colonel tried to console him, because of the way he handled Booth. You know, they were asking a battalion to go across an open area and capture this line of resistance where the Germans were dug-in."[220]

After the company officers had been briefed, the platoon leaders were informed of the upcoming attack. Lt. Richard Durkee received the news from Lieutenant Booth: "At 2100 Lieutenant Booth called the officers in and told us we were to attack, take and hold Rochelinval the next morning, the 7th. I had reconnoitered the area around the town and it was just suicide to attack it with our small company. I told Booth how I felt and said a few words that can't be printed. There were plenty of Krauts in that town. Booth told me he had already spoken words of the same effect to the Colonel, but the Colonel said that these were the orders handed down by General Gavin, so that was that. Booth then gave us his attack order, which directed that my platoon would bring up the rear. Buckenmeyer's platoon was to lead, and that made me happier, but it didn't turn out that way."[221]

C Company platoon 1st Lt. Richard R. Hallock recalled they had been alerted on the night of January 6 that they were to attack to the river line early in the morning and capture Rochelinval. "Lieutenant Colonel Joerg's plan of attack involved one platoon of C Company attacking and destroying the road block at 'A' while Company A attacked the town from the left and Company B swung to the high ground on the right. The remainder of Company C was to initially support the attack by fire and then to attack the town frontally. The machine guns to support the attack were emplaced in a small patch of woods which had previously been outposted to the front of our company. Lieutenant Colonel Joerg also planned to use this patch of woods as his forward command post since it was the farthest point forward and overlooked our objective. It had always been his practice to be well forward."[222] The hours remaining before the battle were spent catching some well-needed sleep, although several men were unable to do this due to cold weather and the prospect of the attack. Mail had arrived, but the paratroopers had been unable to read it. Many would never get the chance.

Private First Class David Finney, Regimental Communications Platoon, cleans his Thompson submachine gun after a recon patrol at Grand Halleux, January 9, 1945. *Courtesy: David Finney*

CHAPTER 10

VICTORY AT A HIGH PRICE
FARNIÈRES, MONT AND ROCHELINVAL,
JANUARY 7, 1945

First Lieutenant Richard Harris' 1st Platoon, in F Company, jumped off at dawn and moved out east towards Farnières. Emerging single file from the woods, they approached the tiny hamlet's most prominent feature, the Château de Farnières. In 1929, a baroness, Madame Louis Orban de Xivry, had graciously donated the château to the Salesian Fathers, who used the buildings for educational purposes. The gardeners, students and most of the Salesian Fathers had been evacuated shortly after the beginning of the Battle of the Bulge, but the château soon filled with hundreds of refugees from surrounding farms and villages, and as Harris and his platoon approached on the morning of January 7, it sheltered nearly 800 civilians. The remainder of the hamlet had been rocked by shell fire, but the château had been spared. Some of the Salesian Fathers, seeing the platoon had their weapons ready, ran outside to avert them that all present were Belgian civilians.[223]

The 1st Platoon quickly searched the other buildings in the hamlet and reported the capture of the town. First Lieutenant Sweet, the F Company commander, ordered Lieutenant Harris to continue his attack eastwards. Captain Campana describes the subsequent events: "When it commenced its advance beyond the town over exposed rolling terrain, the platoon was subjected to machine-gun and small-arms fire. Lieutenant Harris was killed almost immediately and two or three of his men were killed attempting to recover his body. Observing the platoon's difficulty, 1st Lt. Martin E. Middleton of F Company, who was not a participant in the attack, immediately set out to locate a hidden enemy machine gun. He fired several rifle grenades and put it out of action. The 1st Battalion later assisted F Company's advance by dispatching some men to destroy enemy outposts."[224]

Lieutenant Harris' posthumously awarded Silver Star Citation describes the heroic death of a gallant platoon leader: "First Lieutenant Harris and his platoon had the hazardous mission of clearing a road and were fired upon from a woods. First Lieutenant Harris skillfully deployed his platoon and led the assault in a successful attack, killing three of the enemy and capturing the remainder. Continuing down the road with First Lieutenant Harris still in the lead position, the patrol approached a small clump of trees on a high knoll from which dug-in enemy automatic weapons trapped them in a hail of fire. With complete disregard for his own personal safety, First Lieutenant Harris again led the attacking force toward the enemy positions. Far in the lead of his platoon and firing as he advanced, he was wounded seriously by enemy fire. Despite his wounds, he valorously drove himself forward to within grenade range before he was finally shot to death."[225]

First Lieutenant Middleton, the company executive officer and acting 3rd Platoon leader, had gathered a number of F Company troopers and led a flanking assault on enemy positions by personally destroying a machine-gun nest and firing smoke grenades with a rifle grenade launcher. Lieutenant Harris' platoon had been held up by a well-concealed German strongpoint of the 3rd Company, 190th Grenadier Regiment, consisting of 12 Germans and two machine guns. Opening fire at close range on the point of the platoon, they killed Lieutenant Harris and wounded several others. Sgt. Frank J. Salkowski, one of the most experienced rifle squad leaders, jumped up, moving to draw enemy fire away from his wounded comrades. About 20 minutes later he picked up a BAR and laid down a base of fire from the front. Both he and Middleton received the Silver Star for their courageous performance. Middleton's citation describes how the platoon leader "immediately and without orders, organized a rescue patrol for a flanking attack on the enemy positions. This action was met by fierce enemy resistance, and First Lieutenant Middleton returned for smoke shells to blind the enemy positions. The smoke laid down permitted the safe withdrawal of only two of the wounded, whereupon First Lieutenant Middleton then laid down a heavy base of flanking fire on the strongpoint. Under heavy return fire he moved into the area raked by enemy fire and personally directed the evacuation of all the stragglers and wounded. He himself carried one seriously wounded man to safety and killed two Germans who were attempting to loot our dead. Through First Lieutenant Middleton's personal and voluntary efforts, a total of eight enemy were either killed or wounded, and all the members of the beleaguered combat patrol returned to safety. His gallant conduct reflects highest credit on the Armed Forces."[226]

Another rifle squad leader, Sgt. John C. Chamberlin, who was seriously wounded in his arm while evacuating some of the wounded, also received the Silver Star: "During an attack on an enemy strongpoint, Sergeant Chamberlin's squad came under extremely heavy and accurate small-arms and machine-gun fire which caused numerous casualties. Sergeant Chamberlin unhesitatingly rushed across approximately 100 yards of open terrain in the face of this fire in an effort to move the wounded man back. The enemy laid down a barrage of mortar fire, but he succeeded in moving the man to partial cover and returned to his original position. After the barrage had abated, he again rushed out across the open field and was again met with a heavy barrage, which forced him back after being wounded seriously in the arm. Refusing evacuation, he remained in an open position directing his squad's withdrawal until he collapsed from loss of blood."[227]

Like several of his platoon mates, Pvt. William L. Aston, Jr. was decorated later with the Silver Star: "Private Aston, a bazooka man in Company F, exposed himself fearlessly to accurate enemy small-arms and machine-gun fire which was causing many casualties in his company during an attack on an enemy strongpoint in an effort to fix his bazooka fire on the enemy position. Seeing two of his comrades become casualties, he unhesitatingly advanced about 100 yards through enemy fire in an effort to aid the two wounded men. In this attempt, he was hit three times by enemy bullets. He returned to his squad, took a rifle from the hands of another fallen comrade and continued the fight until loss of blood and exhaustion forced his evacuation. Through this entire action, Private Aston displayed a singular devotion to duty and unselfish heroism which was an inspiration to all who witnessed his actions."[228]

F Company rifleman Pvt. Fred L. Kincaid also received the Silver Star "for gallantry in action on 7 January 1945, near Mont, Belgium," when he "voluntarily exposed himself to intense close-range enemy fire to cross approximately 100 yards of terrain in order to retrieve badly needed machine-gun ammunition from a dead ammunition bearer. Early in this attempt, he was painfully wounded but continued on despite his wound until his mission had been completed. He then unhesitatingly returned in the face of the same fire to get a wounded man to a place of safety. This was successfully achieved with the aid of two other men."[229]

One man from the 2nd Platoon, Pfc. Donald E. Morain, was wounded by shell fragments: "On January 7 it was my twenty-sixth birthday. We were moving through a bunch of trees and the Germans threw in aerial bursts and some shrapnel got me. I was taken to a hospital and after some days they loaded me on a railroad car and I was taken to the 203rd General Hospital in Paris. I rejoined the company in Camp Laon."[230] Killed were Cpl. Robert L. Righthouse and Privates Russell Christman, William Meyer and Eugene Stigler. The 2nd Platoon assistant platoon leader, 2nd Lt. Robert E. Bramson, reacted intensely to the deaths and wounding of so many brave brothers-in-arms: "I knew Lieutenant Harris fairly well and when I heard the news I went to the collection area to see his body—all of them lying together in the snow in below-zero weather—a sad sight."[231]

Led by 1st Lt. Hanz K. Druener, D Company's 2nd Platoon participated in the attack on Mont from the west. Lead scout Pfc. William G. Lanseadel emerged from the woods at 0700 hours, and headed down a slope northwest of the town. "Three hundred yards from the jump-off point, the platoon was met by heavy enemy fire from a well-concealed machine gun," Captain Komosa later wrote. "Instead of taking cover, Private First Class Lanseadel moved aggressively and boldly forward in the face of this fire; his actions so upset the enemy that they abandoned the position. Six of the fleeing Germans were killed by members of the platoon."[232]

Firing his tommy gun and hurling a grenade, rifle squad leader Sgt. William S. Kendrick knocked out an enemy heavy machine-gun position, and received the Silver Star: "Sergeant Kendrick's platoon was making a frontal attack on enemy positions when, directly in front of his squad, a machine gun opened fire and pinned the men down. Sergeant Kendrick sprang up without thought of personal safety and moved forward with a tommy gun in one hand and a grenade in the other. Thrown to the ground by a blast from an enemy grenade and momentarily stunned, Sergeant Kendrick struggled doggedly on toward the machine-gun nest in the face of murderous point-blank fire. Hurling his grenade from close range and firing as he advanced, he leaped into the entrenchment and engaged the crew, killing two and wounding one. Sergeant Kendrick's courageous action eliminated the machine gun, enabling the platoon to move forward and accomplish its mission."[233]

Reaching the outskirts of Mont at 0845 hours, the platoon received sniper fire from a house and a half-track. "While the platoon fired at the snipers, Private First Class Lanseadel ran 50 yards through a hail of bullets, into the house and up the stairs, where he killed one of the snipers and captured the other. Farther on, in town, the platoon was temporarily halted by another machine-gun nest. While his comrades poured heavy fire into it, Private First Class Lanseadel ran boldly forward to within hand-grenade distance and wiped out the nest with a Gammon grenade, killing two of the enemy and wounding several more.

"While Private First Class Lanseadel was advancing further towards a house near the far end of the town, he was wounded by a cleverly concealed sniper. Despite the wound, he kept moving in advance of his platoon until hit again by the same sniper. Though seriously and painfully wounded, he was able to point out the location of the sniper to the leading rifle squad leader, who shortly thereafter killed the sniper. A few minutes later, Private First Class Lanseadel died. The platoon continued mopping-up operations in the town, capturing a total of 48 and killing 40 others."[234] Lanseadel posthumously received the Distinguished Service Cross "for extraordinary heroism in action" in which he "voluntarily exposed himself to intense sniper and machine-gun fire as he single-handedly destroyed enemy positions that threatened to delay his platoon's advance. Fierce and accurate fire pinned his comrades to the ground, but Private First Class Lanseadel, ignoring the devastating fire, closed with the enemy, killing a sniper with his rifle and destroying two machine guns with hand grenades. Although painfully wounded, Private First Class Lanseadel deliberately moved about in the open, drawing fire away from his comrades and forcing the enemy to reveal their positions until he was struck again and fatally wounded."[235]

Cpl. John A. Schaebler, one of Lieutenant Druener's squad leaders, moved forward and pulled the mortally wounded Lanseadel to a safer spot. He then took command and led his men forward in a successful charge, during which he "maintained contact with supporting units and control of his squad in such an exemplary manner that his actions were highly instrumental in his platoon's annihilation of a vastly superior force. Corporal Schaebler continually exposed himself to heavy enemy machine-gun and sniper fire in order to better direct and exhort his squad in its advance. In the midst of a fierce enemy mortar barrage, Corporal Schaebler saw one of his machine gunners fall wounded. Without a moment's hesitation, he rushed forward and moved the wounded man to a place of safety. He then retrieved the machine gun and led his squad forward in the face of enemy fire, firing the machine gun from the hip. Inspired by the brand of fearless leadership which Corporal Schaebler displayed, his squad advanced 1,200 yards, routing the enemy with losses of 40 enemy dead and 48 prisoners. During this entire action, Corporal Schaebler exhibited a brand of leadership in keeping with the highest traditions of the United States Armed Forces."[236]

The Silver Star Citation for Lieutenant Druener reads: "First Lieutenant Druener's platoon had the mission of attacking towards Mont, thereby drawing out enemy fire to facilitate large-scale attacks on his platoon's flanks. Although recent casualties had left his platoon far under strength, First Lieutenant Druener led it aggressively, and by brilliant leadership and skillful maneuvering, he reached the town of Mont approximately 30 minutes before adjacent forward elements closed in. The speed and drive of his platoon's attack overran numerous positions. Approximately 40 enemy were killed or wounded, and an additional 48 surrendered to First Lieutenant Druener, whose loud and clear exhortations in German convinced them that further resistance was useless. This unusually high toll of enemy was gained with a minimum of casualties. First Lieutenant Druener's personal leadership and relentless aggressiveness resulted in the perfect accomplishment of the platoon mission."[237]

"About 0930 hours," recalled Captain Campana, "D Company reported that Lieutenant Druener's platoon had seized Mont ahead of the 3rd Battalion. Under the aggressive action and leadership of this platoon leader, the platoon had covered approximately 2,000 yards of woods and open terrain, by-passing and destroying enemy outposts in their advance until they had seized the regimental objective. The platoon, however, sustained several casualties."[238] Casualties included three dead, among them Pfc. Paul R. Nageley, who died of a wound sustained when D Company entered the village. Further weakened by a number of wounded, the 2nd Platoon was relieved at the end of the afternoon by the 3rd Platoon under 2nd Lt. William D. Sachse.

Around 0430 hours the 3rd Battalion, less G Company, set out to capture Petit-Halleux, Captain Kappel's H Company in the lead. Kappel placed Megellas' 3rd Platoon, supported by two tank destroyers, up front. Some 30 minutes later the platoon came under heavy fire. Among the leading elements of the platoon was 2nd Lt. Ernest P. Murphy, the assistant platoon leader, who received the Silver Star for his leadership in the frontal attack after "one of his two supporting tank destroyers was knocked out by an enemy mine, causing heavy casualties among his platoon. His platoon's attack stopped by the intense enemy machine-gun fire, Lieutenant Murphy, with utter disregard of the curtain of fire, crawled through the enemy to a point of vantage and directed the fire of the remaining tank destroyer, silencing two enemy machine guns.

"Returning to his platoon, Lieutenant Murphy quickly reorganized his men, and under the curtain of fire led them in the assault, taking a leading part in flushing the enemy from their positions. The gallant and courageous actions displayed by Lieutenant Murphy were instrumental in the success of the seizure of the town and the capture of 250 of the enemy, with a minimum of casualties. His conspicuous gallantry was an inspiration to his men and was in keeping with the highest standards of the United States Armed Forces."[239]

As 30-year-old Pfc. Eddie R. Hiebert, a rifleman in the 3rd Platoon, recalled: "One of our two supporting tank destroyers struck a teller mine and was knocked out about 800 yards from the town. Six of our men near the tank destroyer were killed or wounded. At this point enemy machine guns opened up on us and we were pinned to the ground. I saw Lt. Murphy crawl forward for about 50 yards under a curtain of murderous machine-gun fire, and called for the remaining TD to come up to him. Two of the enemy machine guns were silenced by the TD. Lieutenant Murphy then returned and organized us into two squads and personally led our assault. Once inside the town Lt. Murphy ran from house to house firing his Thompson submachine gun and throwing hand grenades, forcing many of the enemy to surrender."[240]

Private James H. Moore was killed when the tank destroyer ran over the mine and exploded. Walking nearby, Pfc. John O. Prieto still felt the force of the explosion: "I was about 10 feet away from the tank [destroyer] when a tremendous explosion slammed me to the ground, completely burying me in soil. When I climbed out of the premature grave, I realized all six men were dead."[241] Private First Class Cletus J. Shelton was probably killed at the same moment, perhaps by the same explosion. Shelton was with Pfc. Joseph Jedlicka and Pvt. Simon L. Renner searching a barn when what they later believed to be mortar shell fragments penetrated the wooden wall. A large piece struck Shelton in the forehead above his eyes, and took the top of his skull off, killing him instantly. Smaller fragments simultaneously hit Renner in the head and shoulder.

Shelton's death was not only a devastating blow for his family—he had been the only son—but also for his squad mates. Private Jedlicka, who was slightly wounded that day, wrote a letter to their mutual friend, Pfc. Hugh Wallis, who had been hospitalized with trench foot since December 28. Shelton, Wallis, Jedlicka and Renner had all four been assigned together to the

3rd Platoon of H Company on the Anzio Beachhead. Jedlicka knew that Wallis and Shelton remained especially close, as they made up the platoon's bazooka team. Renner would eventually rejoin H Company two months later, after being evacuated to a field hospital in England.[242]

Wallis' squad leader, Sgt. John J. Foley, Jr., wounded by a sniper, only learned about the details months later in a stateside hospital: "Staff Sergeant Richmond told me in Alabama that it was a sniper that got me, who was up in a chimney. When I was walking back to find an ambulance the German prisoners were streaming back by the hundreds."[243] The previous day, Sergeant Tarbell, Captain Kappel's radio operator, had been admitted to the battalion aid station due to frozen feet, but Pfc. Philip J. Foley took his place. This in a sense turned out to be life-saving for Tarbell when Kappel and Foley were hit by fragments of an exploding artillery shell. Foley was killed outright, while shrapnel penetrated Kappel's stomach and caused intestinal damage. He was rushed to the battalion aid station, where Sergeant Tarbell learned what had occurred, and was taken by an ambulance to a field hospital. This made 1st Lt. Edward J. Sims once more acting company commander.

After Captain Kappel was wounded, Private First Class Prieto did his best to comfort him. In agony, the captain asked him to see if his wounds were any lower than his stomach. Prieto looked down to where the captain was bleeding and said with watering eyes that as far as he could tell, the wounds were no lower than the abdomen. When the stretcher bearers carried the captain away, it took a moment for Prieto to gather himself. He was confused as to why he had become emotional—he had seen so many of his comrades killed or suffer agonizing wounds, like Sergeant Rosenkrantz and Private Baldassar in Holland. The tears he shed were not just for the captain, but for all his comrades fallen in battle.[244]

At the end of the day, H Company had taken 13 casualties: Privates First Class Foley and Shelton and Privates Kalagian and Moore were KIA, and Captain Kappel and eight enlisted men wounded. These latter were Sergeant Foley, T/5 Wrobleski, Privates First Class Gays, Jedlicka, Krueger and Prieto, and Privates Hollar and Rhea. Prieto later recalled picking up the grenades the Germans were throwing, and throwing them back to prevent their detonation at close range. One blew up as it left his hand, seriously wounding him and putting an end to his war. Another trooper, Pvt. Joseph E. McBurnett, was captured by the Germans during the battle. Company strength dropped to seven officers and 90 other ranks.

I Company had the same objective as H Company. Leading the 2nd Platoon, 2nd Lt. George A. Amos, supported by two tank destroyers, advanced to the town of Petit-Halleux. Led by Captain Burriss, the rest of the company followed Amos' platoon. A tank destroyer was demolished when it ran over three mines during the advance, and the explosion mortally wounded S/Sgt. Curtis L. Sims of the 2nd Platoon.[245] Walking behind the tank destroyer, Lieutenant Amos' feet were badly injured, but he refused medical aid and kept leading his men forward. Reporting to the aid station hours later, he was evacuated to a field hospital. He returned a few months later and was awarded with the Silver Star for his heroic action.[246]

German antitank mines had by now knocked out two of the three supporting tank destroyers. Captain Keep, 3rd Battalion S-3, personally led a group of men and the remaining tank destroyer into the attack. His medal citation, for which he received an Oak Leaf Cluster to his Silver Star, sums it all up: "The battalion's dawn attack upon the town was encountering great difficulties when two of the three tank destroyers attached to the battalion were knocked out and a considerable portion of the attacking infantry were casualties. Captain Keep quickly reorganized the attacking force and, with the remaining tank destroyer, personally directed the assault. In spite of heavy enemy artillery and small-arms fire, he led the foremost attacking elements with great skill and courage, advising and encouraging the men by his own example to further their efforts. Later in the morning when the town was under an artillery barrage, he went to the center of the village and evacuated a trapped clean-up detail. Captain Keep's gallant and heroic action, besides saving many lives, insured the success of the attack and reflects credit on the Airborne Forces of the United States Army."[247]

Sgt. Darrel D. Edgar, squad leader in I Company, earned a Silver Star for his aggressive leadership on the right flank while "serving as right-flank protection for his battalion when an enemy strongpoint defending a nearby house opened fire on his position. Sergeant Edgar's return fire killed one German and forced the remaining enemy into the cellar of the house. Positioning his machine gun to cover the entrance, Sergeant Edgar worked his way to the rear of the house and threw a grenade into the cellar, forcing eight Germans to surrender. Then with another man he rushed the house across the street, forcing six more enemy to surrender. Sergeant Edgar then called for tank destroyer fire on a roadblock 100 yards away, after which his squad rushed this group of enemy, capturing 23 more prisoners."[248]

A forward observer of the 376th Parachute Field Artillery Battalion, 1st Lt. Harold A. Stueland, who relayed the request for artillery support for the

3rd Battalion, also received a Silver Star for gallantry in action on 7 January: "First Lieutenant Stueland, acting as Battalion Liaison Officer and Forward Observer, played an outstanding part in the success of a coordinated attack on the town of Petit-Halleux from two directions. Forced by exigencies of combat, First Lieutenant Stueland laid one-half mile of wire through sniper-infested territory to maintain communications, vital for effective close artillery support. First Lieutenant Stueland personally killed three enemy and assisted in the capture of ten more while carrying out his assigned job. His outstanding industry and fortitude under fire made possible the capture of Petit-Halleux and over 200 prisoners, with relatively few casualties by the American forces."[249]

T/4 Kenneth F. Nelson and Cpl. Clemens J. Slepekis, the other two members of Stueland's observer group, were also decorated for bravery: the Silver Star Citations for both are fairly similar, excepting that Nelson was also wounded in action after the two leading tank destroyers were knocked out in the attack at Petit-Halleux. "Technician Fourth Grade Nelson, assisted by another member of the artillery liaison party, laid a vital line of communication over a distance of 2,000 meters, half of it through terrain in the process of being neutralized, and which was continuously under heavy fire from enemy artillery, machine guns and small arms. Several times during the attack Technician Fourth Grade Nelson had to fight off enemy snipers with rifle fire, and, although wounded by artillery fire, continued to lay and service his line until the mission was accomplished. This gallant action not only provided communication for the artillery forward to render very close artillery support for the attacking infantry, but also kept the infantry headquarters informed, materially assisting in the accomplishment of the mission."[250]

First Lieutenant James H. Goethe's G Company advanced to the town of Mont, southwest of Petit-Halleux, the second unit to enter the village. Although Lieutenant Druener's D Company platoon was already in the northern outskirts, G Company's entry to the village met stubborn resistance from German defenders. Staff Sergeant John D. Hamilton and Pfc. Woodrow W. Yarborough were both killed in the attacking platoon. The acting executive officer, 1st Lt. James R. Pursell from Birmingham, Alabama, was later awarded an Oak Leaf Cluster to his Bronze Star when "en route to the attacking platoon [...] he was fired on by several machine guns from the right flank. Gathering a few men he attacked across the open field firing his submachine gun and calling on the Germans to surrender. Reaching a position about 30 feet from two of the machine-gun nests, First Lieutenant Pursell threw several grenades into their position, killing three and wounding two others. He then charged the other positions, capturing 17 Germans. The courageous action of First Lieutenant Pursell eliminated an enemy threat against the remainder of the battalion and served as an inspiration to all who saw him."[251]

Led by Capt. Wade H. McIntyre, Jr., C Company attacked the village from the south with one fatality, Pvt. Robert H. Davis. First Lieutenant John N. Pease's A Company was in 1st Battalion reserve that day. They were to follow B Company towards the Salm River. Private First Class Bayley, 1st Platoon, described the attack through snow-covered woods and over frozen, slippery fields: "The next morning we were on the way again. Some of us drew outpost duty, where we walked through the deep snow a fair distance into the woods as side guards during the advance. Keep in mind that these guards are expendable. They may be killed while warning the main body of troops of danger. Due to the deep snow the outposts were changed frequently.

"At one point the order came down to fix bayonets for hand-to-hand combat. When we got to the place the Germans were expected, they had already left. We marched down a wide paved road and came to a farm near the junction of a north–south road and the village of Vielsalm. Another part of the division was already engaged in battle at this point, so we dispersed into the woods to occupy foxholes previously dug by others. A very busy machine-gun battle was taking place not far from where we were.

"After dark some of us were asked to carry ammunition to the other fighting unit ahead of us [B Company] and to help in bringing out the wounded. We brought in the ammunition and were told the wounded were already gone, but that we were urgently needed to cover gaps in their line where the Germans might attempt a breakthrough during the night. At the gaps, among the widespread troops, there were no foxholes and not much brush cover. The ground was rock-hard and snow-covered and we had no blankets or anything else to keep warm on this very frigid night."[252]

The machine-gun battle was waged by 1st Lt. John M. Randles' B Company near Mont. Commanding the 1st Platoon, 1st Lt. Reneau Breard was recommended for the Silver Star for his part in the assault. He recalled later that "my platoon was on the right of B Company, while B Company was positioned in the direction of Petit-Halleux. Lt. [Leo] Van De Voort's 2nd Platoon was on my left."[253]

The citation for his Silver Star reads as follows: "First Lieutenant Breard's 17-man rifle platoon had just reached its objective when it was fiercely attacked by a company of German panzer grenadiers. With one of his squads, First Lieutenant Breard immediately attacked frontally, temporarily halting the enemy. Dashing across an open field under heavy grazing fire, he then led 13 men against the foe's flank.

"With the enemy temporarily disorganized, First Lieutenant Breard then led the initial squad in another frontal attack, driving back the enemy which had penetrated up to 25 yards of his MLR. With the other squad, he then attacked the opposite flank, whereupon the enemy withdrew in disorder.

"Throughout the initial action, First Lieutenant Breard himself fought as a rifleman, and in the latter phases with a machine pistol which he took from a German he had killed. His under-strength platoon killed 15, wounded 14, and captured six of the enemy with the loss of only two men wounded. The courage, leadership and sound judgement displayed by First Lieutenant Breard contributed directly to his platoon's unusual accomplishment."[254]

As Breard later commented: "We jumped off and went down to the river. I got in a big fight down there up at the railroad. The snow was so deep that I crawled up to the railroad embankment. The Germans had their guns right at me, and fired, and the bullets hit between me and the ground. I started backing up and was trying to grab a grenade. I lobbed two grenades and they missed me anyway."[255] Only "a few minutes later, […] a German soldier came by and I took him prisoner. He carried a rifle. While I was disarming him, one of my men shot him in the shoulder. So we had to let his wound be fixed by my medic before we could have him escorted to the rear."[256]

The platoon sergeant, James M. Boyd, also earned a Silver Star: "Staff Sergeant Boyd, Platoon Sergeant, had just moved his under-strength platoon of 17 men to its objective when it was attacked by a company of German infantry. When part of the enemy attempted a flanking movement, Staff Sergeant Boyd took four men and forced them back 200 yards, during which action Staff Sergeant Boyd personally shot one and captured two of the enemy. Returning to his platoon, Staff Sergeant Boyd then selected four fresh men to drive off a thrust on his opposite flank.

"Dashing 200 yards across an open field in rear of the enemy, Staff Sergeant Boyd killed a motorcycle dispatch rider and two more infantrymen from a range of 25 yards. His ammunition gone, he picked up an enemy weapon and wounded two more of the enemy and captured two. With the enemy in retreat, Staff Sergeant Boyd returned to his unit, carrying a wounded comrade through sniper fire. His gallant action greatly inspired all his men and was a dominant factor in the successful defense of his position."[257]

Second Lieutenant James Douglass' 3rd Platoon was alerted when Breard's platoon was first attacked. Private Bonning recalled: "I was on an outpost with Pfc. Donald Graham and a runner came down from the left, from the 1st Platoon, and said, 'They have the Krauts surrounded,' so I told Graham to stay there and I took the BAR and ran down to give the 1st Platoon some help. Right when I hit the opening of this wooded area, a machine gun opened up. I saw some K ration boxes, a BAR standing against a tree and a foxhole, and I hit the hole.

"I got pinned down and fired about 200 rounds of ammunition. [Corporals] Thomas Holliday [Jr.], Turk Nersesian and Hilton Holland went around to knock the machine gun out. Holland got hit in the stomach. It was about three o'clock in the afternoon. It would get dark early in the Battle of the Bulge.

"Krauts came up from the machine gun firing at our hole and I would let a burst go of the BAR and get down in the hole. One time I stuck my head up and fired a burst, a Kraut threw a potato masher right at me and it hit a tree beside the hole. There was another BAR man in the hole. When the Kraut machine gun opened, he dove in his hole and left the BAR against the tree. But he had his ammo with him so I was using his ammo firing at the Krauts as they were attacking at the left side of the machine gun. I got a couple of Krauts right in front of the hole and I couldn't go by them the next few days. It was something I felt real bad about, killing somebody or get killed. You just can't walk by the bodies. I had to go around them.

"Holland got hit, Turk knocked the machine gun out and then we went down—it was starting to get dark—trying to find Holland. In the meantime he had crawled through the woods about 30 or 40 yards trying to get to our line and it got dark. We couldn't call out his name. [...]

"When Holland got hit there were other casualties too. [Cpl. Fred A.] Faidley heard about us having the Krauts surrounded, which really wasn't true. [...] Faidley came down the trail, the machine gun opened up on him, and he hit a slit trench on the right side of the hole. He didn't make it to my hole where that other BAR man was. I never did find out his name. I met him on a truck sometime going to town in France or Belgium, and he asked me if I was the BAR man that landed in his hole.

"Faidley got machine-gunned in the legs. I was screaming at Faidley and he was only about three or four feet away from me but the machine-gun fire was so loud I couldn't find out where he was hit. The machine gun subsided and I didn't know if he was moving or what. I jumped out of the hole and carried Faidley to a deeper hole on the left side of us, and got Faidley in that hole.

"Then Turk came walking out of the woods with a prisoner. He had killed a Kraut and captured one and then we summoned the medics. Two medics came and took care of Faidley. When Lieutenant Douglass heard about the Kraut attack he and his runner came down the trail. The machine gun opened up on him and knocked the tommy gun out of his hands. He got wounded in the hands and arms and was gone for the rest of the war. But he did rejoin us in Berlin about four or five months later.

"I don't know if Lieutenant Douglass' runner got hit or not. I discovered when everything was over that I had killed about three Krauts in front of my hole and Turk had killed one and I don't know if Holland and Holliday got any. There were three guys in holes behind me that were not firing one round. And I just raised raw hell. I went back to the outpost where I was at with Donald Graham. I never found out what happened to Faidley and always wanted to contact him to find out where he was from. Because of that incident that day and me carrying him to a safer hole."[258]

Corporal Holland died on January 9 and was posthumously decorated with the Silver Star. The citation explains his platoon, reduced to only 17 men, had been setting up a defensive position. "Before this could be completed, it was attacked by a company of enemy supported by a section of enemy mortars. Realizing the seriousness of the situation, Corporal Holland unhesitatingly started out alone to an exposed firing position from which he killed two and captured an additional two enemy. Overwhelming numbers having forced his withdrawal from this position, he then led three men in a flanking counterattack through intense enemy small arms fire which forced the flank platoon of the enemy to retreat in disorder, leaving two more prisoners.

"Corporal Holland then voluntarily led another flanking attack and personally knocked out an enemy machine-gun crew of two men. During this action, he was seriously wounded in the abdomen. Throughout the entire engagement, Corporal Holland displayed a brand of courageous initiative and intelligent leadership which was an inspiration to his comrades. His actions were largely responsible for the successful defense of his platoon's position and typify the highest standards of the United States Armed Forces."[259]

A few miles to the north, the 551st Parachute Infantry Battalion got up early on January 7 to attack the town of Rochelinval. A Company paratroopers woke at 0300 hours and prepared themselves for the upcoming battle. The platoon leaders made sure their men had a full load of ammunition and a working weapon: their platoons were less than 20 men strong. Lt. Richard Durkee recalled starting out "at 0400 with Lieutenant Buckenmeyer in the lead with Platoon B and my platoon following. We had got all the available men for the attack, including the company clerk and the supply sergeant. As we moved up to the Line of Departure, Buckenmeyer went straight ahead with his platoon when he should have turned left, and by the time I got word ahead, I had already led my platoon down there, so Booth [the A Company CO] told me to keep the lead. That was why my platoon got the lead in the attack. At a fork in the trail we picked up Lt. [Joseph W.] McNair, who had a light machine-gun section and was to give us supporting fire.

"We arrived at our Line of Departure and sent up a yellow flare so the other companies would know we were there. Booth then had our attached forward observer Lt. Chuck Minietta of the 376th PFAB] call for the concentration to be laid down on the objective. There was plenty of static on our SCR-300 radio, and contact was very poor."[260]

"Company B was on our far right," 1st Sgt. Roy McGraw remembered, "and Company C was in reserve. We went through a wooded area to where we could look right up a hill to the small town of Rochelinval. We put out security, set up our machine guns, and everything looked very quiet. Then somebody came in from left flank security and said he thought there was a German machine gun up on the hill in the woods."[261]

Lieutenant Joseph Kienly, the assistant platoon leader of Platoon B, recalled that the A Company troopers "were supposed to have jumped off at 0600 but Booth called for artillery preparation and it was a long time coming. When it did, it was only a few rounds and was ineffective. We didn't attack until almost 0800.

"Rochelinval was only a few brick houses sitting on a ridge which overlooked the Salm River. A shallow valley ran between the back road into Rochelinval and the line of woods we followed up to the line of departure. There was a dug-out section of the ridge where an American Browning water-cooled machine gun was positioned, manned by the Germans. That gun was the one that killed Booth and everyone else near our own machine gun. It had an excellent field of fire and was so close to us I could hear the German crew talking. We moved directly across in front of that gun. I never found out what happened to Dahl's platoon. Some of them might have made it almost to the ridge. Those guys and most of the men of my platoon were piled up along a path that led to the village."[262]

A brick house at the edge of Rochelinval was Lieutenant Kienly's prime target before he and his men regrouped to attack the rest of the village. The machine-gun fire, however, pinned the platoon down. "When I followed Dahl's platoon out of those woods and up that path toward the brick house, I sent my men out in two's," Kienly recalled. "That captured American machine gun then opened up on us and pinned us down, with half of us starting up the hill and the rest caught in the open between the woods and the bottom of the valley. Several people, probably including Booth, then hollered at me to get the hell out of there, and I then called to the men ahead of me to come back.

"One small redheaded kid [Cpl. Robert H. Hill] looked up to where they were shouting at me—then up toward the brick house. I could not stop him. He jumped up and ran to where my BAR man [Pvt. Robert R. Mowery] had fallen, scooped up the BAR and headed up the path. He was knocked down twice before he finally threw himself on that horrible pile of killed and wounded men. I wish I could remember his name but I had only been with the platoon one day."[263]

For "extraordinary heroism in action against the enemy on 7 January 1945," Corporal Hill would receive the Distinguished Service Cross. His citation reads as follows: "When his platoon was pinned down and suffered heavy casualties from merciless enemy machine-gun fire, Corporal Hill moved through heavy fire and secured an automatic rifle. Standing erect, fully exposed to hostile fire, he advanced toward the hostile emplacement, firing his weapon as he moved forward. Twice he was hit by enemy fire, but undeterred he continued to advance. As the fire from his weapon silenced the hostile machine gun, he was struck a third time by enemy fire and mortally wounded. By his superb courage and unhesitating action, Corporal Hill enabled his platoon to successfully extricate itself from the trap, reflecting the highest credit upon himself and the military service. Entered military service from Ohio."[264]

Casualties sustained in the woods when Lieutenant Booth was killed included several machine gunners killed or wounded. One who lived to tell the tale was Sgt. Don Garrigues: "We were supporting A Company in elevated terrain that sloped down to our front through some woods then gradually opened into a little valley. On the far side was a cleared area, maybe under cultivation, and then the land sloped up and there was this little settlement on top, a very small place with just a few buildings behind a big stone wall.

"It was still dark when we got there, but you could make out a few things. We called for some mortar and artillery support. Then I think we got some artillery but it just succeeded in waking the Germans up. We were close enough to hear them chattering and carrying on.

"After the machine shelling, word was given to start the attack. I had planned to put my machine gun in a small depression where I had some protection but could still see the field of fire. Well, Lieutenant Booth didn't like that location and he had me move the gun over to another spot right out in the bare open.

"Then here went the riflemen off in front of us, through the brush and trees, across the valley and up the hill. We held our fire until the Germans opened up and then we started. [...] Every fifth bullet was a tracer, and our tracers and the German tracers were crossing. I could see riflemen in front of us getting hit and falling down."[265]

Sergeant Garrigues was wounded by a bullet in his back shortly after an assistant gunner had been hit, and both were evacuated to the aid station. Back at the Headquarters Company CP, Lt. John Milt Hill anxiously awaited relays for fire missions for the Mortar Platoon: "The mortars were assigned to certain target areas and as far as I know, the 81mm mortars were OK for ammunition. I think we had been resupplied since 3 January. The Colonel was in an observation post where he had a good view of the entire area of the attack; he just had to step forward a few paces to come clear of the trees. We were dug-in and ready to fire any mission as directed, and I was in the Headquarters Company command post waiting for requests for fire. I think [Capt.] Bill Smith had already gone to the rear then." Word of the disaster in the A Company sector first reached Lieutenant Hill when 1st Lt. Phil Hand moved over to the A Company area to view the progress of the attack. "He had seen what happened and was so upset he could hardly talk. Booth had been killed, along with many of his men." [266]

While Lieutenant Colonel Joerg was at his observation post on the edge of the woods to the left of Rochelinval, Major Holm sat in a jeep at the battalion command post in Dairomont to the rear of the battle area. The 551st PIB aid station was still set up in Fosse, near the 504th Regimental Aid Station. A sudden German artillery concentration rained down, killing or wounding several men from battalion headquarters and C Company. Lieutenant Hallock was sitting near his battalion commander as the enemy rounds came in: "The attack jumped off in half-darkness with Lieutenant McKay of our company attacking the roadblock and Company A moving toward the town across an open ravine into very heavy fire. Almost immediately the wire and radio to Company A were shot out, preventing Lieutenant

Colonel Joerg from committing the remainder of Company C until contact could be regained.

"Meanwhile, our light machine guns had to maintain their supporting role and drew very heavy mortar, artillery, and small arms fire into the conspicuous patch of woods, causing heavy casualties in Company C and Lieutenant Colonel Joerg's command post group. We later estimated that three light machine guns fired 15.000 rounds from this position without moving. During this time, Lieutenant Colonel Joerg walked coolly among the men offering encouragement by word and presence. It would have been difficult to tell from looking at him that a serious crisis had arisen and that he was gambling his life and the lives of his command group in order to retain contact.

"Part of the plan was to keep contact with Lieutenant [Roy] McKay's platoon by means of telephone wire laid down by a man following the platoon. A second man was sitting at our end of the phone somewhat to the rear and to the right of the emplaced machine guns. When he was hit, I sat down at the phone to keep contact with Lieutenant McKay. Meanwhile, the Colonel was awaiting news from runners whom he had sent to Company A and word from Lieutenant McKay that the roadblock had been taken.

"Lieutenant [Leroy] Sano (who had taken over Company C two days previously when Captain Quinn was hit), while waiting the order to attack, sat down beside me at the phone. In a few moments, Colonel Joerg came over and sat down between us. He asked me what was the word from Lieutenant McKay and, as we all three bent over the phone in my hand, a round of artillery fire scored a direct hit on the middle machine gun and crew; and, then, as I turned back to the phone a second round burst in the tree directly above our heads.

"At that very instant, I was looking directly at the Colonel. A large spark flashed from the top of his helmet, and without a word he fell on his right shoulder from his sitting position. His helmet rolled off and I saw that he had died instantly without a word or movement. A medic reached him at once and he was evacuated.

"It is a tribute to Lieutenant Colonel Joerg's training of the battalion that those men who were left carried out his plan and captured the town to complete the mission. Major Holm took over the battalion, and Company C (totalling less than 25 men) under Lieutenant Sano's fine leadership, supported by two light tanks and fire support from Company B, attacked frontally and captured the town, killing 150 Germans and capturing over

300. (Company A, except for one officer and a half dozen men, had been destroyed.)"[267]

There has been some controversy about the role of the platoon attached from the 740th Tank Battalion. Lt. Lloyd P. Mick's 1st Platoon, D Company, consisted of two M5A1 Stuart tanks and two larger M24 Chaffee tanks. According to the After Action Report of the 740th TB, the platoon was attached to the 551st at 0200 hours on January 7, and moved into a reserve position at 0530 hours "due to woods and narrow trails. The infantry battalion was subjected to heavy fire soon after jumping off by automatic weapons and mortar and artillery fire. The Battalion CO ordered the M24 to fire five rounds into the town of Rochelinval and pull back again. By the time the tank was in position the Battalion CO was killed and the machine-gun section had to move its position.

"From this point S/Sgt. [Roy] Parks fired the entire combat load of 75mm and all but one belt of .30-cal. into the town. At this time mortar fire came down around the tank and it had to withdraw. The other two M5A1's were called up and the M24 withdrew for a resupply of ammunition. As there had been no AT fire it was decided to run the two tanks into town with the infantry about a squad. The M24 furnished a base of fire and the M5 tanks moved in to about 400 yards from the town and sprayed positions and hedgerows with .30 cal., then moved up 200 yards.

"The enemy began coming out of their foxholes and surrendering. The two tanks moved into town 100 yards apart firing .30-cal. and 37mm in all likely positions and basements. At this time so many were surrendering that Staff Sergeant Parks and Sgt. [Clayton] Curtiss manned AA guns to avoid hitting friendly infantry while they exposed themselves to the volume of small arms fire that a tank naturally draws. At 1130 the town was occupied. About 200 prisoners were taken and escorted to the rear. When tanks had taken a defensive position the crews dismounted and assisted in flushing foxholes that had been by-passed."[268]

The second 551st Parachute Infantry Battalion history (1997), written by Gregory Orfalea, differs significantly from the 740th Tank Battalion After Action Report. According to the PIB history, the tanks did not show up at dawn at the start of the attack. Lt. John Belcher was called to Lieutenant Colonel Joerg, who yelled, "We're supposed to have three tanks. Where the hell are they? Go find them!"[269] Belcher showed up hours late with one tank, which had a malfunctioning turret.[270] The 740th Tank Battalion After Action Report mentions that four tanks were in the tank platoon, but only three tanks actively took part. The fourth one may well have had a malfunctioning turret, and so be the tank located by Lieutenant Belcher.

The question remains why the other three tanks had no communication with Lieutenant Colonel Joerg as the attack on Rochelinval began. What might have happened if they had been able to support A Company? Who knows how many men who were killed in that brave, but futile attempt would have survived with tank support? The original history of the 740th Tank Battalion (1945) states: "The 551st Parachute Infantry Battalion had suffered severely through the absence of a plan of attack."[271] The second battalion history (2007) sheds light on the controversy. After Staff Sergeant Parks withdrew his M24 tank, "the situation was confused when D Company's commander, Capt. Raymond R. Smith, arrived. Although small-arms fire was heavy, there had been no antitank fire; so the two M5 light tanks were called up. Smith then had Parks' M24 set up in a defiladed position to provide a base of fire while the M5's made flanking attacks from left and right with infantry."[272]

Lieutenant Hill recalled that after a "light tank came up the road" the attack went smoothly. "When it went into the town with our men, the Germans began to surrender and we got the town. We weren't in too good a frame of mind then. We got in there and dug in—what was left of us, and that wasn't a hell of a lot."[273]

T/5 Jack Affleck, a battalion medic attached to C Company during the attack, requested and received permission from Lieutenant Sano to visit A Company's zone of attack: "I made my way over to the west side of the town and at first it seemed entirely deserted. Where a sunken road entered I came across several machine-gun emplacements, one with its abandoned weapon still in position. Perfectly situated, its field of fire covered every foot of a narrow, almost straight, dirt road that ran down from the town to a jutting neck of woods 150 yards or so to the northwest.

"The reason for Company A's failure was now all too apparent. A single body [Cpl. Robert Hill] lay almost even with the first house, face down with arms outstretched. Behind it at intervals all the way back to the woods were sprawled clumps of olive-drab-clad figures, starkly outlined against the snow-covered road. Caught in the open, Company A's assault elements had been mowed down and then apparently riddled again after they fell.

"I identified the first body by dog-tag and rank insignia as Lieutenant Dahl. Well out in front of the nearest men, he had made his first and only attack in true World War I style. He was armed only with a .45 automatic pistol, still clutched in his right hand. Drained completely of the elation I had felt earlier, I moved mechanically down the road, checking each of group of bodies for any sign of life. Stiffened already, their faces had a sallow, wax-like hue and were contorted with open mouths and wide, staring, sightless eyes. This ageless stamp of the wartime dead made them all similar and hard to recognize as the individuals they had once been.

"In one group I came across a friend I had known since jump school days. Half his face had been shot away and his helmet had come loose and lay by his head. In it, badly stained by his blood, were several unopened letters which he had apparently received the night before but had not had time to read before the attack. I hoped the Graves Registration people would not return them to the senders. Finally, at the edge of the wood line and half in the open, I found Lieutenant Booth. He had been nearly cut in two by bullets, and from the location of his body it looked as though he might have been trying to recall his men when he was hit. Courageous and competent, Booth was an officer I'd always admired who truly cared about the welfare of his men.

"It was a long, grim walk back up that bloody road to the village. A surprise attack, I thought, made in a dash and under cover of darkness, might have had some chance of success—but in broad daylight, and without adequate covering fire, it had never really had any chance at all. About mid-afternoon that day the battalion aid station was moved into town and set up in the same house being used by the German medics. They were cooperative and helpful and later took me to a number of fresh graves, each with a rough cross with dog-tags hanging on it. One set of tags bore Lt. [Joseph A.] Farren's name."[274]

Captain Louis Hauptfleisch accompanied Colonel Tucker on his visit to the regimental aid station in Fosse in the early afternoon: "We stopped at the medical aid station to which Colonel Joerg had been evacuated. Perhaps we were there because Colonel Tucker had been advised that Colonel Joerg had been wounded, but on that point I am not certain.

"At the aid station we found Colonel Joerg still breathing, as evidenced by his warm breath hitting the cold wintry air. He was laid on a makeshift sawbuck-and-wooden-pallet bed in the open area outside the building then serving as the aid station. One can only assume that he had been placed outside for lack of room within the station—and perhaps more importantly, because it had been determined that he was beyond help and would soon expire. On that count I would have to concur, since it was obvious he had suffered

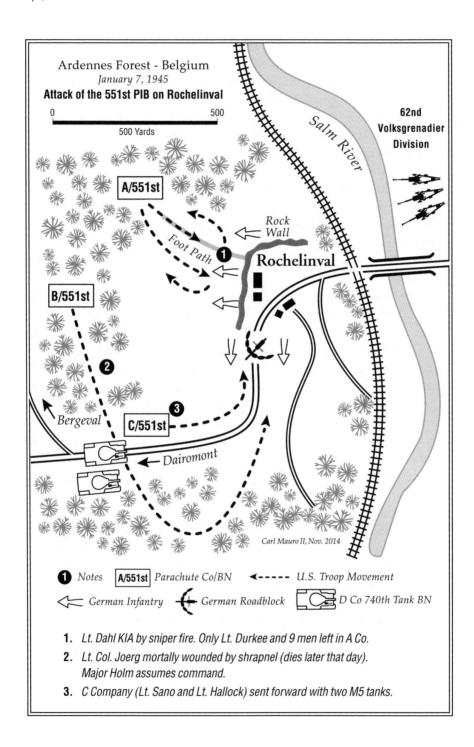

Ardennes Forest - Belgium
January 7, 1945
Attack of the 551st PIB on Rochelinval

0   500

500 Yards

62nd Volksgrenadier Division

Salm River

A/551st

Rock Wall

Foot Path ❶

Rochelinval

B/551st

❷

Bergeval

C/551st ❸

← *Dairomont*

Carl Mauro II, Nov. 2014

❶ *Notes*   A/551st *Parachute Co/BN*   ◀----- *U.S. Troop Movement*

⬅ *German Infantry*   *German Roadblock*   *D Co 740th Tank BN*

1. Lt. Dahl KIA by sniper fire. Only Lt. Durkee and 9 men left in A Co.
2. Lt. Col. Joerg mortally wounded by shrapnel (dies later that day). Major Holm assumes command.
3. C Company (Lt. Sano and Lt. Hallock) sent forward with two M5 tanks.

serious head wounds, presumably from mortar or artillery fire, and was un-conscious.

"I can clearly remember the emotional upset my commander evidenced when he viewed Colonel Joerg in that scenario. Colonel Tucker, a hard-nosed and tough combat officer, was not given to that type of display, so I was understandably surprised. I was surprised even more when he attempted to remove Colonel Joerg's West Point ring, saying, 'I want to make damn sure this gets back to his home.' Recognizing that his impulsive action was prob-ably not proper, I softly but firmly reminded my Colonel that there were proper procedures for the personal effects of a deceased military person fol-lowing him, and that individual actions related thereto were not authorized. He grudgingly backed away then, throwing expletives in every direction against the Krauts (the enemy to him was always "those goddam Krauts"), and we left the scene. My recollection is that this was early afternoon on 7 January, and that Colonel Joerg expired soon thereafter."[275]

The death of the beloved battalion commander of the 551st made Major Holm's command permanent, but only for a couple of weeks. The battalion was a shell of its former self. Out of the original 839 paratroopers present for duty on New Year's Day, only 110 officers and enlisted men were left. Major General Gavin learned about the appalling losses of the decimated battalion and withdrew the remnants from the front lines on January 9. The 551st was sent to a rear area in Juslenville, Belgium.

With the attached 551st PIB, the 504th RCT managed to take all its assigned objectives on this day, except one: Petit Halleux. While his para-troopers were establishing and consolidating positions on the west bank of the Salm River, Colonel Tucker received orders to take Petit Halleux the fol-lowing day and to clear the entire west side of the riverbank. Other regiments, operating on a much smaller front, had also pushed forward from Trois Ponts in the north to Vielsalm and Grand Sart in the south.

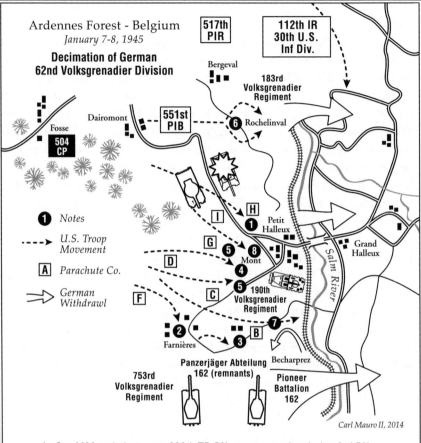

Carl Mauro II, 2014

1. *One M36 tank destroyer, 628th TD BN, runs over mine during 3rd BN attack on Petit-Halleux.*

2. *Lt. Harris' 1st Platoon, F Co. takes Farnières about 0715 hrs.*

3. *Lt. Harris (KIA) and men pinned down by enemy fire. Lt. Middleton (XO) saves situation by a flanking assault.*

4. *Lt. Druener's 2nd Platoon, D Co., reaches Mont ahead of neighboring units in frontal assault, 0845 hrs.*

5. *C and G companies attack Mont from north and south.*

6. *551st PIB takes Rochelinval, sustaining severe casualties.*

7. *Understrength company, 190th VGR, counterattack at 1720 hrs. on 1st Platoon, B Co. Lt. Breard leads flanking assault—20 Germans KIA, 5 POW.*

8. *Petit-Halleux captured by 3rd Battalion, January 8.*

CHAPTER 11

TWIN TOWNS
PETIT HALLEUX AND GRAND HALLEUX,
BELGIUM, JANUARY 8–11, 1945

Writing in the 3rd Battalion journal on January 8, Maj. Abdallah K. Zakby, the Battalion XO, reported: "0900—Has been snowing for past 12 hours. Companies report situation well in hand." Earlier that morning at daybreak, Pvt. Bill Bonning was finishing up guard duty near his B Company outpost between the town of Mont and the Salm River. "They sent two other men up to our outpost. [Pfc. Donald] Graham and I walked back to the company CP to find out where the rest of my platoon was, which were very few, and there were about ten guys around the CP. I raised hell there. I didn't make any points for myself, but I said, 'Why aren't you guys on line instead of back here at the CP?' I couldn't believe it. Like about 10 percent are doing all the damn fighting.

"Don't get me wrong, the paratroopers are one brave bunch. I'm just saying that after so many days of combat you start getting scared, thinking your number is up next. But I did discover that you get careless after about two or three months. After we had crossed the Roer, Rhine and Elbe Rivers and I still couldn't believe I was still alive, I all of a sudden got one of these feelings that nothing can happen to me. It's just not right, you should not ever get that, but I got it for a whole day. That I could do anything in the world and that I would not get killed.

"You finally get so reckless, it's unbelievable. I got a Bronze Star and a Purple Heart but sometimes I think that the guys that really got lots of medals—the guys that got DSCs [Distinguished Service Crosses] and Silver Stars—finally get that feeling too, that nothing is going to happen to them.

It is a crazy feeling—just like you are king of the earth and nothing, nothing can bother you.

"I went back [to the 1st Platoon area] to see if they had found [Cpl. Hilton] Holland, and they did find him. He had crawled up close to our lines and he went back to the hospital. He was still alive, but he died there soon after [on January 9]."[276]

Tucker's troopers still had two towns to capture, the twin towns of Petit- and Grand-Halleux, separated from one another by the Salm River, which is almost fordable at that point. The attack on Petit-Halleux itself resumed, spearheaded by the 3rd Platoon of G Company. The platoon commander, 2nd Lt. James R. Allmand, Jr., was awarded a Silver Star for leading the assault on heavily fortified positions in the heart of the town. Almand's 3rd Platoon "knocked out many enemy strong points and succeeded in reaching their objective. His group was subjected to enemy artillery fire and pounded by small-arms fire from every direction. The advance was held up at one point by an enemy machine gun, but First Lieutenant Allmand crawled close to the position and succeeded in knocking it out with hand grenades, killing the three-man crew. First Lieutenant Allmand's bravery and leadership reflects the highest credit upon himself and the United States Airborne Forces."[277]

Severely wounded in the attack, Pvt. Roger E. Chapin of G Company died the same day of his wounds. In 3rd Battalion Headquarters Company, Pvt. James R. Herman died of sustained wounds. The 3rd Platoon of H Company, led by First Lieutenant James Megellas, was pinned down by small-arms fire as they tried to fight their way from the outskirts to the central part of the town. Pvt. David E. Ward, Jr., a 3rd Platoon rifleman, was wounded while dragging a severely wounded fellow soldier to the rear under heavy enemy fire. His Bronze Star Citation reads:

"While pinned down in a shell hole by heavy small-arms fire, one of our men was seriously wounded through the neck and was losing a considerable amount of blood. Private First Class Ward, in the face of murderous fire, dragged the wounded man from the hole and by crawling and carrying him, started to the rear and medical aid. Under complete enemy observation and heavy fire, and even though he had been wounded in the right leg, Private First Class Ward refused to take cover and continued until he found medical aid for the wounded man."[278]

While H Company was attacking Petit-Halleux from the north and northwest and G Company attacked from the southwest, four 2nd Battalion troopers from Headquarters Company died due to what the Regimental S-

TWIN TOWNS • 179

3 journal describes as "a mine accident." Corporals Oliver J. Bohlken and George B. Ellzey and Privates Wallace R. Jones and Paul R. Reynolds were all killed instantly. The 2nd Battalion also lost Pvt. Manuel D. Orozco of D Company and Pfc. Casmir A. Klamut of Headquarters Company, both of whom died of wounds. Klamut had been wounded on December 30 in the vicinity of Bra.[279]

Private First Class Bayley and a small group of 1st Platoon, A Company men were still positioned in the B Company area. "Nothing happened during the night or in the early morning. We were asked to stay in position throughout most of the day. Some of our own soldiers were so cold that they violated one of the principle warnings, 'Do not build a fire at the front.' They withdrew several hundred feet back up the steep hill and lit a bonfire just to get their feet thawed and get a bit of warmth into their bodies. Nothing happened.

"During the day some of us ran out of drinking water, so two or three brave souls went into no-man's land to the Salm River and filled some of the canteens. We always used water purification tablets when taking water from a brook or river since we had learned from experience that sometimes there would be dead bodies in the water upstream from our dipping point. Late in the afternoon we were sent back to our company area."[280]

In Company B, Private Bonning also made also a few trips to the Salm: "The next couple of days we ran out of water. There was a creek at the bottom of the hill and on the other side were the Krauts. You could see them across the creek. They were moving very little but you could see them. Harold [Florey] and I would go down to get our canteens filled. Ours were in a canteen cover, and when you took your canteen out of the cover, it was still hooked on your belt. You would rattle the canteens as you went down, filled up the canteens, and came back up. The Krauts didn't want to get into a firefight because we had just had a big one and they'd lost quite a few guys. When they went down to fill up their canteens they couldn't rattle theirs because their canteen cover was glued right on it."[281]

In the 2nd Battalion area the Battalion S-3, Captain Campana, was ordered to personally deliver a written attack order to 2nd Lt. William Sachse's 3rd Platoon of D Company in Mont. The order required him "to cover the open terrain between Mont and our positions in the woods as a further check against any possible enemy groups still remaining there. The message was carried by foot and transmitted to Lieutenant Sachse. He was given three tank destroyers from the 3rd Battalion. After seeing that Lieutenant Sachse was well on his way, I returned to the CP on foot, exhausted."[282]

At 2200 hours on January 8, Major Zakby recorded in the After Action Report: "Sgt. [Earl G.] Oldfather (G patrol leader) reports to CP. Went all through town. No sign of life or noise. River not very wide or deep, can walk across. Bridge out. Civilians this side of river report Krauts pulled out tonight."

A few dozen paratroopers developed trench foot or got frozen feet because of the extremely cold weather at night. Although they did have blankets, one—or if they were lucky, two—did nothing to prevent their feet from freezing. "A lot of people lost their feet," recalled Private Bonning. "You had to keep moving. That's what the problem was—you would get exhausted because you had to keep moving at night to keep your feet warm, and you wouldn't get any sleep. In the daytime, you were in combat and after not getting any sleep, about the third night, you would be exhausted and fall asleep on guard and all that stuff. It was terrible."[283]

On January 9 H Company sent out a ten-man patrol at 1100 hours to scout Grand-Halleux. They returned at 1500 hours reporting that the town was deserted by the Germans and they had seen an abandoned American jeep and truck. Late in the afternoon, 1st Lt. Harold A. Stueland and six men from the 3rd Battalion S-2 section were dispatched to Ennal, a small hamlet some two miles east of Grand-Halleux. They returned at 1830 hours, having observed enemy troops in Ennal and plotted down the positions of the German observation posts. Pvt. David R. Smith, Headquarters Company, 3rd Battalion, died that day of wounds.

At 1030 hours on January 10, officers of the relieving U.S. 75th Infantry Division showed up at the regimental and battalion command posts. With their clean uniforms and shiney shoes, they seemed to come from another world. It was their first time on the line, and the officers seemed nervous. Runners guided them around the different company positions, which the relieving forces were to take over identically as occupied by the 504th—A Company of the 75th ID relieving A Company of the 504th PIR, B Company of one relieving B Company of the other, and so forth.

Relieved by 2300 hours, the 3rd Battalion boarded trucks headed for a rest area. The enlisted men in the 1st Battalion sector could hardly believe their ears when the news got through. They assembled their gear and marched through the woods, relieved by the 75th U.S. Infantry Division. "We were told to be ready to move out as we were being relieved," recalled Bayley. "A few days before, a German prisoner had already named the time we would be relieved and the unit that would replace us, and these were exactly as he had said. This made us a bit uncomfortable since we wondered what else the Germans knew and how they were getting the information."[284]

Staff Sergeant John B. Isom, 2nd Platoon, felt miserable on that freezing cold night as A Company emerged from the woods out onto a road: "I thought I was going to die, I thought that I was going to freeze to death that night. It was so bad, I was almost crying like a baby. They came to a road in open trucks and said, 'We are getting out of here.' I didn't know where we were going. It was a short ride but the wind made it even worse and I thought, 'Oh my God, I can't stand it much longer.'

"We drove to the woods and made a right turn and all of a sudden we came into a village and they stopped. I was almost crying. We unloaded and each group went to different homes. We entered the house of a Belgian couple and they had a nice fire burning and gave us food. We just sacked down in the living room and stayed there overnight."[285]

At 0300 hours on January 11, the 504th PIR detrucked in Remouchamps, miles away from the front lines. The past weeks in the Ardennes region had cost the regiment 447 casualties: one officer and ten enlisted men were captured; 82 officers and men killed; a further 354 paratroopers wounded. Bayley recalled receiving combat infantry badges as they unloaded in the center of Remouchamps, awarded for their part in blocking the German assault and the counterattack toward the Salm River: "Much to our surprise there was a line of trucks waiting for us. After climbing aboard, we got the welcome news that we were being taken to a town a few miles back for rest, showers, clean clothes, refitting and training in operating light tanks. We unloaded just after daylight in Remouchamps, Belgium, a town located in a deep valley surrounded by low mountains.

"As we unloaded, we were given combat infantry badges, and also discovered that some troopers that arrived a few minutes ahead of us had already had their first sexual intercourse. It was incredible how these guys did this, but it seemed that every place we went those few always made it within 15 minutes or so of arrival.

"Six or eight of us were assigned to share a small two-story house with Belgian civilians, a husband and wife, a couple of kids, and an older person or two. They made us very welcome. My first memory is going upstairs to a bedroom with no furniture, laying my sleeping bag on a bare board floor and passing out in deep sleep. The house did not have a central heater but there was plenty of heat in the kitchen and other downstairs rooms. The soldiers in our group were extremely well behaved, and we shared what we could in the way of food and other luxuries such as candy or cigarettes with the civilians."[286]

First Lieutenant James R. Allmand, Jr. of G Company
earned a Silver Star for knocking out a German machine
gun position at Petit-Halleux on January 8, 1945.
Courtesy: James R. Allmand III

CHAPTER 12

RECUPERATION
REMOUCHAMPS, BELGIUM,
JANUARY 12–24, 1945

A lthough everyone knew that the next winter objective—breaching the vaunted Siegfried Line—it was located several dozen miles away. As not only Tucker, but Gavin realized, this was too far for the battered 504th RCT to go without proper rest and reorganization. Accordingly, the 504th PIR moved to Remouchamps, the 307th AEB company led by Capt. Wesley D. Harris was sent north to the small town of Deigné, and the 376th PFAB went to La Reid, several miles east of Remouchamps.

Tucker's depleted regiment needed far more than a general bunch of replacements—riflemen, mortar gunners, runners, radiomen, medics and junior officers: it now lacked experienced troopers. The majority of the cadre in B and C Companies had been casualties at Cheneux, and experienced company commanders like Captains Thomas Helgeson, Carl Kappel and Albert Milloy had to be replaced. Combat-wise platoon leaders like Lieutenants George Amos, Robert Magruda, Harry Rollins, Joseph Shirk and Richard Smith were equally hard to find.

The decision to disband the American–Canadian First Special Service Force [FSSF] came as a blessing in disguise. The unit had participated in the unopposed invasion of the Aleutian Islands and the battle for the Winter Line in Italy, had fought on the right flank of the 504th RCT at Anzio, and taken part in the invasion of Southern France. By November 1944, they had suffered such heavy losses that the Canadian government decided to withdraw the Canadian contingent, leading to the deactivation of the FSSF in December.

Captain John F. Gray, a former FSSF company commander, was entrusted with the command of H Company. Twenty-year-old Sgt. Arthur E. Duebner from Medford, Wisconsin, joined the 3rd Platoon of E Company as a replacement. "Those of us who were airborne-trained were allowed to transfer in grade. I was a buck sergeant by that time so I went to the 504th by my own request. I had heard of, and knew of the 504th's reputation as a great fighting outfit, and had served near them at Anzio in the FSSF. So it was my kind of outfit.

"I was assigned to E Company, 3rd Platoon, in a small town in Belgium. The platoon was short of NCO's and so I was made squad leader of the 1st Squad. This was a relatively tough spot for a stranger to walk into, it being an old, established outfit, but in a very few days I was accepted as one of them! Weapons seemed to be in very short supply and all that was available was an old .03-A4 sniper rifle, and that is what they issued me."[287]

D Battery of the 376th Parachute Field Artillery Battalion was disbanded on January 17, freeing a few dozen gunners. Some, like 1st Lt. John W. Spooner, transferred to the 504th PIR, while Pvt. Joseph E. Jobora of C Company, 307th Airborne Engineers, changed his unit for I Company, 504th, on his own request. But these additions, although extremely valuable, were still insufficient to provide the required number of replacements. Quartermaster personnel were even transferred to the airborne troops from the Normandy Base Section in France, including Sgt. Frank Juback and T/4 Elmer C. Wincentsen, who joined D Company on January 16.

If the 82nd Airborne Division was to be kept on the line, the high number of casualties it had sustained in the first six weeks of the Bulge presented little alternative other than disbanding the independent 509th and 551st Parachute Infantry Battalions. These battalions had lost more than 600 men each: numbers in the 509th were down to 54, and the 551st had 110 paratroopers at the time it was withdrawn from the front lines. Some of the survivors had already joined the 504th PIR by this time, and others joined a few days or weeks later.

"We were billeted for a week or ten days in living quarters above a bakery," recalled Private Bill Bonning, 3rd Platoon, B Company. "We would drop a grenade from a footbridge over the river that runs through the town and scoop the fish out and cook them, of course not realizing that it was also a food source for the townspeople during the war. That was quite disastrous for them. But I went back in 2004 with my family to apologize.

"I was made a staff sergeant and Harold Florey and I decided we would go to Liège, Belgium. We had just got out of the Battle of Bulge and wanted some free time, but we couldn't get a pass. We hitchhiked to Liège, which was about 50 or 60 miles away and had a great time. The bars were open and would have live music—the war was still going on—but they would play a tune and everybody would start dancing. When a buzz bomb came overhead the music would stop and the buzz bombs would explode in a different area and then the music would start and everybody would start dancing again.

"That night the MP's rounded the paratroopers all up and put us in a Liège jail. There were about a hundred of us and they missed the .45 I had in a shoulder holster in my ETO jacket. Major Gorham came with six or eight six-by-six trucks, got us out of the prison and put us on the trucks back to Remouchamps. I got busted and lost my stripes in Remouchamps."[288]

When Tucker's troopers woke in Remouchamps on January 12, it was the first time in weeks they did not have to fear incoming mortar or artillery fire. Almost just as good, they could smoke cigarettes after dark! They did, however, hear the nightly buzzing of V-2 rockets aimed at Antwerp and London. The weather had brightened and S/Sgt. John Isom, A Company, was surprised to hear that they were to going to take a test drive in a tank. "The next morning it cleared up and there were American tanks out on the roadside. They said, 'Sometime you may have to drive a tank.' So one by one we got in the tank. We drove it up and down the road, came back, then somebody else took over and drove the tank. It was steered by stick. I found it fairly easy."[289]

Edwin Bayley of the same company recalled that "a tank was provided for training purposes, so if we perchance found an unused, serviceable tank in combat we would be able to drive and use it. The men took turns driving it up the hill to above the town center then back down again, at which point another driver took over. The only thing they didn't teach us was how to fire the cannon."[290]

First Lieutenant Breard, a platoon leader in B Company, found the experience a little more adventuresome than Bayley and Isom. When his turn came, he drove down the street and "hit the door of a house with the gun. It came right on it, hit the door, and broke it open. There were people in there eating breakfast! I backed down and got back on the road, and we drove back. But I was not a good tank driver after just one lesson!"[291]

Several men left the regiment with trench foot or frostbite, like Sgt. Mitchell E. Rech of A Company: "They hadn't developed the type of footwear that we really needed. I suffered from frostbite and they shipped me back to England to thaw me out. Then they sent me back again. So I had about two weeks in England and then I was back with the unit again."[292]

Sgt. George Leoleis, a non-commissioned officer in I Company, was evacuated by ambulance to a field hospital in Reims due to frozen feet. From there he was flown to London and admitted to a large hospital. His ward was full of men with the same condition, with feet that slowly turned from purple to black before being amputated. Unwilling to submit to this fate, Leoleis asked a nurse for some warm oil, and rubbed his feet all night long to bring the circulation back: "The nurse would come over every hour or so and talk to me while the others slept. She tried to get me to get some sleep, but all I would say to her is 'Get me some more hot oil,' and I continued to rub. Morning came and the doctor made his rounds. He stopped at the bed next to mine and told the guy that today was it for him. Just like that. I saw him fold his arms across his eyes to cover them and not let anyone see him. I bit my teeth a little tighter and silently promised myself that they would not cut off mine.

"The doctor then came over to me and after chatting for a minute or two looked at my feet. I watched him very closely and tried to read everything in his eyes and expression. He then told me that if my feet didn't start getting back to normal in the next couple of days that they would have to amputate mine, too. I looked at him and shook my head. 'No way!' I said in a loud voice.

"Two days passed and when the doctor came to see me that morning, he showed surprise that my feet had started to improve. Some of the deep blue color was fading. 'What did you do for him, nurse?' 'Nothing, doctor, we just gave him the oil and he's been rubbing them practically day and night,' she told him. He just shook his head and left. The following day my feet felt real good and the doctor allowed me to take some steps. The hurt was almost gone. Another two days and I was walking around. The color of my feet returned to normal and I kept rubbing. The circulation came back. A week went by, and by this time I was walking around like new. The doctor saw me that day and told me that was good enough to be sent to a replacement camp area and probably back to my outfit."[293]

Sergeant Leoleis eventually rejoined I Company in Remouchamps: "There were a lot of new men I had not met before and they wondered who the hell I was. The company had gone through a lot of changes but you never realized it 'till you left and then came back. I almost felt like an outsider. If you stopped and looked too close you would realize there weren't many men left who started out in Africa. Maybe a handful and a lot of the men were being replaced by new men.

"At this stage of the war you really didn't think of that anymore, and some replacements became bodies that filled out your roster. It's a hard thing to admit, but we were being fed as fodder so fast that we did not get to know each other. The thing that counted was that even though these men had just come in, they always gave a good account of themselves and did their jobs as well as any of the old-timers."[294]

First Lieutenant Kiernan, A Company, recalled that the men "just kind of lulled around and rested" in Remouchamps. "We stayed with a very old man and a younger wife. We were able to get coal and they were very happy, as it was virtually unavailable for the civilian population then. So we burned it in their stove and kept the room we were in warm and their house as well. So she was glad to have us. Plus we were able to give a few rations and that made her very happy. It was a very nice break in that town. The other thing I remember is that buzz bombs used to fly right over. Remouchamps was deep in a valley so we had no fear of a buzz bomb ever hitting it there, even though some that malfunctioned sometimes did. About all I ever did there was sleep and rest up."[295]

Lieutenant Breard was disappointed about the meagre rations distributed to the 1st Battalion. He got the idea to drive to an American supply depot and ask the officer in charge if he could make a trade: "I had good bottle of scotch and I asked [Maj. John] Berry if I could go trade the scotch for some rations. Berry said, 'Get all the meat you can get.' So I took a truck and I went down to a rations dump. There was four feet snow up there near Verviers. I went in and put it down and said, 'I'll trade you this for all the meat I can carry back to my battalion. We are just back from the lines and can't get the rations we need.' He said, 'For that, you can take all you want.'

"It was an American depot, situated on a railroad track with rations on either side. So we drove down there and loaded as much meat as we could and tried to get some eggs and some other things too. We really did do a good job. They were happy and the goods were fine. But I didn't have my bottle of whisky then."[296]

Captain Bruns recalled that "to my complete astonishment the citizens opened their doors and took us into their homes like long-lost relatives. The mayor, a medical doctor, had the 504th doctors to his home for dinner. We pledged that when the war was over we would exchange children for their language and cultural education."[297]

Major Ivan Roggen, the regimental surgeon, and Major Abdallah Zakby, 3rd Battalion XO, received a seven-day recuperation leave on the French

Riviera. "A wonderful week!" recalled Roggen. "I went with one of the line officers, Major Zakby. He spoke the language well and was what we call a real 'operator.' I remember the black market was in full force, and everything was very expensive. Major Zakby had a number of souvenir pistols which he sold to the French (I believe at $700 each), and was active in the black market. I helped him with a personal medical problem, and he returned the favor with a bacon and egg breakfast that cost about $100 on the black market."[298]

On January 17 Colonel Tucker learned that Captain Wade H. McIntyre, C Company, had not been able to use his left arm since he had been wounded in Holland. He relieved McIntyre from his command and sent him back to the hospital. The executive officer, 1st Lt. James E. Dunn, assumed command of C Company and led over the next couple of weeks. That same day, Tucker wrote to McIntyre: "I wish to commend you for your actions during the last eleven months while a member of this organization. Your loyalty, devotion to duty and conscientious application to your work is deserving of the highest praise. It is unfortunate that the wound received in action during the Holland Campaign should deprive this unit of your service."[299]

The 82nd Airborne Division spent 12 days in Corps Reserve while the XVIII Airborne Corps attacked in the direction of St. Vith. In Remouchamps the men were re-equipped and trained in the use of the German panzerfaust (a bazooka which can be fired only once) and taught how to zero in the newly issued weapons. Meanwhile, the war seemed miles away, and the veterans wondered when they would be called up again. They knew from experience that the 504th RCT would not be long held in reserve. Their intuition would soon prove to be right.

CHAPTER 13

ADVANCE BY ATTRITION
HUNNANGE AND HERRESBACH,
BELGIUM, JANUARY 25–29, 1945

O n January 25, S/Sgt. William V. Rice, the H Company, 2nd Platoon platoon sergeant, wrote in his secretly kept diary: "Regular camp duties. Be ready to move out at any given time. Have been briefed to jump off point St. Vith—doesn't sound too bad. Lots of woods before the Siegfried Line though. First heard of Lieutenant Rivers losing his brother in France."[300] Lt. Roland La Riviere, the only brother of 1st Lt. Richard G. ("Rivers") La Riviere, had been killed in France. When the Red Cross informed Chaplain Kozak of his death, the chaplain asked 1st Lt. Megellas, Rivers' best friend, to give his buddy the terrible news. Rivers was watching a movie in Remouchamps when Megellas tapped his friend on the shoulder and motioned him to come outside, where he told him that Roland had died.

Second Lieutenant Charles E. Zastrow of E Company was in a small group of officers and men trucked the next morning, January 26, to the Belgian town of Hunnange to prepare an assembly area. He recalled the movement in a letter to his parents: "Certainly hated to leave the little Belgium town I last wrote from—swell little place. I left about 12 hours before the rest—advance party—to find a place for the battalion to stay that night. Anyhow, when the whole bunch left, they tell me the people wept and kissed them as if they were their own sons."[301]

That evening the remainder of Colonel Tucker's 504th PIR were transferred from Remouchamps to Hunnange by truck. But there was still no news on any objectives in the upcoming attack. It had been made clear that the regiment would be committed on short notice, although no indication had been given as to when and where.

At 0900 hours on January 27 Lieutenant Colonel Cook, Captain Keep and 1st Lt. James H. Goethe (G Company) drove up to Division Headquarters to find out more about the situation. Returning to the 3rd Battalion CP at 1335 hours, Cook held an officers' conference with his company commanders and battalion staff. At 1500 hours Captain Keep, 1st Lt. Virgil F. Carmichael (Battalion S-2) and one officer from each rifle company were to acquaint themselves with the route, move to a forward assembly area, and locate points to place guides. Meanwhile, Lieutenant Colonel Cook flew over the battalion objective in an L-4 Piper Cub reconnaissance plane from the 376th Parachute Field Artillery Battalion.

Cook returned after a few hours and was summoned to Division Headquarters at 1925 hours to receive the final details on the attack order. He returned an hour and a half later and shared the news with his company commanders: that night the battalion would move to the forward assembly area, and jump off at 0600 hours. There would be no accompanying artillery barrage; the plan was to surprise the Germans in their sleeping bags. First Lieutenant Goethe's G Company would be in the lead, followed by Captain Burriss' I Company, and Capt. George M. Warfield's Headquarters Company and the Battalion Staff. Acting as battalion reserve, Capt. John F. Gray's H Company would bring up the rear. Two squads of engineers from the Regimental Demolition Platoon, a company of 4.2-inch mortars, and the 3rd Platoon of C Company, 740th TB, would be in support. Their ultimate objective was a wooded hilltop about a mile from Herresbach, the 2nd Battalion objective.

The 3rd Battalion received some last-minute replacements, survivors of the disbanded 551st Parachute Infantry Battalion. The other two battalions also received some replacements, but the majority were needed to spearhead the regimental attack. Cpl. John M. ("Mel") Clark and Privates Cooper Blakeney and George Regan were among those to join the 3rd Battalion. Arriving on the 27th at approximately 2200 hours, they had only eight hours to get to know their new commander and brothers-in-arms before being sent into battle.[302]

At 0335 hours that night the battalion closed out of the assembly area some two miles northeast of St. Vith and moved to the forward assembly area to prepare for the attack. Precisely at 0600 hours G Company pushed off in an easterly direction through knee-deep snow-covered fields, which were almost invisible in the darkness and fog. Almost 30 minutes later Lieutenant Goethe radioed Cook that his men had broken through the enemy defenses, killing six Germans and capturing seven others.

Lieutenant Goethe had a strange encounter as he talked to one of the German prisoners captured in the approach to the Siegfried Line. The prisoner shared the same last name and was also a parachutist.[303] The citation for the Bronze Star he later received for his actions in the Battle of Bulge reports that Goethe "led his company as the spearhead unit of the Regimental attack towards the Siegfried Line through a heavily wooded area covered with snow, overrunning all enemy fortifications, ammunition dumps and command posts for 2000 yards, capturing 50 prisoners and killing scores without a casualty."[304]

The 1st Platoon led by 1st Lt. Harry J. Frear spearheaded the G Company attack. According to the citation for his Silver Star, Frear "distinguished himself by establishing himself as the point of his platoon, which was the spearhead of his battalion's assault upon the outlying fortifications of the Siegfried Line. In an action lasting 11 hours and fought in waist-deep snow drifts, First Lieutenant Frear displayed a high order of aggressive and courageous leadership by personally entering enemy occupied bunkers on five different occasions and killing and routing the occupants with hand grenades. He killed seven Germans who were attempting to hold up the advance of his platoon with his Thompson submachine gun, one of whom was later identified as the battalion commander of the enemy troops in the vicinity.

"Throughout the entire action he completely disregarded all consideration of his personal safety as he directed BAR and machine-gun fire upon enemy strongpoints. By his exhibition of fearless disregard of the intense enemy fire, he instilled great confidence in his men and inspired them to the successful completion of a hazardous mission under the most trying conditions of weather and terrain. His conduct during this action was such to reflect highly upon himself and the United States Airborne Forces."[305]

At 1030 hours the battalion had reached point 11 on Lieutenant Colonel Cook's phase line map. They made contact with a patrol of the neighboring 325th Glider Infantry Regiment, but an attempt to locate E Company failed. Lieutenant Zastrow of E Company recalled advancing "about seven miles" that first day. "Ours was the only company from our battalion that was in on the attack—we were right flank security for one of the other battalions of our regiment. Started at 0500 in the morning, and kept marching until 2100 at night—continually—with snow above our knees all the way. Never once were we on a road. If you wanted to see a bunch of weary boys, you should have seen us after marching those 16 hours. All we ran across was a patrol of 12 Germans—got 5—guess they kept retreating in front of us."[306]

In the 3rd Battalion sector, Lieutenant Colonel Cook realized that the G Company troopers were getting tired. He ordered them to halt at 1300 hours, when I Company started to pass through. "Snow waist-deep, can advance only 1000 yards per hour," wrote Major Zakby in the 3rd Battalion log. Meanwhile a press photographer took photos of G Company advancing alongside Sherman tanks.

By 1600 hours some 20 Germans and five vehicles were spotted on the left flank of the battalion column about 500 yards away. Major Zakby ordered Captain Gray of H Company to dispatch a patrol to investigate. About 30 minutes later, during the time they were out, the battalion reached its objective and started to prepare for the night. It then transpired that the bedrolls and backpacks, which had forcibly been left behind at the forward assembly area, could not be brought up. This meant little to no protection against the extreme cold.

The H Company patrol returned around 1700 hours and reported that the Germans seemed to be preparing a counterattack. As his battalion dug in on the wooded hill overlooking Herresbach on the valley floor about a mile and a half away, Lieutenant Colonel Cook got a new idea. He ordered his company commanders to meet him at his makeshift battalion headquarters, which was then being set up in some slit trenches. "That town there is in Wellems' zone," said Cook as he pointed down to the village, "but Ed's been held up far to our right rear by heavy opposition. So if your boys want to sleep in those houses tonight, we're going to have to chase the Krauts out of town."[307]

Cook's idea to capture Herresbach to get warm billets for the night impressed his company commanders, who consented to the idea. He then radioed Colonel Tucker for permission to launch an attack. Tucker agreed and came forward with Majors Fordyce Gorham (Regimental S-2) and Mack Shelley (Regimental S-3) to overlook the objective from the hilltop. He conferred with Lieutenant Colonel Cook and they decided to use the 3rd Battalion reserve, H Company. First Lieutenant Charles B. Powers' four Sherman tanks from the 3rd Platoon, 740th TB, would provide the fire support and transport from the base of the hill to the village of Herresbach. Two depleted platoons of paratroopers could be placed on them. There were three platoons in H Company, but it was easy to choose the ones to go: the

Privates Willard Pike and Johnny Collins of D Company in Sicily, 1943. Pike was killed by mortar fire near Fosse on January 4, 1945.
Courtesy: Brenda Taylor

Monument for the 551st Parachute Infantry Battalion in Rochelinval, Belgium. Although the depleted battalion took the village against all odds, it would be a Pyrrhic victory.
Author's collection

German dead lay strewn along a road between St. Vith and Büllingen,
late January 1945. Across the road is a two-man outpost of the 504th
Parachute Infantry Regiment. *Courtesy: Mandle family*

Close-up photo of the two-man outpost. *Courtesy: Mandle family*

First Lieutenant Harry Frear of G Company. His platoon spearheaded the regimental counterattack on January 28 until Herresbach. For his bravery and able leadership he received the Silver Star. *Courtesy: Joy Frear*

PFC Oscar Smith of H Company was decorated with a Bronze Star for delivering an urgent dispatch under fire for resupply of ammunition at Herresbach. *Courtesy: Mary Gagliano*

Lieutenant Leonard Harmon Jr., Sergeant Al Vrabac and Lieutenant
Hubbard Burnum Jr. in Nijmegen, October 1944. Vrabac shot the German
who mortally wounded Lieutenant Kemble. *Courtesy: Tom Vrabac*

Angus Giles Jr. (right) and his brother Oscar,
1942. Angus served with A Company and was
killed at Manderfeld. *Courtesy: Greg Korbelic*

PFC Julius Lasslo of A Company
wrote to Angus Giles' sister, to tell
her how her brother was killed at
Manderfeld. *Courtesy: Michael Lasslo*

Sergeant Ervin Shaffer of A Company was promoted to squad leader on the day the regiment attacked the Siegfried Line. He was evacuated the next day with frozen feet. *Courtesy: Ervin Shaffer*

Right: Private Henry Girard, Jr. of A Company was one of six men in the 3rd Platoon of A Company who were still standing after crossing open fields toward Manderfeld. *Courtesy: Robin Holick*

The 3rd Platoon of B Company on the railroad tracks, waiting for transportation. Seated first left is PFC Bill Bonning, standing with his hands in his pockets is PFC Jack Cocozza. *Courtesy: Bill Bonning*

Captain Herbert Norman of E Company, photographed in 1942. Norman was severely wounded in both arms at the Siegfried Line and died of wounds. *Courtesy: Ken Norman*

PFC Arthur W. Bates, Jr. of A Company was killed on the Mertesrott Heights. His daughter Bonnie was born one month later. *Courtesy: Bonnie Skiles*

Protestant Chaplain Delbert Kuehl (left) and Lieutenant Vincent Voss of the Grave Registration (right) at the Siegfried Line, Feburary 1945. *Courtesy: Robert Stern*

Three rows of dragon's teeth near Schmithof, Germany, February 1945. *Courtesy: David Finney*

Sergeant Sylvester Barbu, radio operator in F Company, used Lieutenant Bramson's .45 pistol to shoot the two Germans who had wounded his assistant platoon leader. *Courtesy: Craig Caba*

CAPT. JACK M. BARTLEY, 30, paratrooper who died in action Dec. 21 in Belgium, began his military training at 17, while still a student in Mount Clemens High school. He attended Citizens' Military Training Camp several s u m m e r s, continuing w   ROTC work at the University   f Michigan, and becoming a member of the National Guard. He was commissioned a second lieutenant in the army in October, 1939, and had been overseas 22 months, taking part in the campaign in Africa, the invasion of Sicily and Italy, and went to England for D-Day last June, entering continental warfare by way of Holland. He had made 22 successful parachute jumps, he told his parents, Mr. and Mrs. Otto Bartley, in a late letter. His wife, Mrs. Mary Bartley makes her home in Kankakee, Ill.

Captain Jack Bartley was killed while leading a platoon of replacements at Monceau. *Courtesy Joni Bartley*

First Lieutenant G.P. Crockett was killed by machine-gun fire at Neuhof while leading B Company of the 325th GIR. *Courtesy Joseph Bass*

The devastated town of Bergstein, where the 1st Battalion
CP was established. *Courtesy: Moffatt Burriss*

Paratroopers in a truck drive through the shell-torn village
of Huertgen, February 1945. *Courtesy: Moffatt Burriss*

Second Lieutenant Myles Abramson of F Company recuperating in Paris from frozen feet, February 1945. Note his sad eyes—he wrongly believed for weeks that his good friend Robert Bramson had been mortally wounded at the Siegfried Line. *Courtesy: Victor Abramson*

Captain Louis Hauptfleisch, Regimental S-1 officer, in Belgium. *Courtesy: Mandle family*

Sergeant First Class John B. Isom of A Company while on leave in England, early April 1945. *Courtesy: John Isom*

First Lieutenant James A. Kiernan of A Company on leave in Liège, March 1945. His decision to assault another hill at Manderfeld and flank the German guns saved many lives. *Courtesy: James Kiernan*

First Lieutenant Vincent P. Ralph of the OSS joined I Company in early February 1945 as a platoon leader. *Courtesy: Elizabeth Doyle*

Sergeant Meldon Hurlbert of C Company, 307th Airborne Engineers Battalion, participated in all the WWII campaigns of the 82nd Airborne Division, and was often attached to the 504th Parachute Infantry Regiment. *Courtesy: John Cutright*

Lieutenant Colonel Albert Marin, Colonel Ira Swift, Colonel Robert Weinecke, Colonel Charles Billingslea and Major General James Gavin ready to toast at a Prop Blast party in early March 1945. *Courtesy: Mandle family*

The new officers drink from high-stemmed glasses as part of their initation ceremony. Colonel Tucker stands behind the table on the right. *Courtesy: Mandle family*

Lieutenant Colonel Julian Cook sits in the rear, setting the cadence with his boot while Lieutenant Richard LaRiviere behind him counts with his fingers. *Courtesy: Mandle family*

Major General James Gavin in March 1945 pinning the Presidential Unit Citation to the guidon of Headquarters Company for their gallant action at Cheneux. *Courtesy: Mandle family*

First Lieutenant Reneau Breard of A Company is awarded the Silver Star by Major General Gavin, March 1945. *Courtesy: Reneau Breard*

Second Lieutenant Wayne
Fetters of C Company is
decorated by Major General
Gavin. *Courtesy: Beth Tweed*

Major General James M. Gavin, commanding the 82
'All-American" airborne division is shown pinning
silver star medal on 2nd. Lt. Wayne M. Fetters, of this ci
A member of the 504th parachute infantry, Lt. Fetters v
decorated for heroic action during the battle of the "bulg

The 1st Battalion marches past Major General Gavin and Colonel
Tucker in Camp Laon, March 1945. *Courtesy: Mandle family*

Private George Silvasy of
G Company and his bride
Winnie on their wedding
day in Leicester, England.
Courtesy: Karen Wald

Staff Sergeant Paul Mann of B Company and his fiancée Josephine
upon his return to the United States, 1945. *Courtesy: Cody Mann*

Second Battalion staff in June 1945. Left to right: Captain Victor Campana, Lieutenant Colonel Edward Wellems and Major William Colville. Officers in the back unidentified. *Courtesy: Mandle family*

The 504th Regimental Honor Guard presents the colors at Tempelhof Airfield on the occasion of the award of the Belgian Fourragère 1940 for their brave actions during the Battle of the Bulge. *Courtesy: Mandle family*

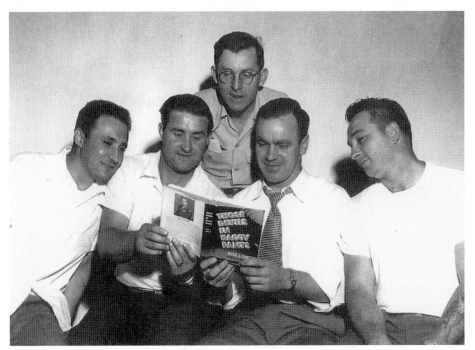

Dominic Ciconte, Dan Serilla (Sokal), George McAllister (Winters) and Albert Feroni with Boyd Carter at top reading a 1952 edition of Ross Carter's classic war memoir *Those Devils in Baggy Pants. Courtesy: Feroni family*

The author during a visit to the American Cemetery at Henri-Chapelle, Belgium, in August 2014. *Author's collection*

2nd Platoon led by La Riviere and the 3rd led by Megellas, seasoned commanders who had both been with the company longer than the leader of the 1st Platoon.

At 1800 hours the attack jumped off with Megellas' platoon in the lead, followed by Lieutenant La Riviere and his men. Before they made it half way into town, the column ran into a company of Germans counterattacking down the road towards the 3rd Battalion position. This clash started a series of sharp engagements cumulating in the capture of Herresbach within an hour.

Silver Stars were awarded for many brave acts that took place during the battle. Lieutenant Megellas' citation reads as follows: "After breaking a trail across country for 12 hours in deep, dry snow, First Lieutenant Megellas, a platoon leader, was ordered to advance with his platoon and two supporting tanks along the main road leading into Herresbach. About one mile from the town, his platoon was fired upon by about 200 Germans forming for a defense. Quickly grasping the situation, he led a frontal assault on the startled enemy who attempted to fight back. First Lieutenant Megellas' direction and leadership of his men was so superb that within ten minutes the entire force of enemy was either killed or captured, or fled into the town. He then reorganized his platoon, and with the two supporting tanks followed the enemy into the town. Braving heavy enemy sniper and rifle fire, he personally took a leading part in flushing the enemy out of their houses, killing eight and capturing five enemy. As a result of First Lieutenant Megellas' fearless leadership and skillful handling of his men, over 100 enemy were killed, 180 captured, and large amounts of valuable equipment fell into our hands. This feat was accomplished without the loss of a single man wounded or killed. First Lieutenant Megellas demonstrated a remarkable degree of tactical skill and a brand of courageous leadership which reflects highly upon himself and the Airborne Forces."[308]

Pvt. Harold J. Sullivan, a rifleman in La Riviere's platoon recalled meeting the German company on the way to Herresbach as they "came down the same road to attack us. I don't know who was more surprised. But I know who had the best firepower. I was on the left-hand side of a tank and everybody was firing to the side and out front. Clips seemed to pop out of the M1 very fast. A lot of dead Germans were on the road and alongside the road."[309]

As soon as the German company had been disposed of, the advance continued on the tanks through the knee-deep snow-covered road into Herresbach. Cpl. Frederic P. Andrews was wounded while lying "in the shadow of the tank turret, aiming through my rifle sight. One of them [the Germans] turned around and shot back. I got a piece of shrapnel in my eyeball. They said the whole side of my face crinkled up and was bleeding. My buddies thought I had been shot in the head. One of them said, 'Well, damn, they shot old Andy!' And the other one said, 'What was the idiot sitting up there for, anyhow?' It knocked me off the tank, too. I bet that German sniper marked one off, thinking for sure he shot me, too."[310]

During the ride Pfc. Gordon V. Brewer, the 3rd Platoon machine gunner, told Lieutenant Megellas that he had expended two bandoliers of .30-caliber machine-gun rounds. Jumping off the tanks at the outskirts of the town, Megellas learned that most of his men and he himself were low on ammunition after the shootout. He summoned his radio operator, Pfc. Oscar Smith of Milwaukee, Wisconsin, to radio Captain Gray that they needed an ammunition supply. Smith tried to raise contact but failed to get through. Megellas knew they would not be able to continue without replenishing their ammunition, and decided the only option was to send Smith back to the wooded hill with a hand-written message, knowing that the remainder of H Company was following on foot. Smith dashed back with the note across snow-covered fields, making a perfect target for German snipers. For his bravery in delivering the message, he was later awarded the Bronze Star.

While Smith was gone, the Germans in town counterattacked, supported by a Mark V tank. The machine gunner opened up on the waiting Americans, who ducked for cover in front of their Shermans. Megellas recalled that the tanks "were behind us and not in position to engage the enemy tank. Instinctively I charged toward the oncoming tank. Taking advantage of available cover along the side of the road, I was able to get close enough to throw a Gammon grenade; it hit the side of the tank, knocking out its tracking mechanism and stopped it cold. With the tank disabled, I charged up to its side and dropped a fragmentation grenade down the open hatch of the turret. We now had removed the last obstacle to our entrance into Herresbach, but we still had not received more ammunition."[311]

Meanwhile Lieutenant Powers managed to maneuver his tanks into better position and provide covering fire, but his own tank soon ran out of ammunition. Powers dismounted and directed the action of his other tanks on foot under heavy enemy fire. After his ammunition was brought up, he climbed back into his tank and led his platoon forward in another attack, knocking out another German tank. For his bravery he was awarded the Silver Star.

Their tanks firing at every possible target in town, Lieutenants La Riviere and Megellas led their men through Herresbach, shooting as they went. The 3rd Platoon runner, Pfc. Julian Romero, was disarming a German soldier when Lieutenant Megellas appeared and cut the German down with a tommy gun to revenge the death of his buddy La Riviere's brother.

"Town in our hands," Major Zakby recorded around 1900 hours in the 3rd Battalion log. "Approximately 100 dead Krauts and about 100 PW's. PW's still coming in. We have no casualties." Captain Gray and 1st Lt. Edward Sims brought up the remainder of H Company in Herresbach and congratulated Lieutenant Megellas on the capture of the town. They also brought the news that H Company was to set up a defensive position in the northern part of town, while G Company would defend the southern half. I Company would be in battalion reserve. Lieutenant Megellas took Brewer and his assistant gunner, Pfc. Enrico S. Malizia, and placed them in a foxhole on an outpost position with their .30-caliber machine gun a few hundred yards outside town.

At 1950 hours Major Zakby recorded: "H patrol in: contacted enemy— had small arms fight. Enemy withdrew. Also contacted 325 [Glider Infantry]—they are behind us but are getting along fine." Meanwhile a G Company patrol was dispatched to make contact with the 1st Battalion. Lieutenant Colonel Wellems' 2nd Battalion followed the 3rd into Herresbach at 2030 hours, thankful for a warm place to spend the night. Lieutenant Zastrow was impressed by the heroic action of the two H Company platoons in Herresbach, which he thought was a German town. He wrote to his parents that they had reached their phase line, the high ground around the town, about 2100. "Had been planned for two battalions to take the town. Instead two platoons of the battalion for whom we were flank security decided they should sleep in houses that night—pretty cold and snowing hard. So they started out with two tanks for the town. As they started down the road they ran into about a battalion of Germans coming from town with the intention of attacking us. First thing the Germans knew, half of them were lying in the ditch and most of the remainder was captured. Killed about 250 and captured as many more—that in itself was a miracle—about 65 men against 700—but the most miraculous part of it was that our casualties were zero. Didn't lose any men until we got into town—sniper fire."[312]

As the 1st Platoon of G Company neared the outskirts of Herresbach, it became clear that there was still some mopping-up to do. Bringing up the rear, the platoon sergeant, T/Sgt. Paul Grear, knocked out an enemy strongpoint that took the advancing Americans under heavy fire from a house on their flank. According to the citation for his Silver Star, "The platoon was pinned down and suffered several casualties. Quickly moving towards the enemy position, with a BAR taken from a wounded man, he opened fire on an enemy machine-gun emplacement in front of the house, killing the three-man crew. Picking up a bazooka, he moved to within 50 feet of the house, despite the intense small arms fire striking all about him. With three rounds he silenced the enemy guns. Then with the aid of another man he rushed the building, capturing five of its occupants and killing four who attempted to resist capture. The bravery of Technical Sergeant Grear reflects great credit upon himself and the Armed Forces."[313]

Major Berry's 1st Battalion, in reserve during the attack toward Herresbach, nevertheless had no easy day. German artillery fire caused several casualties in A Company, 2nd Platoon: the platoon leader, 1st Lt. Earl V. Morin; his platoon medic, Pfc. Fidenceo Lujan; and five other platoon members were all wounded by shrapnel and evacuated to the rear. Morin nevertheless died of wounds the next day. At dawn on January 28, Private First Class Bayley, 1st Platoon, recalled being informed that his unit was "invading Germany and heading for the Siegfried Line. We were moving out with the 1st Division on our left and the 87th Division, Third Army, on our right. In later years I wondered about this. It seemed as if it was preordained that I should be in this area at this time. I had trained for a long time in the United States with the 87th. Here I was in virtually the same area but with a different division several hundred feet away.

"We proceeded into the woods and waited. Finally, a flare was seen in the sky and we moved out. We met no opposition as we moved through the woods and finally onto a road in a wide cut in heavy woods on both sides. The snow was deep and it also began snowing heavily. Men sent off into woods to patrol for enemy [positions] had it very rough as they had to walk through about 24 inches of deep snow. Some of our officers were trying to ride at the head of the line in a jeep. They weren't doing too badly at first, being dug out now and then. I think they finally had to abandon it.

"Some of the Germans must have anticipated a long stay in the woods as some very substantial log cabins had been constructed. There were signs that the Germans had been there but left some time before we arrived. Sporadic artillery fire bore down on us in the road. Once in a while someone would be hit by a several-inch-sized piece of shrapnel. Often the hits were in the abdomen. Many of these men immediately lost consciousness. Someone would stop, open up the man's clothing, and look at the large wound, which usually was not bleeding externally. Sulfa drug would be powdered over and into the wound, a gauze compress applied and stuck down, and the man tagged for a medical pick-up—hopefully before he died.

"Usually we never saw these men again, possibly because of long hospital stays in France, England, or even the United States. Sometimes a man would emit eerie shrieks when grievously wounded. We did everything to get this out of our minds. [...] Because of the deep snow, we didn't know when the medical evacuation team would show up or even if the poor soldier would be buried in the new snow to the extent that he might be overlooked. A rifle attached to a bayonet could be stuck in the ground to indicate that a soldier was under the snow.

"In at least one event where a trooper received a serious abdominal injury from shrapnel, I remember that Lieutenant Kiernan showed care and concern for his men, as he was the person who immediately went to the man's assistance, dressed out the wound, bandaged it, and tagged the unconscious man, whom we had to leave lying in the snow. [...] I remember at this time that the lieutenant's eyeglasses fell off [...] and we all had a few anxious moments while probing through the snow and eventually finding them."[314]

The company's mail orderly, T/5 Michael Farrell, Jr., from Massachusetts, was severely wounded by German artillery fire during the advance across the open fields. Being in a non-combatant assignment, Farrell could have stayed behind, but he requested to stay with his buddies. He died the same day of sustained wounds. The communications sergeant, T/4 Harland A. Tempel, was also wounded.

The 376th Parachute Field Artillery Battalion suffered a terrible loss when one of their jeeps took a full hit. The shell killed the driver, Pfc. John R. Gugerty, and 1st Lt. Whitney S. Russell, and seriously wounded T/4 Edward D. Savaria and Pfc. Richard Hunt. Russell's forward observation team had been on the way to relieve Capt. Frank D. Boyd and his observers when they were surprised by enemy artillery fire.[315]

As darkness fell on January 28, the 1st Battalion bedded in for the night. The men had trudged all day through heavy snow and were very tired. It was all but impossible to dig foxholes with the ground as hard as rock and covered with a thick carpet of snow. "After an extremely trying day," wrote Bayley, "we put in for the night. Some of us joined our shelter halves to make a small tent for protection against the continually falling snow in bitterly cold weather. Foxhole buddies among the group seemed to change almost from day to day because of personnel changes due to combat fatalities and wounding. We had lost a few troopers during the day to [German] artillery or exhaustion. In civilian life one doesn't realize the punishment and fatigue one's body can take and survive when necessary. Digging in was nearly impossible in the heavy snow and frozen ground."[316]

Late that same evening at Herresbach, Lieutenant Megellas decided to check on Privates First Class Brewer and Malizia at the outpost, but found only an empty foxhole. "They had just been assigned to my platoon as replacements the day before the attack on Herresbach. There was no sign of casualties, so I reported them as missing in action [MIA]. After we were relieved from front-line duty in the Battle of the Bulge, I learned that they had been captured and were being held in a prisoner-of-war camp in Germany. In May 1945, when the war was in its final days, American forces overran the camp and freed them."[317]

By midnight it was possible to take good stock of the outcome of the battle for Herresbach. American losses had been extremely light: Sgt. James J. Wright of H Company wounded in the stomach and Brewer and Malizia MIA, compared to 138 German dead and 182 prisoners.[318] Most of the Germans belonged to *Hauptmann* (Captain) Egon von Peller's 2nd Abteilung of the 3rd Fallschirmjäger Artillery Regiment, 3rd Fallschirmjäger Division. The German counterattack on H Company as they moved on towards Herresbach was most likely their last, futile attempt to defend the 75mm guns in the town. This unbelievable achievement was brought to the attention of the press, and newspaper reporters were sent to interview Maj. Fordyce Gorham. The incident was big news all over the U.S. and along the Allied front lines. For security purposes the 504 RCT was never mentioned by name.

During the cover of darkness, the Germans tried to fool H Company outposts in the northeastern sector by identifying themselves as the 325th GIR. They had probably pulled the same trick when they captured Brewer and Malizia. This time, H Company men let them come in, capturing five Germans and chasing away the rest with well-placed artillery, machine-gun, and tank fire.

At 0400 hours Colonel Tucker shifted G Company to the north, making the 2nd Battalion responsible for the defense of the southern sector of Herresbach. Lieutenant Colonel Cook received orders to resume the attack to the north the following morning at 0600 hours, with G Company on the left and H Company on the right flank. Four tanks from C Company, 740th TB, would support H Company. Shortly after 0400 hours, he instructed his company commanders to prepare for the upcoming assault.

At 0600 hours on January 29 it appeared impossible to start the attack: the tanks were not yet ready and there was a delay in lifting supporting artillery fire. This delay proved fatal for two H Company men waiting to move out at daybreak in the northeast sector of Herresbach. "I had taken cover behind one of the buildings next to the road, waiting for the lead platoon to move out," recalled Lieutenant Megellas. "My platoon would be next, and the rest of H Company would follow. I edged just beyond the building [...] to observe where the gunfire was coming from. Private First Class Romero, the platoon runner, and Sgt. Sus J. Gonzales were standing behind me. We moved about a foot outside the building next to the road, looking in the direction of the enemy automatic fire. A German machine gun opened up. The trajectory of the bullets followed alongside the building. Gonzales, Romero, and I were within an arm's length of one another when the fire hit Romero and Gonzales, standing on both sides of me, but missed me completely. Both dropped at my feet on the edge of the road. I pulled Gonzalez behind the house and called for a medic.

"Then I dragged Romero [...] behind the house. He had been shot through the neck, and his carotid artery was severed. Blood was spurting out of his neck like a fountain, and his entire body was quivering. I placed my hand over the jugular, applying pressure. It was an instinctive reaction, but a futile gesture; the blood just kept spurting out, covering both of us. In a matter of minutes, he stopped quivering; his body drained of blood, he died in my arms. Gonzales had been shot in the chest. The medics placed him on a stretcher and evacuated him to a field hospital. The following day he died of his wounds."[319]

La Riviere's 2nd Platoon had received a new assistant platoon leader the previous day when 2nd Lt. Donald M. Crooks was transferred out of the Regimental Reconnaissance Platoon. Crooks had earned a battlefield commission at Anzio, jumped with Gavin in Normandy, and served in the Recon Platoon in Holland and during the first weeks of the Battle of the Bulge. He was now to take charge of the leading elements of the 2nd Platoon, spearheading the H Company assault. But when German artillery, machine-gun, and mortar fire scattered the 2nd Platoon men, who tried to take cover behind the Shermans, Crooks himself dove under a tank, refusing to come out or lead the attack when Lieutenant La Riviere ordered him to do so.

Livid at this cowardly behavior, La Riviere pulled out his .45 and threatened to shoot him on the spot. Luckily, Lieutenant Sims, the company XO, persuaded La Riviere to put his pistol back in his holster. Still furious, La Riviere relieved Crooks on the spot and sent him to the rear. Crooks had survived several campaigns without a scratch, but now had reached the breaking point. S/Sgt. William Rice, the platoon sergeant, recorded on January 31: "Lieutenant Crooks transferred from outfit." There was no further elaboration.

The attack finally began at 0735 hours. All went well until H Company reported at 0900 hours that they were pinned down by sniper fire from some high ground to their north. Lieutenant Colonel Cook and Captain Keep moved forward to personally assess the opposition. They radioed back to Major Zakby at 0945 hours that the situation had improved: H Company had split up into two parts, and moved through the enemy lines, cutting off a group of Germans. At 1000 hours G Company reached its position, followed an hour and a half later by Captain Gray's confirmation that his men had also taken their objective. He also reported to Lieutenant Colonel Cook that he had by-passed a small pocket of Germans between his line and Herresbach. Cook instructed Captain Burriss in I Company to dispatch 1st Lt. Harold G. Weber's platoon to deal with them, operating under Captain Gray's command.

Fifteen minutes later Major Zakby recorded in the battalion log that 76 Germans had been captured so far and only 12 American casualties, mostly wounded, had been sustained. That afternoon, several smaller groups of Germans were spotted and their positions were radioed back to the 376th PFAB. Lieutenant Weber and his platoon returned to I Company at 1700 hours, reporting that they had only seen 12 dead Germans and very little enemy activity. The other rifle companies all pulled back to Herresbach at dusk.

One platoon-strength German counterattack was repulsed that day by a two-man outpost of G Company, as described by the Silver Star Citation of Pfc. Warnie R. Sims. Sims was "on a two-man machine-gun outpost when the German infantry counterattacked through his position. Although heavily outnumbered, he refused to withdraw, and stayed by his post. When his companion was wounded, Private First Class Sims took over the gun, repeatedly reloading and firing. When the counterattack was finally repulsed, 17 dead and eight wounded enemy were found in front of Private First Class Sims' position. His great display of courage and his refusal to withdraw in the face of a vastly superior force was a main factor in the ultimate defeat of the enemy attack."[320]

On the southern edge of Herresbach, the 2nd Battalion had suffered mortar-fire casualties on the morning of January 29. Sgt. Arthur Duebner, E Company, recalled several Germans in a farmstead complex tried "to escape by moving along a hedgerow about 200 yards from my position. Here I made real good use of my sniper rifle. None of them made it to the security of the nearby woods! At the same time this was going on, one of my friends, Walter Nulty, who had transferred in with me from the FSSF, lost his leg to a mortar round. He was in the 2nd Platoon. This did not help my attitude toward the enemy trying to escape the area."[321]

In the D Company sector, the 2nd Platoon under 1st Lt. Hanz K. Druener was sent out to occupy a ridge on the northern side of the town. During the attack, both Druener and his platoon sergeant were wounded. T/Sgt. Augusta F. Billingsley moved over to the 2nd Platoon and led them in another attack up the ridge. His Silver Star Citation sums up: "After a severe and bloody battle, Technical Sergeant Billingsley led his men to the crest, and immediately deployed them defensively. The enemy opened up on the hill with 20-mm flak guns, mortars, artillery and small arms and launched a counterattack. Technical Sergeant Billingsley, with utter and complete disregard for his own personal safety, took a Thompson submachine gun and charged the enemy forces by himself. Firing his weapon from the hip and throwing hand grenades, he succeeded in killing at least nine of the enemy and wounded several more, took two prisoners, and forced the remaining enemy to leave the field of battle in complete disorder. Technical Sergeant Billingsley's actions were an inspiration to all who saw him, and in keeping with the highest standards of the Airborne Forces."[322]

The same day, January 29, Colonel Tucker received new attack orders from Division Headquarters. At 1810 hours, he briefed his officers on their next-day assignments. The 2nd Battalion was to push out east to capture the village of Eimerscheid, supported by a tank platoon, while the 1st Battalion would advance further on their left alongside the 508th PIR. Cook's 3rd Battalion was to defend Herresbach, looking southwest, with H Company on the left and I Company on the right flank. G Company would be in reserve.

Colonel Tucker and Lieutenant Colonel Cook were both well aware that the 3rd Battalion positions in Herresbach would be vulnerable to German counterbattery fire or attacks. To prevent such actions, it was especially important to take the high ridge east of town. A platoon of G Company, supported by a tank platoon of C Company, 740th Tank Battalion, was to take the ridge, shoot up some woods, and possibly take a couple of prisoners. This action would facilitate the 2nd Battalion's attack, scheduled for the following day, and divert German attention to the east side of Herresbach so H Company could more easily take up defensive positions in the south.

The task of executing the plan fell to 2nd Lt. Chester R. Anderson from Sioux Falls, South Dakota. Anderson's 3rd Platoon set off at 2155 hours accompanied by four Sherman tanks from 2nd Platoon, C Company, 740th TB, under the command of 2nd Lt. John E. Callaway. Cook and Keep followed in their tracks. By 2300 hours, the assault force had moved almost halfway up the deeply snow-covered ridge, when several German machine guns opened fire. One tank lumbered over a landmine and was put out of action. Miraculously, no crew members were killed or wounded by the explosion. The other three tanks moved forward to successfully subdue the machine-gun nests, but in the process Lieutenant Callaway's lead tank slid into an artillery shell crater and upended, injuring Callaway so badly he had to be was evacuated. S/Sgt. Homer B. Tompkins took command of the remainder of the tank platoon, which was down to just two tanks.

Lieutenant Anderson received a Silver Star and a promotion to first lieutenant for his part in the action in Herresbach on 29 January. "First Lieutenant Anderson, a platoon leader, was given the mission of capturing and holding a large ridge to the east of the town. At a point halfway up, he and his men came under intense small-arms and artillery fire. First Lieutenant Anderson almost immediately suffered a severe and very painful shrapnel wound to the shoulder. Refusing medical aid, he continued to lead his men to the crest of the ridge, where the platoon was immediately counterattacked by a force estimated at battalion strength.

"First Lieutenant Anderson, with complete disregard for personal safety, and ignoring his wound, personally killed 13 of the enemy and captured three more. His courageous actions were an inspiration to all who saw him and reflect great credit upon himself and the Airborne Forces."[323] Anderson rejoined his company two months later.

At 2340 hours Cook and Keep returned to the 3rd Battalion CP to inform Major Zakby that G Company was on the high ground and that two tanks were out of action. The other two tanks withdrew an hour later, after Germans used flat-trajectory fire. This left one of Anderson's platoons and another G Company platoon with the two knocked-out tanks situated on the high ground. The 3rd Platoon leader, Lieutenant Allmand, who had been promoted to first lieutenant in the hospital, had just rejoined the 3rd Battalion. Cook immediately sent him forward to take command of his platoon. Fortunately, no new German counterattack took place during the night.

North of Herresbach, the 1st Battalion had a fairly quiet day. Meanwhile, the neighboring 508th PIR pushed on in the direction of Holzheim. "The morning dawned clear and bright," recalled Private First Class Bayley of A Company. "During the day we sat around in small groups chatting and dining on old field rations. Little did we know that by the next day many of the gang would no longer be together. Some had become very close friends during many months of sharing thoughts, dreams and family information. I remember one trooper making arrangements with another to have his family renew his supply of Mail Pouch chewing tobacco.

"It appeared that we would have a second night in this reasonably quiet, concealed spot off the road, but in the evening our non-coms called a little gathering and said we were going in to take a small road bridge [across Manderfeld Creek]. If we captured the bridge, we were to destroy it. If we had to retreat, the bridge would be left intact. We argued this point, as it did not seem to make sense.

"[…] We started out well after dark. A small group of six or so, including myself, was selected to lead the single-file line of advance. S/Sgt. Frank Heidebrink (a person with always an upbeat attitude, respected and liked by all who knew him), with two others following, took the lead. I was the fourth man in the column.

"A short while into the march, tracer bullet shots rang out as we approached a sharp, right-angle bend in the road and Heidebrink and the second man were instantly killed. I managed to drop and roll into a shallow ditch while several more tracers passed just above my body. Several troopers tried to shoot rifle grenades in the direction of the shots, only to have them fail to detonate as they landed in the soft snow. Another two soldiers who were very close friends of the sergeant ran forward to see if they could help him. I yelled for them to stay down or they would be killed. Both were shot dead. By now, my hands and feet began to get really cold from lying in the snow."[324]

Proceeding on point, Pvt. Ignatius W. ("Ziggy") Wengress also met sudden death that night. "I remember Ziggy turning around and asking if there were supposed to be Germans in that area. It was the last thing he said," First Lieutenant Kiernan remembered. "I must have been fairly close to the point man to have heard what he said and therefore fairly close to Bayley. Staff Sergeant Heidebrink shouldn't have been there. He was the kind of a person who always headed toward the action."[325]

Bayley decided to crawl back to get some help: "I crawled back some distance where there was a tracked jeep-type vehicle [a weasel] with the motor running. I went to this with two or three others to get thawed out, and spoke to a major to try to get mortar fire at the approximate area from which the shots had come. He said he had been by the area earlier in the day and there were no Germans there, and he *refused to take any action*. [Emphasis in the original.] We told him the Germans were definitely there because they had yelled at us in German, and that they could have moved in after he had gone by. The site was at a right-turning bend in the road I estimate to be about half a mile before we got to Holzheim."[326]

Although Bayley did not succeed in persuading the major to take action, Pvt. Albert Rosner of Headquarters Company had meanwhile managed to talk the Germans out of their concealed position: "He yelled something in the direction from which the shots had come and two Germans emerged and came to him. At first they would not talk. He hand-whipped them across the face several times and finally they talked. We found out that they were the only ones there.

"After a delay of maybe two or so hours we moved on and came to a crossroads and a small village, probably Holzheim. We halted here for a while in the center of the town. American troops had been here earlier, leaving a number of dead Germans lying about in the snow and destroyed German vehicles."[327]

Another A Company veteran killed that day was Pfc. Angus J. Giles, Jr., from Denison, Oklahoma. Giles served as a BAR gunner in the 2nd Platoon. As his assistant, Pfc. Julius Lasslo, recounted later: "Our company moved out on the night of January 29 to get ready to go into the attack the next morning. Our squad led out the company, and of course we were the first to hit action. We established ourselves behind a wall of snow and began firing. Giles, myself, and four others kept up a base of fire, so the rest of the company could advance down a road to our right.

"Our objective was to capture high ground for the purpose of observation and a tactical strongpoint. We were keeping up a steady stream of fire when Giles, who was on my right, was suddenly struck by a burst of machine-gun bullets. I don't think he knew what hit him, because when I leaned over and rolled him on his back, he was already dead. Instant hate filled our hearts. We were all prepared to charge the enemy and kill everyone in sight, but our squad leader, using wise judgement, held us back. We finally did succeed in capturing the position later that afternoon with heavy loss of life.

"It was a sad day for us all, even though we were victorious. Down deep in my heart, I pray that my eyes will never witness such horror of bloodshed. Giles and all the rest that died that fateful day gave their blood so that all the rest of us could live in peace and security and have the pursuit of happiness."[328]

Tank from the 740th Tank Battalion and G Company paratroopers
advancing on January 28, 1945. *Courtesy: U.S. Army*

CHAPTER 14

DECIMATION AT MANDERFELD
Holzheim, Eimerscheid and Manderfeld,
Belgium, January 30–31, 1945

At 0500 hours on January 30, the 1st Battalion advance continued east on the mission to take the bridge across Manderfeld Creek, not far from the German town of Manderfeld. Lt. Col. Warren Williams again ordered 1st. Lt. John Pease to lead the advance with A Company, which had a little over 100 men left, while B and C Company each numbered only about 65 men. It seemed to A Company like they were "the only company in the battalion" that had to lead advances.

As PFC Bayley remembers the attack: "A Company was told to advance down one of the roads to find what was down there and launch an attack against the bridge. The snow banks at the sides of the road were several feet high where the Germans had plowed the road. The snow in the fields was about 24 inches deep. It was now January 30. We were initially told that several minutes of artillery fire would take place before we attacked the bridge area and that we would be accompanied by tanks. Neither of these events occurred."[329]

The snow was waist deep and the temperature was sub-zero. With no tank support from the 740th Tank Battalion or the 643rd Tank Destroyer Battalion and no artillery support, A Company had to assault the bridge across Manderfeld Creek under the eyes of *Generalleutnant* (Major General) Richard Schimpf's 3rd Fallschirmjäger Division, situated in entrenched positions on the high hills around Manderfeld. Remnants of the 3rd Fallschirmjäger Division Battleschool, along with the depleted 3rd Fallschirm Panzer-Jäger Abteilung, commanded by *Oberleutnant* (First Lieutenant) Siegfried

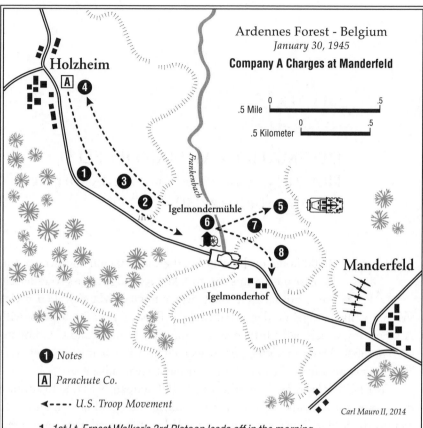

Ardennes Forest - Belgium
January 30, 1945
Company A Charges at Manderfeld

Holzheim

Igelmondermühle

Igelmonderhof

Manderfeld

Frankenbach

0	.5
.5 Mile	

0	.5
.5 Kilometer	

❶ *Notes*

Ⓐ *Parachute Co.*

◀---- *U.S. Troop Movement*

Carl Mauro II, 2014

1. *1st Lt. Ernest Walker's 3rd Platoon leads off in the morning.*

2. *Many wounded and KIA by 88mm gunfire on the open slope.*

3. *1st Lt. Henry Dunavant and Pfc. Clarence Sonntag killed during withdrawl.*

4. *Lt. James Kiernan receives order to lead a second A Company attack with his 1st Platoon in the afternoon.*

5. *German 20mm flak wagon fires from left hill on medics who try to retrieve wounded in morning assault.*

6. *Lt. Kieman's platoon, led by Kiernan and Pfc. Edwin Bayley with a BAR, reach Igelmondermühle and stone bridge.*

7. *Lt. Kiernan sends Pfc. Harold Freeman back to collect Sherman tanks from C/740th Tank Battalion. He decides to attack the left hill to silence enemy small-arms fire and 20mm gun.*

8. *3rd Platoon remnants with Sherman tanks, followed by B Company, take the Igelmonderhof and silence five 88mm guns.*

Junghans, defended the Igelmondermühle—a saw mill not far from the bridge across the creek. Junghans' successor, Major Max Härtle, had been killed the previous day in Holzheim in a firefight with the 508th Parachute Infantry Regiment.[330]

Beyond the bridge, the road to Manderfeld curved by the Igelmonderhof, a large farm complex belonging to the Heinzius family, where the 8th Fallschirmjäger Regiment headquarters and aid station were located. The regiment, with strays from the SS-Panzergrenadier Regiment 2 attached, was under the command of *Oberst* (Colonel) Egon Liebach, who had withdrawn from the Igelmondermühle the previous day. Four Russian guns from the 3rd Abteilung of the 3rd Fallschirmjäger Artillerie Regiment were situated nearby, and *Hauptmann* (Captain) Steinbeck's 1st Abteilung was positioned between Holzheim and the Igelmondermühle—right on A Company's route of advance.

As 1st Lt. James Kiernan recalled the morning attack, "Company A was leading the advance, with the second Platoon (Lt. Ernie Walker) in the lead, followed by the 3rd Platoon, and then the 1st Platoon. The 1st Platoon was last, as we had been shot up the night before and needed time to reorganize as best we could on the move. We were all going down a large hill toward the bridge when the Germans opened fire."[331]

The company received heavy small-arms fire and several paratroopers began returning fire. The enemy group trying to hold up their advance seemed to be small, similar to the two soldiers who had killed Staff Sergeant Heidebrink and Privates Galitza, Wengress, and Stone in the 1st Platoon. Private First Class Bayley fills in the details: "As we went forward and started a small descent around a curve down to the small river, rifle shots rang out. No one was hit. As we advanced further, more intense rifle firing began and our troopers, finding targets, began to shoot back. One was Pvt. Theodore Brown, an expert rifleman. He was somewhat deaf and couldn't hear too well, but it seemed like all his bullets hit the target. I guess some of the troopers were hit, as I could not see all of them. Some had spread out as skirmishers in the field to the left."[332]

German forward observers dug-in on the hills around Manderfeld on the opposite side of Manderfeld Creek had a perfect view of the fields below them as A Company trudged through the waist-deep snow towards the bridge. They called in artillery fire on the assaulting paratroopers, blowing several men to bits, while shrapnel killed or wounded numerous others. Lieutenant Kiernan recalled that the 1st Platoon, in the rear of A Company, also received artillery fire: "The fire was heavy and included direct fire from artillery emplaced on the hill east of the creek. Initially the 2nd Platoon received the heaviest fire as they were in the lead, but very quickly the entire company was under fire. It was a difficult time since we were all exposed and in plain view of the Germans."[333]

With no available cover, A Company's situation quickly became chaotic. Bayley remembered some men "froze," some turned around, and others moved forward. He himself had a close call: "Some [artillery shells] hit the road and exploded. Some landing in the soft snow in the fields did not explode. Others hitting the snow skipped across like small stones skipping on water. All the time a captain on the top of the street rise kept yelling for the troopers to advance under withering rifle and deadly artillery fire. More of the shells landed in the roadway.

"Suddenly the captain was seen no more and a lieutenant ordered us to pull back, as nothing but death and grievous wounds were being obtained. We turned, and as I was running, I saw some of my close friends lying dead in the road, their bodies torn asunder by the artillery. The last time I saw [Pvt.] Clarence [Sonntag] was just after he had been killed on the road sloping down to the river during the attack.

"At that time a heavy shock lifted me off the road and several feet into the air. My backside stung as if from a hornet. I landed on it suddenly on the icy road and quickly got up and ran again with the others to get out of there. Later I realized that an artillery shell had exploded beneath my feet and that I had survived without even a cut."[334]

The lieutenant who ordered Bayley and others to pull back may have been 1st Lt. Henry C. Dunavant, the company executive officer. Lieutenant Kiernan was not far from Dunavant when a German shell came in: "We began to withdraw (1st Platoon first), followed by the others who were further down the hill. I remember doing my best to keep people from bunching up, as a bunch would draw a direct artillery round. Lt. Hank Dunavant, our Company XO, was near me trying to help with the withdrawal when he received a direct hit from an artillery shell, killing him instantly. Ultimately, we reached the reverse side of the hill where we were out of view of the Germans with their small arms and direct artillery fire."[335]

Out of breath, A Company regrouped behind the hill. Many people were missing; most of the wounded had been left behind during the withdrawal. Pfc. Edwin Bayley, 1st Platoon, witnessed several medics running back with a Red Cross flag to evacuate the wounded: "We pulled back and regrouped while the Germans continued to shoot 20mm antipersonnel flak shells over our heads. Shortly, medics and volunteers with a big Red Cross flag went down into the shoot out area to retrieve the wounded. We couldn't believe it, but the Germans shot and wounded several of these men. We were supposed to have had an artillery barrage and a couple of tanks assist us with this operation but this did not occur.

"During the several minutes this tragic event lasted, we lost several more of the veterans to death. It seemed a shame that some of them had come all the way from Africa, Sicily, Italy, France and Holland to be killed in what would be the last days of the war. Taking into account Cheneux and other battles of the previous weeks, a large number of the old-time veterans had been killed. Some had been badly wounded but were still alive, although we never saw them again."[336]

Among these "old-time veterans" was Pvt. Louis C. Bosher, 2nd Squad, 2nd Platoon. Seeing a fellow paratrooper manning a machine gun struck by enemy fire, Bosher ran over to his wounded comrade and took up the machine gun, continuing to fire on the same German position. An 88mm shell landed right on top of him, killing him instantly. Corporal Baldino, Bosher's close friend and assistant squad leader, did not learn what had happened to him until after the war. "He was just a peach of a person. In a terrible fight against the Germans, Bosher came over to one guy manning a machine gun and said, 'Let me take that over for a while.' No sooner had he done this than an (I think) 88mm shell hit him and the machine gun and of course killed him. I forget the name of the man he relieved. I met him at the conventions and he was always appreciative that Bosher came over and relieved him."[337]

As Pfc. Ervin E. Shaffer, 3rd Platoon, was attempting to evade incoming artillery fire, one trooper was blown to bits within four to six feet of him. Shaffer, who received shrapnel in his right hand, began shifting from position to position. When the majority of A Company turned and headed back up the hill, the Germans seem to have misidentified Shaffer as the commander of the attack because he was wearing a snow cape. Concentrating all their firepower on Shaffer, they fired ahead of him as he ran. Shaffer doubled back, then stopped until they fired, then again ran down the road and doubled back as the enemy fired eight to twelve rounds but failed to hit him. They fired their last shell into a tree on the left side of the road to create an air burst just as Shaffer went over the top of the hill.[338]

Having fought against all odds until ordered to withdraw, A Company reorganized, again assembling squads and platoons on the other side of the hill. Many killed and wounded men were missing: the company's casualties were extremely high, especially in the 1st Platoon, which had already lost Heidebrink and three other men early that morning, so the men did not expect the company would be sent up front again. However, the order to make another assault came down that afternoon. Lieutenant Kiernan was to lead his platoon across the Manderfeld Creek and capture a hill on the right: "Our platoon lost some fine men in this action, in addition to those we had lost the night before. I don't remember the exact losses suffered by the 2nd and 3rd Platoons, but they were greater than ours. This left us as the strongest platoon in Company A, which made us the strongest in the 1st Battalion. Thus, it was no great surprise to me that when the order came to make another assault on the hill, the 1st Platoon was to lead. I wasn't very happy when I gave the platoon the news, but they took it well. Possibly, like me, they were too numb with fatigue to react."[339]

The exhausted 1st Platoon could hardly believe the shocking news when Kiernan told them they would return to spearhead the attack. Bayley was in the lead with his Browning submachine gun: "After a couple of hours or so (now in the afternoon) we were told we were going in again. This time there was a short artillery barrage and the tanks showed up behind us. Then I got the worst command that any soldier in combat can get: 'BAR man, lead the attack in.' There was nothing I could do but go. Rifle bullets were coming in but I could not take this into account. I had to lead the attack. Not trusting anything for snipers, etc., I shot up everything I saw, including the electric transformers on the poles and vehicles beside the road. Nothing was left to chance.

"I briefly saw two or so German soldiers in the road near a truck. I completely shot up the truck as there might be someone hiding in there. I later learned where the Germans I had seen had gone. They had gotten into the truck and I had gotten them. I came around the corner and was face to face with a large farmhouse and the associated buildings of a small mill. I peppered the house from top to bottom and side to side as well as the other buildings."[340]

Lieutenant Kiernan assembled as many of his men as possible near the Igelmondermühle farm buildings at Manderfeld Creek and sent a runner, Pfc. Harold J. Freeman from Willimantic, Connecticut, to the 740th TB to request tank support: "We made our way back down the hill, past the same area where we had been only a couple of hours before. We had received a good artillery barrage on the target when we were about halfway down the hill and that helped a lot, though we still receiving small arms fire.

"When we reached a farmhouse down by the creek, I was able to gather most of the platoon and gave the order to continue east to the high ground on our left, although my original orders had been to take the hill on the right. It looked to me like we would have been completely exposed to fire from two sides if there had been any Germans on the hill on the left.

"About this time I had shouted to someone, 'Send down the tanks!' This perhaps was not wise from a tanker's point of view, but it certainly was a great boost that we could well use. The tankers did respond. Also, at this time I sent a message back to 1st Lieutenant Pease telling him I was going left and would provide fire support for whoever was going to the right. First Lieutenant Pease later told me that when he saw that messenger his heart sank, for he was afraid he was going to hear that we were withdrawing. He happily acknowledged that going left was a good idea."[341]

The company was still held up by enemy artillery fire from a well-placed German battery on top of a hill. Bayley spotted these guns and called a warning out to Freeman, who had meanwhile come up with the tanks: "At this time I looked up behind me and saw one of the tanks on the cliff above me and also my close friend Pfc. Harold Freeman. Looking about a quarter mile up the far hill, I saw an artillery piece and German soldiers rushing to get it. This was probably the gun that had killed so many of our troopers early in the day.

"I called to my friend and he notified the tank crew who took care of the artillery piece and the soldiers in seconds, before the artillery piece could be loaded and fired. (In later years I learned he got a Silver Star for this and I got nothing, although I was the one telling him to relay my message to the tanks.) One of the tanks tried to cross the small bridge and fell into the river. The other one dashed quickly up the hill with some troopers and the battle was all over. We took well over 100 prisoners."[342]

Tanks belonging to 1st Lt. Charles B. Powers' 3rd Platoon, C Company, 740th Tank Battalion, rolled towards Holzheim, their hulls and sides loaded with B Company troopers. According to the 740th TB battalion history, "Third Platoon tankers thought they were getting a break as they moved with infantry against nothing more than small-arms fire into the town of Holzheim. However, when they pushed on through to Chateau Igelmonderhof at the top of a hill, they ran headlong into a hornets' nest. As the lead infantry broke out of the woods across open ground, the attack was unexpectedly bushwhacked by powerful, flat-trajectory weapons fire—antitank guns! The tanks spread out: First Lieutenant Powers, the platoon leader, and S/Sgt. [Charlie W.] Loopey led the charge up the hill, blasting away with everything they had.

"The attack was bold and devastating. Loopey's tank set two trucks filled with Germans afire with star shells. And when the tanks reached the chateau, the bow gunners jumped from their front right hatches with tommy guns spitting fire and rounded up the Germans who were left alive. When the infantry arrived to take over, the prisoner count varied from 100 all the way up to 200."[343]

While B Company and the tanks charged down the road, the majority of Lieutenant Pease's A Company, less the 1st Platoon, charged frontally across the snow-covered fields towards the Igelmonderhof. The 3rd Platoon pressed on in the lead, despite having lost its platoon leader hours earlier. The price had been high for the morning assault: out of about 40 men who started the attack, some 18 were still capable of fighting, and the platoon was without a single officer. Pvt. Henry R. Girard was one of only four men still standing after his platoon had crossed 700 yards of open fields. Assuming the initiative while the enemy was temporarily disorganized, Girard had obtained the surrender of six German officers and 59 soldiers. For this action under enemy artillery fire he received the Bronze Star.

The acting platoon sergeant, Cpl. John H. Stubbs, was also decorated for his leadership that day. His Silver Star Citation reads: "When his platoon leader and platoon sergeant became casualties, Staff Sergeant Stubbs took command of the platoon and, despite intense fire which reduced his command to only four men, reached the objective. Cornering sixty-five enemy in a group of buildings, he returned 600 yards under heavy fire to guide tanks forward. After killing six Germans, whom he had flushed from concealed positions, Staff Sergeant Stubbs persuaded the balance of the enemy to surrender. The gallantry, courage and aggressiveness displayed by Staff Sergeant Stubbs were in keeping with the highest traditions of the Airborne Forces."[344]

According to the 3rd Fallschirmjäger Division history, the American airborne infantry had landed at Holzheim on January 29, 1945. This account is purely fictional: the 508th and 504th Parachute Infantry Regiments approached on foot. The German historian recounts that the four Russian guns at the Igelmonderhof fire opened fire around 1000 hours on the morning of January 30 as A Company advanced, seemingly casually, in a column from Holzheim down to the Igelmondermühle. *Oberst* Liebach supposedly ordered his guns to cease fire when the medics in Red Cross jeeps tried to evacuate the wounded.[345]

That afternoon, *Oberst* Liebach and the 8th Fallschirmjäger Regiment staff had taken refuge along with the Heinzius family in the basement of the main building in the farm complex when American artillery fire peppered the immediate area with explosions. The cellar soon began to fill with smoke as the Americans shelled the building at close range. A German soldier ran down the steps and called out, "*Herr Oberst*, the entire complex is surrounded!" An SS officer present in the cellar barked out, "This citadel is to be defended to the last man!" but Liebach squarely told the soldier, "Run up the white flag!" In all, some 300 Germans, including several wounded, surrendered at the Igelmonderhof. They were marched to Holzheim, where Liebach and a few others managed to slip away during the night.[346]

Meanwhile, the 1st Platoon had been more fortunate than the 3rd. "We took the hill on the left with little difficulty," recalled Lieutenant Kiernan, "and were able to provide fire support for the troops who took the hill on the right. Later that afternoon I went to the area where the Germans had the artillery and saw what remained. There were eight to ten dead Germans in the area, several wounded, and several prisoners. For some reason, I can't remember which unit took the hill on the right, but I believed it was a platoon from Company A, probably the 3rd Platoon. I can't recall if we got any sleep that night, but we must have. It had been a harrowing 24 hours, but 1st Platoon, though badly battered, was still intact."[347]

As he later mused about the second attack, Bayley stated he "wondered at times about the situation. The Germans may have decided that we had been so badly mauled in the morning that we would not attack later that day. I say this because when I led the attack down the hill [...] I was surprised to see two German soldiers casually walking up the hill towards us, and just after I shot many bullets into the big farmhouse, a bunch of civilians and some German soldiers emerged from the building. The soldiers were not carrying weapons."[348]

B Company, led by 1st Lt. Reneau Breard's platoon, had followed close behind A Company. "The snow was waist deep. We were in single file, the first man breaking the way until exhausted. He would then fall out and get to the tail end of the squad, while the next man would break the way and so on. We followed A Company towards Holzheim, taking a road to Manderfeld. Crossing a creek, A Company was hit by direct artillery fire. B Company assisted with tanks. The guns were overrun and no prisoners were taken. This is the place where Lieutenant Dunavant was killed."[349]

Private First Class Bayley remembered that the 1st Squad slept soundly that night, exhausted by combat: "After the hill on the right was taken (some 1st Platoon men were there when I arrived), we went into the farm buildings. While about four of us were in a shed behind the barn looking at the road beyond, two Germans came walking toward us, dragging an apparently wounded German on the snowy surface of the road. Two of the troopers shot at the Germans but evidently did not hit either of them, because they quickly dropped the guy and ran away down the road from the farm buildings. The 1st Platoon at least then withdrew back to the hill on the left just across from the creek and moved into foxholes that someone had previously dug there.

"About four of us occupied one very large foxhole. I remember a new addition to the platoon I had not noticed before, Pvt. [Raymond] Tate. I remember him especially because in civilian life he was a baker. His ambition when he got home was to establish his own bakery and name it Tate's Tasty Pastries. Our foxhole group slept very soundly that night except when we had to do outpost duty."[350]

In addition to the Russian guns, another five 88mm guns were taken out of action and most of the crews were either killed or captured. Just outside of Holzheim at the Igelmondermühle, A Company captured 39 members of the 1st Abteilung, 3rd Fallschirmjäger Artillery Regiment commanded by *Hauptmann* Steinbeck.[351] One severely wounded gunner, the only man the Germans had been able to evacuate after the morning attack, escaped capture.[352] Five communication men from 3rd Fallschirm Nachrichten Abteilung 3 were also taken prisoner near Holzheim.[353] The casualty rate for the 8th Fallschirmjäger Regiment and Fallschirm Flak Regiment 12 is unknown, but must have been considerable. The author estimates German total losses (killed, wounded and prisoners) to be at least 400 men.

The victory at the Igelmonderhof and Igelmondermühle had nevertheless decimated A Company. Nine men were killed on January 29 and 30 and numerous more were wounded. In the 2nd Platoon, Private Bosher and Private First Class Giles had been killed. Private First Class Galitza and Privates Stone and Wengress were killed when the 1st Platoon had been ambushed. First Lieutenant Dunavant and Privates McFadden and Sonntag were killed during the morning attack. All were initially buried in the Henri Chapelle Cemetery, and their remains were later repatriated.

Ironically, exactly one year before he was killed in the Bulge, Staff Sergeant Heidebrink had been wounded at Anzio while still a corporal. Heidebrink's death was a great loss to the company: an inspiring and courageous leader, who volunteered for many dangerous patrols and led by example, he had risen through the ranks from private to staff sergeant and was well liked by everyone who knew him. Another squad leader temporarily replaced him as acting platoon sergeant.

Lieutenant Dunavant's death was another blow to the company. Although he had recently joined the company at Camp Sissonne, he had been with the 1st Battalion since Venafro, Italy, in the fall of 1943. An officer who had often demonstrated he concern for the safety of his men, Dunavant was well liked and sorely missed in A Company.

Private First Class Bayley again encountered Private Rosner, who had been assigned to escort prisoners taken at Manderfeld to a collection point for POW's in the rear. "An escort guard was assigned to take the prisoners to a collecting point. The foreign-looking person [Private Rosner] was placed in charge along with a few troopers. When the troopers returned, they were laughing about the episode. They said that when the detail got out of sight of the officers that [Rosner] stopped the group and reminded the Germans that if they tried anything out of line that they were now under the command of a Czechoslovakian Jew. With that, they said, he fired his submachine gun into the ground and said that is what he would do to them.

"Later on, while we were chatting, he joined our group. He had taken up with the 504 somewhere along their travels and apparently was not an American soldier. [Rosner was a member of HQ/I Company.] He pulled back his sleeves to display wrist watches on both arms from the wrist to nearly the elbow. These had all been taken from German prisoners.

"The remainder of January 30, January 31 and February 1 we stayed in this area. During the night of January 30 we heard that another outfit had passed through our lines to carry on the attack. During these days we acquired some new men from other paratroop outfits that were being deactivated after losing too many members to remain in active status."[354]

Major Wellems' 2nd Battalion also had to fight its way forward through the snow, heading towards the town of Eimerscheid. Captain Komosa's D Company was leading the column. In support were two tanks from 1st Platoon, C Company, 740th TB commanded by S/Sgt. William H. Nemnich, which destroyed two German horse-drawn artillery pieces on the way to Eimerscheid. Captain Komosa was awarded the Silver Star "for gallantry in action" that day: "Captain Komosa, his exhausted and decimated company pinned down by four machine guns as he led it across open and exposed terrain, dashed with his submachine gun and silenced one enemy gun. To perform this action, which enabled the company to advance, Captain Komosa voluntarily exposed himself for five minutes to a raking stream of accurate and interlocked enemy automatic weapons fire. Having disposed of one enemy machine gun, he called forward his own, and so skillfully directed their emplacement and operation that the three remaining enemy guns were destroyed.

"Captain Komosa then placed himself at the head of the company and led it forward in a smashing attack against well-emplaced enemy infantry that yielded 80 prisoners and caused many enemy casualties. His personal example of determination, devotion to duty and forgetfulness of self-safety inspired the men of this company and was a major consideration in the success of the attack."[355]

The 3rd Battalion remained in Herresbach during the day. This, however, was no safe spot: it was here that G Company mortar man Pvt. Francis L. Allen was hit by a German sniper and died that same day. Only the day before he had stated to his close friend, Pfc. Donald R. June, "I know I am going to get killed," and June had been unable to convince Allen to put the thought out of his mind.[356]

At 1200 hours Colonel Tucker instructed Lieutenant Colonel Cook that his unit would be relieved by the 32nd Cavalry Squadron and then move immediately to Medendorf. Five hours later he called Cook again to inform him that whether or not they had been relieved, the 3rd Battalion was to move out by 1800 hours to set up defenses at Medendorf. That night Staff Sergeant Rice, the platoon sergeant of 2nd Platoon, H Company, wrote in his secret diary: "Ready to move out at 1800, where to now? Marched till 0400. Hills, snow, everyone dead tired. One-mile march turned into 10-hour one instead."[357]

The 3rd Battalion moved to Lanzerath in the early hours on January 31. First Lieutenant Goethe's G Company received the order to set up a roadblock outside town, while the remainder of G Company and I Company were positioned on either side of the town. H Company was in reserve at Lanzerath near the Battalion CP. Before daybreak, Goethe called to inform the Battalion CP that his roadblock had been shelled by enemy armor. First Lieutenant Harold A. Stueland, a forward observer from 376th Parachute Field Artillery Battalion, called for fire support and knocked out one German tank. H Company was placed at standby at 0800 hours, but this proved unnecessary.

Throughout the morning, radio contact was maintained with the neighboring 508th PIR, which was expecting a German counterattack. They requested their tanks, which had been left near Lanzerath. The attached 508th tanks were relieved shortly after 1000 hours when three other tanks arrived, two of which were placed at the roadblock. The third remained in battalion reserve in Lanzerath. At 1130 hours 1st Lieutenant Marshall W. Stark's 1st Platoon, C Battery, 80th Airborne Anti-Aircraft Battalion, arrived, considerably strengthening the 504th defensive position. His armament consisted of two 57mm antitank guns and four .50-caliber machine guns. Lieutenant Colonel Cook directed the entire platoon to the roadblock.

Just before midday a seven-man contact patrol was dispatched from H Company to get in touch with the neighboring 1st Battalion to the south. They returned at 1600 hours to report having talked to Major Berry in the 1st Battalion CP near Manderfeld, to make him aware that the 3rd Battalion would dispatch a contact patrol every two hours. At 1800 hours, I Company sent in two prisoners, apparently German deserters, who stated that the Germans would withdraw during the night. The patrol was changed every four hours, and it did indeed prove to be a quiet night with no enemy activity. A pleased Staff Sergeant Rice recorded that H Company was "gettin' to sleep in a house—first night's sleep since we've started."[358]

The 1st Battalion sector was less quiet that day: B Company lost their company radio operator, T/4 William H. Jandran, who was hit in the head by 88mm shrapnel. "He was a spit and polish kid," observed Private Bill Bonning. "He was really always shaved, clean-dressed and had shiney boots at all times. He became a buck sergeant and a SCR-500 radio man. Eighty-eights came in when we were in a woods—the Krauts had spotted us—and [Sgt.] Harold [Florey] got hit the second or third time. Bill Jandran got hit behind his head—an 88mm landed right behind them. We lost about two or three guys there, casualties from wounds. I think Bill was the only one that was killed that day."[359]

At 1700 hours 1st Lt. John Spooner, Sgt. Donald E. Wolfgang and Privates First Class John Ince and William Zeller from the Regimental Reconnaissance Platoon departed the Regimental CP on a mission to reconnoiter a junction with a view to establishing a roadblock. Moving into enemy territory from a 3rd Battalion outpost, they proceeded southwest to a tip of the woods, where they heard men coughing, talking and stomping their feet to their right front. Ince and Zeller then walked east to the road, where they heard the sound of moving vehicles coming from a nearby house, the metallic clangs of German boots on the pavement and the sounds of men digging in. The patrol also heard a German convoy. From the sounds of it, trucks and at least two tracked vehicles were coming from the southwest and running northeast on the Hassenen–Merlscheid road. The convoy continued until it reached another crossing, at which point the sounds disappeared. Motor noise seemed to indicate that the convoy had turned off the road. The patrol safely reported back to the 3rd Battalion OP at 1950 hours.

Over the previous days, casualties in the 504th had soared. The spearhead of the 1st Battalion attack at Manderfeld, A Company had paid the price of having been left out of the battle for Cheneux. The smallest company in the entire regiment, A Company underwent a quick reorganization: it now numbered just two understrength platoons, and was down to two officers, Lieutenants Kiernan and Pease. By late January 1945, only a sprinkling of old-timers were left. Pitted against a better-equipped, stronger opponent, and fighting in ferocious weather, Tucker's troopers had nearly reached the breaking point, and yet they had still accomplished their missions.

A similar performance could be expected from veteran replacements transferred in to help bring A Company back to strength. Among them were five paratroopers from the recently disbanded 551st Parachute Infantry Battalion: 1st Lt. Richard R. Hallock, Privates First Class Fred Chalfant and Frank E. Gould, and Privates William Amann and Harold J. McNeilly. Born on November 23, 1919, in Oxford, Pennsylvania, Lieutenant Hallock had been valedictorian of his class, graduating in in 1937 from the oldest preparatory school in the United States, West Nottingham Academy in Colora, Maryland. Four years later he graduated from Oberlin College in Ohio, and joined the U.S. Army as a second lieutenant in 1942.

After qualifying as a paratrooper at Fort Benning in the summer of 1943, 2nd Lieutenant Hallock was assigned to the newly formed 542nd PIR, under the command of Col. William T. Ryder, who had led the original Test Platoon in 1940. The 542nd was trained to make the first combat jump across the Rhine River into Germany, which was to take place after a firm bridgehead had been established in Normandy. However, by March 1944 this plan had been scrubbed, and the 542nd PIR was far below strength, having sent hundreds of its men and officers as replacements for the 504th PIR at Anzio and the 511th PIR in the Pacific. When Colonel Ryder transferred out to become Gen. Douglas MacArthur's airborne adviser, Lt. Col. Wood G. Joerg, the regimental XO, returned to his former command, the independent 551st PIB. He asked Lieutenants Dick Durkee, Charles Buckenmeyer and Richard

Hallock to accompany him, and all three accepted. Joerg assigned Bucken-meyer and Durkee to A Company and Hallock to Headquarters Company as platoon leaders. Hallock's first combat jump came in August 1944 with C Company as part of Operation Dragoon, the Allied invasion of Southern France. Wounded in the French Alps by a bullet in the thigh (a bullet he carried for the rest of his life), he recovered in time to fight in the Bulge.

Having survived the fierce fighting at Dairomont and Rochelinval in early January 1945, Hallock was transferred to A Company, where he led the 3rd Platoon. "In the attack to the Siegfried Line the platoon had lost two officers, six out of eight NCO's and two thirds of its numbers," Hallock recalled. "Squad identities had been lost; and the men were suffering from frozen feet, hunger and exhaustion from the hard climb over slippery trails. However, it was a veteran platoon, proud of its fighting record and proud of its regiment and division, and long enured to change and hardship."[360]

The fighting in January 1945 had cost the 504th dearly: battle casualties for the month totalled three officers and 53 enlisted men; four officers and 36 enlisted men had been killed in December 1944. These figures do not include losses in attached units. Many more weeks of fighting still lay ahead: February would take the lives of another five officers and 34 enlisted men.[361]

Major General Ridgway, the XVIII Airborne Corps commander, had meanwhile decided to penetrate the notorious Siegfried Line to enter Germany. On February 1 he issued orders to Major General Gavin: the 82nd Airborne Division was to push on through the formidable German defenses. These orders contradicted General Eisenhower's decision to cancel the planned offensive from St. Vith to Euskirchen on February 1.[362]

The 82nd ABD, and especially the 504th PIR, was nearly 50 percent understrength due to casualties both in and out of battle. Ridgway thus attached the 629th TDB and the independent 517th RCT to the 82nd. The 517th, which joined the division at Honsfeld, had already suffered high casualties in the first weeks of the Bulge, including two battalion commanders. These additions to the division, however, did nothing to change the fact that Colonel Tucker's troopers were still greatly understrength.

On February 1 Lieutenant Colonel Cook and Captain Henry B. Keep (Battalion S-3) observed the Germans withdrawing with vehicles near a crossroad to the 3rd Battalion's southern front and requested an artillery barrage. At 1140 hours a G Company patrol reported that the crossroads were deserted except for eight abandoned trucks, four tanks, and ammunition and jerry cans left along the road. Lieutenant Goethe decided to outpost the crossroads with 1st Lt. Harry Frear's 1st Platoon and four tanks.

At 1730 hours Colonel Tucker called to report the 87th Cavalry Squadron was approaching Manderfeld in an hour and would check on the G Company platoon at the crossroads. Lieutenant Frear called at 1825 hours to report the sighting of some 55 soldiers digging several hundred yards away, and requested permission to fire on them if they proved to be Germans. Half an hour later they appeared indeed to be enemy troops, since no other friendly forces were in the area, and artillery fire was placed on the location. That evening, Lieutenant Frear dispatched one sergeant and three enlisted men to contact the 87th Cavalry Squadron. Two hours later they reported back that they had gone as far as the first houses in Manderfeld, where the lights were on and they heard babies were crying. They had not spotted any friendly forces, but had observed artillery fire falling onto the town.

That same day, February 1, Pvt. William E. Barber, Headquarters Company, 2nd Battalion, was killed. One officer and 27 men from the 82nd's Reconnaissance Platoon made a long patrol of 26 hours to reconnoiter the Siegfried Line and captured seven Germans from the 33rd Volksgrenadier Regiment. They reported finding empty bunkers and no evidence of large enemy activity. Confidence at division headquarters mounted: it would be possible to break through the "impassable barrier" after all! Based on the information from his recon platoon, Major General Gavin and his staff planned the assault on the Siegfried Line. Colonel Billingslea's 325th GIR was tasked to capture the towns of Udenbreth and Neuhof in the north. The 1st Battalion of the 517th PIR would guard their left flank and the 3rd Battalion would be kept in reserve. Colonel Ekman's 505th PIR was to seize ground southeast of Losheimergraben, while the 508th PIR actively patrolled to the southeast.

Gavin chose the 504th PIR to attack the Mertesrott Heights. The most formidable defensive position between the objectives of the 325th and 505th Regiments, the heights dominated the terrain for many miles around. Control of this area would greatly facilitate an assault on the Dalhemer Ridge towards two U.S. First Army objectives, the towns of Blankenheim and Marmagen. The fortified minor road junctions at Udenbreth, Neuhof, and Scheid could be difficult to capture. In order to cut off and encircle each of these road junctions the 504th would need to cut off the Scheid–Neuhof Road, and thus deprive the Germans of contact between the two towns, which were situated just north and south of the Mertesrott Heights.

The operational instructions for the seizure of the Mertesrott Heights came down at 2400 hours on February 1 as follows: the 2nd Battalion was to attack, supported by the Regimental Reconnaissance Platoon; one platoon from the 629th Tank Destroyer Battalion; one platoon from C Company, 307th Airborne Engineers Battalion; and one platoon from Battery C and one from Battery D of the 80th Airborne Anti-Aircraft Battalion. Contact was to be maintained during the assault with the 325th GIR on their left flank.

The 1st Battalion was to follow through the gap created by the 2nd Battalion and swing southeast to capture the lower part of the Mertesrott Heights just north of Scheid, where they would link up with the 505th. Like the 2nd Battalion, the 1st would need to clear all fortifications it encountered. The Regimental Demolition Platoon was thus attached, as well as two 629th Tank Destroyer Battalion platoons; one C Company, 307th Airborne Engineers Battalion platoon; and one platoon from Battery C and one from Battery D of the 80th Airborne Anti-Aircraft Battalion. Fire support would be provided by Lt. Col. Robert Neptune's 376th Parachute Field Artillery Battalion. Lieutenant Colonel Cook's 3rd Battalion, one platoon of tank destroyers, and a platoon of antitank guns from Battery A, 80th AAAB were kept in regimental reserve.

That same evening two replacement officers arrived fresh from West Point and the Parachute School at Fort Benning. Second Lieutenants Thomas O. Mahon and Larkin S. Tully were both graduates of the West Point Class of 1944 who had applied successfully for a transfer to the Parachute School. Their classmate John S. Eisenhower's acceptance into the paratroops had been denied because Gen. Dwight Eisenhower feared he might be severely injured or killed during a jump.[363] Having qualified as paratroopers that summer, both officers briefly joined the 515th PIR, 13th Airborne Division, before being sent to Europe as replacement officers a few months later. Tully was assigned as assistant platoon leader, 1st Platoon, in A Company and Mahon was assigned to 3rd Platoon, G Company, as assistant platoon leader to 1st Lieutenant James R. Allmand, Jr. Both Mahon and Tully were about to experience their first combat mission.

HOME FROM THE WARS—The first of this area's World War II dead to return home from overseas graves arrived in Denison yesterday morning. It was the body of Pfc. Angus N. Giles Jr., 23, son of Mr. and Mrs. Angus Giles of Colbert, shown here being escorted from the train by an American Legion and VFW honor guard. Funeral services will be held Sunday at 2 p. m. at the Denison Funeral Home, with graveside ceremonies at the Colbert Cemetery. (Herald staff photo)

Post-war newspaper clipping of the return of Angus Giles' body for reburial in his hometown. *Courtesy: Greg Korbelic*

CHAPTER 15

THE BATTLE FOR THE MERTESROTT HEIGHTS: MERTESROTT HEIGHTS, GERMANY, FEBRUARY 2, 1945

In the early hours of February 2, the 32nd Cavalry Reconnaissance Squadron moved up from Herresbach to relieve the 2nd Battalion, selected to lead the next attack. Lieutenant Colonel Cook's 3rd Battalion had spearheaded the assault on Herresbach and Major Berry's 1st Battalion had led the way from Holzheim toward Manderfeld, and so were kept in initial reserve.

The few available trucks transported the 2nd Battalion to the immediate assembly area 2000 yards north of Losheimergraben. The area was established on the left side of the road that ran parallel to the Scheid–Neuhof road on the other side of the Mertesrott Heights. During the shuttle Sergeant Arthur Duebner's 1st Squad, 3rd Platoon of E Company accidentally destroyed one of the much-needed deuce-and-a-half trucks: "My squad was in a six-by-six truck. There were two 'Jerry-cans' full of gas in the back with us. Most of us were sleeping. Someone near the cans lit a cigarette and dropped the spent match into some spilled gas that was leaking from one of the cans. Needless to say our awakening was rude and fast—the fastest de-trucking in history—resulting in one lost two-and-a-half-ton truck. Subsequent investigation proved only that 'no one saw anything'!"[364]

An assistant platoon leader in E Company, 2nd Lt. Charles E. Zastrow received word in the staging area that his platoon would spearhead the attack: "They loaded us on trucks and hauled us about ten miles. Whenever we rode it meant trouble—this time was no exception. Arrived about 2300 at night—[they] told us at 0500 in the morning we were going to take a crack at the Siegfried Line. Didn't sleep well that night."[365]

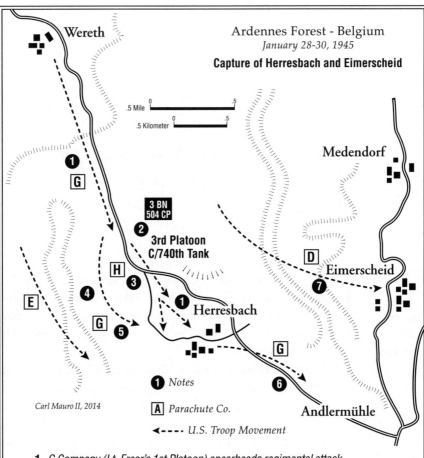

Ardennes Forest - Belgium
January 28-30, 1945

Capture of Herresbach and Eimerscheid

Wereth

Medendorf

Eimerscheid

.5 Mile 0 — .5
.5 Kilometer 0 — .5

3 BN 504 CP

3rd Platoon C/740th Tank

Herresbach

Andlermühle

Carl Mauro II, 2014

❶ *Notes*

Ⓐ *Parachute Co.*

◀---- *U.S. Troop Movement*

1. *G Company (Lt. Frear's 1st Platoon) spearheads regimental attack.*
2. *Location 3rd BN CP at 1800 hrs. January 28, 1945. Lt. Col. Cook receives permission to take Herresbach.*
3. *Two platoons, H Company and 3rd Platoon, C/740th Tank Battalion, advance on Herresbach and encounter German troops on their way.*
4. *PFC Oscar Smith of H Company runs back through open field under fire to deliver an urgent message for ammunition resupply.*
5. *G Company attacks the western edge of Herresbach. T/Sgt. Grear knocks out machine-gun position.*
6. *G Company seizes high hill east of Herresbach with tank support from C/740th.*
7. *Captain Komosa's D Company successfully attacks Eimerscheid with tank support from 740th Tank Battalion, January 30, 1945.*

Lieutenant Colonel Wellems divided his battalion into two assault waves before they entered the Mertesrott Heights from the Losheimergraben–Udenbreth road. Captain Herbert Norman's E Company would attack on the left flank with 1st Lieutenant William Sweet's F Company on the right. Captain Adam Komosa's D Company and Captain Robert Cellar's Headquarters Company would follow and support them by every available means. The 81mm Mortar Platoon would not go forward, because it was all but impossible to fire shells between the tall, densely growing fir trees. The officers and enlisted men had only a few hours to rest before the attack began.

It was still dark when the 1st and 3rd Battalions were respectively relieved by the 32nd Cavalry Reconnaissance Squadron and the 1st Battalion, 508th PIR. Owing to the ever-present lack of transportation for airborne troops, only six deuce-and-a-half trucks without trailers and two borrowed weasels [small infantry carriers on tracks] from division artillery were available.[366]

Third Battalion troopers waited while Major Berry's 1st Battalion was transported for the assault. As Berry's men packed their gear and boarded nearby trucks, nobody except the senior officers knew where they would be taken. "We were waked up early in the morning of February 2 and told we were moving out, but not where," recalled Private First Class Bayley. "We were told to carry plenty of ammunition. I had so much ammunition in BAR clips and also a heavy pocket load of field rations that I had to have a man on either side of me help me into the truck. However, I had no trouble walking with this weight and bulk. I was in great condition at this time.

"As we were loading the trucks, several names were called out, and these men were told to stand down and not get into the trucks. They received the unbelievable news that they had sufficient service points to be sent back to the United States for long-term leave. What a wonderful break for them. We rode for quite a number of miles north and got off the trucks at a town at the German border."[367]

The 1st Battalion was dropped off near the German border town of Losheimergraben, just across the Belgian–German border. Glancing at the surrounding countryside, Bayley suddenly realized their next task. "The road seemed to be a main thoroughfare lined on one side by a few substantially built two-story houses. On the other side was a small, wooded road leading into a forest. To our left was an open field or brush containing rows and rows of the concrete dragon-teeth antitank barricades that I had read about in the Sunday paper magazine section a few years before the war. We now knew that our assignment was to crack the Siegfried Line."[368]

Meanwhile, 2nd Battalion and Regimental Reconnaissance Platoon scouts plunged into the forest with their comrades close behind them. The Mertesrott Heights were almost uncannily silent as 504th troopers moved forward in approach march formation with 1st Lt. Roy L. James' 1st Platoon leading the attack. At first only occasional small arms fire was exchanged among the dense fir trees. It was very hard for the scouts to determine where the sniper and automatic weapons fire was coming from. The foliage, combined with well-dug foxholes, zigzag trenches, and log-covered bunkers provided perfect concealment for the defenders. D and Headquarters Companies followed the lead elements into the woods.

As the 2nd Battalion moved deeper into the forest, it became increasingly difficult to exercise command at the levels of company and platoon. Deep in the center of Mertesrott Heights, orientation proved extremely difficult. The huge amount of snow and ice were certainly no help either, as the lead companies slowly progressed under increasing enemy fire. Advancing through a firebreak, E Company encountered barbed wire at an open space in front of a streambed. The ground rose steeply behind the stream, where the Germans had dug in on the ridge, giving them a perfect field of fire. Leading the attack, the 1st Platoon emerged from the forest and onto open ground. Standing out against the low vegetation, the troopers made ideal targets. The ground rose on either side of the firebreak, and the extremely well-camouflaged pillboxes and bunkers above were aptly covered with logs and snow. The defenders waited patiently until they spotted Captain Norman talking to Lieutenant James.

Suddenly machine-gun fire broke loose, killing James instantly and severely wounding Norman in the arm. As assistant platoon leader, Lieutenant Zastrow recalled: "All hell broke loose. [...] Looked pretty black for awhile. Ran into about eight pillboxes across a creek from us on high ground—darn things were camouflaged so you could hardly see them. All the heavy stuff we had with us were bazookas and rifle grenades—not much against seven feet of reinforced concrete—pretty rough."[369]

Captain Norman's posthumously awarded Silver Star Citation succinctly resumes the action: "Without regard for his personal safety and under heavy machine-gun and small-arms fire, Captain Norman crawled forward well ahead of his men to analyze the defensive installations and plan his attack in the company sector of the attack on the Siegfried Line fortifications. He directed the emplacing of machine guns so they could cover the apertures of the enemy pillboxes, then moved forward again on an exposed slope to plot the fire trench system. While doing this, Captain Norman was fatally wounded but, despite his wound, continued to direct and advise his unit, ensuring the successful storming of the line. His courage and devotion to duty were in keeping with the highest traditions of the Airborne Forces."[370]

Private First Class Leonard H. Dennison, an E Company machine gunner, opened counterfire with his .30-caliber machine gun so the medics could pull Captain Norman to safety. He was later awarded the Silver Star for having "set up his machine gun in an open unprotected position so that he could lay fire on an enemy pillbox in the Siegfried Line from which the Germans had seriously wounded his company commander who lay in an exposed position. His covering fire enabled medical men to reach the company commander, administer first aid, and evacuate him. After the commander had been evacuated, he kept up the covering fire, allowing friendly troops to flank the pillbox and eliminate it. His quick thinking and courageous, unselfish action undoubtedly saved the life of the company commander and led to the knocking out of a vital enemy fortification."[371]

Because Captain Norman's wound required special surgery, he was transferred to a hospital in England. The operation went wrong, however, and he died of wounds on February 8, six days after the battle. Norman's death was a great blow to his close friend 1st Lt. Lauren Ramsey, whose 81mm Mortar Platoon had been left behind because the dense forest prevented them from rendering fire support.[372]

While a medic escorted Captain Norman to the rear, the company executive officer, 1st Lt. John Thompson, took command of the company. Casualties mounted quickly: the squad leader of the 1st Platoon, S/Sgt. Diego Lisciani was killed and the remainder of the lead platoon was pinned down. The platoon sergeant, T/Sgt. Robert Lemery, then assumed command of the platoon with such skill and bravery he was awarded the Silver Star. "Technical Sergeant Lemery bravely led his men across open terrain under intense fire so skillfully that few casualties were sustained. Exposing himself to intense automatic weapons fire, Technical Sergeant Lemery set such an inspiring example for his men that five pillboxes were reduced and 27 prisoners taken. The courageous gallantry and aggressive initiative displayed by Technical Sergeant Lemery in this action were dominant features in the success of the mission and in keeping with the highest traditions of the Airborne Forces."[373]

Meanwhile Pfc. Louis H. Tuthill had seen his squad leader go down. Running zigzag through the intense machine-gun fire to within 75 yards of the pillbox containing the gun, he fired all his ammunition clips into the apertures, then ran up close with a Gammon grenade and tossed it inside. The explosion convinced the five remaining defenders to come out and surrender. Tuthill took them back and delivered them to Thompson, his company commander, before moving to Lisciani's body to pick up his Thompson submachine gun. For his action Tuthill would be decorated with the Silver Star.

With one pillbox taken, Lieutenant Thompson ordered S/Sgt. Frank L. Boersig to lead his 1st Platoon rifle squad to the right to find another route. Going forward, Boersig ran into a minefield and machine-gun fire and his seriously wounded body was carried back by his men. He died of wounds three days later.

Reviewing the company's horrendous situation and many losses, Lieutenant Thompson realized that an advance would be suicidal without the use of mine detectors. He called Lieutenant Colonel Wellems around 0700 hours to make the request, but no detectors were available and the attack had to continue. Knowing that speed is often the key to a successful attack, Wellems came forward to survey E Company's situation, and quickly concluded that Thompson's objection was valid. Changing tactics, Wellems ordered Lieutenant Sweet to bring F Company up to the right of E Company to make a combined frontal assault against the pillboxes.

Lieutenant Sweet briefed his platoon leaders; 1st Lieutenant Stuart McCash's 2nd Platoon was to lead. The platoon approached its objective in deployed formation with bazookas and machine guns on either side, ready to counterfire when needed. Both Sweet and McCash led the platoon in assaulting the enemy strongpoints and bunkers. Firing rifles and heavy BAR's from the hip, all charged onto the enemy-held ridge. They here put Panzerfausts captured in Holland to good use, firing at apertures and heavy steel rear doors, blowing them open. Soon the company had taken 30 prisoners.

According to McCash's assistant, 2nd Lt. Robert E. Bramson, the platoon advanced through "a hilly wooded area that I now know to be the Mertesrott Heights. I didn't know that name at the time—all I saw was single trail path slopping up through a lot of trees in deep snow […]. As I recall, the recon patrol out in front of us met some sort of opposition on the trail and I was ordered to take over the advance single file up the trail with my platoon. We had to proceed cautiously as there were a lot of trip wires strung across the path. We came upon a small clearing with a concrete pillbox about 25 or 30 yards directly ahead at the base of a hillside under a stand of trees— they commenced firing at us as we entered the small clearing.

"We tried to contain the pillbox with bazooka- and rifle-fire while others in the platoon moved close around the flanks to take it out. While firing, I was wounded about 20 yards from the pillbox even though I had some cover from a small tree. The bullet entered my stomach and went out my back, and I lost control of the platoon as I was in deep shock. Shortly thereafter I was wounded again in the upper right thigh as I lay spread-legged open toward the pillbox. A medic I didn't really know who had just been transferred to the company worked on me while they were shooting at us, and I probably owe him my life.

"The flanking troops managed to capture the pillbox and the prisoners were used to carry me back, how far I don't know, to where a snow weasel was available to take me to the nearest aid station. Conditions were such that it was impossible to have even traction vehicles in that area of the Mertesrott Heights. Two men from my platoon [Sgt. Alva R. Thompson and Pfc. James W. Weeks] were killed February 2, 1945, although I have no knowledge of when or where. Private First Class Weeks may have been killed in front of the same pillbox where I was wounded."[374]

Avenging his wounded assistant platoon leader, Sgt. Sylvester Barbu, the radio operator, took Bramson's .45 pistol and used it in the assault on the pillbox.[375] Bramson's platoon leader, too, capably rose to the task, earning a Silver Star for leadership: "Leading his platoon in an attack on the Siegfried Line, Lieutenant McCash planned and carried out a most brilliant assault. Without support of artillery or heavy weapons, he placed his light machine guns and rocket launchers in the most advantageous positions and personally led the assault upon the pillboxes and the mopping-up of infantry behind them. He then reorganized immediately and secured a route of advance for his company. The following counterattack of two battalions of enemy was beaten off. Throughout the entire action Lieutenant McCash displayed a high order of physical courage and intrepid leadership in the face of deadly enemy fire."[376]

On E Company's left flank, 1st Lt. William Sharp's 2nd Platoon simultaneously assaulted, descending a wooded slope toward the open streambed to charge the pillboxes on the other side. Lieutenant Sharp, who had voluntarily led many successful night patrols, was now again on point when machine-gun fire from the pillboxes raked his platoon, instantly killing him and Pfc. Robert A. Lynn. The platoon took over and led the assault up the slope, taking five pillboxes and capturing 27 Germans. For his courageous leadership and example Lieutenant Sharp posthumously received the Silver Star.

Colonel Tucker came up to the front line. Having witnessed E Company's difficulties with his own eyes, it was evident to him that the 2nd Battalion had taken too many casualties to be able to continue the attack. At approximately 0800, he thus committed the 1st Battalion with orders to enter the forest and attack the bunker line on F Company's right flank. Meanwhile, E Company's 3rd Platoon remained pinned down by a pillbox. "As we moved into the line again my squad was involved in trying to reduce a pillbox," Sergeant Duebner recalled. "Our bazooka team was scoring hits full on, but succeeded only in knocking off some cement—along with some of the ice caked on it. As this was going on, a group of officers came up behind me. The leader, a short fellow with a mustache, asked, 'Where is the front line, sergeant?' I replied, 'Sir, you are 50 yards past it!' Thus was my first meeting with Colonel Tucker, the regimental commander!

"At that time we found a guy in the platoon who could pitch real good left handed. He pitched a Gammon grenade into one of the gun ports on the bunker. This brought out the entire 12 Germans that had been inside in a hurry! We had successfully breached the vaunted and feared Siegfried Line!"[377]

The man with the mean left arm, Pfc. Eugene G. Strutzenberg, received the Silver Star for "gallantry in action […] three miles from Neuhof, Germany": "During the assault on the Siegfried Line, when his company was pinned down by very heavy defensive fire from enemy pillboxes, Private First Class Strutzenberg set out voluntarily to neutralize one of the fortifications in the enemy line. He crawled through snow-covered minefields in the face of heavy small-arms fire to within ten yards of his objective and threw a Gammon grenade which blew off the door of the pillbox, killing two of the enemy and stunning the others. The elimination of this critical obstacle permitted the company to resume its advance. Private First Class Strutzenberg's bold demonstration of courage and aggressiveness contributed materially to the accomplishment of his unit's mission."[378]

Two large groups of German troops, thought to be two battalions, moved along the ridge from the southeast around 0830 hours, threatening to split the 2nd Battalion. Lieutenant Sweet rapidly shifted McCash's 2nd Platoon to meet the Germans on the right flank, using the other two platoons to counterattack the enemy to the east. Sweet himself was wounded in the process, but remained with his company and received a Silver Star for his actions. "Personally leading his company in an attack on strongly defended pillboxes and fortifications of the Siegfried Line, Captain Sweet so inspired his men by his courage and gallantry that they swept forward undaunted by the intense fire, neutralized the positions, and took 30 prisoners. When the enemy counterattack threatened to split the battalion, Captain Sweet so committed his company as to confuse the enemy and disorganize their attack. Although wounded, he refused to be evacuated and continued to expose himself fearlessly as he directed the efforts of his men. The gallant leadership of Captain Sweet was a prime factor in the success of his battalion and in keeping with the highest traditions of the Airborne Forces."[379]

Technician Fifth Grade Marvin Dixon, F Company's senior medic, was killed outright as he went forward in the open to render first aid to a wounded paratrooper. He posthumously received the Silver Star: "Technician Fifth Grade Dixon, a Company Aid Man, unhesitatingly crossed 200 yards of wooded terrain under extremely heavy enemy fire to administer first aid to a wounded soldier in an exposed position. While administering first aid to a wounded man, Technician Fifth Grade Dixon was instantly killed. His sacrificial devotion to duty and utter disregard for extreme danger upholds the traditions of the Medical Corps in which he served."[380]

F Company paid a high price for its success that day in repulsing the enemy counterattack, for it lost more men than any other company in the regiment. Twelve non-commissioned officers and privates were killed: S/Sgt. Douglas C. Shuit; Sergeants John Opitz and Alva H. Thompson; T/5 Marvin Dixon; Privates First Class Thomas W. Auck, Robert P. Devine, John A. Patton, and James W. Weeks; and Privates Edward J. Beaton, Willard A. DeVore, Earl G. Meagher, and Paul D. Vukmanic. Shuit was an original F Company member and Opitz came from the disbanded 551st PIB; Thompson had transferred in three weeks earlier from the First Special Service Force. D Company and Headquarters Company, in support, counted no fatal casualties.

Lieutenant Colonel Wellems received a Silver Star for his leadership. "During a critical period in the attack on the Siegfried Line, [Lieutenant Colonel Wellems] ignored heavy artillery and concentrated small-arms fire delivered from well-concealed positions, and moved forward to personally reorganize units shattered by heavy casualties and led them again into the attack. On at least three occasions, Lieutenant Colonel Wellems, finding platoons losing their forward impetus as a result of casualties among officers and non-commissioned officers, personally took command and, without regard for his own safety, conveyed to the units his own fearless determination. During the entire attack, he moved from company to company, encouraging, supervising, and issuing orders, continuously under enemy fire. His calm and courageous leadership, and his unyielding fortitude made possible the successful attack by his battalion."[381]

The engineers from 2nd Platoon, C Company, 307th Airborne Engineers Battalion attached to Wellems' battalion were there to assist with clearing mines and blowing up enemy bunkers. Sgt. Meldon F. Hurlbert and his good friend Pvt. Paul Mennen passed through the dragon's teeth in the outer ring of the Siegfried Line and proceeded through the woods, weapons at the ready. Suddenly coming on a clearing in the woods, Hurlbert hit a trip wire. Both men instantly froze—they had walked into the middle of a minefield! The lay of snow and frost on the mine was likely all that saved them.[382]

Unknown to the Americans at the time, their opponents once more included the battered remnants of the 3rd Fallschirmjäger Division, as well as the 9th Panzer Division, the 18th Volksgrenadier Division, and other smaller units.

CHAPTER 16

BREACHING THE SIEGFRIED LINE
MERTESROTT HEIGHTS, GERMANY,
FEBRUARY 2, 1945

M ajor Berry's 1st Battalion had been dropped off on the Losheim-ergraben–Udenbreth road at first light, and rapidly assembled into squads and platoons. While they were forming up in the forest, Private First Class Bayley got a glimpse of Major General Gavin: "As we gathered our group together, I saw General Gavin on the opposite side of the street conversing with some of our officers. It was encouraging to see that Gavin was with us as we grouped for our mission. He regularly went to the front, sometimes by himself or with one or two others on patrol, to see firsthand what was taking place and to help in planning. He believed that he could best command a battle when he knew the ground and the troops."[383]

Major John Berry briefed his company commanders on the route of attack and their objectives. They, in turn, briefed their platoon leaders. Some of the junior officers were about to experience their first combat with a platoon that was totally unknown to them. Others like 24-year-old 1st Lt. Edward F. Shaifer, Jr., from San Antonio, Texas, had been in command for only a few weeks. A graduate of West Point, Class of 1943, Shaifer had succeeded 2nd Lt. James Douglass as the leader of 3rd Platoon, B Company, after Douglass had been wounded in early January, and was thus still relatively green. "Orders for the employment of the battalion were framed tentatively," he remembered. "Each company was assigned a general portion on the lower Mertesrott Heights which had been designated as the battalion objective. C Company would lead out in the tracks of the 2nd Battalion, turn right after entering the line and center itself on the battalion objective. A and B Companies, following in column, would then position themselves

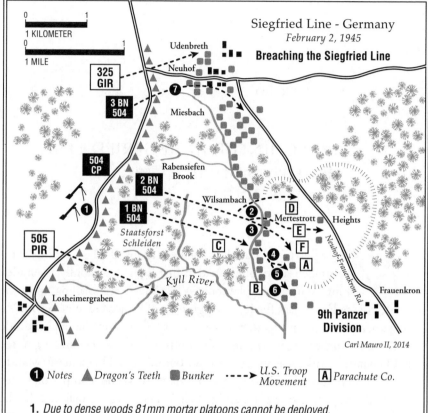

1. Due to dense woods 81mm mortar platoons cannot be deployed.

2. Leading 1st Platoon E Co. (1st Lt. Roy James) is fired upon. Lt. James is killed and Capt. Herbert Norman severly wounded. 1st Lt. John Thompson assumes command of E Co., 2nd Lt. Charles Zastrow the 1st Platoon.

3. In frontal assault on pillbox, 2nd Lt. Robert Bramson (2nd Platoon, F Co.) is severly wounded.

4. Pvt. John McLaughlin (B Co.) killed. His BAR is found about 20 minutes later by Pfc. Edwin Bayley.

5. Newly promoted Sgt. Ervin Shaffer (3rd Platoon, A Co.) leads attack on pillbox. Pfc. Arthur Bates, Jr. and several other men KIA.

6. 1st Lt. Edward Shaifer, Jr., Pfc. Jack Cocozza (3rd Platoon, B Co.) and an interpreter frontally assault and capture a pillbox.

7. Around 1340 hrs. the 3rd BN is held up by vehicles from the 325th GIR as Lt. Col. Julian Cook leads them to Neuhof to carry out a flanking assault from the north.

on the left and right of C Company respectively, thus forming a battalion perimeter on the objective. Mortars and machine guns of the Battalion Headquarters Company would remain under battalion control and be employed on opportunity.

"With no further delay the battalion went into the march, struggling, slipping and sliding up the precipitous route. […] All men were heavily burdened with ammunition and the high proportion of automatic weapons always carried by parachute units. For all individuals the constant climbing and sliding was a hardship. Some men, had they not been closely supervised, would have thrown away the extra ammunition they carried."[384]

The 1st Battalion advanced for some 2000 yards into the forest. Sounds of scattered rifle shots and the occasional staccato of a BAR came from the woods. Shaifer sent Privates William L. Bonning and David Amendola ahead to scout the right flank and check developments in the first 1st Platoon, leading B Company's advance. Bonning recalled that "there was a BAR man firing ahead of me and magazines lying on the snow. He kept firing short bursts and I thought, 'Man, this guy is really good. He is really a hell of a good BAR man.' You could tell from the firing that it was a BAR and you would come across a magazine lying on the snow.

"All of a sudden the firing stopped. Amendola and I kept moving forward and one Kraut came out of the woods, bleeding from his mouth. We at that time were told to take no prisoners, and that is a fact. Most of us did take prisoners, but we didn't have anybody to send this Kraut back with. He was only about 16 years old. He didn't have a helmet on, his shirt was open and his overcoat was open. He had his hands up and his eyes were just huge—he was scared to death. I just told him, 'Zurück, zurück—Go back!' because we couldn't do anything else.

"As we moved forward I saw a figure leaning against a small tree of brush. I came closer and closer, and here it was [Pvt. John W.] McLaughlin. He got shot by a sniper right in the forehead of his helmet. His BAR was stuck in the snow. The medics of course were behind us and they couldn't do anything for him. […] That same day, later, is when [Pvt. Sydney] Redburn got killed. They were both killed at the same day, but one death is dated February 2nd and one is February 3rd. I visited both their graves when I went to Europe on the [60th] anniversary of D-Day. The dates are different on their gravestones but their deaths were the same day."[385]

At approximately 0800 hours, the company reassembled. Although the men could not fathom why, the reason was no mystery to Lieutenant Shaifer:

"Word came back from the Regimental Commander, who was well forward with his lead battalion, that despite the earlier reconnaissance reports, the Siegfried Line was occupied by the enemy in force. The 2nd Battalion had shot its way through the first line of bunkers, suffering heavy casualties, but was now moving forward to its objective against increasing resistance. It was also seriously tied up with heavy counterattacks from the south. The 325th GIR at Neuhof to the north had stirred up a hornet's nest [...]."[386]

First Battalion officers received a quick word concerning the fate of the 2nd Battalion that had gone before them. Wellems' men had captured the central portion of the Mertesrott Heights, but had been counterattacked in battalion strength on their left flank, and also received small-arms fire on their right flank. As soon as trucks were available to bring them up, the 3rd Battalion would be sent through the 325th GIR's sector in the north to attack enemy units now threatening the left flank of the 2nd Battalion.

The 1st Battalion received the order to pass F Company to the right of the 2nd Battalion and attack to the south to relieve pressure on the 2nd Battalion. It was next to seize the southeastern portion of the Mertesrott Heights and cut the Scheid–Neuhof road which ran parallel to the Losheimergraben–Udenbreth road on the west side of the vast forest. First Lieutenant Randles, Shaifer's company commander, called the lieutenant forward for a briefing by Major Berry, who gave orders as follows: "I want B Company to enter the line through the gap created by the 2nd Battalion and attack to the south to take the pressure off that battalion. Your specific objectives are these two pillboxes. Knock them out, then change direction to the southwest and drive to the Wilsam Brook, clearing out any other installations in your path. [...]

"C Company will enlarge the gap made by the 2nd Battalion by turning on the shoulder of the Siegfried Line and attack south along the Wilsam Brook, clearing out all installations as it goes. [...] A Company will follow you until you return to the Wilsam Brook. At that point it will take up your old direction of assault and will make a limited attack to the east."[387]

A soldier of Czechoslovakian origin was sent to accompany Lieutenant Shaifer as an interpreter for occupants of any pillboxes that might surrender. A section of light machine guns was also attached. The 81mm Mortar Platoon was left out of battle because they could not properly deploy in dense forest. A forward artillery observer from the 376th PFAB was attached to 1st Lieutenant James E. Dunn's C Company. His unit would lead out, followed by B Company. The order of march for B Company was: Shaifer's 3rd Platoon; 1st Lieutenant Randles and Company Headquarters; 1st Lt.

Leo Van De Voort's 2nd Platoon; and 1st Lt. Reneau Breard's 1st Platoon bringing up the rear. A Company and Headquarters Company followed B Company. Due to unfavourable terrain, they would not be accompanied by tank destroyers from the 629th TDB. Gunners from the 80th AAAB likewise had to be left behind.

C Company moved out, passing by two bunkers that had been taken by the 2nd Battalion. Signs of a recent violent fight were obvious and demoralizing. A great many dead Germans were strewn about on the ground—and interspersed among them lay several F Company troopers. C Company continued in the lead until Wilsam Brook, when they swung to the right to reduce a pillbox south of a draw and the 3rd Platoon took the lead: "Sporadic mortar and artillery fire was interdicting the area," Lieutenant Shaifer stated. "To prevent casualties and prepare itself for the assault, the platoon was organized into sort of a dispersed column. […] Owing to the denseness of the timber in the area, and the thorough concealment of the German positions it was a certainty that contact with the enemy would come by surprise. The option of opening fire would be all his."[388]

Private Ortega, a recent replacement, was placed diagonally to the front of the platoon.[389] Shaifer knew he would make a perfect target. Ortega was moving forward, but more slowly than Shaifer wanted, so he shouted to him several times, getting him to move from vantage point to vantage point. Checking the route by map proved useless to the young platoon leader, for "it soon became obvious that the wintry terrain corresponded little with the details of the map. This area had never before been occupied by Allied troops and all chartering had been done from aerial photographs. As a consequence each map contained numerous errors. Pillboxes appeared where none were supposed to be and vice-versa."[390]

Private Bonning became "a refugee from the law of averages" that day when Ortega, sent out as a scout, was wounded, and Bonning was ordered to follow him. "The Kraut let Ortega pass, but the Kraut was behind a tree and shot Ortega in the back of the head. Ortega survived, but he was severely wounded. The only way to get back to the aid station was to hitchhike by himself. He was conscious, but nobody could go back with him—we were too short-handed.

"When Ortega got hit I was about 15 or 20 yards behind Lieutenant Shaifer, and he looked at me and he pointed at me to go out as scout. I have had a guilty problem ever since for over 60 years because at the time Amendola was my ammo carrier, and I was BAR man. I lifted up my BAR to show the lieutenant that I had a BAR and shouldn't be going out as a scout. He then pointed at [Pvt. Sydney] Redburn."391

Lieutenant Shaifer continues his account: "The 3rd Platoon was half across a second ridge and had progressed into a forward draw when sweeping rifle fire from a smaller ridge just to the front drove most of the exposed men to the ground. There was no time to turn and regain the cover behind the ridge we'd just traversed. To do so would have been to get shot in the back. One course only was open, a single straight rush at the enemy. The logic was simple. Drive them off the ridge and they wouldn't fire at you.

"I yelled a short order to my men. 'Come on, you guys! Let's get 'em!' There was no time for troop-leading procedures or other control measures. I led off the sudden counterattack myself, firing as I ran. Two veteran men went with me. The rest lay where they had hit the ground, not moving and not shooting. […] Suddenly from the heights to the left a powerful, sustained burst of fire from an American light machine gun ripped into the German position to the front, enfilading the entire ridge. Both I and the two troopers with me recognized the fire as friendly and hit the ground to wait for a lull in the flying bark and armor-piercing ricochets. The enemy fire ceased completely. Twisting back, I yelled to my men: 'When I stand up, all you guys get up here and help us out!' Individual instructions were also shouted to two of the non-coms at the rear to police up the tail of the platoon. The two men who had gone forward with their lieutenant were two of the platoon's three squad leaders. The thing that had sent them forward was the same thing that had made them squad leaders.

"The remainder of the men to the rear were a study in contrasts. Two new machine gunners were crawling backwards from their gun assemblies as if they were more afraid of it than they were the enemy. Only one of the scouts was visible. He lay in a trench of snow with a look of unbelieving horror on his face. At the top of the ridge to the rear appeared two faces— the platoon's veteran sergeants coolly reviewing the situation. Hearing their lieutenant, they shifted forward and called to the men to get ready to move. Control had been reestablished.

"Abruptly the flanking machine-gun fire ceased and I cautiously got up, hoping that the lull would be a long one. It was. Long enough me for to yell, 'Come on, 504, let's get them!' Accompanying shouts and yells rose up and the platoon sprinted forward. About half of it, that is. Many men did not get up until the situation on the top of the hill was proved safe.

"As a matter of fact it was so safe that the platoon had to waste few rounds improving it on the few shadowy forms disappearing into the trees to the front. On the position itself only one German moved. He was in a sitting position with his hands in the air, screaming for his life. He couldn't get up. One of his legs was a twisted, bleeding shambles. Every other German on the ridge lay dead, arrayed in a perfect skirmish line, each behind a tree, many with their brains leaking out of their helmets. The machine-gun fire had been decisive and accurate. It is not often that such completely effective use can be made of an automatic weapon. This cooperative move prevented the 3rd Platoon from receiving a single casualty."[392]

Lieutenant Shaifer reoriented himself on the ridge and surveyed the surrounding area. The two pillboxes he was ordered to take out were nowhere to be seen. Thinking he might have come forward a few hundred yards too far, he turned the platoon to the southwest and headed for Wilsam Brook, where he would have a better chance to orient his position. The B Company command group continued to follow Shaifer and his men, and the 1st Platoon was shifted to Shaifer's left rear to guard the 3rd Platoon's flank.

"The 3rd Platoon continued with the same two reluctant scouts forward," recalled Lieutenant Shaifer. "Their recent performance did not justify replacing them with better men. Progressing downhill, this time more rapidly than before, the platoon had covered about 600 yards without finding a pillbox when it began to receive aimed small-arms fire from the front. The enemy was more distant than in the previous encounter, and thereby allowed the platoon more cover and time with which to prepare a coordinated attack. I called for the platoon sergeant to come forward. Both scouts had been driven down and would not return fire even though repeatedly ordered to do so."[393]

As always in combat, every man sees the action around him differently. "Redburn hit the ground when he saw a machine gun," remembered Private Bonning. "It opened up and Redburn rolled over and raised up his rifle to signal 'machine gun.' Right at that time he got hit. It was an instinctual move—you were trained at the infantry school to raise your rifle over your head when you have seen a machine gun. Redburn was very inexperienced—they broke up Service Company and divided the men [...] and we got Redburn in the 3rd Platoon in Remouchamps, Belgium. Redburn carried everything. Any time you needed something Redburn had it. A needle and thread? He had it. A button? He had it. He carried everything. A can opener? He had it.

"I was told by Lieutenant Shaifer that Amendola and I and [the recently promoted] Sgt. Bob Waldon were to go on the left flank and attack the pillbox on the left. As we were going around, Bob Waldon was to my right front, then there was me, and then Amendola on my left to the rear. We were only three to four yards apart. All of a sudden coming over the rise were two Krauts carrying a litter with a third Kraut on the litter. Waldon held his hand up not to fire. Right then they dropped the litter, the Kraut rolled off, opened fire with a burp gun, and missed all three of us. He didn't hit any of us! I pulled the trigger on the BAR and it went 'clunk.' I'd been carrying it for about an hour in cold, cold weather and it just didn't fire. So I pulled it back and pulled the trigger again and it fired. I spread the top of the snow with bullets, because I was lying down, and we don't know if we got any Krauts at all because we had to turn right at that time to hit the pillbox.

"It was [Pfc.] Jack Cocozza from Philadelphia, Pennsylvania, who attacked the pillbox. The three of them, the interpreter, Cocozza and Lieutenant Shaifer charged that pillbox. I saw them do it through the woods."[394]

Lieutenant Shaifer picks up the story: "This small thrust momentarily caused the Germans to reduce their fire. Several other troopers began to move forward. The impasse was broken and the platoon began to get into action. A group of men came up carrying panzerfausts. One of the light machine guns from the rear began to fire into the tops of the trees in the direction in which I had gone. There wasn't much chance of this gun hitting anybody, but its fire combined with riflemen now in action was effective firepower, for field-gray-clad soldiers could be seen abandoning their positions and fleeing through the trees.

"Suddenly from an open concrete fire pit just to the left of the pillbox, which the interpreter had located and attacked, a group of trapped Volksgrenadiers led by a parachute captain rushed from behind each side of a concrete apron. Somebody let a panzerfaust go perfectly into their midst, and pieces of German soldiers were splattered in liberal quantities all over the landscape. Those of the enemy who were able surrendered on the spot.

"The interpreter, in the meanwhile, almost sprayed his way into the pillbox, which he had rushed all alone, but the Germans who had been out of it defending its rear, shut it in his face as he jumped for the entrance. Screaming in German he fired a full clip into the outer passage in which he was standing, completely unaware of any danger from his own ricochets. He was unharmed.

"Several more panzerfausts were brought up, and security elements were placed to the north and south. In the rear, the platoon sergeant was asking the occupants of the pillbox silenced by the platoon guide to surrender. He was successful shortly thereafter, and four prisoners were taken. One German was dead inside, hit full in the face by the fire the platoon guide had delivered through the aperture. The surrender of the bunker, assaulted singlehandedly by the interpreter, became a cat-and-mouse game. The two embrasures were blown in with panzerfausts in a hurry, but the Germans inside would not readily surrender, because their officer inside would not permit it.

"Several B Company men were standing on top of this pillbox when two bazooka rounds were fired at them by C Company, which had come from the north. This was a mistake in identification. One round exploded in the center of the group but wounded nobody. Recognition was made through the medium of loud protests voiced by B Company. The pillbox surrendered soon after and swelled the company's total for this single action to 22 Germans taken prisoner."[395]

Private Bonning remembered that "when we got the two pillboxes a lot of fire was going on and when we got back and assembled, Murad ("Turk") Nersesian, a long combat vet, was standing right there in the group. There weren't many of us left in the platoon. He said, 'Lieutenant Shaifer, Redburn has got a wristwatch. I think it would be valuable for the platoon to have.' Lieutenant Shaifer allowed Turk Nersesian to get the wristwatch.

"Well, Turk found Redburn and rolled him over. The medic had earlier thought that Redburn was hit in the shoulder, but he wasn't. He was hit in his shoulder but it went through his body and out his side. A little hole out his side. Redburn screamed furiously for about 15 or 20 seconds, and you could hear it all through the woods. He died instantly, but it is not true that he died of shock. My wife and I a few years later visited Redburn's mother in Kentucky, but we did not reveal what had happened. She thought he had been hit in the shoulder and had died of shock."[396]

Following B Company, A Company's advance through the woods also proved to be "no walk in the park." Shortly after assembly, the company moved out under radio silence, advancing nearly without a sound except for low-voiced orders and the crunch of snow underfoot. "There was a narrow road down through the dragon's teeth," recalled Bayley. "We started down this road behind an open cab bulldozer plowing the deep snow in front of it; soldiers would take turns walking ahead with a mine detector. When a soldier got tired walking in the deep snow, another would take his place. We proceeded slowly down the road in a gentle downhill direction. There was firing elsewhere, but nothing in our immediate area. After several hours we saw German prisoners walking back parallel to our advance. That indicated that someone else was operating ahead of us, but had gone in by a different route.

"Finally we arrived at a clear area through which a shallow, narrow river flowed. We were told to stay on the path through this area because of the probability of mines. We had no problem crossing the river. Our feet didn't get wet because we stepped over the rocks. As we crossed the area we could see a three-story reinforced concrete pillbox. It was empty. There were zigzag trenches on the sides of the pillbox—they were empty. We didn't know whether those ahead of us had taken the pillbox or if it was not manned. We saw no soldiers from any other outfit and were told to spread out in lines and climb the steep hill."[397]

As 1st Lieutenant Richard Hallock, 3rd Platoon leader, A Company, recalled the situation, "the 1st Battalion started for its objective in a column of companies, C, B, A. It was out of supporting distance of its 81mm mortars. Its artillery forward observer was with C Company. When the head of the battalion arrived at the draw, however, C Company was at the Wilsalm River, where it had dropped off to reduce a pillbox to permit the passage of the Battalion; and B Company, for some reason, had turned southeast at the draw. [...] A Company arrived at the draw as a two-platoon company, with its platoon in column, 1st, 3rd. It had reorganized into two platoons earlier in the attack. Its strength now was three officers and 59 enlisted men, including an aid man.

"As the company commander arrived at the head of his column, he noted that F Company on his left, deployed on the right flank of the 2nd Battalion objective, was receiving small-arms fire from across the draw. He also noted that his company was leading the Battalion. He was temporarily out of radio contact with Battalion. Knowing that speed was paramount, he decided to proceed with the Battalion mission. He ordered the 1st Platoon to attack across the draw at once.

"The 3rd Platoon, in support, arrived at the draw in platoon column between F Company and 1st Platoon. Sporadic fire from a machine gun and several rifles was being received from the area in front of A Company. This fire seemed unaimed and was not sufficient to deter movement, most of it being directed at F Company. No enemy could be seen, but the platoon leader assumed that he was occupying a blocking position across the draw in platoon, or greater, strength.

"The platoon consisted of an officer, a platoon sergeant, and 21 enlisted men organized as an eight-man rifle squad (the '1st Squad'), a ten-man rifle squad (the '2nd Squad') and a three-man light machine -gun team. The 1st Squad, armed with two Browning Automatic Rifles, one Thompson submachine gun and five rifles, had been organized the day before from remnants of all of the rifle elements of the platoon. The 2nd Squad, armed with two Thompson submachine guns and eight rifles, had been organized a half mile down the road from the remnants of the platoon's mortar squad and six men from the company's dissolved 2nd Platoon. [...]

"The draw in front of the platoon was about 100 yards wide and 50 feet deep with gently sloping sides [...]. The head of the draw was thinly wooded and open to observation from the enemy side. The draw deepened toward the south, and the woods on the far side extended more toward the bottom of A Company's right."[398]

Private Frist Class Shaffer suddenly found himself promoted to sergeant as his unit moved into the area on the outer part of the Siegfried Line that had already been captured. "We walked through the dragon's teeth and into the area where they had the bunkers. [...] Some of our men were already up there [...] shooting at the Germans that were on top of a small hill in front of us. Lieutenant Hallock called all of the sergeants and me over, and that is where he promoted me to sergeant. He said, 'Sergeant Shaffer, you take your squad and you lead the attack up the hill. When you get on top of the hill there is a road—go to the right.' Now he didn't know it, but that was the main bunker we were taking [...] inside the Siegfried Line. It was one of the main bunkers that were built up along there.

"We got in place and I led the attack up the hill. I saw the man that was carrying the automatic rifle, the BAR, lying down. I went right over to him, and he said, 'I can't get up. I hurt my back.' I said, 'Well, get up.' He said, 'I can't get up.'

"I said, 'Give me your BAR,' and I took the BAR and some ammunition. I told the ammunition carrier to come with me. I opened up and sprayed the whole mountainside and started running up the hill again. I looked over to my left and there were two Germans lying behind a machine gun. They had been shooting at us. I turned and held the gun on them and made a run for them and came over to the emplacement and kicked it out of their hands. We made them stand up and took those two prisoners.

"As we started on [further up the hill] another German jumped up and started running. I let him have a burst with the BAR and he was down. We got up to a road, went down the road, and Germans opened up on us again. A German machine gun that I could not see [was] behind a snow bank firing all over to the distant position on our right. I jumped in a trench and I could see where the gun should lead to. I started firing in that trench as far away as 5000 feet to the place where the machine gun was and stopped that machine gun right away.

"Lieutenant Hallock came running over to me and he said, 'Turn your gun this way and keep shooting, we've got to get two men out.' I covered him while he went out to help them. And a German in front of me in a foxhole jumped out and came running straight toward me. He was running for a hole in front of me that I hadn't seen. I opened up with the BAR and I gave it to him. I think it killed him." [399]

Lieutenant Hallock remembered this action as well: "In a few yards the line reached level ground above the draw. About 40 Germans could be seen prone behind trees, their positions exposed to the advancing line. The skirmish line almost halted as the men fired flatfooted into the nearest Germans, who were only a few feet away, some returning fire and some already dead. On the right, a German crawled forward, pushing a MG34 ahead of him in the snow, and was killed as he tried to put it into action. A second German, moving as though in a trance, tried to man the gun, but it was kicked out of his hands and he was killed as he reached for it a second time." [400]

As acting Sergeant Shaffer and his squad charged up the hill, Pvt. Ervin L. ("Pop") Prechowski was wounded: "I found him and he had fallen to his knees. When he fell back I called him and it looked like a bullet had hit him in the heart area because he was all bloody. I laid him down and thought, 'for sure, he is dead now.' Anyway I said, 'The medic will be along soon.' I was leading the charge so I couldn't stop."[401]

The 3rd Platoon medic, Pfc Benjamin P. Walker, was indeed directly following Shaffer. His posthumously awarded Silver Star Citation describes his actions as he administered aid to Prechowski: "During an assault upon a strongly defended enemy position one of the assault squad was seriously wounded. Private First Class Walker, an Aid Man, with no thought for his personal safety, left his position of comparative safety and rushed forward to the wounded man despite intense machine-gun and sniper fire. Disregarding the hail of enemy bullets, he administered first aid in the exposed position. When he attempted to carry the casualty to safety, Private First Class Walker was seriously wounded himself. The supreme heroism and high conception of duty displayed by Private First Class Walker were a tribute to himself and the Medical Corps."[402]

Private First Class Arthur W. Bates, Jr., from Pennsylvania, was killed while assisting Shaffer to fire at a German bunker. "He was my very good friend and he had been my ammunition carrier for quite a long time when I had the bazooka, the rocket gun," Shaffer recounted. "He was killed going up this hill which turned out to be a big bunker under the ground."[403]

Meanwhile, Bayley and others in the 1st Platoon also started up the hill. The snow hid a veritable quilt of lethal antipersonnel mines. Bayley remembered no resistance during the first part of the difficult advance up the steep, frozen hill. Everything was quiet, except for the sound of breaking twigs, climbing parachute boots, and heavily breathing men: "The hill was covered in icy snow and we had to climb almost hand-by-hand by grabbing small trees. At the top of the hill were countless log-covered gun emplacements that were high enough to use guns from, but with tops just above ground level so that they might be hard to see and to attack. They were empty.

"In a few minutes, we met a large group of Germans heading through the heavy woods, apparently to reach the emplacements. We sensed that the enemy was close by and got ready to attack. I test-fired the brand-new BAR that I had picked up a few days ago and it would not work. Nothing is scarier than facing imminent combat with a useless weapon. It was just about unbelievable that when I looked to my left I found an old-issue BAR resting against a tree.[404] Somebody had been there some time before us and left the gun. Happily, the gun worked well when test-fired.

"We now met the Germans head-on in a very intense and heavy firefight. Many soldiers on both sides were getting hit, as this was practically a hand-to-hand battle. I could see smoke-tracing bullets as they passed close to me. Finally, I got hit by a bullet which made a long, deep wound in my left shoulder.

"About three paratroopers fired at the soldier who had shot me and killed him. I retain thanks for those who killed the person who wounded me, and yet feel compassion for that person, who died crying out for his mother. I could not continue to fire my BAR, so I propped it against a tree and went looking for help. While walking back for medical assistance, I met a close friend, Pvt. Ernest LaCroix, who had been shot through the throat. He was not bleeding badly and could talk okay. We continued to walk back along the narrow road and came to the small river we had crossed an hour or so before.

"On the far side was a group of airborne soldiers who stopped before advancing into the battle behind our troops. The [2nd] Battalion Surgeon, Captain Bruns, had set up a temporary treatment table and was ministering to those needing assistance. A group of German prisoners with a German medic was in line nearby.

"Several troopers were sitting in a circle, apparently eating field rations and chatting. Another trooper jumped over the heads of the others and landed in the middle of the circle, apparently tripping a mine. He and several others were grievously injured. Pieces of metal also struck Captain Bruns. The German prisoner medic broke ranks and opened his medical case and began immediately administering to the fallen troopers. Just after this event LaCroix and I reached a jeep that picked us up and took us to a front-line emergency hospital."[405]

Captain Bruns was wounded in the head, and would later receive the Bronze Star: "Captain Bruns, while working at his forward aid station, was struck and rendered unconscious by fragments of a hand grenade thrown by an enemy soldier. Regaining consciousness, Captain Bruns refused evacuation or treatment until the attack was successfully completed, all wounded evacuated, and another medical officer was brought forward to relieve him. Captain Bruns' devotion to duty reflects credit upon the highest traditions of the Medical Corps in which he served. Entered military service from Sioux City, Iowa."[406]

Bruns has blurred memories of what happened: "I don't remember getting hit or treating my wounded soldiers, but I do recall a GI standing close to me having his leg blown off. I remember being loaded into a 'meat wagon' at night, having a long, bumpy ride before awakening on an operating table. It seems that two young, inexperienced surgeons like me were exploring my right neck region. One said: 'I think that's the carotid artery. Let's get the hell out of here.'

"I believe my next stop was a hospital in Paris, the Hotel Dieu, and from there a hospital in England. I remember physicians making rounds and commenting: 'He's been sleeping for three days like most of the others.' Incidentally, when the War Department informed [my wife] Gert that I was wounded in battle, it was the first time she found out I had joined the paratroopers. I thought it would worry her unnecessarily if I told her I had transferred from the safety and solitude of the Air Force."[407]

As Bayley and Bruns were evacuated to a hospital, the remainder of A Company captured the top of hill. In the words of Bayley's platoon leader, 1st Lieutenant James A. Kiernan, "It was really a kind of small-arms battle. There was an enlisted man nicknamed Tex who couldn't see too far. At some point I knew that some were shooting at me too. [...] Bullets were zipping by and I moved over about three or four feet and here was this damn Tex. He couldn't see who it was [...]. He was shooting at me [from] 20 or 30 yards away, but didn't hit me. And then he said, 'Geez, lieutenant, I thought you were a German.'"[408]

A Company's Lt. John Pease contacted his counterparts in B and C Companies by radio and learned they were already assembled not far away at the battalion objective. Casualties had been high on the German side, but Pease had several men wounded in action and one killed, Pvt. George W. Strohmaier. Shortly later, the company moved on to join the other two rifle companies. The day had made Kiernan proud: "The 1st Platoon did not fail or falter [...]. Rather, it acquitted itself well in a difficult situation. We had fought long and hard that day until we took the objective. We reorganized on the objective and almost immediately were given a new mission of establishing contact with the 2nd Battalion. Our Battalion said we had taken our objective, but in fact we had not. I had been given the job to contact the 2nd Battalion."[409]

Lieutenant Kiernan made his way to the 2nd Battalion CP, located in a pillbox, and got himself orientated on a map. With that, he returned to A Company to give the correct coordinates to Lieutenant Pease, who shared them with his colleagues and platoon leaders. "As a matter of fact, the battalion had failed by some 600 yards to reach its proper objective," recalled Lieutenant Shaifer. "This error, however, gave little tactical advantage to the enemy, for the 2nd Battalion had successfully cut of the Neuhof road. Moreover, the 1st Battalion in its present location could do a fair job of defending the regimental sector from the south." A serious problem nevertheless remained: "A supply-carrying weasel, riskily squeezed through Neuhof by B Company's supply sergeant, was trapped by the enemy as it searched for the misplaced battalion on the Neuhof road. This vehicle carried a trailer loaded with ammunition and odds and ends of a few ration boxes scavenged from the 740th TB, which supported the division. Food was beginning to become a real problem. Every man's belly was gnawed by hunger.

"Company B went into position on the south flank of the battalion perimeter, and immediately dispatched patrols to its front. These patrols were short-lived: they had gotten no farther than 125 yards when one [...] caught a group of Germans in the open between two pillboxes. They drove [the Germans] inside one of the bunkers and returned with the story that a line of the forts lay to the south. [...]

"As the last daylight faded, the northern half of the company was plastered with salvo after salvo of 155mm artillery fire continually bursting in the tree tops. The occupants of the pillboxes that B Company patrols had contacted had undoubtedly called for the fire. Several men were wounded in the initial barrage: one man who lost most of his lower legs received more wounds seconds later, even while others bent closely over him. This shook morale, for the wounded man was one of the legendary heroes of the unit.

"The incessant fire lasted all night, perhaps because the enemy had few other targets. The volume was so heavy that when dawn arrived, the forest Company B had occupied the night before was now only an open clearing of slashed and jagged stumps. Branches and tree limbs continuously showered down on us all night long. The wounded were evacuated by strong patrols that made contact with the enemy both coming and going."[410]

The 3rd Battalion had been in regimental reserve for most of February 2, waiting from 0830 hours on the Losheimergraben–Udenbreth road. Lieutenant Colonel Cook and Captain Keep went forward to the 2nd Battalion area to get an update on the attack and confer with Colonel Tucker. They returned to the battalion at 1100 hours with new orders. "Colonel Tucker changed our mission," wrote Major Zakby in the battalion journal. "We will make a flanking attack from the north, attacking south down the road from Neuhof. By doing so we will be behind the main installations of the Siegfried Line—sweep down road clearing high ground to our right, therefore relieving pressure from 1st and 2nd Battalions."[411]

Cook called for his company commanders and gave them the order of attack: Captain. Gray's II Company leading, followed by Captain Burriss' I Company, Battalion staff, Captain Warfield's Headquarters Company, and 1st Lieutenant Goethe's G Company in the rear. Both H and I Company would receive an attached machine-gun squad; a squad of engineers, four medium tanks and eight tank destroyers would accompany the battalion. The battalion column set off for Neuhof by 1330 hours, but was soon stopped behind vehicles from the 325th GIR and attached units.

Annoyed by the traffic jam, Cook and Keep headed for Billingslea's Regimental CP in quest of more information. The battalion meanwhile remained in position along the road, ducking in ditches due to heavy shelling. Frequent radio messages were received from Colonel Tucker, urging the battalion to move out to aid the rest of the regiment. Colonel Billingslea informed Cook and Keep that Neuhof was partially in American and partially in German hands. Lt. Col. Edwin J. Ostberg, commanding 2nd Battalion, 325 GIR, had been fatally struck by a German tank round while standing on an American tank to better direct fire against German tanks at a junction between Neuhof and Udenbreth.

Just before the fighting near Udenbreth, 1st Lieutenant G. P. Crockett, liaison officer of the 504th to the 325th Glider Infantry Regiment, had been made acting commander of B Company when all the officers were wounded on February 1. Sgt. Clinton Riddle, 325th GIR, recalled that Lieutenant Crockett sent for him. "He said, 'You have been with the company long enough you ought to know what you are doing. I want you for my runner or messenger and I want you to help me out. I have not had much combat experience.' I thought that strange for an officer, asking an enlisted man to help him, besides it was a paratrooper asking a gliderman to help him with his leadership. (There wasn't much love between a paratrooper and a gliderman in the beginning; they counted us glidermen as second-class troopers.) 'Yes Sir, I will help you all I can.' The day before the attack was a busy day. I helped give out the rations and supplies after dark for the next day. It was about midnight by the time I got my foxhole dug in the snow-covered frozen ground and got to sleep.

"About 0230 or 0300 o'clock in the morning, Lieutenant Crockett sent for me [...] to go on patrol with him. Just he and I were all that were going. (This showed the lack of combat experience. Most of the time six or eight men would make up a patrol.) We walked several hundred yards to within sight of the dragon's teeth on the Siegfried Line near the village of Udenbreth. We walked parallel with the line quite some distance. We could just make out the outline of the bunker on the side of the road leading through the rows of dragon's teeth into Germany. Pill boxes dotted the hillside, arranged to cover each other with crossfire. [...]

"We made an attack the next morning. A Company went first and was pinned down, B Company went next and was pinned down, C Company, in reserve, came up next. We crawled and crawled in the snow, then would get up and run a short distance. During one of the short runs a burst of machine-gun fire knocked a big hole in the tail of my overcoat. We made it up to the road after almost taking the whole morning. When we reached the road Lieutenant Crockett looked back over his shoulder and said, 'Come on Riddle, let's go to the other side of the road.' Those were the last words he said. He ran toward the other side of the road. When he was half-way across, the Germans had the road covered and he never knew what hit him. I hit the snow and waited a while before getting up to go again."[412]

Brig. Gen. Ira P. Swift, the assistant division commander, ran into Lieutenant Colonel Cook, and asked him why his battalion was not carrying out the flanking movement through Neuhof into the Mertesrott Heights. "How can I? The 325th GIR is still far from taking Neuhof!" Cook replied.

Not until 1930 hours that evening could the attack be carried out. H

Company, in the lead, was "held up by a bunker with a machine gun," Sergeant Tarbell recalled, which finally "must have run out of ammunition. They started coming out of there, holding up their hands. And, boy, were they crying. These were old men—30 years old, 40—not the young kids we were used to."[413] To the amazement of Tarbell and his comrades, the Germans removed their wedding rings and gave them to the Americans, along with pictures of their families. "They must have thought we were going to kill them all. We didn't. We captured them. They put up a good fight for old guys."[414]

Cpl. John ("Mel") Clark, recently transferred to the 3rd Battalion from the disbanded 551st PIB, was attacking a bunker when he "fell through ice in a creek and got wet up to the waist. Another kid and I got 21 prisoners out of the bunker, including a girl. […] I was evacuated on 5 February from Eimsert, Germany, with blast injury from a grenade and frozen feet. I went to the evacuation hospital in Liège."[415]

With three medium tanks and seven tank destroyers attached to the battalion, the advance across the road from Neuhof to the south and through the Mertesrott Heights went swiftly. Little opposition was encountered, and armor soon silenced any resistance there was. At 2130 hours the 2nd Battalion was contacted and a patrol was sent to locate the 1st Battalion. The patrol made contact and after its return, tanks and tank destroyers were sent down the road to join the 1st Battalion. Meanwhile, Major Zakby had set up the 3rd Battalion CP next to that of the 2nd Battalion for the rest of the night.

The attack that day been had successful: all division objectives—Udenbreth, Neuhof, and Mertesrott Heights—were taken by nightfall. Tucker's troopers had advanced 6000 yards and seized the Mertesrott Heights, organized positions, and repulsed enemy counterattacks. The regiment spent the next two days consolidating the heights. It had been a costly day with three officers and 20 non-commissioned officers and enlisted men killed, many of whom were veterans of earlier campaigns. Private First Class Jesse L. Mitchem from F Company was also taken prisoner that day. Fortunately, several of the mines and booby traps the regiment had encountered did not explode because freezing temperatures, snow and ice had corroded their detonating mechanisms. The seemingly impregnable Siegfried Line had been breached: the next battle would be deeper into German territory.

CHAPTER 17

FROM ONE FOREST TO ANOTHER
HUERTGEN FOREST, GERMANY, FEBRUARY 3–21, 1945

The night of February 2–3, "the temperature dropped considerably and the men's wet clothing froze on their bodies," recalled Lieutenant Shaifer. "There was no warmth of any kind. Blankets, shelter halves and raincoats had all been left in the assembly area. Many men slept with their arms around each other trying to keep warm. Company officers were to endure all night the moaning of their men fighting the cold. [...]

"The labor of traversing areas without coats in blinding snow storms, through waist-deep drifts, in sub-zero temperatures without rest, shelter or food took its inevitable toll. Men's feet were beginning to bleed and ooze fluid from the alternate freezing and friction of halts and marches. Feet and hands both were beginning to turn the blue-black of frostbite or trench foot. Some of the serious cases were asked to return to the rear. This they refused to do, claiming that they were good for at least a few days more. Some men removed their boots and found that they could not put them back on again. They wrapped their feet in parts of enemy uniforms, asking not to be evacuated."[416]

The 1st Battalion Surgeon suggested that the troopers rub their feet with Barbasol shaving cream. The battalion aid station was set up in a pillbox. B Company men would visit in groups of two or three, get a tube of shaving cream (of which whole cases were available) and receive two new pairs of socks. "That night they realized how much moisture there was in this stuff and it froze. Our feet were freezing. We were using *Stars and Stripes*, brown toilet paper, to get it off our feet, but it ruined one pair of

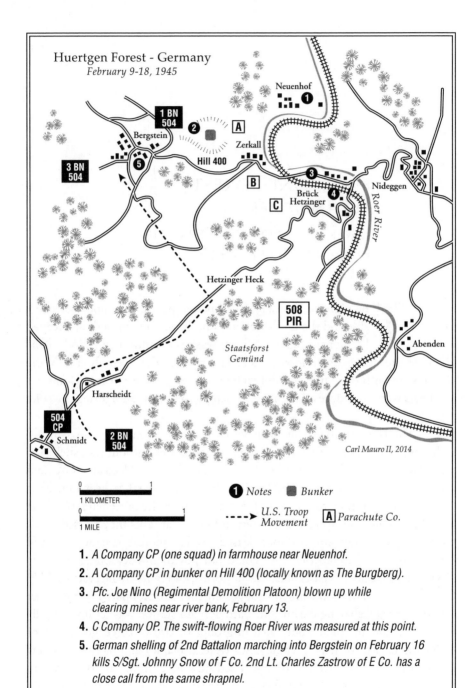

Huertgen Forest - Germany
February 9-18, 1945

Carl Mauro II, 2014

1 KILOMETER

1 MILE

1 Notes ▪ Bunker

----▸ *U.S. Troop Movement* Ⓐ *Parachute Co.*

1. *A Company CP (one squad) in farmhouse near Neuenhof.*
2. *A Company CP in bunker on Hill 400 (locally known as The Burgberg).*
3. *Pfc. Joe Nino (Regimental Demolition Platoon) blown up while clearing mines near river bank, February 13.*
4. *C Company OP. The swift-flowing Roer River was measured at this point.*
5. *German shelling of 2nd Battalion marching into Bergstein on February 16 kills S/Sgt. Johnny Snow of F Co. 2nd Lt. Charles Zastrow of E Co. has a close call from the same shrapnel.*

socks. We had two pairs on. It was terrible. GI's were having an awful time trying to get the frozen stuff off. We wrapped our feet in newspapers, *Stars and Stripes* and so on, to keep them from freezing. But it was a farce to use that shaving cream.

"When we had that shaving cream episode [...], I went back by myself. I had to go west, south and then east. There were small flags stuck in the snow to find the aid station. When I got there Major Berry asked if there was anybody there from B Company. He had a map on a table in the pillbox. I said, 'Yes, I am in B Company.' He said, 'Can you read a map and tell me where B Company is, compared to where we are here?' I said, 'Sir, if I go out the door, and instead of following the flags, go straight across and go north, I'll go straight to B Company.' He said, 'What?' and I said, 'Yeah, I went east and then I went south and then I went west and you're right on the line.' He said, 'We can't be on the line.' I answered, 'Well, yes, you are,' and I showed him on the map exactly the way we went. He said, 'We have got to get the hell out of here.' When I went to the aid station, there was something I didn't notice [until] I walked out [...]. I was then facing south and there must have been 40 dead GI's all lined up with raincoats and canvas covers over them. [...] All you could see were their boots. That really hit me."[417]

That same day, 1st Lt. Vance C. Hall, Jr., a platoon leader in F Company, reported back to the 2nd Battalion CP after being hospitalized for several days due to frozen feet. As he was about to enter the farmhouse where the CP was located, he saw a pile of frozen bodies stacked up like firewood in the snow. Freezing temperatures had prevented the U.S. Army from properly burying their dead. Taking a closer look, Hall recognized some of the soldiers—they were men from his platoon! His return to his battalion was a bitter one, and he would never forget seeing his fellow soldiers stacked up like firewood.[418]

In the evening the Germans counterattacked the Mertesrott Heights in an attempt to regain the high ground they had lost the day before. The German infantry was supported by numerous artillery pieces of various calibers. Some of the fighting was vicious, as demonstrated by the Bronze Star Citation for C Company's Cpl. Forrest L. Smith, from Grand Rapids, Michigan. Smith "voluntarily manned a machine gun whose operator had been killed and which was still the target of the enemy's concentrated fire. With his group reduced from 23 to nine men, and with four machine guns knocked out and under a hail of fire that ricocheted off his gun, Smith fearlessly exposed himself to almost certain death to cut down wave after wave of on-rushing Germans. He remained at his post until blinded by an exploding Panzerfaust. His courage and devotion to duty saved the position from annihilation and was responsible for the security of his Battalion's flank."[419]

The attack was repulsed, but the list of the dead is long. In C Company, T/4 Christ Buchikos, a former member of the disbanded 1st Special Service Force; Privates First Class Philip J. Huber, Rene R. Pelletier, and John E. Whalen; and Pvt. Don P. Asbury were killed. A Company lost Pfc. Bruce P. Gibson and Headquarters Company, 1st Battalion, lost William A. Preston. Sgt. Arthur M. Wright, Headquarters Company, 1st Battalion, and Pvt. Alfred J. Zurlino, D Company, died of wounds.

"During the night [of February 2–3] enemy infantry had not been idle," recalled Lieutenant Shaifer. "[The enemy] had fully developed the battalion's position, and with daylight he launched heavy, coordinated counterattacks, preceded by masses of artillery fire, principally against A and C Companies. These were repelled only after severe fighting. Company B was struck by a flanking unit of about a platoon in size, and this attack was quickly repelled, mainly by the actions of one of the attached machine-gun crews."[420]

Although the 1st Battalion had repulsed the counterattack, Colonel Tucker was dissatisfied that the battalion's original February 3 objective was yet to be achieved. Late in the afternoon of February 4, he ordered Major Berry to continue his attack, now that the 508th PIR had moved up closer to the 504th positions. "A wide gap existed between the 1st and 2nd Battalions," recalled Shaifer, "and because of the unremitting German counterattacks, it was essential that the 1st Battalion position be improved. Having had the major portion of its front pinched out by the 508th, Company B was free to be used for this purpose. It constituted the only unit in the entire regiment that could be spared. The 3rd Battalion was completely employed in mopping up the defenses between Neuhof and the Jagerhauschen Farm. Both A and C Companies were desperately resisting well-supported countertattacks from the south and could not possibly be disengaged. They were to be under constant pressure for the next 37 hours."[421]

First Lieutenant Breard, 1st Platoon, B Company, was ordered to lead his company's advance: "In this late afternoon attack my platoon of 17 men, reinforced with an M10 tank destroyer, moved out down a trail in the forest. The snow was about two feet deep, with two scouts out front and squads on either side of the M10. At a bend in the trail we came under a sudden intense mortar barrage. Within minutes my platoon was decimated. The

M10 backed up fast. Four men and myself were the only ones not wounded [… and] we had one man killed. After getting the wounded out, I reported the action to Lieutenant Randles and he called Battalion on the phone.

"Major Berry then talked to me on the phone and ordered me to take the 2nd Platoon and continue the attack. Berry ordered me to take the 2nd Platoon up. I told him, 'I am not sure what I am going to run into. I went on this one in such a hurry that we made no reconnaissance whatsoever. They could hear that tank destroyer. They only had a gun and a .50-caliber.'

"He said, 'Are you refusing?'

"I said, 'Major Berry, I am not refusing. I will go either way. I will take the platoon out if you want me to. But I'd like to make a reconnaissance first and see what I can find out and take that platoon leader with me.'

"Randles was right there. He wasn't listening but he was there standing behind. Berry said, 'All right, wind it up and see what you can come up with on a reconnaissance.' Right after [that] I got Lieutenant Randles to alert the 2nd Platoon and I went to that platoon to see Lieutenant Van De Voort, the platoon leader. He was a replacement officer and had received the DSC with the 116th Infantry Regiment, 29th Infantry Division, on D-Day in Normandy, and was sent to B Company as a replacement right after me."[422]

First Lieutenant Shaifer, leader of B Company, 3rd Platoon, also recalled that night. "It was now dark. While we were preparing for the recon with two men, a runner came up and said 'Lieutenant Randles wants to see you.' I went back in and Randles told me the attack was cancelled and we would be relieved by a battalion of the 99th Infantry Division before dawn. That's when word came down by phone that we could send four men on rest and recuperation to Paris. I suggested my four remaining men that I had left on an outpost. He said, 'Yeah, but that will leave you without a platoon.' I said, 'I lost a platoon up there.' The four men left and they made me executive officer of B Company."[423]

Private Bonning watched as members of the 1st Platoon straggled back: "The 1st Platoon had received many casualties and their walking wounded were walking back. I was 10 to 15 feet from Lieutenant Randles when he was arguing on the radio—he was standing behind a tank destroyer—and he was having a heck of a time with Battalion, saying that we had to stop the attack because we were receiving so much flat-trajectory fire. I was very proud of our officer at that time. He really, really knew that if we went further our whole company would have been annihilated. I have to give it to Lieutenant Randles for arguing. It was sincerely justified. He was a heck of a man."[424]

As Shaifer recalls, at that moment, the leader of the 2nd Platoon broke. First Lieutenant Van De Voort was by any man's measure a hero and a very experienced soldier and officer who had withstood some of the worst tests of the war. He had survived the landing of the 116th Infantry Regiment on Omaha Beach and earned a DSC for leading a rifle company a few days later. He had been wounded in Normandy and volunteered for the airborne troops in England. But now, seeing so many men suffering in the freezing cold, without proper food, clothing or shelter from the elements, he could take no more. According to Shaifer, Van De Voort "stayed [in the CP] only long enough to hear the battalion commander on the SCR-300 radio change his plan and order the company to defend in its present position. Deserting his platoon, he returned to the safety of a pillbox to the rear. He no longer had the courage required to lead his men."[425]

After another cold night, the 289th Infantry Regiment from the 99th Infantry failed to show up in the morning. Colonel Tucker's troopers would be longer on the line. This cost the life of one trooper, Pvt. Philip Alberts of Headquarters Company, but on many occasions that day, it was just plain luck that other men managed to escape fatal hits. Private Bonning was on an outpost with his assistant BAR gunner, Private Amendola, and Pfc. Charles E. Mizzi: "A flat-trajectory was going over our heads from a tank. We couldn't spot the tank and we would take turns jumping out in a firebreak and jump back into the woods. Mizzi would jump out, I would jump out and then Amendola would jump out and jump back in. The three of us were lying in a slit trench because we didn't know how long we were gonna be there, and in fact the trajectory was just peeling the bark off all the trees.

"It was just horrible how many guys were getting hit. The three of us were lying together: Mizzi, Amendola in the middle and myself. We got our hands and arms over our heads and Amendola got hit. He was screaming for a medic and wanted to take his sulfa pills and I was trying to discourage him because he just got hit in the arm. Then I jumped up in the firebreak and went to look for Johnny, our medic. He came running up and flat-trajectory was flying over his head and exploding. I motioned for Johnny to go back, but he couldn't figure out why because there was Amendola screaming 'Medic, medic!' And I was yelling at Amendola: 'You can walk back! You can walk back!' because we were going to get our medic killed. So Amendola finally got up and ran, crouched down, and the two of them ran back all the way on the firebreak and neither got hit.

"Then they sent Smitty up to replace Amendola as my ammo bearer. I didn't know him but they sent him out, and he was a hell of a combat guy too. Boy, I tell you, you can tell who is a good combat guy and who isn't, and who you *can* be with and who you *cannot* be with, and you try to avoid and stay away from those who will get you killed."[426]

The stubborn defense of the 504th PIR had permitted the division to consolidate its defensive positions on the Mertesrott Heights, Neuhof and Udenbreth, and to eliminate the scattered groups of enemy soldiers encountered in the rear area. "Still waiting for the relief," Staff Sergeant Rice, 2nd Platoon, H Company, recorded: "Left pill-box at 1930. Stumbled in the dark [for] three miles. No trucks—staying here all night—in bed 0020! Damn near froze. Pine forest. Rain, snow, thawing mud."[427]

The morning of February 5, the exhausted paratroopers could finally sleep in, sheltered by the pup tents set up in a rear area. "Breakfast 0930. Sick call—1300—lost six men from Plt. to hospital with trench foot. Hands cold. Lots of letters from everyone—no packages. Froze two big toes," wrote Rice in his diary.[428] That same day a former member of the Office of Strategic Services [OSS], 1st Lt. Vincent P. Ralph, reported to the 3rd Battalion CP. Born in Cleveland, Ohio, Ralph had been an original member of the 464th PFAB before attending OCS to become an officer and joining the OSS, arriving in North Africa in April 1944. Sent on several missions in Operation Group Helen [an OSS outfit operating in Italy and France], Ralph wanted to rejoin a regular airborne outfit. He was assigned to I Company to command the 2nd Platoon.

Colonel Tucker favored veteran officers as replacements for wounded senior officers and captains. On February 5, E Company received a new company commander, 1st Lt. Leo L. Rodrigues. A former C Company platoon leader in the disbanded 509th PIB, Rodrigues soon earned the respect of his men. An inexperienced replacement officer, 2nd Lt. William L. McDaniel, was assigned to G Company as assistant platoon leader.

On February 6, the regiment was trucked to the vicinity of Petit-Halleux, the scene of fighting in early January, where the 3rd Battalion reorganized and refitted to move to another sector in the front lines. The remainder of the regiment was billeted in the nearby town of Grand Halleux. Ironically the men received shoepack boots, which they could have used to better advantage in the freezing weather of previous weeks. The snow had begun to melt, so there was little use for them now. Promotions also came through, noted by Sergeant Rice: "Official rating S/Sgt came thru today—effective as of Jan 19th. Resting—how long?"[429]

On February 7, the 3rd Battalion received bad news. The 505th and 517th Parachute Infantry Regiments had been engaged in fierce fighting in the Huertgen Forest, a large wooded area to the north in the triangle between the German cities of Aachen, Monschau, and Düren. The 505 and the 517 had suffered many casualties, and Colonel Tucker had been ordered to send up one of his battalions to act as division reserve. The task fell to the 3rd Battalion, which had suffered fewer casualties than its two sister battalions and was thus in better shape. A meeting for company commanders at the Battalion CP disclosed that the new assembly area was near the Belgian town of Eupen. The move was scheduled for that evening.

At 1600 hours the 3rd Battalion learned their destination would instead likely be a village in Germany. The move was called off until 0400 hours on February 8. Five hours later, at 0900 hours on February 8, the 3rd Battalion closed in at the railway station in the small village of Schmidthof, Germany. Long, successive rows of dragon's teeth lined the countryside, indicating the outer ring of the Siegfried Line at its strongest point.

On the morning of February 9, the remainder of the 504th PIR and other units of the 82nd ABD were trucked to the Huertgen Forest to join the 505th and 508th Parachute Infantry Regiments. The Division Command Post was established in Rott and the Regimental CP was in Schmidthof. That same day the 1st and 2nd Battalions received badly needed replacements. In A Company, 28 green replacements came straight from Parachute School in Fort Benning.

Nineteen-year-old Pvt. David L. Haushalter and Pvt. Charles W. Hofmeister had become close friends on the trip to Europe, and the two were lucky enough to be assigned to the same rifle squad in the 3rd Platoon of A Company. Haushalter, born in February 1926, grew up in New Jersey, graduated from high school in autumn 1944, and volunteered for the paratroopers after basic training at Camp Blanding, Florida. "Three or four of us went at the same time and had a physical examination. Getting into the paratroopers you had to have a certain weight and height and things like that. They turned me down for the paratroopers for being too tall and having a heart murmur, a very slight one. A couple of buddies and I talked to the doctor. I said, 'You know, I'd like to go and you passed all my buddies and now I can't go.' I explained that I played all kind of sports and then he said 'OK,' and they finally passed me."[430]

Private Hofmeister from Baltimore, Maryland, was the same age as Haushalter. Hofmeister's brother William had been killed in November 1943 at

Venafro, Italy, while serving with Colonel Darby's Rangers. Although he had not yet been drafted, Hofmeister asked his mother if she would sign his application papers for the army, and she finally consented. He finished basic training and was sent to Fort Benning. Arriving fresh on the front, Hofmeister and his fellow replacements found themselves assigned to foxholes. Sitting alone in the dark, he wondered where the others were and to which outfit he belonged. The next morning he learned he was now a member of A Company, 3rd Platoon, and met his squad leader, Sgt. Henry R. Girard, Jr., from Taunton, Massachusetts.[431]

The night of February 9-10, the Germans blew the Schwammenauel Dam and the Roer River overflowed in the U.S. First and Ninth Army sectors of the Huertgen Forest, causing the river crossing to be postponed until the water level dropped. Tucker's troopers spent their days waiting in various captured pillboxes and foxholes, while battalion and regimental staff officers straightened out the Morning Reports and wrote medal citations, and promotions came through.

On February 10, one day after A Company had received its replacements, 1st Lieutenant Breard was reassigned as the company's executive officer. Encountering many new faces, he realized that a number of changes had taken place in the command structure. First Lieutenant Pease was still in command, but many other men he had known in A Company in December 1944 were gone.

Breard was shocked to learn that his former platoon sergeant, S/Sgt. Frank Heidebrink, the company executive officer; Lieutenant Dunavant; and Lieutenant Morin had all been killed, and that Sgt. Gordon Gould from his own platoon had been badly wounded. Although he was back with his old unit, its composition had drastically changed over the last seven weeks. A Company now consisted of only two depleted platoons: the 2nd Platoon had temporarily disbanded, and would not be reconstituted until the company returned to France. Survivors were now serving in the 3rd Platoon.

On February 12 new officers arrived, assigned from the 3rd Replacement Depot. Among them was 2nd Lt. James S. Kessler, who was assigned as an assistant platoon leader. At 1000 hours Lieutenant Colonel Cook and Captain Keep were called to the Regimental CP where Colonel Tucker told them that the battalion was to prepare to cross the Roer River.

The following day, the regiment moved to the west bank of the Roer, the 2nd Battalion remaining in division reserve at Schmidthof. The 3rd Battalion took up positions west of Bergstein, and 1/504 relieved 1/508 about

1800 yards southeast of the town. "We were facing east on the Roer River," recalled Lieutenant Breard. "The dams were blown near Schmidt and the river was at flood stage. We patrolled the west side. I'm glad we did not have to cross it, as the current was too strong. We were in the vicinity of Bergstein, which was completely levelled. There was nothing left there except the cellars."[432]

Reconnoitring the river bank, the Regimental Demolition Platoon asked for volunteers to swim across with a cable. Privates Cocozza and Bonning from B Company volunteered for the job: "Jack Cocozza—and this is why I know him so well—was a terrific swimmer and I was a Red Cross life-saving instructor, so we both volunteered to take a cable across the Roer River. We would have to swim across with a rope and pull a cable across for a boat crossing. We […] both would get a Bronze Star and a three-day pass to do it. We kept moving closer and closer to the Roer and it was pouring down with rain. The combat engineers were trying to get through a minefield. Every once in a while there would be an explosion. They were detonating some.

"The next morning we came across a combat engineer whose intestines and everything were hanging from a tree. They gathered what was left of his body—two guys were carrying this heap of body on the litter. There were so many minefields there that they called it off. Jack Cocozza and I did not cross the Roer River."[433] The explosion had killed Pfc. Joe A. Nino from the Regimental Demolition Platoon, a long-time veteran of several campaigns. Staff Sergeant Rice, H Company, wrote that day in his diary: "Went to see a demonstration river crossing—assault boats. Doesn't look so good. Another Waal River???"[434]

On February 14, Rice witnessed "another boat demonstration—not so bad—*if* it works. Another patrol tonight. Somebody certainly screwing up. This is the closest we've been to the front without getting into a fight. Everything cancelled—believe we're being relieved. Moving out at 0100 morning of 18th."[435]

Earlier on, Capt. Wesley D. Harris' C Company, 307th AEB, which had supported and fought alongside the 504th during the Battle of the Bulge, had started preparations for an assault across the Roer River. According to the Battalion After Action report: "Reconnaissance of the Roer valley started February 11th. The river was found to be only 100 to 200 feet wide. However, the water was very swift, 10 to 12 miles per hour, rushing from the demolished gates of the Schwammenauel Dam. Further reconnaissance during the following days revealed all bridges in our division sector were completely destroyed except the highway bridge leading to Nideggen. This bridge had one of its three spans blown. The water gap was 40 feet. Roads leading to the river were badly cratered and were under enemy observation.

"Practice with assault boats on the Kall Creek began February 14th. The creek was as swift as the river. During the night Company C detail was unsuccessful in an attempt to cross the Roer. A gauge was set in the river to measure the rise or fall in the water. An OP nearby gave hourly readings.

"Reconnaissance and improvement of concealed routes to the Roer was made. Training with assault boats continued. Nightly, more attempts to cross the Roer were made—all without success. Reconnaissance and additional marking of minefields in the division sector progressed. There were casualties almost every day from the extensive and dense minefields in our area."[436]

At 1200 hours on February 15, Lieutenant King, 1st Platoon, C Company, 90th Chemical Mortar Battalion, reported to the 1st Battalion CP in Bergstein. His 4.2-inch mortars were to lay down a smoke screen for the upcoming river crossing. King's battalion had just arrived in Europe two weeks earlier and were about to enter the front line for the first time. Lieutenant Colonel Williams indicated their sector and Lieutenant King moved back to Schmidt to bring his platoon forward. The battalion history, *The Story of the Ninetieth in Training and in Action*, describes their arrival: "In the meantime, the 1st Platoon had gone into position on the same day at Bergstein, a ghost town with here a lone wall, there a chimney, and around it all, the damaged vehicles and unburied dead of both sides tangled up amid the debris. At Bergstein the 1st Platoon was attached to the 504th Parachute Infantry Regiment."[437]

At 2300 hours Colonel Tucker and his S-3 officer, Capt. Mack C. Shelley, walked down to the river to observe the preparations of a C Company river patrol. The first attempt to cross the swift-flowing Roer with the aid of a 70-foot-long pole failed when the pole broke. Tucker then decided to try to cross in boats. At 0815 hours on February 16, 1st Lt. Henry B. Ziegler, C Company, 307th AEB, called the 1st Battalion CP to request additional equipment. According to the Regimental S-3 journal, he needed "600 feet of fishing cord on reel, 300 feet of 1/4 inch feet rope, and cable for crossing the river. Lieutenant Ziegler has found a boat which he is fixing up. Notified Captain Harris."[438]

German forward artillery observers had registered their guns on Bergstein for several months in a row. Shells landed on a regular basis in town. No fatalities were sustained until 1300 hours on February 16 when the 2nd

Battalion arrived after a long foot march from Schmidt. S/Sgt. Johnny L. Snow from F Company was killed when an artillery shell landed alongside the marching paratroopers. As 2nd Lieutenant Zastrow, E Company, wrote to his parents: "Had a close one right before we were relieved. Moving along a road when Jerrie starts dropping a few shells on us. One landed about ten feet behind me. Took me off my feet and threw me about 15 feet. Ears were ringing and my head felt as if the top had been used as a battering ram—otherwise no scratches. Four men ahead of me were wounded and one behind me wounded and one killed, so I was pretty lucky.

"When I took off my equipment that afternoon, I noticed shrapnel holes through my shovel. Searching further I noticed a piece that had gone through the shovel, pistol belt, leather case in which I carry cleaning material, two jackets I had on, and through my first pair of pants. There I found a piece of shrapnel about as large as a nickel. Sort of close."[439]

First Lieutenant Harold Roy, 376th PFAB, was glad that galoshes were made available before the 504th RCT was deployed in the Huertgen Forest, because his "feet had been frozen earlier in the winter." Roy and his fellow officers received orders from Lt. Col. Robert H. Neptune to prepare prefixed reference points for artillery fire to be used during the river crossing. Junior infantry officers "were brought up and shown the adjusted points for the Roer River crossing."[440] Even company commanders were informed about the upcoming assault.

Preparations to cross the Roer River were suddenly cancelled in the early morning of February 19, when a regiment of the U.S. 9th Infantry Division arrived to relieve the 504th RCT. The veterans of the Battle of the Bulge and the Siegfried Line were very glad to receive the news that they were returning to France for some well-deserved rest and recuperation. After an overnight stop in Schmidthof, near the German city of Aachen, the regiment loaded onto 40 & 8 boxcars and travelled back to their old base camp in Sissonne, northeast of Paris.

After tired H Company troopers had been assigned to tents at Camp Sissonne on February 21, Staff Sergeant Rice finally found the time to scribble a few words in his diary: "Camp Sissonne—tents. 0430—Taking up regular garrison duties. Another campaign behind us. Is this the last?"[441]

POSTSCRIPT United States, January, 1946–January, 2015

After the war, many 504th RCT veterans remained in the army as career soldiers. Others studied law or went into politics. Several founded their own construction companies or became building contractors. Then there were those who decided to teach history, art or English. But regardless of career, all had one thing in common: they did not brag about their accomplishments during the war. On the contrary, many decided to remain silent—even with wives and children—about what they had experienced. In writing this book I contacted over a hundred veterans, and on any number of occasions I was the first person to whom they had ever spoken about the war.

Many paratroopers in F Company believed 2nd Lt. Robert Bramson had been mortally wounded. He was hospitalized for months and wrote a letter to fellow officer Lt. Myles J. Abramson in the spring of 1945. Abramson replied on May 17: "Dear Bob, sure glad to get your letter. We knew that you were back in the States, but that was all. Glad to hear that you're coming along fine. I sure was worried when the Krauts carried you past me. You looked like a sheet—you were so white. That sounds like a pretty soft touch now with a 30-day sick leave and then another month in the hospital. Maybe you can get another leave after the hospital, for to my knowledge sick leave does not count against regular leave time. You certainly deserve it, so don't get me wrong. I'll bet the gal friend was sure glad to see you back. What's the score there—any momentous decisions?"[442]

Just six days after Abramson wrote his letter, Bramson's engagement to Beverly Marcus was announced in *The Nebraska State Journal*. A little over four weeks later, on June 27, Robert and Beverly were married in Beth El Synagogue in Omaha, Nebraska. He worked as a legal assistant in the Nebraska State Attorney General's Office from 1947 to 1950, and later served as a special agent with the Federal Bureau of Investigation in New York City and Washington D.C. until 1954. Bramson then became attorney and marketing executive for MCA Inc., retiring as president of MCA TV International. He subsequently worked a few more years as consultant for MGM Studios before retiring in 1992. He currently resides in California.

By the time Lt. Col. Willard E. Harrison was discharged from the hospital, the war in Europe had ended. He received orders to ship for the Pacific to command another parachute infantry battalion, but just before he left the United States for his new command the war in Japan came to an end as well. Harrison stayed in the army and during the Korean War spent six months in Korea as a regimental executive officer. He commanded the 10th Special Forces Group at Bad Tolz, Germany, from 1956 to 1958. In 1959, he became the commander of the Parachute School at Fort Benning, a post he loved. In 1967 he retired from Fort Leonard Wood with the rank of colonel and moved to Springfield, Missouri. He died on June 11, 1980 at 67 and is buried at the National Cemetery in Springfield, plot 34, grave 72.

Colonel John Berry remained with the regiment after the New York Victory Parade and commanded the 1st Battalion until he was posted elsewhere. In the early 1960's he served as chief of staff of the 101st Airborne Division in Fort Campbell, Kentucky. He retired in the late 1960's as a colonel. He has the distinction of serving in more airborne units than any other 504th veteran of World War II: 504th Parachute Battalion; 2nd Battalion, 503rd Parachute Infantry; 2nd Battalion, 509th Parachute Infantry Regiment; 508th Parachute Infantry Regiment; 82nd Airborne Division Headquarters; and XVIII Airborne Corps Headquarters. He made combat jumps in North Africa, Normandy and the Netherlands. Colonel Berry died on February 24, 1993, in his hometown of Arkadelphia, Arkansas, at age 76 and is buried at block 4 in the Rose Hill Cemetery in Arkadelphia.

Captain Louis Hauptfleisch left the army as the war ended to pursue a career in business administration. He worked for Halsey Stuart, Goldman Sachs and Smith Barney as vice president of municipal finance. From 1976 to 1977 Hauptfleisch was president of the Municipal Bond Club of New York. He was also very active in the 504th Parachute Infantry Regiment Association, editing the 2nd Battalion Unit Journal for the Sicily and Italy Campaigns in the 1980's, compiling a regimental Roll of Honor for the association with fellow veteran Bennie Weeks, and writing for decades the "Devils In Baggy Pants" column in *The Static Line*.

Hauptfleisch also contributed to books by Clay Blair, William Breuer, and Cornelius Ryan, to Dan Morgan's history of the 551st PIB, and to the *Roll of Honor of the 82nd Airborne Division in WWII* compiled by the Liberation Museum in Groesbeek, the Netherlands. From 1988 to 1997, almost every year he visited former battlefields in the Belgian Ardennes during the February Commemorative Marches organized by the Belgian Chapter of the C-47 Club. Captain Hauptfleisch passed away on December 14, 2006 at age 88 in his hometown of Summit, New Jersey.

Two veterans who remained in the army after World War II had the privilege of commanding the 504th Parachute Infantry Regiment. The first was former C Company commander Col. Albert Milloy, who briefly commanded the regiment from February to May of 1964. Milloy rose quickly through the ranks, commanding the 1st and 23rd Infantry Divisions in Vietnam and retiring as a major general. He lives in Henderson Falls, Nevada. Col. Hanz Druener, a former D Company platoon leader, commanded the regiment from September 24, 1969, until September 30, 1970, and retired shortly afterwards. He died in April 1984 in his hometown of Merritt Island, Florida, at age 63.

A Company 1st Lt. Richard Hallock also stayed in the army, but as many other junior officers also had the same idea, he had to accept a commission in the Reserves. On June 27, 1946, he was promoted to captain, taken into the regular army, and transferred to the Military Intelligence Division at the Pentagon. The high grades Hallock received before entering the Military Intelligence Division soon brought him to the attention of Gen. Lucius D. Clay, who selected him be his Personal Aide for Intelligence in Berlin. Hallock served during the Berlin Airlift and throughout the post-war reconstruction of Germany until 1949.

During the Korean War he was the youngest major to command a battalion of the 32nd Infantry Regiment and fought on Hill 598 during the Triangle Battle. Hallock also battled behind the scenes for nearly ten years to convince the army to adopt the M16 as its standard rifle, during which time he became the first member of Secretary of Defense Robert McNamara's "Whiz Kids" advisors. Hallock retired as a colonel in 1967, having received five Bronze Stars, one Silver Star, a Purple Heart, the Haile Selassie Medal (Ethopia) and the Legion of Merit.

Hallock became a successful entrepreneur, establishing two corporations, Intrec and Quaestor. During the Nixon and Ford administrations he served as the personal representative of Defense Secretary James Schlesinger to the

Shah of Iran. Invited to attend the 55th Anniversary of the Berlin Airlift In 1998, he also planned to visit the village of Hitdorf where he had been captured during the war, but became ill and passed away on July 27, 1999, at the age of 79.[443] Colonel Hallock is buried in the Fort Benning Post Cemetery at Section J, grave 587. Professor Dan Crosswell of the Columbus State University is currently writing Hallock's biography.

As victory in Europe was celebrated in May 1945, Sgt. Ross S. Carter, C Company, was one of only three men left from the original 3rd Platoon as it had landed in Casablanca, the others being S/Sgt. Sergeant Frank Dietrich and Sgt. George McAllister. Discharged in the summer of 1945, Carter returned to Duffield, Virginia, along with his close friend Dietrich, an orphan, who was soon adopted by the Carter family. Encouraged by Dietrich and his family, Carter began to record his remembrances of the war, and thought about going back to school to study history, but in November 1945 he and Dietrich reenlisted in the paratroops and were assigned to the 505th PIR. En route to maneuvers in Alaska he was discovered to have cancer in his back. After surgery, he continued to Alaska to join the training maneuvers, but additional surgery soon became needed.

In February 1947 Carter was admitted to Walter Reed Hospital for further treatments. His younger brother Boyd brought along the manuscript during his visits, which they edited and completed together before Carter's death at 28 on April 18, 1947. He is buried in the family cemetery between Duffield and Pattonsville. In 1951, his mother Viola and brother Boyd published his book as *Those Devils in Baggy Pants*, which also appeared in condensed form in *The Readers Digest* and was translated into several languages, including Danish, French and Spanish. Over a million copies of the U.S. paperback edition were sold in 1952 alone. In 2006 veterans and friends of the 504th Parachute Infantry Regiment founded the Ross S. Carter Endowed Scholarship Fund.

For decades readers have wondered about the real identities of the men who appear under pseudonyms in Carter's book. The character "Arab" appears to be a pseudonym for Ross himself. "Berkeley" is Frank Dietrich, "Winters" is Sgt. George McAllister, and "Toland" is 1st Lt. Horace Carlock. "Freisinger" is actually Lt. Vern Frisinger, and "Master Termite" is Pvt. John Parsons. Others are as follows: William ("Dan") Serilla (Sokal); S/Sgt. Andrew Pompey (Pompey), Albert Feroni (Feroni), Cpl. Fred Gruneberg (Gruening), Sgt. Leon Duquette (Duquesne), Pfc. Raymond Levy (Finkelstein) and Pvt. Thomas Gugliuzza (Glutz). I am indebted to Mike St. George, secretary of the Colonel Reuben Tucker Chapter, for identifying many of the characters.

The popularity of Ross Carter's book and the effect it has had on many readers is perhaps best exemplified by retired Danish baker Jörgen Rosenquist, who first read *Those Devils in Baggy Pants* in 1952 and subsequently travelled to the United States where he worked as a baker in California for several years. Before returning home he drove across the United States to Duffield, Virginia, to see Ross Carter's grave in July 1967 and visit with his mother Viola. Back in Denmark, Rosenquist settled down and raised a family, but his interest in Carter's story never faded. When a new edition of the book appeared in 1978, Rosenquist hunted down Boyd Carter's address and wrote to him. Boyd replied: "My mother told me of your visit. She died November 2, 1969, at age 83."[444] Rosenquist later travelled several times to Cheneux, Belgium, and Altavilla, Italy, to visit Carter's former battlefields. In 1978 a farmer in Cheneux presented him with the barrel of a German 20mm gun he had found on the battlefield in 1945. Rosenquist donated it to the December 44 Museum in La Gleize, Belgium, in 2006. Now retired, Rosenquist still travels to Belgium and the Netherlands for annual commemorations. Characteristically, he always asks people to whom he is there introduced, "Do you know Ross Carter?"

Carter's best friend, Staff Sergeant Dietrich, attended OCS after the war and fought as a company commander in Korea. He also served in the 25th Infantry Division in Japan and attended the Command and General Staff College, the Armed Forces Staff College, and the Air War College. During the Vietnam War, Dietrich made two tours in Vietnam as a battalion and brigade commander and was awarded the Distinguished Service Cross in 1967 for exceptionally valorous actions on November 9-11, 1966, while commanding the 2nd Battalion (Airborne), 502nd Infantry, on a search and destroy operation near Tuy Hoa. His personal leadership and tactical maneuvers led to the destruction of a full North Vietnamese battalion. The 1st Battalion of the 502nd Infantry was led at the time by Lt. Col. Jack Bishop, who served in B, A and F Companies as a company first sergeant during World War II. Dietrich retired as a colonel in 1975 and was later made Honorary Colonel of the 504th PIR. He named his oldest son Ross Carter after his wartime friend. Dietrich passed away on September 22, 1997, in Anderson Memorial Medical Center in Clemson, South Carolina, at age 76, and was buried with full military honors at Arlington National Cemetery in Section 31, grave 5690.

APPENDIX A
DISTINGUISHED SERVICE CROSS RECIPIENTS

RANK	FIRST NAME	INITIAL	LAST NAME	COMPANY	PLACE OF ACTION
PFC	Daniel	T	Del Grippo	B	Cheneux
PFC	Raymond	S	Holsti	G	Cheneux
S/SGT	William	P	Walsh	B	Cheneux

APPENDIX B
PRISONERS OF WAR CAPTURED IN THE BATTLE OF THE BULGE

RANK	FIRST NAME	INITIAL	LAST NAME	CO	DATE	PLACE OF CAPTURE
PVT	Warren	H	Anderson	C	Jan 2	Bra sector
PVT	Horace	M	Biddle	C	Jan 2	Bra sector
PFC	Gordon	V	Brewer	H	Jan 29	Herresbach
PVT	George	P	Haydu	C	Jan 2	Bra sector
CPL	Jack	C	Larison	D	Dec 26	Floret
PFC	Enrico	S	Malizia	H	Jan 29	Herresbach
PFC	Jesse	L	Mitchem	F	Feb 2	Mertesrott Heights
PVT	Joseph	E	McBurnett	H	Jan 7	Petit-Halleux
2LT	Harry	W	Rollins	D	Dec 26	Floret
PFC	Edward	C	Rosella	D	Dec 26	Floret
PVT	Marvin	C	Scroggins	D	Dec 26	Floret
PVT	Kenneth	G	Shelton	D/medic	Dec 26	Floret
PFC	Kenneth	M	Smithey	D	Dec 26	Floret
PVT	David	J	Sturgeon	D	Dec 26	Floret
PFC	Vernon	P	West	D	Dec 26	Floret

APPENDIX C
B COMPANY REPLACEMENTS AT
CHENEUX, DECEMBER 22, 1944

RANK	FIRST NAME	INITIAL	LAST NAME	COMPANY	JOINED AT
PVT	Harold	A	Black	B	Cheneux
PVT	Harold	R	Dudley	B	Cheneux
PVT	John	V	Fox Jr	B	Cheneux
PVT	William	T	Frame	B	Cheneux
PVT	James	G	Garner Jr	B	Cheneux
PVT	Keith	E	Harper	B	Cheneux
PVT	Charles	C	Johnston	B	Cheneux
PFC	Alfred	R	Lindeman	B	Cheneux
PVT	Frank	X	McAvoy	B	Cheneux
PVT	Oliver	NMI	McClorey	B	Cheneux
PVT	John	W	McLaughlin	B	Cheneux
PVT	Charles	P	Mikell	B	Cheneux
PVT	William	NMI	Persowich	B	Cheneux
PVT	James	N	Price	B from F	Cheneux
PVT	Milous	G	Rains	B	Cheneux
TEC5	James	R	Reagan	B	Cheneux
PVT	Sydney	J	Redburn	B	Cheneux
PVT	Anthony	NMI	Saracelli	B	Cheneux
PVT	Arthur	L	Southworth	B	Cheneux
PVT	Joseph	N	Shepard	B	Cheneux

APPENDIX D
C COMPANY REPLACEMENTS AT
CHENEUX, DECEMBER 22, 1944

RANK	FIRST NAME	INITIAL	LAST NAME	COMPANY	JOINED AT
PVT	Robert	H	Allard	C	Cheneux
PVT	Alfredo	C	Castillon	C	Cheneux
PVT	Frederick	A	Green	C	Cheneux
PVT	Henry	NMI	Furgal	C	Cheneux
PVT	Paul	E	Hawkins	C	Cheneux
PVT	George	P	Haydu	C	Cheneux
PVT	Joseph	P	Hillanbrand	C	Cheneux
PVT	Paul	E	Jacobson	C	Cheneux
PFC	Robert	J	Kelly	C	Cheneux
PVT	Roy	NMI	Kidd	C	Cheneux
PVT	Harold	C	King	C	Cheneux
PVT	Pierre	NMI	Latreille	C	Cheneux
PFC	Arthur	J	Lazbur	C	Cheneux
PVT	Emerson	R	Lee	C	Cheneux
PVT	Sol	J	Mirmow	C	Cheneux
PVT	Bernard	J	Muncy	C	Cheneux
CPL	Stephen	H	Parry	C	Cheneux
PVT	Lyle	G	Raymond	C	Cheneux
PVT	Peter	NMI	Villalobos	C	Cheneux
PVT	Chester	J	Wisniewski	C	Cheneux

APPENDIX E
ORDER OF BATTLE FOR THE BATTLE
OF THE BULGE, DECEMBER 18, 1944

REGIMENTAL STAFF

Colonel Reuben H. Tucker III	Regimental Commanding Officer
Lieutenant Colonel Warren R. Williams, Jr.	Regimental Executive Officer
Captain Louis A. Hauptfleisch	S-1 (Personnel)
Captain Fordyce Gorham	S-2 (Intelligence)
Captain Mack C. Shelley	S-3 (Operations)
Captain William A. B. Addison	S-4 (Supply)
Major Ivan J. Roggen	Regimental Surgeon
Captain Delbert A. Kuehl	Protestant Chaplain
Captain Edwin J. Kozak	Catholic Chaplain

1ST BATTALION

Lieutenant Colonel William E. Harrison	Battalion Commander
Major John T. Berry	Executive Battalion Commander
Captain Paul D. Bruns	Battalion Surgeon Capt. Charles B. Zirkle, Jr.
1st Lieutenant Percy E. Schools, Jr.	Assistant Battalion Surgeon
1st Lieutenant G.P. Crockett	S-1 (Personnel)
1st Lieutenant William W. Magrath	S-2 (Intelligence)
Captain Charles W. Duncan	S-3 (Operations)
1st Lieutenant George F. Taliaferro	S-4 (Supply)
1st Lieutenant John N. Pease	A Company
Captain Thomas C. Helgeson	B Company
Captain Roy E. Anderson	C Company
Captain Albert E. Milloy	HQ Company

2ND BATTALION

Lieutenant Colonel Edward N. Wellems	Battalion Commander
Major William Colville	Executive Battalion Commander
Captain Paul D. Bruns	Battalion Surgeon
1st Lieutenant Chester A. Garrison	S-1 (Personnel)
1st Lieutenant George H. Fust	S-2 (Intelligence)
Captain Victor W. Campana	S-3 (Operations)
1st Lieutenant Ross I. Donnelly	S-4 (Supply)
Captain Adam A. Komosa	D Company
Captain Herbert H. Norman	E Company
1st Lieutenant William J. Sweet	F Company
Captain Robert J. Cellar	HQ Company

3RD BATTALION

Lieutenant Colonel Julian A. Cook	Battalion Commander
Major Abdallah K. Zakby	Executive Battalion Commander
Captain William W. Kitchin	Battalion Surgeon
1st Lieutenant Thomas F. Pitt	S-1 (Personnel)
1st Lieutenant Virgil F. Carmichael	S-2 (Intelligence)
Captain Henry B. Keep	S-3 (Operations)
1st Lieutenant Thomas S. Utterback	S-4 (Supply)
Captain Fred H. Thomas	G Company
Captain Carl W. Kappel	H Company
Captain T. Moffatt Burriss	I Company
Captain George M. Warfield	HQ Company

APPENDIX F
ORDER OF BATTLE FOR THE BATTLE OF THE BULGE, JANUARY 5, 1945

REGIMENTAL STAFF

Colonel Reuben H. Tucker III	Regimental Commanding Officer
Lieutenant Colonel Warren R. Williams, Jr.	Regimental Executive Officer
Captain Louis A. Hauptfleisch	S-1 (Personnel)
Captain Fordyce Gorham	S-2 (Intelligence)
Captain Mack C. Shelley	S-3 (Operations)
Captain William A.B. Addison	S-4 (Supply)
Major Ivan J. Roggen	Regimental Surgeon
Captain Delbert A. Kuehl	Protestant Chaplain
Captain Edwin J. Kozak	Catholic Chaplain

1ST BATTALION

Major John T. Berry (acting)	Battalion Commander
Captain Albert E. Milloy (acting)	Executive Battalion Commander
Captain Paul D. Bruns	Battalion Surgeon
1st Lieutenant (name unknown)	S-1 (Personnel)
1st Lieutenant William W. Magrath	S-2 (Intelligence)
Captain Charles W. Duncan	S-3 (Operations)
1st Lieutenant George F. Taliaferro	S-4 (Supply)
1st Lieutenant John N. Pease	A Company
1st Lieutenant John M. Randles	B Company
Captain Wade H. McIntyre, Jr.	C Company
1st Lieutenant Peyton C. Hartley	HQ Company

2ND BATTALION

Lieutenant Colonel Edward N. Wellems	Battalion Commander
Major William Colville, Jr.	Executive Battalion Commander
Captain Frederick E. DePriest	Battalion Surgeon
1st Lieutenant Rexford O. Stribley	S-1 (Personnel)
1st Lieutenant George H. Fust	S-2 (Intelligence)
Captain Victor W. Campana	S-3 (Operations)
1st Lieutenant Ross I. Donnelly	S-4 (Supply)
Captain Adam A. Komosa	D Company
Captain Herbert H. Norman	E Company
1st Lieutenant William J. Sweet	F Company
Captain Robert J. Cellar	HQ Company

3RD BATTALION

Lieutenant Colonel Julian A. Cook	Battalion Commander
Major Abdallah K. Zakby	Executive Battalion Commander
Captain William W. Kitchin	Battalion Surgeon
1st Lieutenant Thomas F. Pitt	S-1 (Personnel)
1st Lieutenant Virgil F. Carmichael	S-2 (Intelligence)
Captain Henry B. Keep	S-3 (Operations)
1st Lieutenant Thomas S. Utterback	S-4 (Supply)
1st Lieutenant James H. Goethe	G Company
Captain Carl W. Kappel	H Company
Captain T. Moffatt Burriss	I Company
Captain George M. Warfield	HQ Company

APPENDIX G
ORDER OF BATTLE FOR THE BATTLE
OF THE BULGE, JANUARY 26, 1945

REGIMENTAL STAFF

Colonel Reuben H. Tucker III	Regimental Commanding Officer
Lieutenant Colonel Warren R. Williams, Jr.	Regimental Executive Officer
Captain Louis A. Hauptfleisch	S-1 (Personnel)
Captain Fordyce Gorham	S-2 (Intelligence)
Captain Mack C. Shelley	S-3 (Operations)
Captain William A.B. Addison	S-4 (Supply)
Major Ivan J. Roggen	Regimental Surgeon
Captain Delbert A. Kuehl	Protestant Chaplain
Captain Edwin J. Kozak	Catholic Chaplain

1ST BATTALION

Lieutenant Colonel Willard E. Harrison	Battalion Commander
Major John T. Berry	Executive Battalion Commander
Captain Paul D. Bruns	Battalion Surgeon
1st Lieutenant (name unknown)	S-1 (Personnel)
1st Lieutenant William W. Magrath	S-2 (Intelligence)
Captain Charles W. Duncan	S-3 (Operations)
1st Lieutenant George F. Taliaferro	S-4 (Supply)
1st Lieutenant John N. Pease	A Company
1st Lieutenant John M. Randles	B Company
1st Lieutenant James E. Dunn	C Company
Captain Albert E. Milloy	HQ Company

2ND BATTALION

Lieutenant Colonel Edward N. Wellems	Battalion Commander
Major William Colville, Jr.	Executive Battalion Commander
Captain Frederick E. DePriest	Battalion Surgeon
1st Lieutenant Rexford O. Stribley	S-1 (Personnel)
1st Lieutenant George H. Fust	S-2 (Intelligence)
Captain Victor W. Campana	S-3 (Operations)
1st Lieutenant Ross I. Donnelly	S-4 (Supply)
Captain Adam A. Komosa	D Company
Captain Herbert H. Norman	E Company
1st Lieutenant William J. Sweet	F Company
Captain Robert J. Cellar	HQ Company

3RD BATTALION

Lieutenant Colonel Julian A. Cook	Battalion Commander
Major Abdallah K. Zakby	Executive Battalion Commander
Captain William W. Kitchin	Battalion Surgeon
1st Lieutenant Thomas F. Pitt	S-1 (Personnel)
1st Lieutenant Virgil F. Carmichael	S-2 (Intelligence)
Captain Henry B. Keep	S-3 (Operations)
1st Lieutenant Thomas S. Utterback	S-4 (Supply)
1st Lieutenant James H. Goethe	G Company
Captain John F. Gray	H Company
Captain T. Moffatt Burriss	I Company
Captain George M. Warfield	HQ Company

APPENDIX H
ORDER OF BATTLE FOR THE 551ST PARACHUTE BATTALION, JANUARY 7, 1945

551ST PARACHUTE BATTALION

Lieutenant Colonel Wood G. Joerg	Battalion Commander
Major William N. Holm	Executive Battalion Commander
Captain John Y. Battenfield	Battalion Surgeon
1st Lieutenant Paul F. Koch	S-1 (Personnel)
Captain Edward W. Hartman	S-2 (Intelligence)
Major Charles R. Hermann	S-3 (Operations)
1st Lieutenant Glen A. Slucter	S-4 (Supply)
1st Lieutenant Donald A. Booth	A Company
1st Lieutenant Richard Mascuch	B Company
1st Lieutenant Leroy C. Sano	C Company
Captain William G. Smith	HQ Company

APPENDIX I

THE PRISONER OF WAR EXPERIENCE
OF 2ND LIEUTENANT HARRY ROLLINS

The platoon leader of the 1st Platoon of D Company, 2nd Lt. Harry W. Rollins, was captured in Floret, Belgium, late in the evening of December 26, 1944. He was the first officer from the 504th who was sent to Oflag XIIIB rather than to Oflag 64. From a provisional POW camp in a warehouse full of sick, dying and dead prisoners in Gerolstein, Rollins was put on a transport train to Hammelburg in Bavaria: "En route to Hammelburg by train we passed some Russian women—forced laborers—working on the railroad bed. Oflag XIIIB at Hammelburg was very unlike the way it was depicted on *Hogan's Heroes*. When we arrived we were issued a chocolate bar, blanket and a little food and could shave. For most of our stay we ate grass soup, sometimes with a little potato."[445]

Rollins would not have to wait long for the anticipated liberation. Late on the night of March 25, General Patton ordered XII Corps to provide a task force from the German city of Aschaffenburg to attack Hammelburg, 60 miles away through enemy-occupied territory, to liberate 300 American officers. Patton made no mention of his son-in-law, Lt. Col. John Waters, the actual target of the operation. At XII Corps the order was passed on to the 4th U.S. Armored Division, where this difficult task was delegated to Capt. Abraham Baum, the 10th Armored Infantry Battalion S-3 officer, who was of Jewish origin. Maj. Alexander Stiller, aide to General Patton, would accompany him as an observer. Twenty-one-year-old Captain Baum was not at all happy with the assignment, which he considered to be certain suicide for his small force of men. It would be no easy task to cover so many miles through enemy terrain, with no more than 291 officers and men and 53 vehicles. The vehicles and other detachments included three M7 Priest 105mm self-propelled assault guns, five light M3 Stuart tanks, ten medium M4 Sherman tanks and a rifle company in half-tracks.[446] The task force moved out late in the evening of the same day, battling its way through the German front line near Schweinheim.

Back in Oflag 64, on the afternoon of March 27, 2nd Lt. Rollins and Lt. Col. Waters were unaware of the planned liberation. Task Force Baum was attacked by a company of German *Ferdinand* tank destroyers as they came around the curve of the highway at Untereschenbach and were about to take the exit to drive on to Hammelburg. The *Ferdinand* tank destroyers fired their deadly 88mm shells but

281

missed Baum's column, which was driving at full speed. The Americans immediately returned fire, knocking out two *Ferdinands* and driving off the remaining six.

Captain Baum placed his remaining two M7 assault guns on a hill to give supporting fire while the remainder of the column rolled on across the intersection road that ran towards the camp through the Reussenberg hills. The lead Shermans were just going up the first hill when they were hit by the German tank destroyers, which destroyed three tanks and a couple of half-tracks carrying extra fuel. At the bottom of the hill some soldiers abandoned even the undamaged vehicles and Baum had a hard time reorganizing his men and getting them to remount. Meanwhile the American gunners destroyed six trucks transporting fuel and ammunition to the German tank destroyers.

After the *Ferdinands* withdrew, the column again moved forward toward Oflag XIIIB. At 1630 hours a group of cadre and engineers from the nearby Lager Hammelburg, a training area attacked Task Force Baum with panzerfausts, but the Americans eventually won the chaotic battle that ensued. American shells were accidentally fired on the Serbian prisoner of war compound, where some 4000 communist and royalist Serbian officers were housed. Major General Von Goeckel, the German camp commander, called Colonel Goode and Lieutenant Colonel Waters to his office, as well as the highest-ranking Serbian general and an interpreter, Capt. Hans Fuchs. Goode was informed of the shell fire on the Serbian housing, and Von Goeckel advised him to keep all American officers inside their barracks, for fear of more casualties. He said he was willing to surrender the camp to the Americans. Seizing the opportunity, Lieutenant Colonel Waters volunteered to leave the camp with a white flag to negotiate the surrender. Von Goeckel complied and sent Captain Fuchs along as Waters' interpreter, should they run into any Germans.

Accompanied by Captain Fuchs and three American lieutenants, Lieutenant Colonel Waters walked out of the front gate and was challenged and shot by a German guard. Captain Fuchs, who tried to interfere and order the soldier to lower his rifle, was almost fired upon before the German soldier realized that Waters had been sent out by Von Goeckel.[447]

In the early evening the firing outside the camp subdued and the prisoners broke out. "We all jumped on the tanks to escape," recalled Rollins. "I was with [2nd Lieutenants] John [L.] Bundy [Jr., 434th Armored Field Artillery Battalion] and Tom [Thomas M.] Galloway [109th Field Artillery Battalion]. As we were heading back to the west, German tanks showed up to engage. The tank commander told us that we would be better off on our own and pointed in the direction of friendly lines. We got up to the top of a small hill and watched the tank battle, including some little self-propelled, tracked vehicles that would get beside the tanks and explode.

"We had to cross the river to get back to our lines. By the time we got into the little town of Gemunden we were exhausted. John was sick and neither Tom nor I could swim. We decided to rest for a while and come back that night and float across the river under a bridge (which was being guarded by Germans). We found a barn and a Dutch forced laborer. The Dutchman brought us some frozen sugar beets, blankets, and a large tub of hot water. Here we were, sitting naked, wrapped in blankets, with our feet in this large tub when a squad of Germans came into the barn just to get out of the rain. Back to Hammelburg.

"After just a few days, we were crowded into boxcars. Only half could sit down. We would try to get close to the doors to pee and had to poop in a #10 can. We scraped frost from the metal to try to get a little moisture. To make matters worse, the train was strafed by American P-40's. We were all herded into the Nuremberg Sports Palace and ran into some Russian pilots who had trained to fly in Texas.

"We were to be marched to the Berchtesgaden area, Hitler's last redoubt. Our presence in the area of the Eagles Nest could limit the use of American air power against Hitler and we could be used as bargaining chips for favorable surrender terms. Our guards were old or wounded, sometimes both. We would stop at farms in the evening. […] I would spot the henhouse at each of these stops. Tom was especially good at sneaking into the henhouse without disturbing the chickens and usually came out with two or three eggs while Bundy and I would keep watch.

"We could find seeds in the roof area of the barns. I would tie them up in handkerchiefs and throw them down to Bundy and Galloway. You could hold the seeds in your mouth for a while to soften them but the oats would tear you up. When we could, we would cook the wheat seeds with the eggs in a can and share our food with Father [Paul W.] Cavanaugh [422nd Infantry Regiment, 106th Infantry Division].

"During the march, I pointed off to the side of the road and told the guard *scheissen*, indicating that I had to go to the bathroom. Tom and I wandered off toward the west and the sounds of distant fire. After a short while, we ran into a German captain guarding five Americans. They were also heading toward American lines with the idea that the Americans were his prisoners until they found the Allied lines, and then he would be our prisoner. We stopped at a farm and slaughtered a hog. A woman at the farm made blood sausage. A little later a sergeant from the 14th Armored Division busted into the farmhouse with a tommy gun and our war was over."[448]

Once Rollins and Galloway were liberated, they faced the challenge of rejoining their units. How could they find them? Both divisions had been moved across the European landscape for many, perhaps hundreds, of miles. Galloway and Rollins came upon a jeep with a chaplain and his assistant, who offered to take them along. "They were en route to Paris for rest and recuperation. Near Kaiserslautern, on the 8th of May, Tom spotted the guidon from his field artillery battery from the 78th Division."[449]

At 78th Infantry Division headquarters "another interrogation" followed before Rollins was sent from Kaiserslautern "to Brussels and quarantined. There I was deloused several times. We received a partial pay here and ice cream. The place where we were staying had a 14-foot wall. I snuck out. From Brussels, I went to Camp Lucky Strike. This was the camp for RAMP's (Repatriated Allied Military Personnel). We would stand in line for two hours to get a milk shake and get back in line to wait for the next one. There were a lot of Air Force [crews] there."[450]

Camp Lucky Strike was situated in the small village of Janville, five miles northeast of Cany-Barville in the northern region of Normandy. It was still several miles from Le Havre, where thousands of ex-prisoners of war were hoping to get on a ship to the United States. Rollins decided after a couple of days not to stay any longer than necessary in the camp. His unit might get him back much sooner! He learned to his surprise that the 82nd Airborne Division was stationed in Berlin, hundreds of miles away!

Hearing that Chartres and the surrounding region had several American air-fields, he hitchhiked to the city to arrange a flight to England, guessing he could probably leave much sooner from there than from a port in France. In Chartres he found a friend who was going to England and hitched a ride to London, where he "roomed with a journalist at a Red Cross villa. He took a lot of notes and was writing a book about me. We spent a lot of time at a very famous hotel, Claridge's. They had an English officers' mess."[451]

Several days later all the RAMP's in Rollins' group were moved to Tidworth Barracks on the Salisbury Plain, from where their voyage continued shortly later to Bournemouth, a popular English resort. "Each day, we would call in at 1200 noon. After several days, I sailed from Southampton on the *Santa Rosa*. Cabins were for the wounded. Everybody else was in the hold. We sailed into New York City and were housed at Camp Shanks.

"I took the train to Fort Sheridan in Chicago. After 30 days at home I was sent to Miami Beach for another 30 days of leave. Here everything was free (hot dogs, milk shakes, coke). A lot of folks were mustered out from here and returned to civilian life."[452]

Rollins did not leave the army, but was promoted to first lieutenant and eventually retired with the rank of lieutenant colonel. He kept in touch with Colonel Reuben Tucker until the latter's death in 1970. His son Harry Jr. was a classmate of Colonel Tucker's son Scott at the Citadel.

NOTES

Author's note: Unpublished sources were sometimes also untitled or unpaginated, or both; every effort has been made to document these and other sources as fully as possible. Unpaginated works are indicated as "n.p." (no page) on first reference. Translations from German to English are my own unless otherwise stated. I have indicated my own questionnaires and interviews with the initials FVL; sources from the Cornelius Ryan Collection are designated CRC.

INTRODUCTION / ACKNOWLEDGMENTS
1 Clay Blair, *Ridgway's Paratroopers: The American Airborne in World War II.* (Annapolis, MD: Naval Institute Press, 2002), 384.
2 Mark King, Email to FVL, January 9, 2013.

CHAPTER 1
3 Hugh D. Wallis, Questionnaire, FVL.
4 Edwin R. Bayley, "Ed's Army Days." Unpublished memoir (2004), 3–8. Courtesy of Edwin Bayley.
5 Ibid., 12–17.
6 Ibid., 21–28.
7 Edwin R. Bayley, Email to FVL, January 5, 2006.
8 William D. Mandle, Letter to his parents, November 16, 1944. Courtesy of his son, Steve Mandle.
9 Reneau G. Breard, Letter to FVL, February 24, 2005.
10 James A. Kiernan, Telephone interview with FVL, November 13, 2005.
11 Ibid.
12 Henry B. Keep, Letter to his mother, November 20, 1944. Courtesy of Margaret Shelly, niece of the late Pvt. Robert T. Koelle.
13 Abdallah K. Zakby, Questionnaire, CRC, 1968.
14 James Megellas, *All the Way to Berlin* (New York, NY: 2003), 175–176.
15 Bayley, "Ed's Army Days," 29.
16 Wayne Pierce, *Let's Go! The Story of the Men Who Served in the 325th Glider Infantry Regiment* (Chapel Hill, NC: Professional Press, 1997), 228–230.
17 Wayne M. Fetters, Letter to a friend in Wisconsin, November 23, 1944. Courtesy of his daughter, Beth Tweed.
18 Charles E. Zastrow, Letter to his parents, December 11, 1944. All letters from Lieutenant Zastrow courtesy of his daughter, Susan Repke.
19 Robert E. Bramson, Email to FVL, July 4, 2012.
20 Ibid.
21 Paul D. Bruns, "Flight Surgeon," Unpublished memoir (1987), 12. Courtesy of Charlotte Baldridge, 359th Fighter Group Historian.
22 Bayley, Email to FVL, May 7, 2008.

23 Bruns, 11.
24 Ibid.
25 Morris ("Mike") Holmstock, Telephone interview with FVL, February 10, 2012.

CHAPTER 2
26 David Cooke and Wayne Evans, *Kampfgruppe Peiper at the Battle of the Bulge* (Mechanicsburg, PA: Stackpole Books, 2005), 51–52.
27 James A. Kiernan, Telephone interview with FVL, November 13, 2005.
28 Breard, Letter to FVL, February 24, 2005.
29 Bayley, "Ed's Army Days," 31.
30 Ervin E. Shaffer, Telephone interview with FVL, March 29, 2004.
31 Meldon F. Hurlbert, Interview with his son-in-law, John Cutright, July 2009, n.p. Transcript courtesy of John Cutright.
32 George H. Mahon, Interview with his daughter, Eileen Mahon, November 15, 2014. Audiotape courtesy of Eileen Mahon.
33 Robert E. Bramson, Email to FVL, November 17, 2014.
34 Victor W. Campana, "The Operations of the 2nd Battalion, 504th Parachute Infantry (82nd Airborne Division) in the German Counteroffensive 18 December 1944–10 January 1945." Unpublished manuscript, 5–6. Donovan Research Library, Fort Benning, GA.
35 Ibid., 6–7.
36 Megellas, 177–178. French boxcars emblazoned with 40 & 8 on their sides had the capacity to carry forty men or eight horses.
37 Bayley, "Ed's Army Days," 32.
38 Campana, 8–9.
39 Bayley, "Ed's Army Days," 32.
40 Breard, Letter to FVL, February 24, 2005.
41 Bayley, "Ed's Army Days," 32.
42 Mahon, Interview with Eileen Mahon.
43 Breard, Letter to FVL, February 24, 2005.
44 Bayley, "Ed's Army Days," 33.
45 Hubbard D. Burnum, Jr., Questionnaire FVL.
46 Herbert C. Lucas, Questionnaire, FVL.
47 Walter E. Hughes, Unpublished account, n.p. Courtesy of Walter E. Hughes.
48 Chester A. Garrison, *An Ivy-League Paratrooper* (Corvallis, OR: Franklin Press, 2002), 159.
49 Campana, 9.
50 David K. Finney, "My Time with the 504th," Privately published memoir (Santee, CA, 2006), n.p.
51 Campana, 10.
52 David E. Pergrin with Eric Hammel, *First Across The Rhine. The 291st Combat Engineer Battalion in France, Belgium and Germany* (St. Paul, MN: Zenith Press, 2006), 118–119.
53 Ibid, 127–128.

54 Kenneth Hechler, "An Interview with Obersturmbannführer Jochen Peiper, 1st SS-Pz Regt 11–24 Dec." (Historical Division, September 7, 1945), 21. National Archives: Ethint 10. Accessed through <www.fold3.com>.

55 Jochen Peiper, "Kampfgruppe Peiper 15–26 December 1944" (Historical Division, European Command, 1949), 9–10. National Archives: C-004. Accessed through <www.fold3.com>.

56 Campana, 10–11.

57 Breard, Letter to FVL, February 24, 2005.

58 Bayley, "Ed's Army Days," 33–34.

CHAPTER 3

59 Marshall W. Stark, "The Operations of the 1st Platoon, Battery C, 80th Airborne Antiaircraft Battalion (82nd Airborne Division) in the Battle of the Bulge," 12–14.

60 Campana, 11–12.

61 Stark, 14–15.

62 Robert E. Waldon, cited from <http://home.comcast.net/~b504pir/waldonmeM-1.html>. Accessed August 4, 2008.

63 Ibid.

64 Ibid.

65 Ibid.

66 Cooke and Evans, 102.

67 Stark, 15.

68 Thomas C. Helgeson, "Narrative of Action of the First Battalion, 504th Parachute Infantry at Cheneux, Belgium on December 20–21, 1944." Unpublished manuscript. Donovan Research Library, Fort Benning, GA. Copy courtesy of Mike Bigalke.

69 Cooke and Evans, 104.

70 Helgeson, "Narrative of Action of the First Battalion," 1.

71 Morning Reports for the 504th PIR for November and December 1944 and January and March 1945 were posted on <www.fultonhistory.com> and accessed in 2012–13. Since late 2014, they have no longer been accessible. The website is run by Tom Trynisky.

72 Helgeson, "Narrative of the Action of the First Battalion," 2.

73 Ibid.

74 Morris ("Mike") Holmstock cited in Phil Nordyke, *All American All The Way. The Combat History of the 82nd Airborne Division in World War II* (St. Paul, MN: 2005), 602.

75 Distinguished Service Cross Citation for S/Sgt. William P. Walsh. First U.S. Army, General Order No. 34, 27 February 1945.

76 While O'Neal recalls that he was a technical sergeant when assigned to B Company, the Morning Reports list him as a private. As I have seen errors in ranks in Morning Reports, I believe that O'Neal was an acting sergeant at the time and have listed him as such.

77 Military Medal Citation for Pvt. Mack Barkley. Headquarters, First U.S. Army, Letter, April 18, 1945.

78 Silver Star Citation for 1st Lt. Richard A. Smith. 82nd Airborne Division, General Order No. 22, February 26, 1945.
79 Distinguished Service Cross Citation for Pfc. Daniel T. Grippo. First U.S. Army, General Order No. 32, February 23, 1945.
80 Holmstock cited in Nordyke, 603.
81 Distinguished Service Cross Citation for S/Sgt. William P. Walsh. First U.S. Army, General Order No. 34, February 27, 1945.
82 Silver Star Citation for Cpl. Henry B. Klee. 82nd Airborne Division, General Order No. 75, May 22, 1945.
83 Silver Star Citation for 1st Lt. Richard A. Smith. 82nd Airborne Division, General Order No. 36, March 19, 1945.
84 Dock C. O'Neal, Sr., Telephone interview with FVL, February 10, 2012.
85 Silver Star Citation for Pfc. Arley O. Farley. 82nd Airborne Division, General Order No. 31, March 10, 1945.
86 Holmstock cited in Nordyke, 605. The medic may have been Pvt. Theodore S. Watson, attached to Headquarters Company, 1st Battalion, who received the Silver Star for safely evacuating five men under enemy fire.
87 Holmstock, Telephone interview with FVL, February 10, 2012. Former Lt. Hubbard D. Burnum, Jr. of Headquarters Company also stated that "the battle got to Helgeson mentally and that night they assigned someone else to be in charge of B Company due to the mental stress he was experiencing." David Burnum, Email to FVL, February 25, 2015.
88 Silver Star Citation for Capt. Thomas C. Helgeson, 82nd Airborne Division, General Order No. 3, January 6, 1945. Courtesy of Thomas A. Helgeson.
89 Silver Star Citation for 1st Lt. Harold E. Allen, 82nd Airborne Division, General Order No. 14, February 2, 1945.

CHAPTER 4
90 Ross S. Carter, *Those Devils in Baggy Pants* (Kingsport, TN: Kingsport Press, 1978), 183.
91 Frank L. Dietrich cited in Nordyke, 604.
92 Edwin J. Kozak, Letter to Valeria Seborg, March 12, 1945. Courtesy of the veteran's grand niece, Chelsea Williams.
93 I am indebted to Steve Howerter, a good friend of the Stevenson family, for biographical information about Harold D. Stevenson. Stevenson is buried in Wiley Cemetery, Ellisville, Illinois. According to the Roll of Honor of the 82nd Airborne Division (Liberation Museum: Groesbeek, the Netherlands), Stevenson was killed "while engaging tanks."
94 Albert E. Milloy, Telephone interview with FVL, November 30, 2008.
95 Robert Magruda cited in William B. Breuer, *Geronimo!* (New York, NY: St. Martin's Press: 1992), 388.
96 Charles W. Duncan cited in Breuer, 388.
97 Cooke and Evans, 102.
98 Karl-Heinz Nehring is buried at the War Cemetery Bad Münstereifel, row 4, grave 23.

99 Silver Star Citation for 2nd Lt. Wayne M. Fetters. 82nd Airborne Division, General Order No. 17, February 15, 1945.

100 Elmer W. Swartz, Telephone interview with FVL, November 19, 2007.

101 Carter, 186.

102 Karl Laun, Diary, December 21, 1944. The diary was translated into English in December 1944 and copies were handed out in the 1st Battalion. I am greatly indebted to Cody Mann, grandson of S/Sgt. Paul V. Mann, B Company, for providing scans of the translation.

103 Jan Bos, *Circle and the Fields of Little America. The History of the 376th Parachute Field Artillery Battalion, 82nd Airborne,* Privately published DVD Book (2007), 246.

104 Stanley S. Kaslikowski, "Stanley Kaslikowski," The Stamford Historical Society. <http://www.stamfordhistory.org/ww2_kaslikowski.htm>. Accessed 20 January 2009. Kaslikowski cited from an Interview with Tonia Pavia, 1995.

105 Silver Star Citation for Pvt. Paul E. Hayden. 82nd Airborne Division, General Order No. 31, March 10, 1945.

106 Silver Star Citation for Pfc. Robert M. Kinney. 82nd Airborne Division, General Order No. 31, March 10, 1945.

107 Silver Star Citation for 2nd Lt. William G. Yepsen. 82nd Airborne Division, General Order No. 61, April 18, 1945.

108 Silver Star Citation for 1st Lt. Howard A. Kemble. 82nd Airborne Division, General Order No. 14, February 2, 1945.

109 Edwin J. Kozak, Letter to George and Alice Kemble, 16 March 1945. Courtesy of Howard's nephew, Frederick M. Lindley.

110 Bronze Star Citation for Sgt. Al N. Vrabac. 82nd Airborne Division, General Order No. 105, July 5, 1945. Copy courtesy of his son, Tom Vrabac, who reported that his father spoke several times about how Lieutenant Kemble was killed, and that he was the sergeant who had "shot the German who had killed my lieutenant."

111 Military Medal Citation for Pvt. Mack Barkley. Headquarters, First U.S. Army, Letter, April 18, 1945.

112 Hubert A. Wolfe cited in Jennifer Bush, "Battle of the Bulge Stands Out for Woodlake Veteran," *Visalia Times-Delta,* December 16, 1994, Section A, 1–2. Article courtesy of Hubert's son, Robert Wolfe.

113 Silver Star Citation for Pfc. Albert S. Ianacone. 82nd Airborne Division, General Order No. 14, February 2, 1945.

114 Silver Star Citation for S/Sgt. Norman B. Angel. 82nd Airborne Division, General Order No. 14, February 2, 1945.

115 Willard E. Harrison cited in Nordyke, 606.

116 "Operations with 82nd Airborne Division, 20 December 1944–January 1945," After Action Report, 740th Tank Battalion, 3 January 1945. Cited hereafter as "After Action Report, 740th TB."

CHAPTER 5

117 Harry J. Frear, Letter to Mrs. Lambert (sister of John E. Allen, Jr.), March 25, 1945. Courtesy of her son, Mark King.

118 Silver Star Citation for Pvt. Francis J. Bardon. 82ns Airborne Division, General Order No. 97, June 28, 1945.
119 Silver Star Citation for Pfc. Clarence E. Ables. 82nd Airborne Division, General Order No. 75, May 22, 1945.
120 Silver Star Citation for S/Sgt. Marion Shagdai. General Order No. 74, May 22, 1945.
121 Henry E. Schmid, Telephone interview with FVL, July 12, 2012.
122 Silver Star Citation for 2nd Lt. James C. Hesson. 82nd Airborne Division, General Order No. 86, June 6, 1945.
123 Silver Star Citation for 2nd Lt. Paul M. Nance. 82nd Airborne Division, General Order No. 119, September 13, 1945.
124 Distinguished Service Cross Citation for Pfc. Raymond S. Holsti. XVIII Airborne Corps, General Order No. 19, March 14, 1945.
125 According to G Company veteran Donald June, Lawrence Bishop was killed by 20mm fire. Telephone interview with FVL, January 5, 2013.
126 Stark, 16–19.
127 James M. McNamara, written account (1980's). Courtesy of his son, James M. McNamara, Jr.
128 3rd Battalion Unit Journal, December 21, 1944.
129 Harold Roy, Telephone interview with FVL, June 24, 2008.
130 Megellas, 188–189.
131 Albert Tarbell cited in Megellas, 189.
132 George Leoleis, *Medals* (New York, NY: Carlton, 1990), 204.
133 Silver Star Citation for 1st Lt. James Megellas. 82nd Airborne Division, General Order No. 36, March 19, 1945. Copy provided courtesy of Jörgen Rosenquist.
134 Silver Star Citation for Cpl. Eldon F. Young. 82nd Airborne Division, General Order No. 14, February 2, 1945.
135 Silver Star Citation for 1st Lt. Harold Roy. 82nd Airborne Division, General Order No. 32, March 12, 1945. Courtesy of Harold Roy.
136 After Action Report, 740th TB, 3 January 1945.
137 Silver Star Citation for Col. Reuben H. Tucker. 82nd Airborne Division, General Order No. 119, September 13, 1945.
138 Tarbell cited in Megellas, 189.
139 Regimental S-2 Journal, December 21, 1944.
140 Laun, Diary, December 21, 1944.
141 Fordyce Gorham cited in "Nazi Slicker Took In a Boy from the Hills," *Spokane Daily Chronicle* (Spokane, Washington), December 22, 1944.
142 Stark, 19–20.
143 Ed Cunningham, "Meeting the German thrust, the 82nd Airborne turned the Nazis' own guns against them and then went on to retake the village of Cheneux," *Yank Magazine*, January 1945. There may also have been more jeeps of Germans in American uniform heading for Cheneux that day. Stabsfeldwebel Laun mentions a total of 12 in his diary.
144 George D. Graves, Jr., Diary, December 21, 1944. Courtesy of Mike Bigalke.
145 Stark, 19.

146 Peiper, "Kampfgruppe Peiper," 12–13.
147 Cooke and Evans, 119.

CHAPTER 6
148 Bayley, "Ed's Army Days," 37–38.
149 Silver Star Citation for 1st Lt. Harold E. Reeves. 82nd Airborne Division, General Order No. 138, July 1945.
150 Campana, 12–13.
151 George H. Mahon, Questionnaire, FVL.
152 Ibid.
153 Stark, 21.
154 William B. Lovelady, Letter dated June 1, 1989, cited in Albert J. Palfey, "The Trap that doomed Kampfgruppe Peiper." <http://www.criba.be/fr/stories/detail/the-trap-that-doomed-kampfgruppe-peiper-26-1>. Accessed 19 November 2014.
155 Peiper, "Kampfgruppe Peiper," 13–14.
156 Campana, 13–15.
157 Garrison, 159–160
158 Campana, 15.
159 Blair, 392.
160 William L. Bonning, Telephone interview with FVL, June 29, 2008.
161 Ibid.
162 3rd Battalion Unit Journal, December 23, 1944.
163 Peiper, "Kampfgruppe Peiper," 15.
164 Silver Star Citation for 2nd Lt. George A. Amos. 82nd Airborne Division, General Order No. 89, June 9, 1945.
165 Campana, 15–16.
166 Mitchell E. Rech, Email to FVL, December 29, 2009.
167 Peiper, "Kampfgruppe Peiper," 16.
168 Cooke and Evans, 163.
169 Breard, Letter to FVL, February 24, 2005.
170 Bayley, "Ed's Army Days," 39–40.
171 Frank Boyd cited in Bos, *Circle and the Fields,* "Voices of the Veterans, HQ Battery," 12.

CHAPTER 7
172 Bayley, "Ed's Army Days," 40.
173 William L. Bonning, Letter to the *Valley Morning Star,* December 2009.
174 Stark, 28.
175 Herbert Lucas, Questionnaire, FVL.
176 Wilhelm Tieke, *Im Feuersturm letzter Kriegsjahre* (Selent, Austria: Pour le Mérite, 2006), 382.
177 Campana, 16–17.
178 Harry W. Rollins, Sr., Interview with his son Harry Jr., December 2007, n.p. Transcript courtesy of Harry W. Rollins, Jr.

179 Rollins, Interview.
180 Ibid.
181 Ibid. Luther E. Krantz is buried at the American Cemetery in Henri-Chapelle, Belgium, plot A, row 15, grave 15.
182 Dominic T. Biello's nephew was named after him. Biello read in his uncle's Individual Deceased Personnel File that he was found weeks after his death and first identified as Pvt. Michael J. Csakan because Biello was wearing a pair of Csakan's pants. Email to FVL, July 30, 2010.
183 Rollins, Interview.
184 Regimental S-2 Journal, December 26, 1944.
185 Rollins, Interview.
186 Edwin P. Hoyt, *Airborne: The History of American Parachute Forces* (New York, NY: Stein and Day, 1978), 135.
187 Silver Star Citation for Pfc. Bert Davis. 82nd Airborne Division, General Order No. 105, July 5, 1945.
188 Rollins, Interview.
189 Campana, 19–20.
190 Military Medal Citation for Sgt. Harold Dunnagan. Headquarters, First U.S. Army, Letter, April 18, 1945.

CHAPTER 8
191 Johannsen cited in Tieke, 436.
192 Megellas, 204.
193 Frank Boyd cited in Bos, *Circle and the Fields,* "Voices of the Veterans, HQ Battery," 12–13.
194 Silver Star Citation for Pvt. Donald Dukovich. Headquarters, 82nd Airborne Division, General Order No. 122, October 5, 1945.
195 Stark, 29–30.
196 Tieke, 438.
197 Campana, 20.
198 Silver Star Citation for Pvt. Albert C. Lodovici. 82nd Airborne Division, General Order No. 122, October 5, 1945.
199 Campana, 20–21.
200 Hubbard D. Burnum, Jr., Questionnaire, FVL.
201 Garrison, 161.
202 Campana, 21–22.
203 Garrison, 161.

CHAPTER 9
204 Shaffer, Telephone Interview with FVL, February 6, 2006.
205 Bayley, "Ed's Army Days," 42–43.
206 Ibid., 45.
207 Campana, 23.
208 Ernest W. Parks, "The War Years (WWII)." Unpublished memoir, 14.

209 Campana, 23–25.

210 Parks, 15.

211 Campana, 25–26.

212 Recommendation for Award, 23 October 1945. Copy courtesy of Richard F. Blankenship.

213 Campana, 26.

214 Richard Durkee cited in Dan Morgan, *The Last Corner of My Heart* (551st Parachute Infantry Battalion Association, 2007), 417.

215 Morgan, 429.

216 Andy Titko cited in Morgan, 452. In an e-mail to the author on 21 November 2009, former S/Sgt. Douglas Dillard of the 551st Parachute Infantry Association confirmed that there was no telephone line between the 504th and 551st.

217 Bill Hatcher cited in Morgan, 418. Gregory Orfalea believes the senior officer was Major General Gavin. Gregory Orfalea, *Messengers of the Lost Battalion. The Heroic 551st and the Turning of the Tide at the Battle of the Bulge* (New York, NY: Simon & Schuster, 1999), 297.

218 William N. Holm cited in Morgan, 440.

219 Estimate, FVL. Capt. Bill G. Smith, Headquarters Company, estimated the strength of B and C Companies to be 50 officers and men, A Company some 30, and his own company 60. See: Bill G. Smith, "The Operations of the 551st Parachute Infantry Battalion (Attached to the 82nd Airborne Division and 517th Parachute Infantry Regiment) in the Attack, in the Vicinity of Trois Ponts, Belgium, 2–7 January 1945 (Ardennes Campaign)," Fort Benning 1949–1950, 30. Aref Orfalea, a messenger in the 551st, wrote 83 officers and men down for B Company in his diary in the evening of January 5, 1945. See: Orfalea, *Messengers of the Lost Battalion*, 292.

220 J. Milt Hill cited in Morgan, 439.

221 Richard Durkee cited in Morgan, 418.

222 Richard Hallock, Letter to Mrs. Elizabeth Joerg, mother of Wood Joerg, October 8, 1946. Courtesy of his widow, Myriam Hallock.

CHAPTER 10

223 Peter Schrijvers, *The Unknown Dead: Civilians in the Battle of the Bulge.* Lexington, KY: University Press of Kentucky, 2005), 341–343.

224 Campana, 27.

225 Silver Star Citation for 1st Lt. Richard A. Harris. 82nd Airborne Division, General Order No. 113, September 13, 1945.

226 Silver Star Citation for 1st Lt. Martin E. Middleton. 82nd Airborne Division, General Order No. 21, February 24, 1945.

227 Silver Star Citation for Sgt. John C. Chamberlin. 82nd Airborne Division, General Order No. 14, February 2, 1945.

228 Silver Star Citation for Pvt. William L. Aston, Jr. 82nd Airborne Division, General Order No. 14, February 2, 1945.

229 Silver Star Citation for Pvt. Fred L. Kincaid. 82nd Airborne Division, General Order No. 14, February 2, 1945.

230 Donald E. Morain, Telephone interview with FVL, June 16, 2012.
231 Robert E. Bramson, Email to FVL, June 27, 2012.
232 Adam A. Komosa, "Recommendation for Award (Posthumous), Pfc. William G. Lanseadel, January 19, 1945." Copy courtesy of Mike Bigalke.
233 Silver Star Citation for Sgt. William S. Kendrick. 82nd Airborne Division, General Order No. 118, September 5, 1945.
234 Komosa, "Recommendation for Award."
235 Distinguished Service Cross Citation for Pfc. William G. Lanseadel. First United States Army, General Order No. 33, February 25, 1945. Lanseadel is buried at Long Island National Cemetery at H-10647.
236 Silver Star Citation for Cpl. John A. Schaebler. 82nd Airborne Division, General Order No. 14, February 2, 1945.
237 Silver Star Citation for 1st Lt. Hanz K. Druener. 82nd Airborne Division, General Order No. 17, February 15, 1945.
238 Campana, 26.
239 Lt. Col. Julian A. Cook, "Recommendation for Award [for 1st Lt. Ernest P. Murphy], 23 October 1945." The recommendation includes statements by Heibert and Ward. Copy courtesy of Richie Blankenship.
240 Eddie R. Hiebert, statement of October 23, 1945, cited in Megellas, 211–12. Megellas, the platoon leader, misidentifies Hiebert as "Technical Sergeant Eddie C. Heibert." Hiebert was indeed a non-commissioned officer in October 1945, but a Pfc. in January 1945.
241 John O. Prieto, Untitled written account. Courtesy of his son, Eric Prieto. n.p.
242 Hugh D. Wallis, Telephone interview, FVL, January 8, 2010. Wallis first spoke with Simon Renner about the death of Cletus Shelton in 2000, the year before Renner died.
243 John J. Foley, Jr., Telephone interview with FVL, February 25, 2012.
244 Prieto, Untitled account.
245 James M. Gavin, Letter to Mrs. Enus Sims, 23 February 1945. Courtesy of Kathleen Buttke, who received a copy from the Minnesota State Archives furnished by Jane and Ron Brown.
246 T. Moffatt Burriss, Telephone interview with JVL, January 10, 2010.
247 Silver Star Citation for Capt. Henry B. Keep. 82nd Airborne Division, General Order No. 116, August 25, 1945.
248 Silver Star Citation for Sgt. Darrel D. Edgar. 82nd Airborne Division, General Order No. 14, February 2, 1945.
249 Silver Star Citation for 1st Lt. Harold W. Stueland, 82nd Airborne Division, General Order No. 21, February 24, 1945.
250 Silver Star Citation for T/4 Kenneth F. Nelson. 82nd Airborne Division, General Order No. 22, February 26, 1945.
251 Bronze Star (Oak Leaf Cluster) Citation for 1st Lt. James R. Pursell. 82nd Airborne Division, General Order No. 87, June 8, 1945.
252 Bayley, "Ed's Army Days," 45.
253 Breard, Telephone interview with FVL, November 21, 2008.

254 Silver Star Citation for 1st Lt. Reneau G. Breard. 82nd Airborne Division, General Order No. 1, February 24, 1945. Courtesy of Reneau G. Breard.

255 Breard, Interview with FVL, Hotel Courage, Nijmegen, Holland, May 8, 2005.

256 Breard, Telephone interview with FVL, June 20, 2014.

257 Silver Star Citation for S/Sgt. James M. Boyd. 82nd Airborne Division, General Order No. 21, February 24, 1945.

258 William L. Bonning, Audiotape, March 21, 2008. [Ninety-minute oral history taped by the veteran at the request of FVL.] Fred Faidley survived and died in December 1972.

259 Silver Star Citation for Cpl. Hilton M. Holland. 82nd Airborne Division, General Order No. 22, February 26, 1945.

260 Durkee cited in Morgan, 445–447.

261 Roy McGraw cited in Morgan, 440.

262 Joseph Kienly cited in Morgan, 448.

263 Ibid, 449.

264 Distinguished Service Cross Citation for Cpl. Robert H. Hill. First U.S. Army, General Order No. A bronze plaque honoring Corporal Hill was added to the existing monument in Rochelinval and unveiled on 10 July 2010.

265 Don Garrigues cited in Morgan, 442.

266 J. Milt Hill cited in Morgan, 439.

267 Hallock, Letter to Elizabeth Joerg.

268 After Action Report, 740th TB, 7 January 1945.

269 Orfalea, *Messengers of the Lost Battalion,* 302.

270 Ibid., 388.

271 George K. Rubel, *Daredevil Tankers: The Story of the 740th Tank Battalion* (Werk Gottingen: Germany, 1945), 86.

272 Paul L. Pearson, *Into the Breach. The Life and Times of the 740th Tank Battalion in World War II* (Trafford Publishers: Bloomington, IN: 2007), 142.

273 J. Milt Hill cited in Morgan, 439.

274 Jack Affleck cited in Morgan, 450.

275 Louis A. Hauptfleisch cited in Morgan, 453.

CHAPTER 11

276 Bonning, Audiotape. Hilton Holland died on January 9, 1945 of sustained wounds. He is buried at the American Cemetery in Henri-Chapelle, Belgium, plot F, row 10, grave 33.

277 Silver Star Citation for 1st Lt. James R. Allmand, Jr. 82nd Airborne Division, General Order No. 73, May 22, 1945. Courtesy of his son, James R. Allmand III.

278 Bronze Star Citation for Pvt. David E. Ward, Jr. cited in Megellas, 212.

279 There is contradicting information regarding the date of death of Pfc. Casmir Klamut. While his gravestone says January 9, it should be January 8, according to a list compiled by Louis Hauptfleisch for the 504th PIR Association in the 1980's.

280 Bayley, "Ed's Army Days," 45.

281 Bonning, Audiotape.

282 Campana, 27.

283 Candy Allan, "Band of Brothers. World War II Veteran Recalls Fighting Alongside Those Who Never Returned," *Pioneer* (Big Rapids, Michigan), Weekend edition, November 10–11, 2007.

284 Bayley, "Ed's Army Days," 45.

285 John B. Isom, Telephone interview with FVL, February 21, 2005.

286 Bayley, "Ed's Army Days," 46.

CHAPTER 12

287 Arthur E. Duebner, "WWII with the Combined American/Canadian First Special Service Force Until and Including Transfer and Subsequent Service with the 82nd Airborne—504th Regiment, E Company," in Norman H. Stolp, ed., *As You Were. A Book of Memories Told by the Men Who Lived Through Them* (Nekoosa, WI: Badger State Chapter, 1994), 17. <http://www.scls.lib.wi.us/mcmillan/history/82nd/82_05.pdf>. Accessed 23 July 2007.

288 Bonning, Audiotape. Bonning was demoted for going AWOL.

289 John B. Isom, Telephone interview with FVL, June 12, 2005.

290 Bayley, Email FVL, June 14, 2005.

291 Breard, Interview with FVL, May 8, 2005.

292 Mitchell E. Rech, Interview, Veterans History Project, Library of Congress, May 21, 2002. Courtesy of Mitchell Rech.

293 Leoleis, 218–220.

294 Ibid., 220.

295 James A. Kiernan, Telephone interview with FVL, November 13, 2005.

296 Breard, Interview with FVL, May 8, 2005.

297 Bruns, 13.

298 Ivan J. Roggen, Questionnaire, FVL.

299 Colonel Tucker, Letter of Commendation to Captain McIntyre, January 17, 1945. Copy courtesy of Doug MacIntyre, son of Captain McIntyre (who changed the spelling of his name after WWII).

CHAPTER 13

300 William V. Rice, Diary, 31 January 1945. Copy courtesy of Richard Gariepy.

301 Zastrow, Letter to his parents, February 12, 1945.

302 Morgan, 483.

303 James H. Goethe, Questionnaire, CRC.

304 Bronze Star Citation for Capt. James H. Goethe. 504th Parachute Infantry Regiment, General Order No. 87, June 8, 1945.

305 Silver Star Citation for 1st Lt. Harry J. Frear. 82nd Airborne Division, General Order No. 38, March 19, 1945. Courtesy of his daughter, Joy Frear.

306 Zastrow, Letter to his parents, February 10, 1945.

307 Julian A. Cook cited in Breuer, 462.

308 Silver Star Citation for 1st Lt. James Megellas. 82nd Airborne Division, General Order No. 36, March 19, 1945.

309 Harold J. Sullivan cited in Megellas, 226

310 Frederick Andrews cited in Tom Harrison, "Military Actions—Twice Wounded Soldier Kept His Sense of Humor," *Lima News*, September 30, 2012. Accessed at <http://m.limaohio.com/mobile/news/local_news/article_912be50a-0b50-11e2-8edd-0019bb30f31a.html>.

311 Megellas, 227.

312 Zastrow, Letter to his parents, February 10, 1945. [The casualty was Pfc. Lorenzo J. Davis.]

313 Silver Star Citation for T/Sgt. Paul Grear. 82nd Airborne Division, General Order No. 118, September 5, 1945.

314 Bayley, "Ed's Army Days," 47–48.

315 Bos, 258.

316 Bayley, "Ed's Army Days," 48–49.

317 Megellas, 231.

318 Regimental S-2 Journal, January 29, 1945.

319 Megellas, 233.

320 Silver Star Citation for Pfc. Warnie R. Sims. 82nd Airborne Division, General Order No. 119, September 13, 1945.

321 Duebner, 17.

322 Silver Star Citation for T/Sgt. Augusta F. Billingsley. 82nd Airborne Division, General Order No. 118, September 5, 1945.

323 Silver Star Citation for 1st Lt. Chester R. Anderson. 82nd Airborne Division, General Order No. 119, September 13, 1945. Copy courtesy of his son, Jeff Anderson.

324 Bayley, "Ed's Army Days," 49.

325 James A. Kiernan, Email to FVL, February 8, 2006.

326 Bayley, "Ed's Army Days," 49–50.

327 Bayley, "Ed's Army Days," 50.

328 Julius Lasslo, Letter to Frances Barkley, sister of Angus Giles, July 28, 1945. Courtesy of Greg Korbelic, nephew of Angus Giles.

CHAPTER 14

329 Bayley, "Ed's Army Days," 50.

330 Fritz Roppelt, *Der Vergangenheit auf der Spur!* (Niederdorfelden, Germany: 1993), 626.

331 Kiernan, Email to FVL, February 8, 2006.

332 Bayley, "Ed's Army Days," 50.

333 Kiernan, Email to FVL, February 8, 2006

334 Bayley, "Ed's Army Days," 51.

335 Kiernan, Email to FVL, February 8, 2006.

336 Bayley, "Ed's Army Days," 51

337 Fred J. Baldino, Email to FVL, February 7, 2006.

338 Shaffer, Telephone interview with FVL, July 28, 2005.

339 Kiernan, Email to FVL, February 8, 2006.

340 Bayley, "Ed's Army Days," 51.

341 Kiernan, Email to FVL, February 8, 2006.

342 Bayley, "Ed's Army Days," 51–52.

343 Paul L. Pearson, *Into the Breach: The Life and Times of the 740th Tank Battalion in World War II* (Trafford Publishers: Bloomington, IN: 2007), 153–154.

344 Silver Star Citation for S/Sgt. John H. Stubbs. 82nd Airborne Division, General Order No. 59, October 29, 1945.

345 Roppelt, 519–520.

346 Ibid., 520–521.

347 Kiernan, Email to FVL, February 8, 2006.

348 Bayley, Email to FVL, October 16, 2006.

349 Breard, Letter to FVL, February 24, 2005.

350 Bayley, Email to FVL, February 9, 2006.

351 Roppelt, 468.

352 Ibid, 509.

353 Ibid, 495.

354 Bayley, "Ed's Army Days," 53.

355 Silver Star Citation for Capt. Adam A. Komosa. 82nd Airborne Division, General Order No. 103, July 3, 1945.

356 Donald R. June, Telephone interview with FVL, January 5, 2013. Second citation

357 Rice, 30 January 1945.

358 Ibid., 31 January 1945.

359 Bonning, Audiotape.

360 Richard Hallock, "The operations of the 3rd Platoon, Company A, 504 Parachute Infantry (82nd Airborne Division) in an assault across a draw on the Mertesrott Heights, in the Siegfried Line near Neuhof, Germany, 2 February 1945" (Fort Benning, 1949–1950), 7–8.

361 Casualty statistics based on FVL's research and Company Morning Reports.

362 Blair, 427.

363 John Eisenhower, Telephone interview with FVL, December 10, 2007.

CHAPTER 15

364 Duebner, 17.

365 Zastrow, Letter to his parents, February 12, 1945.

366 Edward F. Shaifer, Jr. "The operations of Company B, 504th Parachute Infantry (82nd Airborne) in piercing the Siegfried Line, near Losheimergraben, Germany, 2–4 February 1945" (Fort Benning, 1948–1949), 12.

367 Bayley, "Ed's Army Days," 54.

368 Ibid. Dragon's teeth are rows of conical or wedge-shaped concrete antitank obstacles protruding from the ground.

369 Zastrow, Letter to his parents, February 10, 1945

370 Silver Star Citation for Capt. Herbert H. Norman. 82nd Airborne Division, General Order No. 105, July 5, 1945.

371 Silver Star Citation for Pfc. Leonard H. Dennison. 82nd Airborne Division, General Order No. 69 (1945).

372 Lauren W. Ramsey, Telephone interview with FVL, April 8, 2008. The Herbert E.

Norman Post No. 4830 of the Veterans of Foreign Wars in Moultrie, Georgia, is named after the E Company commander.

373 Silver Star Citation for T/Sgt. Robert Lemery. 82nd Airborne Division, General Order No. 58, April 15, 1945.
374 Robert E. Bramson, Email to FVL, June 27, 2012.
375 Craig Caba, cousin of Sergeant Barbu, Email to FVL, July 19, 2014.
376 Silver Star Citation for 1st Lt. Stuart McCash. 82nd Airborne Division, General Order No. 58, April 15, 1945.
377 Arthur E. Duebner, 17–18.
378 Silver Star Citation for Pfc. Eugene G. Strutzenberg. 82nd Airborne Division, General Order No. 117. September 4, 1945.
379 Silver Star Citation for Capt. William J. Sweet, Jr. 82nd Airborne Division, General Order No. 58, April 15, 1945.
380 Silver Star Citation for T/5 Marvin Dixon. 82nd Airborne Division, General Order No. 32, March 12, 1945.
381 Silver Star Citation for Lt. Col. Edward N. Wellems. 82nd Airborne Division, General Order No. 114. September, 1945.
382 Hurlbert, Interview with John Cutright.

CHAPTER 16
383 Bayley, "Ed's Army Days," 54.
384 Shaifer, 13–15.
385 Bonning, Audiotape.
386 Shaifer, 14.
387 Ibid., 14–15.
388 Ibid., 16.
389 Ortega may have been a paratrooper in the 551st Parachute Infantry Battalion before joining B Company. After the 551st was disbanded in January 1945 its survivors were assigned to the 504th PIR. (For example, Pfc. George Kane, a medic from the 551st, joined B Company's 1st Platoon.)
390 Shaifer, 16.
391 Bonning, Audiotape.
392 Shaifer, 17–18.
393 Ibid., 19.
394 Bonning, Audiotape.
395 Shaifer, 22–23.
396 Bonning, Audiotape.
397 Bayley, "Ed's Army Days," 54–55.
398 Hallock, "The operations of the 3rd Platoon," 6–8.
399 Shaffer, Telephone interview with FVL, July 28, 2005.
400 Hallock, "The operations of the 3rd Platoon," 12.
401 Shaffer, Telephone interview with FVL, July 28, 2005.
402 Silver Star Citation for Pfc. Benjamin P. Walker. 82nd Airborne Division, General Order No. 58, April 15, 1945.
403 Shaffer, Telephone interview with FVL, July 28, 2005.

404 The BAR belonged to Pvt. John McLaughlin, B Company, who had been killed about 15 minutes earlier.
405 Bayley, "Ed's Army Days," 55–56.
406 Bronze Star Citation for Capt. Paul D. Bruns. 82nd Airborne Division, General Order No. 32, March 12, 1945.
407 Bruns, 14.
408 James A. Kiernan, Interview with FVL, August 17, 2007.
409 Kiernan, Email to FVL, November 3, 2006.
410 Shaifer, 24–25.
411 3rd Battalion Unit Journal, December 21, 1944.
412 Clinton Riddle, Email to Joe Bass, February 28, 2015. Copy courtesy of Joe Bass, nephew to the late Lt. G.P. Crockett.
413 Albert Tarbell cited in Michael Takiff, *Brave Men, Gentle Heroes* (New York, NY: Perennial, 2004), 253.
414 Ibid.
415 John M. Clark cited in Morgan, 483.

CHAPTER 17
416 Shaifer, 26.
417 Bonning, Audiotape.
418 Garrison, 164.
419 Bronze Star Citation for Cpl. Forrest L. Smith. General Orders No. 9, 504th Parachute Infantry Regiment, May 14, 1945.
420 Shaifer, 26–27.
421 Ibid., 28–29.
422 Breard, Interview with FVL, May 8, 2005.
423 Shaifer, 26–27.
424 Bonning, Audiotape.
425 Shaifer, 31.
426 Bonning, Audiotape.
427 Rice, Diary, February 4, 1945.
428 Ibid., February 5, 1945.
429 Ibid., February 6, 1945.
430 David L. Haushalter, Telephone interview with FVL, May 14, 2006.
431 Hofmeister, Interview with FVL, August 14, 2007 (personal interview conducted at Severna Park, Maryland).
432 Breard, Interview with FVL, May 8, 2005.
433 Bonning, Audiotape.
434 Rice, Diary, February 13, 1945.
435 Ibid., February 14, 1945.
436 "Historical Narrative of the 307th Airborne Engineer Battalion, 1 January 1945–22 February 1945." After Action Report of the 307th Airborne Engineers, February 14, 1945.
437 Douglas W. Dwyer, *The Story of the Ninetieth In Training and In Action 1944–1945*

(Columbia, SC; R.L. Bryan Company, 1945). <http://www.4point2.org/hist-90.htm #diary>. Accessed July 29, 2014.
438 Regimental S-3 Journal, February 15, 1945.
439 Zastrow, Letter to his parents, February 22, 1945.
440 Harold Roy, Telephone interview with FVL.
441 Rice, Diary, February 21, 1945.

POSTSCRIPT
442 Myles J. Abramson, Letter to Robert E. Bramson, May 17, 1945. Courtesy of Myles Abramson.
443 Myriam Hallock, Telephone interview with FVL, November 11, 2005.
444 Boyd G. Carter, Letter to Jörgen Rosenquist, 28 May 1978. Courtesy of Jörgen Rosenquist.

APPENDIX I
445 Rollins, Interview.
446 Richard Baron, Abe Baum and Richard Goldhurst, *Raid! The Untold Story of Patton's Secret Mission* (New York, NY; 2000), 19–21.
447 Ibid., 148–157.
448 Rollins, Interview.
449 Ibid.
450 Ibid.
451 Ibid.
452 Ibid.

CONTRIBUTING VETERANS

Between 2002 and 2014, I interviewed and/or corresponded with the following veterans. Ranks given are the highest-held during the war. An asterisk indicates veterans who have since passed away. Without their contributions, this regimental history could never have been written.

REGIMENTAL HEADQUARTERS: *Capt. Delbert Kuehl (Protestant Chaplain), *Maj. Ivan Roggen (Regimental surgeon), *Pfc. Warren Tidwell (A Co. and Capt. Fordyce Gorham's jeep driver).

HQ & HQ COMPANY: 2nd Lt. Hubbard Burnum, Jr. (Demolition Platoon), *Pfc. David Finney (Communications Platoon), Pfc. Darrell Harris (Demolition Platoon), *Cpl. Thomas Zouzas (S-2 section).

1ST BATTALION: *Sgt. James Addis (A Co.), *2nd Lt. Charles Battisti (HQ/1 Coy), Pfc. Edwin Bayley (A Co.), Sgt. William Bonning (B Co.), 1st Lt. Reneau Breard (A and B Co.), Pfc. Samuel Comparato (A. Co.), *Sgt. George Cutting (HQ/1 Co.), *Sgt. Virgil Danielson (A Co.), *1st Lt. James Dunn (A and C Co.), *Cpl. Glenn Frew (A Co.), Pfc. Mike Holmstock (B Co.), * S/Sgt. John Isom (A Co.), *Pfc. Marvin Jensen (A Co.), S/Sgt. John Kaslikowski (HQ/1 Co.), 1st Lt. James Kiernan (A Co.), *Pfc. James Lay (HQ/1 Co.), *Sgt. Fred Lilley (A Co.), Pfc. Louis Marino (A Co.), *Capt. Albert Milloy (C Co.), *T/Sgt. Dock O'Neal (B Co.), *T/Sgt. Mitchell E. Rech (A Co.), *Sgt. Ervin Shaffer (A Co.), *Sgt. Elmer Swartz (C Co.), *Sgt. Robert Waldon (B Co.), *Pfc. Elbert Winningham (C Co.), Pfc. Hubert Wolfe (B Co.), *Capt. Charles Zirkle, Jr. (1st Battalion Surgeon)

2ND BATTALION: 2nd Lt. Robert Bramson (F Co.), *Pvt. Henry Covello (F Co.), *1st Lt. Leonard Greenblatt (D Co.), *Pfc. Leo Hart (F Co.), Pvt. Paul Kunde (E Co.), *Pfc. Maurice McSwain (F Co.), Pvt. George Mahon (E Co.) Pfc. Donald Morain (F Co.), Pfc. Albert Musto (F Co.), *Cpl. Louis Napier (E Co.), *S/Sgt. Ernest Parks, *1st Lt. Lauren Ramsey (HQ/2 Co.), *2nd Lt. Harry Rollins (D Co.), Pfc. James Sapp (HQ/2 Co.), Sgt. Willis Sisson (E Co.), Pfc. Werner Speer (F Co.), *Sgt. Roy Tidd (E Co.), *Sgt. Bennie Weeks (HQ/2 Co.), *Pfc. Virgil Widger (D Co.).

3RD BATTALION: Capt. Moffatt Burriss (I Co.), Pfc. Robert DeVinney (H Co.), *Sgt. John Foley, Jr. (H Co.), 1st Lt. Roy Hanna (G Co.), Pfc. John Horvatis (HQ/3 Co.), Pfc. Walter Hughes (I Co.), *Pfc. Donald June (G Co.), Pfc. Melvin Kessler (G Co.), *Pvt. James Legacie, Jr. (H Co.), *Sgt. George Leoleis (I Co.), T/5 Herbert Lucas (HQ/3 Co.), 1st Lt. James Megellas (H Co.), *Pfc. Paul Mentzer (HQ/3 Co.), *T/Sgt. Louis Orvin, Jr. (I Co.), Pfc. Henry Schmid (G Co.), *Pfc. John Schultz (H Co.), *1st Lt. Edward Sims (H Co.), *Cpl. Walter Souza (H Co.), *Sgt. Albert Tarbell (H Co.), Sgt. Don Zimmerman (H Co.).

C COMPANY 307TH AIRBORNE ENGINEER BATTALION: *1st Lt. John Holabird, *Sgt. Meldon Hurlbert. *Pfc. Alexander Nemeth, *1st Lt. Michael Sabia, Cpl. Obie Wickersham.

VETERANS, OTHER AMERICAN UNITS: Sgt. Harold Bradley (740th Tank Battalion), 1st Lt. Rufus Broadaway (82nd Airborne, Division HQ), *Capt. Paul Donnelly (376th Parachute Field Artillery Battalion), *Pfc. Raymond Fary (80th Airborne Anti-Aircraft Battalion), *M/Sgt. Leonard Lebenson (82nd Airborne, Division HQ), S/Sgt. Clinton Riddle (325th Glider Infantry Regiment), *1st Lt. Harold Roy (376th Parachute Field Artillery Battalion).

SELECTED BIBLIOGRAPHY

INTERVIEWS, QUESTIONNAIRES AND AUDIOTAPES

Bayley, Edwin R.
Bonning, William L.
Bramson, Robert E.
Breard, Reneau G.
Burriss, T. Moffatt
Dunn, James E.
Foley, Jr. John J.
Holmstock, Mike M.

Hughes, Walter E.
Isom, John B.
Kiernan, James A.
Lucas, Herbert C.
Mahon, George H.
Milloy, Albert E.
Ramsey, Lauren W.
Rollins, Harry W.

Roggen, Ivan J.
Shaffer, Ervin E.
Sims, Edward J.
Waldon, Robert
Wallis, Hugh D.
Widger, Virgil W.
Zimmerman, Harry D.

ARCHIVAL SOURCES:

Athens, Ohio: Ohio University Library, the Cornelius Ryan Collection (CRC)

Carlisle Barracks, Pennsylvania: United States Army Military History Institute (USAMHI)

College Park, Maryland: National Archives and Records Administration II, Modern Military Reference Branch

Fort Benning, Georgia: Donovan Research Library

Government Archival sources include After Action Reports for: 82nd U.S. Airborne Division Headquarters; the 504th, 505th and 508th Parachute Infantry Regiments; 30th U.S. Infantry Division. Especially noteworthy are the 2nd and 3rd Battalion Unit Journals and the 504th Regimental S-1, S-2 and S-3 Journals, which provided a timeframe for many eyewitness reports.

PUBLISHED WORKS:

Anzuoni, Robert P. *I'm the 82nd Airborne Division!* Atglen, PA: Schiffer Publishing, 2005.

Baron, Richard, Abe Baum and Richard Goldhurst, *Raid! The Untold Story of Patton's Secret Mission.* New York, NY: Dell Publishing, 1981; 2000.

Blair, Clay. *Ridgway's Paratroopers: The American Airborne in World War II.* Annapolis, MD: Naval Institute Press, 1985; 2002.

Bos, Jan. *Circle and the Fields of Little America. The History of the 376th Parachute Field Artillery Battalion, 82nd Airborne.* Privately published DVD book, 2007.

Breuer, William B. *Geronimo!* New York, NY: St. Martin's Press, 1989; 1992.

Burriss, T. Moffatt. *Strike and Hold. A Memoir of the 82nd Airborne in World War II.* Washington DC: Brassey's, 2001.

Carter, Ross S. *Those Devils in Baggy Pants*. Kingsport, TN: Kingsport Press, 1979.

Cooke, David and Wayne Evans. *Kampfgruppe Peiper in the Battle of the Bulge*. Mechanicsburg, PA: Stackpole Books, 2005; 2008.

Cunningham, Ed. "Meeting the German thrust, the 82nd Airborne turned the Nazis' own guns against them and then went on to retake the village of Cheneux," *Yank Magazine*, January 1945, n.p.

Dawson, W. Forrest. *Saga of the All American*. Atlanta, GA: Albert Love Enterprises, 1946; 1978.

———. *Stand Up and Hook Up*. Austin, TX: Eakin Press, 1989; 1997. [Author appears as "Buck Dawson" on the cover of the 1997 edition.]

Devlin, Gerard M. *Paratrooper!* New York, NY: St. Martin's Press, 1979.

Fürbringer, Herbert. *9. SS-Panzer Division. 1944: Normandie–Tarnopol–Arnhem*. Bayeux, France: Editions Heimdal, 1984.

Garrison, Chester A. *An Ivy-League Paratrooper*. Corvallis, OR: The Franklin Press, 2002.

Gavin, James M. *On to Berlin: Battles of an Airborne Commander 1943–1946*. New York, NY: Viking Press, 1978.

Gross, Manfred. *Westwallkämpfe. Die Angriffe der Amerikaner 1944/45 zwischen Ormont (Rheinland Pfalz) und Geilenkirchen (Nordrhein-Westfalen)*. Aachen, Germany: Helios Press, 2008.

Hoyt, Edwin P. *Airborne: The History of the American Parachute Forces*. New York, NY: Stein and Day, 1978.

Harris, Darrell G. *Casablanca to VE Day. A Paratrooper's Memoirs*. Pittsburgh, PA: Dorrance Publishing, 1995.

Leoleis, George. *Medals*. New York, NY: Carlton, 1990.

Liberation Museum Groesbeek. *Roll of Honour 82nd Airborne Division World War Two*. Nijmegen, the Netherlands: Nijmegen University Press, 1997.

LoFaro, Guy. *The Sword of St. Michael: The 82nd Airborne Division in World War II*. Cambridge, MA: Da Capo Press, 2011.

Lord, William G. *History of the 508th Parachute Infantry*. Washington DC: Infantry Journal Press, 1948.

Mandle, William D. and David H. Whittier. *Combat Record of the 504th Parachute Infantry Regiment*. Paris, France: 1946; Nashville, TN: The Battery Press, 1976.

Megellas, James. *All the Way to Berlin*. New York, NY: Random House, 2003.

Morgan, Dan. *The Last Corner of My Heart. The Saga of the 551st Parachute Infantry Battalion*. 551st Parachute Infantry Battalion Association, 1984; 2007.

Mrozek, Steven J., ed. *Propblast. Chronicle of the 504th Parachute Infantry Regiment*. Fort Bragg, NC: 82nd Airborne Division Historical Society, 1986.

Nigl, Alfred J. and Charles A. Nigl. *Silent Wings, Savage Death*. Santa Ana, CA: Nigl & Nigl, 2007.

Nordyke, Phil, *All American All the Way. The Combat History of the 82nd Airborne*

Division in World War II. St. Paul, MN: Zenith Press, 2005.

———. *More than Courage. The Combat History of the 504th Parachute Infantry Regiment in World War II.* Minneapolis, MN: Zenith Press, 2008.

Orfalea, Gregory. *Messengers of the Lost Battalion. The Heroic 551st and the Turning of the Tide at the Battle of the Bulge.* New York, NY: Simon & Schuster, 1997; 1999.

Pergrin, David E. with Eric Hammel, *First Across The Rhine. The 291st Combat Engineer Battalion in France, Belgium and Germany.* St. Paul, MN: Zenith Press, 1989; 2006.

Pearson, Paul L. *Into the Breach. The Life and Times of the 740th Tank Battalion in World War II.* Bloomington, IN:Trafford Publishers, 2007.

Pierce, Wayne. *Let's Go! The Story of the Men Who Served in the 325th Glider Infantry Regiment.* Chapel Hill, NC: Professional Press, 1997.

Roppelt, Fritz. *Der Vergangenheit auf der Spur!* Niederdorfelden, Germany: Privately printed, 1993.

Rubel, George K. *Daredevil Tankers: The Story of the 740th Tank Battalion.* Göttingen, Germany: Werk Göttingen, 1945.

Scherer, Wingolf. *Westwall 1944/45. US–Angriffe und vergeblicher Widerstand im Grossraum Aachen und in der Eifel.* Aachen, Germany: Helios Verlag, 2010.

Schrijvers, Peter. *The Unknown Dead. Civilians in the Battle of the Bulge.* Lexington, KY: University Press of Kentucky, 2005.

Takiff, Michael, *Brave Men, Gentle Heroes.* New York, NY: Perennial, 2004.

Tieke, Wilhelm. *Im Feuersturm letzter Kriegsjahre. II. SS-Panzer Korps mit 9. Und 10. SS-Division Hohenstaufen und Frundsberg.* Selent, Austria: Pour le Mérite, 2006.

Turnbull, Peter. *I Maintain the Right. The 307th Airborne Engineer Battalion in WWII.* Bloomington, IN: Author House, 2005.

Van Lunteren, Frank. *The Battle of the Bridges. The 504th Parachute Infantry Regiment in Operation Market Garden.* Havertown, PA: Casemate Publishing, 2014.

UNPUBLISHED AND PRIVATELY PUBLISHED SOURCES:
MEMOIRS AND HISTORIES
Bayley, Edwin R. "Ed's Army Days (WWII)," Unpublished memoir, 2004.

Bruns, Paul D. "Flight Surgeon." Unpublished memoir, 1987.

Finney, David K. "My Time with the 504th." Privately printed memoir. San Diego, 2006.

Parks, Ernest W. "The War Years (WWII)." Unpublished memoir, 2008.

Van Lunteren, Frank W., "Brothers in Arms: A Company, 504th Parachute Infantry Regiment, 82nd Airborne Division, from North Africa to Berlin." Privately printed company history. Arnhem: The Netherlands, 2007.

UNTITLED WORKS AND SHORTER CONTRIBUTIONS
Bradley, Harold G.
Brown, Earnest H.
Hughes, Walter H.
Mandle, William D.
McNamara Sr., James M. (courtesy of James M. McNamara, Jr.)
Prieto, John O.

INDEX

81mm mortar, 42, 50, 88, 111, 119,
144–146, 149, 169, 227, 229,
238, 244
88mm ammunition (Ger.), 111, 211
88mm gun (Ger.), 111, 118, 123,
216, 219
120mm flak wagon (Ger.), 59, 61–
65, 68–69, 72–73, 75, 81, 85–87,
91–93, 100, 123–124, 131–132
anti-aircraft gun, 171
anti-personnel mine, 24, 135, 247
anti-tank gun, 53–54, 58, 88–89,
98, 106, 131, 214, 223
anti-tank mine, 120, 161
armor-piercing shell (APCBDF),
81, 107, 131, 240
automatic pistol (Ger.), 79
bayonet, 20, 163
bazooka, anti-tank rocket, 56–57,
64, 71, 87, 141, 155, 160, 188,
196, 231–232, 243, 246
Browning Automatic Rifle (BAR),
20, 41, 56, 59, 71, 154, 165, 168,
191, 196, 204, 212, 227, 230,
237, 239–240, 242, 244–247,
258
Browning water-cooled machine
gun, 167–168
bunker (Ger.), 74, 191, 222, 228,
230, 232, 234, 238, 239, 243,
245–246, 249, 251–252
burp gun—MP38/40 submachine
gun (Ger.), 242
buzz bomb (Ger.), 185, 187
carbine rifle, 20
dragon's teeth—concrete dragon-
teeth anti-tank barricade (Ger.),
227, 234, 243, 245, 251, 260
Gammon grenade, 104, 157, 194,
230, 232
hand grenade, 20, 50, 62–63, 71, 73,

75–76, 79, 85–86, 121, 124, 153–
154, 156–157, 159–160, 163–
164, 178, 191, 194, 201, 248
incendiary bomb, 20
K-98 rifle (Ger.), 123
light machine gun, 75–76, 87, 143,
150, 238, 240, 242, 244
M-1 rifle, 20, 30, 61, 65, 98, 193
M-10 tank destroyer, 256–257
M-16 rifle, 267
M24 Chaffee tank, 171–172
M36 tank destroyer, 60
M5A1 Stuart tank, 171–172
machine gun, 20, 40, 42, 50, 57–60,
62–66, 69, 71, 73, 75–80, 82–83,
85–86, 91, 93–94, 96, 99–100,
112, 121, 123, 126, 129, 130–
131, 141, 150, 153–159, 161–
163, 165, 166–172, 178, 191,
196, 198–200, 202, 204, 211,
217–218, 228–231, 237, 240–
241, 244–246, 250–252,
255–256
machine pistol (Ger.), 96, 164
Mark IV tank (Ger.), 39
Mark V tank (Ger.), 194
Mark VI King Tiger tank (Ger.),
98, 100, 106
medium tank, 250, 252
MG34 machine gun (Ger.), 246
MG42 machine gun (Ger.), 58–59,
72, 122, 127
minefield (Ger.), 54, 126, 141, 230,
232, 234, 262–264
Nebelwerfers. *See* 88mm gun (Ger.)
Panther tank (Ger.), 39
Panzerfaust, anti-tank weapon
(Ger.), 81, 96, 188, 230, 242–
243, 256
phosphorus grenade, 135
pillbox (Ger.), 228–232, 238, 239,